2014 SUPPLEMENT TO THIRTEENTH EDITIONS

MODERN CRIMINAL PROCEDURE
BASIC CRIMINAL PROCEDURE

AND

ADVANCED CRIMINAL PROCEDURE

■ ■ ■

by

Yale Kamisar

Clarence Darrow Distinguished University Professor Emeritus of Law,
University of Michigan
Professor Emeritus of Law, University of San Diego

Wayne R. LaFave

David C. Baum Professor Emeritus of Law
and Center for Advanced Study Professor Emeritus,
University of Illinois

Jerold H. Israel

Ed Rood Eminent Scholar Emeritus,
University of Florida, Fredric G. Levin College of Law
Alene and Allan F. Smith Professor Emeritus,
University of Michigan

Nancy J. King

Lee S. & Charles A. Speir Professor of Law
Vanderbilt University Law School

Orin S. Kerr

Fred C. Stevenson Research Professor of Law
The George Washington University Law School

Eve Brensike Primus

Professor of Law
University of Michigan

AMERICAN CASEBOOK SERIES®

Mat #41648364

American Casebook Series is a trademark registered in the U.S. Patent and Trademark Office.

© West, a Thomson business, 1999, 2002, 2005–2008
© 2009–2012 Thomson Reuters
© 2013 LEG, Inc. d/b/a West Academic Publishing
© 2014 LEG, Inc. d/b/a West Academic
     444 Cedar Street, Suite 700
     St. Paul, MN 55101
     1-877-888-1330

Printed in the United States of America

ISBN: 978-1-62810-085-3

PREFACE

This Supplement contains all significant cases decided by the United States Supreme Court in the 2013–14 Term. It also includes some lower court cases and some citations to, or extracts from, recent academic commentary.

YALE KAMISAR
WAYNE R. LAFAVE
JEROLD H. ISRAEL
NANCY J. KING
ORIN S. KERR
EVE BRENSIKE PRIMUS

July 2014

TABLE OF CONTENTS

PART 3. THE COMMENCEMENT OF
FORMAL PROCEEDINGS

TABLE OF CASES

The principal cases are in bold type.

―――――

2014 SUPPLEMENT TO THIRTEENTH EDITIONS

MODERN CRIMINAL PROCEDURE
BASIC CRIMINAL PROCEDURE
AND
ADVANCED CRIMINAL PROCEDURE

PART 1

INTRODUCTION

■ ■ ■

CHAPTER 3

SOME GENERAL REFLECTIONS ON CRIMINAL PROCEDURE AND ITS ADMINISTRATION

■ ■ ■

13th ed., p. 63; after extract from Brandon Garrett's book, add:

Consider, too, Samuel R. Gross & Michael Shaffer, Report by the National Registry of Exonerations,[a] *Exonerations in the United States, 1989–2012,* pp. 3–4 (2012) (http://www.exonerationregistry.org) (analyzing 873 exonerations).

"The most important conclusion of this Report is that there are far more false convictions than exonerations. That should come as no surprise. The essential fact about false convictions is that they are generally invisible: if we could spot them, they'd never happen in the first place. Why would anyone suppose that the small number of miscarriages of justice that we learn about years later—like the handful of fossils of early hominids that we have discovered—is anything more than an insignificant fraction of the total?

"In any event, the exonerations we know about tell us something about the ones we have missed. Eighty-three percent of the exonerations in the Registry were in rape and homicide cases, which together constitute about 2% of felony convictions, but the problems that cause false convictions are hardly limited to rape and murder. For example, in 47 of the exonerations the defendants were convicted of robbery compared to 203 convictions for rape, even though there is every reason to believe that there are many more false convictions for robbery than for rape. For both rape and robbery, the false convictions we know about are overwhelmingly caused by mistaken eyewitness identifications—a problem that is almost entirely restricted to crimes committed by strangers—and arrests for robberies by strangers are at least several times more common than arrests for rapes by strangers. Why so comparatively few robbery exonerations? Because DNA evidence is the factual basis for the vast majority of rape exonerations, but DNA is hardly ever useful in proving the innocence of robbery defendants.

---

[a] The National Registry of Exonerations is a joint project of the University of Michigan Law School and the Center on Wrongful Convictions at Northwestern University School of Law.

"Even among rape and murder cases, only a small minority of false convictions end in exoneration. A quarter of murder exonerees were sentenced to death (101/409), and nearly half of all homicide and sexual assault exonerees were sentenced to death or life imprisonment (345/721). But overall, very few convicted murderers are sentenced to death, and the great majority of rape defendants plead guilty and receive sentences of several years in prison.

"Why do so few rape and murder convictions with comparatively light sentences show up among the exonerations? Most innocent defendants with short sentences probably never try to clear their names. They serve their time and do what they can to put the past behind them. If they do seek justice, they are unlikely to find help. The Center on Wrongful Convictions, for example, tells prisoners who ask for assistance that unless they have at least 10 years *remaining* on their sentences, the Center will not be able to help them because it is overloaded with cases where the stakes are much higher."

CHAPTER 4

THE RIGHT TO COUNSEL

■ ■ ■

SECTION 1. THE RIGHT TO APPOINTED COUNSEL AND RELATED PROBLEMS

A. THE RIGHT TO APPOINTED COUNSEL IN CRIMINAL PROCEEDINGS

13th ed., p. 78; in Note 5, replace the citation to James M. Anderson and Paul Heaton's working paper with the following citation:

James M. Anderson & Paul Heaton, *How Much Difference Does the Lawyer Make? The Effect of Defense Counsel on Murder Case Outcomes*, 122 Yale L.J. 154 (2012).

13th ed., p. 78; after Note 5, add:

5A. *Gideon Vouchers.* Indigent defendants in Comal County, Texas will soon be able to use government vouchers to choose their own attorneys from a list of qualified attorneys. While some believe that *Gideon* vouchers can improve the quality of indigent defense representation, others fear that it will only give an advantage to savvy criminals. For a discussion of the pilot project, see Adam Liptak, *Need-Blind Justice*, N.Y. Times (Jan. 4, 2014). For a discussion of the theory behind *Gideon* vouchers, see Stephen J. Schulhofer & David D. Friedman, *Rethinking Indigent Defense: Promoting Effective Representation Through Consumer Sovereignty and Freedom of Choice for All Criminal Defendants*, 31 Am. Crim. L. Rev. 73 (1993).

13th ed., p. 78; at the end of the first paragraph of Note 6, add:

For additional reflections on *Gideon* fifty years later, see articles in the following symposia: *The Gideon Effect: Rights, Justice, and Lawyers Fifty Years After Gideon v. Wainwright*, 122 Yale L.J. 2106 et seq. (2013); *Gideon at 50: Reassessing the Right to Counsel*, 70 Wash. & Lee L. Rev. 835 et seq. (2013); 25 Fed. Sent'g Rep. 87 et seq. (2012).

13th ed., p. 83; after Note 6, add:

For an argument that courts often use the seemingly-expansive nature of the right to counsel announced in *Gideon* to justify limiting or diluting other criminal procedure rights, see Justin F. Marceau, *Gideon's Shadow*, 122 Yale L.J. 2482 (2013).

13th ed., p. 85; after Note 8, add:

9.   *Shrinking Gideon.* Consider Stephanos Bibas, *Shrinking Gideon and Expanding Alternatives to Lawyers*, 70 Wash. & Lee L. Rev. 1287, 1290 (2013):

"*Gideon*'s problems are deep, structural ones. We have been spreading resources too thin, in the process slighting the core cases such as capital and other serious felonies that are the most complex and need the most time and money. A perfunctory chat with a lawyer is little better than no lawyer at all.

"[W]e must shrink the universe of cases covered by *Gideon* to preserve its core. That would mean excluding nonjury misdemeanors and perhaps probationary sentences from its ambit, for example, and thinking harder up front about which cases need to be charged and pursued as felonies.

"Especially in bench trials, there are other ways to simplify cases to make lawyers less necessary. In particular, civil procedure could learn from inquisitorial systems, in which judicial officers are more active and the parties and their lawyers need do less. Magistrates could lead investigations, discovery, and witness examinations, relying less on the parties to proactively frame and pursue their claims. Inquisitorial procedure sounds like a strange transplant from civil-law countries. But it already has parallels in administrative systems for claiming government benefits, in which claimants commonly pursue their claims without lawyers.

"There may also be ways to loosen the bar's stranglehold so that paralegals, social workers, and others can automate delivery of legal services for routine cases. That change would resemble what we see in health care, as nurse practitioners and physician assistants are providing care in routine medical cases.

"In short, *Gideon* can work in the real world only if lawyers drop their grandest ambitions for lawyerizing the world and instead step back to make lawyers less necessary in the first place. The goal should be to concentrate lawyers' efforts on providing quality legal services in the highest-stakes cases where they are needed most. Quality and support matter more than quantity alone."

See also Donald A. Dripps, *Up From Gideon*, 45 Tex. Tech. L. Rev. 113 (2012) (proposing a number of reforms including (1) exempting some self-representing felony defendants, like their misdemeanor counterparts, from sentences of incarceration if convicted; (2) giving counsel for indigent defendants discretion to decline unpromising appeals; (3) permitting lay representation of juvenile and misdemeanor defendants; and (4) recognizing indigent defense as a separate career track from the general practice of law).

SECTION 2.   THE RIGHT TO APPOINTED COUNSEL IN PROCEEDINGS OTHER THAN CRIMINAL PROSECUTIONS: THE CONTINUED VITALITY OF THE *BETTS V. BRADY* APPROACH

B.   COLLATERAL ATTACK PROCEEDINGS

13th ed., p. 97; after Note 7, add:

For additional discussion of the pros and cons of recognizing a "civil *Gideon*," see articles in the following symposia: *Toward a Civil Gideon: The Future of American Legal Service*, 7 Harv. L. & Pol'y Rev. 1 et seq. (2013) and *The Gideon Effect: Rights, Justice, and Lawyers Fifty Years After Gideon v. Wainwright*, 122 Yale L.J. 2106 et seq. (2013).

13th ed., p. 98; replace Section B at the bottom of the page with the following:

As is discussed more extensively elsewhere (see 13th ed., ch. 29, § 1), the Supreme Court has held that an indigent prisoner typically has no federal constitutional right to assigned counsel in collateral review proceedings. See *Pennsylvania v. Finley*, 481 U.S. 551 (1987). A 5–4 majority held in *Murray v. Giarratano*, 492 U.S. 1 (1989) that this rule applies no differently in capital cases than in noncapital cases. The Supreme Court has left open the possibility of modifying this general rule for "initial review collateral proceedings," defined as postconviction proceedings that provide the first occasion for a prisoner to raise a constitutional claim (such as a claim of ineffective assistance of trial counsel). See *Coleman v. Thompson*, 501 U.S. 722, 755 (1991) (leaving open the question of whether indigent prisoners have a constitutional right to assigned counsel for initial review collateral proceedings); see also *Martinez v. Ryan*, 132 S.Ct. 1309, 1315 (2012) (reiterating that this remains an open question). For a discussion of other aspects of *Martinez v. Ryan*, see infra Supp., p. 151.

CHAPTER 5

THE PERFORMANCE OF COUNSEL

■ ■ ■

SECTION 1. THE INEFFECTIVE ASSISTANCE OF COUNSEL (IAC) CLAIM: BASIC FEATURES

13th ed., p. 135; at the end of the second paragraph of Note 7, add:

But note *Martinez v. Ryan*, discussed at Supp., p. 149 (new paragraph c) and Supp., pp. 151–152 (new paragraph a).

SECTION 2. THE *STRICKLAND* STANDARDS

13th ed., p. 154; after Note 6, add:

6A. In LAFLER v. COOPER, 132 S.Ct. 1376 (2012), the Court was sharply divided as to the appropriate reading of the above cases and the character of *Strickland's* prejudice requirement. The state there conceded that defense counsel had violated the performance prong of *Strickland* by providing deficient advice that led to the defendant's rejection of a prosecution offer to accept a guilty plea to a single count, with a prosecution recommendation of a sentence of 51–85 months. The state argued, however, that the prejudice prong was not established even though defendant was convicted at trial on all three charged counts and received a sentence of 185–360 months.[1] Rejecting that contention, Justice Kennedy's opinion for the 5–4 majority reasoned:

"The question for this Court is how to apply *Strickland's* prejudice test where ineffective assistance results in a rejection of the plea offer and the defendant is convicted at the ensuing trial. To establish *Strickland* prejudice a defendant must 'show that there is a reasonable probability that, but for counsel's unprofessional errors, the result of the proceeding would have been different.' In the context of pleas a defendant must show the outcome of the plea process would have been different with competent advice. * * * In *Hill v. Lockhart*, 474 U.S. 52 (1985), when evaluating the petitioner's claim that ineffective assistance led to the improvident acceptance of a guilty plea, the

---

[1] The state also argued that (1) the AEDPA standard of review precluded reversal based on the interpretation of the prejudice prong that the Supreme Court had previously adopted for federal habeas courts and (2) the federal habeas court erred in fashioning a remedy (assuming a violation of *Strickland*). The Court's responses on these issues are discussed at Note 5, Supp., pp. 157–159 and Supp., p. 120.

Court required the petitioner to show 'that there is a reasonable probability that, but for counsel's errors, [the defendant] would not have pleaded guilty and would have insisted on going to trial.' * * * In contrast to *Hill,* here the ineffective advice led not to an offer's acceptance but to its rejection. Having to stand trial, not choosing to waive it, is the prejudice alleged. In these circumstances a defendant must show that but for the ineffective advice of counsel there is a reasonable probability that the plea offer would have been presented to the court (*i.e.,* that the defendant would have accepted the plea and the prosecution would not have withdrawn it in light of intervening circumstances), that the court would have accepted its terms, and that the conviction or sentence, or both, under the offer's terms would have been less severe than under the judgment and sentence that in fact were imposed. * * *

"Petitioner [the state warden] and the Solicitor General [amicus curiae] propose a different, far more narrow, view of the Sixth Amendment. They contend there can be no finding of *Strickland* prejudice arising from plea bargaining if the defendant is later convicted at a fair trial. The three reasons petitioner and the Solicitor General offer for their approach are unpersuasive.

"First, petitioner and the Solicitor General claim that the sole purpose of the Sixth Amendment is to protect the right to a fair trial. Errors before trial, they argue, are not cognizable under the Sixth Amendment unless they affect the fairness of the trial itself. * * * The Sixth Amendment, however, is not so narrow in its reach. The Sixth Amendment requires effective assistance of counsel at critical stages of a criminal proceeding. Its protections are not designed simply to protect the trial, even though 'counsel's absence [in these stages] may derogate from the accused's right to a fair trial.' *United States v. Wade,* [13th ed., p. 761]. The constitutional guarantee applies to pretrial critical stages that are part of the whole course of a criminal proceeding, a proceeding in which defendants cannot be presumed to make critical decisions without counsel's advice. This is consistent, too, with the rule that defendants have a right to effective assistance of counsel on appeal, even though that cannot in any way be characterized as part of the trial. * * * The precedents also establish that there exists a right to counsel during sentencing in both noncapital and capital cases. Even though sentencing does not concern the defendant's guilt or innocence, ineffective assistance of counsel during a sentencing hearing can result in *Strickland* prejudice because 'any amount of [additional] jail time has Sixth Amendment significance.' *Glover v. United States,* [13th ed., p. 154]. * * *

"Second, petitioner claims this Court refined *Strickland*'s prejudice analysis in *Lockhart v. Fretwell,* [13th ed., p. 153], to add an additional requirement that the defendant show that ineffective assistance of counsel led to his being denied a substantive or procedural right. The Court has rejected the argument that *Fretwell* modified *Strickland* before and does so again now. See *Williams v. Taylor,* [13th ed., p. 154] * * * . [*Fretwell*] presented the 'unusual circumstance where the defendant attempts to demonstrate prejudice based on considerations that, as a matter of law, ought not inform the inquiry.' Ibid. (O'Connor, J., concurring). See also ibid.

(recognizing '[t]he determinative question—whether there is a reasonable probability that, but for counsel's unprofessional errors, the result of the proceeding would have been different—remains unchanged'). It is for this same reason a defendant cannot show prejudice based on counsel's refusal to present perjured testimony, even if such testimony might have affected the outcome of the case. See *Nix v. Whiteside,* [13th ed., p. 153] (holding first that counsel's refusal to present perjured testimony breached no professional duty and second that it cannot establish prejudice under *Strickland*).

"Both *Fretwell* and *Nix* are instructive in that they demonstrate 'there are also situations in which it would be unjust to characterize the likelihood of a different outcome as legitimate prejudice,' *Williams v. Taylor,* because defendants would receive a windfall as a result of the application of an incorrect legal principle or a defense strategy outside the law. Here, however, the injured client seeks relief from counsel's failure to meet a valid legal standard, not from counsel's refusal to violate it. He maintains that, absent ineffective counsel, he would have accepted a plea offer for a sentence the prosecution evidently deemed consistent with the sound administration of criminal justice. The favorable sentence that eluded the defendant in the criminal proceeding appears to be the sentence he or others in his position would have received in the ordinary course, absent the failings of counsel. If a plea bargain has been offered, a defendant has the right to effective assistance of counsel in considering whether to accept it. If that right is denied, prejudice can be shown if loss of the plea opportunity led to a trial resulting in a conviction on more serious charges or the imposition of a more severe sentence.

"It is, of course, true that defendants have 'no right to be offered a plea . . . nor a federal right that the judge accept it.' *Missouri v. Frye,* [Supp., p. 113. In the circumstances here, that is beside the point. If no plea offer is made, or a plea deal is accepted by the defendant but rejected by the judge, the issue raised here simply does not arise. Much the same reasoning guides cases that find criminal defendants have a right to effective assistance of counsel in direct appeals even though the Constitution does not require States to provide a system of appellate review at all. As in those cases, '[w]hen a State opts to act in a field where its action has significant discretionary elements, it must nonetheless act in accord with the dictates of the Constitution.' * * *

"Third, petitioner seeks to preserve the conviction obtained by the State by arguing that the purpose of the Sixth Amendment is to ensure 'the reliability of [a] conviction following trial.' This argument, too, fails to comprehend the full scope of the Sixth Amendment's protections; and it is refuted by precedent. *Strickland* recognized '[t]he benchmark for judging any claim of ineffectiveness must be whether counsel's conduct so undermined the proper functioning of the adversarial process that the trial cannot be relied on as having produced a just result.' The goal of a just result is not divorced from the reliability of a conviction * * *; but here the question is not the fairness or reliability of the trial but the fairness and regularity of the processes that preceded it, which caused the defendant to lose benefits he would have received in the ordinary course but for counsel's ineffective assistance.

"There are instances, furthermore, where a reliable trial does not foreclose relief when counsel has failed to assert rights that may have altered the outcome. In *Kimmelman v. Morrison,* [13th ed., p. 152], the Court held that an attorney's failure to timely move to suppress evidence during trial could be grounds for federal habeas relief. The Court rejected the suggestion that the 'failure to make a timely request for the exclusion of illegally seized evidence' could not be the basis for a Sixth Amendment violation because the evidence 'is typically reliable and often the most probative information bearing on the guilt or innocence of the defendant.' 'The constitutional rights of criminal defendants,' the Court observed, 'are granted to the innocent and the guilty alike. Consequently, we decline to hold either that the guarantee of effective assistance of counsel belongs solely to the innocent or that it attaches only to matters affecting the determination of actual guilt.' The same logic applies here. The fact that respondent is guilty does not mean he was not entitled by the Sixth Amendment to effective assistance or that he suffered no prejudice from his attorney's deficient performance during plea bargaining.

"In the end, petitioner's three arguments amount to one general contention: A fair trial wipes clean any deficient performance by defense counsel during plea bargaining. That position ignores the reality that criminal justice today is for the most part a system of pleas, not a system of trials. Ninety-seven percent of federal convictions and ninety-four percent of state convictions are the result of guilty pleas. See *Frye.* As explained in *Frye,* the right to adequate assistance of counsel cannot be defined or enforced without taking account of the central role plea bargaining plays in securing convictions and determining sentences."

Part I of Justice Scalia's dissent, joined by Chief Justice Roberts and Justice Thomas, responded to the majority's reasoning. Justice Alito, in a separate dissent, agreed that, "for the reasons set forth in Par[t] I * * * of Justice Scalia's dissent, the Court's holding * * * misapplies our ineffective-assistance-of-counsel case law." Justice Scalia reasoned in Part I:

"This case and its companion, *Missouri v. Frye,* raise relatively straightforward questions about the scope of the right to effective assistance of counsel. Our case law originally derived that right from the Due Process Clause, and its guarantee of a fair trial, *United States v. Gonzalez-Lopez,* [13th ed., pp. 122–23], but the seminal case of *Strickland v. Washington* located the right within the Sixth Amendment. As the Court notes, the right to counsel does not begin at trial. It extends to 'any stage of the prosecution, formal or informal, in court or out, where counsel's absence might derogate from the accused's right to a fair trial.' * * * And it follows from this that *acceptance* of a plea offer is a critical stage. That, and nothing more, is the point of the Court's observation in *Padilla v. Kentucky* [13th ed., p. 1315] that 'the negotiation of a plea bargain is a critical phase of litigation for purposes of the Sixth Amendment right to effective assistance of counsel.' The defendant in *Padilla* had accepted the plea bargain and pleaded guilty, abandoning his right to a fair trial; he was entitled to advice of competent counsel before he did so. The Court has never held that the rule articulated in [cases like] *Padilla* * * * extends to all aspects of plea negotiations, requiring not just advice of competent counsel before the defendant accepts a plea bargain and pleads guilty, but also the advice of competent counsel before the defendant rejects a plea bargain and stands on his constitutional right to a fair trial. The latter is a vast departure from our past cases, protecting not just the constitutionally prescribed right to a fair adjudication of guilt and punishment, but a judicially invented right to effective plea bargaining.

"It is also apparent from *Strickland* that bad plea bargaining has nothing to do with ineffective assistance of counsel in the constitutional sense. *Strickland* explained that '[i]n giving meaning to the requirement [of effective assistance], . . . we must take its purpose—to ensure a fair trial—as the guide.' Since 'the right to the effective assistance of counsel is recognized not for its own sake, but because of the effect it has on the ability of the accused to receive a fair trial,' *United States v. Cronic*, the 'benchmark' inquiry in evaluating any claim of ineffective assistance is whether counsel's performance 'so undermined the proper functioning of the adversarial process' that it failed to produce a reliably 'just result.' *Strickland*. That is what *Strickland*'s requirement of 'prejudice' consists of: Because the right to effective assistance has as its purpose the assurance of a fair trial, the right is not infringed unless counsel's mistakes call into question the basic justice of a defendant's conviction or sentence.

"To be sure, *Strickland* stated a rule of thumb for measuring prejudice which, applied blindly and out of context, could support the Court's holding today: 'The defendant must show that there is a reasonable probability that, but for counsel's unprofessional errors, the result of the proceeding would have been different.' *Strickland* itself cautioned, however, that its test was not to be applied in a mechanical fashion, and that courts were not to divert their 'ultimate focus' from 'the fundamental fairness of the proceeding whose result is being challenged.' And until today we have followed that course.

"In *Lockhart v. Fretwell*, * * * [we] determined that a prejudice analysis 'focusing solely on mere outcome determination, without attention to whether the result of the proceeding was fundamentally unfair or unreliable,' would be defective. Because counsel's error did not 'deprive the defendant of any substantive or procedural right to which the law entitles him,' the defendant's sentencing proceeding was fair and its result was reliable, even though counsel's error may have affected its outcome.[2] * * * As the Court

---

[2]   *Kimmelman v. Morrison*, cited by the Court, does not contradict this principle. That case * * * considered whether our holding that Fourth Amendment claims fully litigated in state court cannot be raised in federal habeas "should be extended to Sixth Amendment claims of ineffective assistance of counsel where the principal allegation and manifestations of inadequate representation is counsel's failure to file a timely motion to suppress evidence allegedly obtained

itself observes, a criminal defendant has no right to a plea bargain. * * * Counsel's mistakes in this case thus did not 'deprive the defendant of a substantive or procedural right to which the law entitles him.' Far from being 'beside the point,' *Ante* [Supp., p. 11], that is critical to correct application of our precedents. Like *Fretwell,* this case 'concerns the unusual circumstance where the defendant attempts to demonstrate prejudice based on considerations that, as a matter of law, ought not inform the inquiry.' * * *"

6B. In Part IV of his dissent in *Lafler v. Cooper*, Justice Scalia, joined by Thomas, J., commented further on the significance of recognizing as "prejudice" the loss of a bargained plea. Justice Scalia noted:

"In many—perhaps most—countries of the world, American-style plea bargaining is forbidden in cases as serious as this one, even for the purpose of obtaining testimony that enables conviction of a greater malefactor, much less for the purpose of sparing the expense of trial. In Europe, many countries adhere to what they aptly call the 'legality principle' by requiring prosecutors to charge all prosecutable offenses, which is typically incompatible with the practice of charge-bargaining. * * * Such a system reflects an admirable belief that the law is the law, and those who break it should pay the penalty provided.

"In the United States, we have plea bargaining a-plenty, but until today it has been regarded as a necessary evil. It presents grave risks of prosecutorial overcharging that effectively compels an innocent defendant to avoid massive risk by pleading guilty to a lesser offense; and for guilty defendants it often—perhaps usually—results in a sentence well below what the law prescribes for the actual crime. But even so, we accept plea bargaining because many believe that without it our long and expensive process of criminal trial could not sustain the burden imposed on it, and our system of criminal justice would grind to a halt.

"Today, however, the Supreme Court of the United States elevates plea bargaining from a necessary evil to a constitutional entitlement. It is no longer a somewhat embarrassing adjunct to our criminal justice system; rather, as the Court announces in the companion case to this one, 'it *is* the criminal justice system.' *Frye.* * * * I am less saddened by the outcome of this case than I am by what it says about this Court's attitude toward criminal justice. The Court today embraces the sporting-chance theory of criminal law,

---

in violation of the Fourth Amendment." Our negative answer to that question had nothing to do with the issue here. The parties in *Kimmelman* had not raised the question "whether the admission of illegally seized but reliable evidence can ever constitute 'prejudice' under *Strickland*"—a question similar to the one presented her—and the Court therefore did not address it. Id. (Powell, J., concurring in judgment). *Kimmelman* made clear, however, how the answer to that question is to be determined: "The essence of an ineffective-assistance claim is that counsel's unprofessional errors so upset the adversarial balance between defense and prosecution *that the trial was rendered unfair and the verdict rendered suspect*," Id. (emphasis added). "Only those habeas petitioners who can prove under *Strickland that they have been denied a fair trial* . . . will be granted the writ," Id. (emphasis added). In short, *Kimmelman's* only relevance is to prove the Court's opinion wrong.

in which the State functions like a conscientious casino-operator, giving each player a fair chance to beat the house, that is, to serve less time than the law says he deserves. And when a player is excluded from the tables, his *constitutional rights* have been violated. I do not subscribe to that theory. No one should, least of all the Justices of the Supreme Court."

PART 2

POLICE PRACTICES

■ ■ ■

CHAPTER 6

ARREST, SEARCH AND SEIZURE

■ ■ ■

SECTION 1. THE EXCLUSIONARY RULE

13th ed., p. 250; before Note 5, add:

Police involvement well short of that in *Jacobsen* will sometimes suffice to take the event out of the "private" category, as is illustrated by the repossession cases, collected in *Hensley v. Gassman,* 693 F.3d 681 (6th Cir.2012). As summarized there, while "a police officer's presence during a repossession solely to keep the peace, i.e., to prevent a violent confrontation between the debtor and the creditor, is alone insufficient to convert the repossession into state action," "the likelihood that state action will be found increases when officers take a more active role in the repossession," and even "without active participation, courts have found that an officer's conduct can facilitate a repossession if it chills the plaintiff's right to object," given that a "police officer's arrival and close association with the creditor during the repossession may signal to the debtor that the weight of the state is behind the repossession and that the debtor should not interfere by objecting."

SECTION 2. PROTECTED AREAS AND INTERESTS

13th ed., p. 278; at the end of footnote *l*, add:

For a "property-rights" (rather than "privacy") solution to this problem, see *Florida v. Jardines,* below.

13th ed., p. 286; before *Gouled* case, add:

FLORIDA V. JARDINES
___ U.S. ___, 133 S.Ct. 1409, 185 L.Ed.2d 495 (2013).

JUSTICE SCALIA delivered the opinion of the Court. * * *

[After police received an unverified tip that Jardines was growing marijuana in his home, they took a drug-detection dog onto Jardines' front porch, where the dog "alerted" at the front door. On this basis, police obtained and executed a search warrant at Jardines' residence and seized marijuana plants, but the evidence was excluded below as the fruit of an unreasonable search.]

* * * By reason of our decision in *Katz v. United States*, [13th ed., p. 264], property rights "are not the sole measure of Fourth Amendment violations," but though *Katz* may add to the baseline, it does not subtract anything from the Amendment's protections "when the Government does engage in [a] physical intrusion of a constitutionally protected area."

That principle renders this case a straightforward one. The officers were gathering information in an area belonging to Jardines and immediately surrounding his house—in the curtilage[a] of the house, which we have held enjoys protection as part of the home itself. And they gathered that information by physically entering and occupying the area to engage in conduct not explicitly or implicitly permitted by the homeowner.

The Fourth Amendment "indicates with some precision the places and things encompassed by its protections": persons, houses, papers, and effects. The Fourth Amendment does not, therefore, prevent all investigations conducted on private property; for example, an officer may (subject to *Katz*) gather information in what we have called "open fields"—even if those fields are privately owned—because such fields are not enumerated in the Amendment's text.

But when it comes to the Fourth Amendment, the home is first among equals. At the Amendment's "very core" stands "the right of a man to retreat into his own home and there be free from unreasonable governmental intrusion." *Silverman v. United States*, 365 U.S. 505, 511 (1961). This right would be of little practical value if the State's agents could stand in a home's porch or side garden and trawl for evidence with impunity; the right to retreat would be significantly diminished if the police could enter a man's property to observe his repose from just outside the front window.

We therefore regard the area "immediately surrounding and associated with the home"—what our cases call the curtilage—as "part of the home itself for Fourth Amendment purposes." That principle has ancient and durable roots. Just as the distinction between the home and the open fields is "as old as the common law," so too is the identity of home and what Blackstone called the "curtilage or homestall," for the "house protects and privileges all its branches and appurtenants." This area around the home is "intimately linked to the home, both physically and psychologically," and is where "privacy expectations are most heightened."

While the boundaries of the curtilage are generally "clearly marked," the "conception defining the curtilage" is at any rate familiar enough that it is "easily understood from our daily experience." Here there is no doubt

---

[a]   On the meaning of "curtilage," see 13th ed., p. 270, fn. e.

that the officers entered it: The front porch is the classic exemplar of an area adjacent to the home and "to which the activity of home life extends."

Since the officers' investigation took place in a constitutionally protected area, we turn to the question of whether it was accomplished through an unlicensed physical intrusion. While law enforcement officers need not "shield their eyes" when passing by the home "on public thoroughfares," an officer's leave to gather information is sharply circumscribed when he steps off those thoroughfares and enters the Fourth Amendment's protected areas. * * * As it is undisputed that the detectives had all four of their feet and all four of their companion's firmly planted on the constitutionally protected extension of Jardines' home, the only question is whether he had given his leave (even implicitly) for them to do so. He had not.

"A license may be implied from the habits of the country," notwithstanding the "strict rule of the English common law as to entry upon a close." * * * This implicit license typically permits the visitor to approach the home by the front path, knock promptly, wait briefly to be received, and then (absent invitation to linger longer) leave. Complying with the terms of that traditional invitation does not require fine-grained legal knowledge; it is generally managed without incident by the Nation's Girl Scouts and trick-or-treaters. Thus, a police officer not armed with a warrant may approach a home and knock, precisely because that is "no more than any private citizen might do."

But introducing a trained police dog to explore the area around the home in hopes of discovering incriminating evidence is something else. There is no customary invitation to do that. An invitation to engage in canine forensic investigation assuredly does not inhere in the very act of hanging a knocker.[3] To find a visitor knocking on the door is routine (even if sometimes unwelcome); to spot that same visitor exploring the front path with a metal detector, or marching his bloodhound into the garden before saying hello and asking permission, would inspire most of us to—well, call the police. The scope of a license—express or implied—is limited not only to a particular area but also to a specific purpose. * * * Here, the background social norms that invite a visitor to the front door do not invite him there to conduct a search.

---

[3] The dissent insists that our argument must rest upon "the particular instrument that Detective Bartelt used to detect the odor of marijuana"—the dog. It is not the dog that is the problem, but the behavior that here involved use of the dog. We think a typical person would find it " 'a cause for great alarm' " * * * to find a stranger snooping about his front porch with or without a dog. The dissent would let the police do whatever they want by way of gathering evidence so long as they stay on the base-path, to use a baseball analogy—so long as they "stick to the path that is typically used to approach a front door, such as a paved walkway." From that vantage point they can presumably peer into the house through binoculars with impunity. That is not the law, as even the State concedes.

The State points to our decisions holding that the subjective intent of the officer is irrelevant. But those cases merely hold that a stop or search that is objectively reasonable is not vitiated by the fact that the officer's real reason for making the stop or search has nothing to do with the validating reason. * * * Here, however, the question before the court is precisely whether the officer's conduct was an objectively reasonable search. As we have described, that depends upon whether the officers had an implied license to enter the porch, which in turn depends upon the purpose for which they entered. Here, their behavior objectively reveals a purpose to conduct a search, which is not what anyone would think he had license to do.

The State argues that investigation by a forensic narcotics dog by definition cannot implicate any legitimate privacy interest. The State cites for authority our decisions in *United States v. Place*, [13th ed., p. 433], *United States v. Jacobsen*, [13th ed., pp. 249, 278], and *Illinois v. Caballes*, [13th ed., p. 428] * * *.

[But], we need not decide whether the officers' investigation of Jardines' home violated his expectation of privacy under *Katz*. One virtue of the Fourth Amendment's property-rights baseline is that it keeps easy cases easy. That the officers learned what they learned only by physically intruding on Jardines' property to gather evidence is enough to establish that a search occurred. * * *

JUSTICE KAGAN, with whom JUSTICE GINSBURG and JUSTICE SOTOMAYOR join, concurring. * * *

The Court today treats this case under a property rubric; I write separately to note that I could just as happily have decided it by looking to Jardines' privacy interests. A decision along those lines would have looked . . . well, much like this one. * * *

It is not surprising that in a case involving a search of a home, property concepts and privacy concepts should so align. The law of property "naturally enough influence[s]" our "shared social expectations" of what places should be free from governmental incursions. And so the sentiment "my home is my own," while originating in property law, now also denotes a common understanding—extending even beyond that law's formal protections—about an especially private sphere. Jardines' home was his property; it was also his most intimate and familiar space. The analysis proceeding from each of those facts, as today's decision reveals, runs mostly along the same path.

I can think of only one divergence: If we had decided this case on privacy grounds, we would have realized that *Kyllo v. United States*,

[13th ed., p. 274], already resolved it.[1] The *Kyllo* Court held that police officers conducted a search when they used a thermal-imaging device to detect heat emanating from a private home, even though they committed no trespass. Highlighting our intention to draw both a "firm" and a "bright" line at "the entrance to the house," we announced the following rule:

> "Where, as here, the Government uses a device that is not in general public use, to explore details of the home that would previously have been unknowable without physical intrusion, the surveillance is a 'search' and is presumptively unreasonable without a warrant."

That "firm" and "bright" rule governs this case: The police officers here conducted a search because they used a "device . . . not in general public use" (a trained drug-detection dog) to "explore details of the home" (the presence of certain substances) that they would not otherwise have discovered without entering the premises.

And again, the dissent's argument that the device is just a dog cannot change the equation. As *Kyllo* made clear, the "sense-enhancing" tool at issue may be "crude" or "sophisticated," may be old or new (drug-detection dogs actually go back not "12,000 years" or "centuries," but only a few decades), may be either smaller or bigger than a breadbox; still, "at least where (as here)" the device is not "in general public use," training it on a home violates our "minimal expectation of privacy"—an expectation "that exists, and that is acknowledged to be *reasonable*." * * *

With these further thoughts, suggesting that a focus on Jardines' privacy interests would make an "easy cas[e] easy" twice over, I join the Court's opinion in full.

JUSTICE ALITO, with whom THE CHIEF JUSTICE, JUSTICE KENNEDY, and JUSTICE BREYER join, dissenting. * * *

The Court concludes that the conduct in this case was a search because Detective Bartelt exceeded the boundaries of the license to approach the house that is recognized by the law of trespass, but the Court's interpretation of the scope of that license is unfounded.

It is said that members of the public may lawfully proceed along a walkway leading to the front door of a house because custom grants them a license to do so. This rule encompasses categories of visitors whom most homeowners almost certainly wish to allow to approach their front doors—friends, relatives, mail carriers, persons making deliveries. But it

---

[1]   The dissent claims, alternatively, that *Illinois v. Caballes* controls this case (or nearly does). But *Caballes* concerned a drug-detection dog's sniff of an automobile during a traffic stop. And we have held, over and over again, that people's expectations of privacy are much lower in their cars than in their homes.

also reaches categories of visitors who are less universally welcome—
"solicitors," "hawkers," "peddlers," and the like. * * *

Of course, this license has certain spatial and temporal limits. A
visitor must stick to the path that is typically used to approach a front
door, such as a paved walkway. * * *

Nor, as a general matter, may a visitor come to the front door in the
middle of the night without an express invitation. * * *

Similarly, a visitor may not linger at the front door for an extended
period. * * *The license is limited to the amount of time it would
customarily take to approach the door, pause long enough to see if
someone is home, and (if not expressly invited to stay longer), leave.

As I understand the law of trespass and the scope of the implied
license, a visitor who adheres to these limitations is not necessarily
required to ring the doorbell, knock on the door, or attempt to speak with
an occupant. For example, mail carriers, persons making deliveries, and
individuals distributing flyers may leave the items they are carrying and
depart without making any attempt to converse. * * *

As the majority acknowledges, this implied license to approach the
front door extends to the police. * * * Even when the objective of a "knock
and talk" is to obtain evidence that will lead to the homeowner's arrest
and prosecution, the license to approach still applies. In other words,
gathering evidence—even damning evidence—is a lawful activity that
falls within the scope of the license to approach. * * *

Detective Bartelt did not exceed the scope of the license to approach
respondent's front door. He adhered to the customary path; he did not
approach in the middle of the night; and he remained at the front door for
only a very short period (less than a minute or two). * * *

What the Court must fall back on, then, is the particular instrument
that Detective Bartelt used to detect the odor of marijuana, namely, his
dog. But in the entire body of common-law decisions, the Court has not
found a single case holding that a visitor to the front door of a home
commits a trespass if the visitor is accompanied by a dog on a leash. On
the contrary, the common law allowed even unleashed dogs to wander on
private property without committing a trespass. * * *

The concurring opinion attempts to provide an alternative ground for
today's decision, namely, that Detective Bartelt's conduct violated
respondent's reasonable expectations of privacy. But we have already
rejected a very similar, if not identical argument, see *Illinois v. Caballes*,
and in any event I see no basis for concluding that the occupants of a
dwelling have a reasonable expectation of privacy in odors that emanate
from the dwelling and reach spots where members of the public may
lawfully stand. * * *

In an attempt to show that respondent had a reasonable expectation of privacy in the odor of marijuana wafting from his house, the concurrence argues that this case is just like *Kyllo v. United States*, which held that police officers conducted a search when they used a thermal imaging device to detect heat emanating from a house. This Court, however, has already rejected the argument that the use of a drug-sniffing dog is the same as the use of a thermal imaging device. See *Caballes*. * * *

Contrary to the interpretation propounded by the concurrence, *Kyllo* is best understood as a decision about the use of new technology. * * * A dog, however, is not a new form of "technology" or a "device." And, as noted, the use of dogs' acute sense of smell in law enforcement dates back many centuries.

The concurrence suggests that a *Kyllo*-based decision would be "much like" the actual decision of the Court, but that is simply not so. * * *

The concurrence's *Kyllo*-based approach would have a much wider reach. When the police used the thermal imaging device in *Kyllo*, they were on a public street, and "committed no trespass." Therefore, if a dog's nose is just like a thermal imaging device for Fourth Amendment purposes, a search would occur if a dog alerted while on a public sidewalk or in the corridor of an apartment building. * * *

NOTES AND QUESTIONS

1. *"Curtilage."* Considering *Jardines'* emphasis upon the dog's presence within the "curtilage," as well as pre-*Jardines* authority to the effect that the concept of "curtilage" has little if any application to commercial structures, e.g., *United States v. Elkins*, 300 F.3d 638 (6th Cir.2002) ("areas that adjoin a commercial building but are accessible to the public do not receive curtilage-like protection"), or to multiple-unit dwellings, e.g., *Reeves v. Churchich*, 484 F.3d 1244 (10th Cir.2007) (areas outside individual units of duplex not "curtilage" with respect to either unit if shared with occupants of other unit), what result as to a dog sniff at these doors: (a) at the front door of a former two-story dwelling now occupied by "Jake's Junk," an antique store, on the first floor, though Jake lives on the second floor; (b) at the outdoor storage room door at "Ajax Auto," a car towing-and-repair business, where that room has been converted to sleeping quarters for the tow-truck operator when he is on a 24-hour shift; (c) at the front door of one of a series of zero-lawn, common side-wall, individually-owned row houses, where the door is separated from the passing sidewalk only by a small stoop not used by the dog; (d) at the front door of unit C in a triplex owned by the occupant of unit A, who rents out units B and C, where all three doors are on a common porch; (e) at the front door of apartment 805, facing an unlocked interior hallway used by other occupants and visitors, in an 8-story, 48-unit apartment building; (f) at the front door of unit 211, facing an outdoor walkway, at

"Sanibel Surfside," a 38-unit condominium, where the walkway is part of the "common elements," as to which each unit owner holds an undivided 1/38th share of ownership.

2. **"Trespass."** *Jones*, it will be recalled, held that "[t]respass * * * conjoined with * * * an attempt to find something or to obtain information" constitutes a search. As one commentator has noted, while the "apparent restoration of a pre-*Katz* search doctrine in *Jones* reflects the widely-shared assumption that pre-*Katz* search doctrine was in fact based on trespass law," in actuality "no trespass test was used in the pre-*Katz* era." Kerr, *What Is the State of the Jones Trespass Test After Florida v. Jardines?,* www.volokh.com/ 2013/03/27/what-is-the-state-of-the-jones-trespass-test-after-florida-v- jardines/. Is it significant, then, that the word "trespass" *never* appears in the majority opinion in *Jardines* (as compared to 15 times in the dissent)? Kerr goes on to suggest that thus the issue in these cases "isn't the technicalities of trespass law, but rather the presence of physical intrusion into property owned by the person," as to which "the long-forgotten per curiam decision in *Clinton v. Virginia,"* 377 U.S. 158 (1964) (apparently applying the "physical penetration" test of *Silverman,* relied upon in *Jardines,* to a case involving eavesdropping via a mechanical listening device attached to the wall of an adjoining apartment), may have relevance. Is this so, and, if so, does this change your answer to any of the Note 1 hypos? (For that matter, would any of your answers change if you instead applied the *Jardines* concurrence's "privacy" test?)

3. **Intent, instrumentality, and license limits.** On an anonymous tip that "Smitty is peddling dope at 123 Main St.," police went there in the early evening planning to use the "knock-and-talk" technique, but no one answered the door of the darkened premises. Noting a porch light on at 125 Main, the nearest neighboring house, one officer went there to inquire about Smitty, but just before he stepped onto the porch that light went out; no one answered the door after repeated knocks, although the officer thought he heard a moaning sound and saw a slight movement of the drapes at the window two feet to the left of the door. Entertaining a variety of thoughts (e.g., are the occupants OK? am I in danger if I now turn to leave?) the officer tried to look in the picture window through a one-foot gap in the drapes, but it was dark inside. Taking his standard issue flashlight from his belt, he shined it through the opening and saw drugs and drug paraphernalia on a table in the middle of the room, so he departed and obtained a search warrant which was later executed at those premises. The police then turned their attention back to 123 Main; one officer opted to "stand by" on the porch there while his colleague went to see if a drug dog was available at that hour (1 a.m.). After waiting on the porch about 15 minutes, the officer heard voices, and by moving a foot or two on the porch to an adjacent slightly open window the officer with his naked ear overheard conversations about delivering on-site drugs to other locations the next afternoon. The officer then departed and obtained a warrant, which was then successfully executed at those premises. What result on the motions to suppress the drugs found at

125 Main and 123 Main, respectively, under the Scalia, Kagan and Alito versions of *Jardines*?

4. ***Jardines vs. Caballes.*** What if in *Jardines* the officer had instead found a vehicle parked in the driveway just in front of the garage door, and the dog "alerted" to the vehicle?

13th ed., p. 291; at the end of Note 3, add:

Consider also *Preventive Medicine Associates, Inc. v. Commonwealth,* 992 N.E.2d 257 (Mass.2013), holding, with respect to a post-indictment search warrant for defendant's e-mail account, that where there is a "substantial likelihood that privileged attorney-client communications will be present," upon a "failure to justify the need for a search warrant rather than a * * * subpoena," the judge would have a basis for denying the warrant application, and if the warrant is to be issued, any search under that warrant, "to be reasonable, must include reasonable steps designed to prevent a breach of the attorney-client privilege," such as a "taint team search procedure," whereby a team of attorneys who have not been and will not be involved in the investigation or prosecution of the defendants examines the e-mails and places them into possibly privileged and not privileged categories, after which the defendant is allowed to review and challenge any of the classifications; any objections that cannot otherwise be resolved are then determined by the court.

SECTION 3. "PROBABLE CAUSE"

13th ed., p. 305; before Note 2, add:

1A. In FLORIDA v. HARRIS, 133 S.Ct. 1050 (2013), a unanimous Court, per Kagan, J., overturned a state court ruling that for an "alert" by a drug-detection dog to constitute probable cause, "the State must in every case present an exhaustive set of records, including a log of the dog's performance in the field, to establish the dog's reliability." The Court found such a requirement inconsistent with *Gates*, which looks "to the totality of the circumstance" and rejects "rigid rules, bright-line tests, and mechanistic inquiries in favor of a more flexible, all-thing-considered approach":

"For that reason, evidence of a dog's satisfactory performance in a certification or training program can itself provide sufficient reason to trust his alert. If a bona fide organization has certified a dog after testing his reliability in a controlled setting, a court can presume (subject to any conflicting evidence offered) that the dog's alert provides probable cause to search. The same is true, even in the absence of formal certification, if the dog has recently and successfully completed a training program that evaluated his proficiency in locating drugs. After all, law enforcement units have their own strong incentive to use effective training and certification programs, because only accurate drug-detection dogs enable officers to locate contraband without incurring unnecessary risks or wasting limited time and resources.

"A defendant, however, must have an opportunity to challenge such evidence of a dog's reliability, whether by cross-examining the testifying officer or by introducing his own fact or expert witnesses. The defendant, for example, may contest the adequacy of a certification or training program, perhaps asserting that its standards are too lax or its methods faulty. So too, the defendant may examine how the dog (or handler) performed in the assessments made in those settings. Indeed, evidence of the dog's (or handler's) history in the field, although susceptible to the kind of misinterpretation we have discussed,[aa] may sometimes be relevant * * *. And even assuming a dog is generally reliable, circumstances surrounding a particular alert may undermine the case for probable cause—if, say, the officer cued the dog (consciously or not), or if the team was working under unfamiliar conditions."

The Court then concluded probable cause existed in the instant case, as the state showed the dog "had successfully completed two drug-detection courses and maintained his proficiency through weekly training exercises," while defendant's evidence purporting to show two false alerts to his vehicle might be attributable to defendant, a regular meth user, transferring the odor to the door handle. (Compare the different response to the perceived "false positives" risk in *United States v. Galloway*, 316 F.3d 624 (6th Cir.2003), concluding that while a "canine alert" could elevate pre-existing reasonable suspicion of drug presence up to probable cause, it alone "does not constitute probable cause in a completely random setting, such as an airport, because of its questionable accuracy.")

[aa] As the Court noted earlier: "Errors may abound in such records. If a dog on patrol fails to alert to a car containing drugs, the mistake usually will go undetected because the officer will not initiate a search. Field data thus may not capture a dog's false negatives. Conversely (and more relevant here), if the dog alerts to a car in which the officer finds no narcotics, the dog may not have made a mistake at all. The dog may have detected substances that were too well hidden or present in quantities too small for the officer to locate. Or the dog may have smelled the residual odor of drugs previously in the vehicle or on the driver's person."

13th ed., p. 315; before Note 3, add:

Sometimes—as with visual speed estimates—there is a question as to whether the officer was able reliably to make the judgment about what was occurring before him. Thus, "where an officer estimates that a vehicle is traveling in only slight excess of the legal speed limit, and particularly where the alleged violation is at a speed differential difficult for the naked eye to discern, an officer's visual speed estimate required additional indicia of reliability to support probable cause," such as where the visual estimate is "supported by radar, pacing methods, or other indicia of reliability that establish, in the totality of the circumstances, the reasonableness of the officer's visual speed estimate." *United States v. Sowards*, 690 F.3d 583 (4th Cir.2012) (no probable cause where officer's uncorroborated visual speed estimate was 75 m.p.h. in 70 m.p.h. zone).[c]

c Distinguishing *Sowards*, it was held in *United States v. Mubdi*, 691 F.3d 334 (4th Cir.2012), that there was probable cause regarding an estimate defendant was driving 65 m.p.h. in a 55 m.p.h. zone because there were "two independent and virtually identical estimates as to Mubdi's speed by officers who were required, as part of a radar certification class, to visually estimate the speed of vehicles within a narrow margin of error."

SECTION 4. SEARCH WARRANTS

A. ISSUANCE OF THE WARRANT

13th ed., p. 319; at the end of the second paragraph of Note 3, within the quotation, add:

(12) A description that alone might be insufficient may become particular enough given the context within which it is used. (13) Where the search warrant description of the items to be seized is sufficiently specific and limited, that description cannot be broadened by allegations appearing in the search warrant affidavit.

B. EXECUTION OF THE WARRANT

13th ed., p. 327; before *Muehler* case, add:

In *Bailey v. United States*, 133 S.Ct. 1031 (2013), where the lower court relied upon *Summers* in upholding a detention commenced about a mile from the premises to be searched, the Court held, 6–3, per Kennedy, J., that *Summers* is limited to instances in which "an occupant was detained within the immediate vicinity of the premises to be searched," as this restriction "accords with the rationale of the [*Summers*] rule." For one thing, such a limitation squares with the "three important law enforcement interests" recognized in *Summers*: (1) as for "the interest in minimizing the risk of harm to the officers," an absent occupant such as Bailey "posed little risk to the officers at the scene," and if he returned the police then "could have apprehended and detained him under *Summers*"; (2) as for "the orderly completion of the search," Bailey "was not a threat to the proper execution of the search," and the fact he might "assist the officers" is a consideration applicable only to those "on site," as otherwise "it would have no limiting principle"; (3) as for the "concern over flight," it is limited to "the damage that potential flight can cause to the integrity of the search," and thus "does not independently justify detention of an occupant beyond the immediate vicinity of the premises to be searched." For another, *Summers* emphasized that there "the intrusion on personal liberty was limited," not so as to situations like the instant case, involving a "public detention" that "will resemble a full-fledged arrest" plus "the additional indignity of a compelled transfer back to the premises." Three concurring Justices, per Scalia, J., added that the "interest-balancing approach" of the court of appeals, "endorsed by the dissent," is "incompatible" with *Summers* because that case established "a categorical, bright-line rule," so the government, "having received the advantage of *Summers*' categorical authorization," "must take the bitter with the sweet."

The three *Bailey* dissenters, per Breyer, J., objected that the majority had "offer[ed] no easily administered bright line,"[ff] and had ignored the reasonableness of the police conduct in the instant case, given that Bailey and a companion were "seen leaving the premises to be searched" and were "detained as soon as reasonably practicable," as their immediate seizure could have alerted anyone inside the premises and prompted them to hide evidence, flee or resist the warrant execution, and the stop occurred only a few blocks away as soon as the car left "busier streets" for "a quieter side road."

[ff] They noted that the majority "describes its line as one drawn at 'the immediate vicinity of the premises to be searched,' to be determined by 'a number of factors . . . including [but not limited to] the lawful limits of the premises, whether the occupant was within the line of sight of his dwelling, the ease of reentry from the occupant's location, and other relevant factors.' "

13th ed., p. 327; at the end of Note 5, add:

The lawful duration of the search may be affected by the dissipation of probable cause, as in *State v. Schulz*, 55 A.3d 933 (N.H.2012), where police lawfully present outside a home saw "three long guns near a staircase." Knowing one of the occupants was a convicted felon, the police obtained a warrant to search those premises for "firearms," but early on in the execution of the warrant the police discovered those three weapons were only BB guns and thus lawful to possess, but nonetheless continued with the search and discovered cocaine, deemed inadmissible by the *Schulz* court given the "need for probable cause to exist both at the time the warrant issues and throughout its execution." But the court cautioned that "in many situations involving risky and high-intensity searches, police officers will not have an opportunity to reconsider with sober reflection the basis of probable cause each time a new piece of information comes to light," in which case the *Schulz* rule would not apply.

SECTION 5. WARRANTLESS ARRESTS AND SEARCHES OF THE PERSON

13th ed., p. 347; at the end of Note 1, add:

Consider also *United States v. Edwards*, 666 F.3d 877 (4th Cir.2011), where police arrested defendant on the street at 11:15 p.m. for domestic assault and handcuffed his hands behind him. Before placing defendant in a police van, they conducted a second, more thorough search of his person, which included loosening his belt and pulling his pants and underpants 6–7 inches away from his body and then shining a flashlight into the opening, revealing that defendant had a plastic sandwich baggie tied in a knot around his penis. Concluding that the baggie contained a controlled substance, one officer cut the baggie off defendant's penis with a knife, which the court concluded violated the Fourth Amendment because "the government provides no reason" why the baggie "could not have been removed under circumstances less dangerous" to defendant. The court added there were several plausible alternatives the officer could have used: "untying the baggie, removing it by hand, tearing the baggie, requesting that a blunt scissors be brought to the scene to remove the baggie."

13th ed., p. 347; delete Note 2

13th ed., p. 360; at the end of Note 4, add:

In MISSOURI v. McNEELY, 133 S.Ct. 1552 (2013), the Court "granted certiorari to resolve a split of authority on the question whether the natural dissipation of alcohol in the bloodstream establishes a per se exigency that suffices on its own to justify an exception to the warrant requirement for nonconsensual blood testing in drunk-driving investigations." The majority, per Sotomayor, J., acknowledged "that because an individual's alcohol level gradually declines soon after he stops drinking, a significant delay in testing will negatively affect the probative value of the results," but asserted "it does not follow that we should depart from careful case-by-case assessment of exigency and adopt the categorical rule proposed by the State and its amici. In those drunk-driving investigations where police officers can reasonably obtain a warrant before a blood sample can be drawn without significantly undermining the efficacy of the search, the Fourth Amendment mandates that they do so." Blood testing, the majority asserted, "is different in critical respects from other destruction-of-evidence cases," as the evidence "naturally dissipates over time in a gradual and relatively predictable manner," and "some delay" is "inevitable" in any event because "a police officer must typically transport a drunk-driving suspect to a medical facility and obtain the assistance of someone with appropriate medical training before conducting a blood test." Moreover, there have been "advances in the 47 years since *Schmerber* was decided," as the "Federal Rules of Criminal Procedure [and] well over a majority of States allow police officers or prosecutors to apply for search warrants remotely through various means, including telephonic or radio communication, electronic communication such as e-mail, and video conferencing."

Roberts, C.J., for three Justices, dissenting in part, objected that a police officer reading the majority opinion "would have no idea—no idea—what the Fourth Amendment requires of him," and then concluded that "the proper rule is straightforward": "The natural dissipation of alcohol in the bloodstream constitutes not only the imminent but ongoing destruction of critical evidence. That would qualify as an exigent circumstance, except that there may be time to secure a warrant before blood can be drawn. If there is, an officer must seek a warrant. If an officer could reasonably conclude that there is not, the exigent circumstances exception applies by its terms, and the blood may be drawn without a warrant." (One member of the majority, Kennedy, J., concurring in part, emphasized that the posture of the case—the state had raised *only* the per se exigency claim—meant the Court had only decided that "always dispensing with a warrant" in these kinds of cases "is inconsistent with the Fourth Amendment," apparently meaning he neither embraced nor rejected the Roberts approach.) Thomas, J., dissenting, who "would hold that a warrantless blood draw does not violate the Fourth Amendment," objected that the majority had adopted "a rule that requires police to guess whether they will be able to obtain a warrant before 'too much' evidence is destroyed, for the police lack reliable information concerning the relevant variables," i.e., "how intoxicated a suspect is at the time of arrest" and "how long it will take to roust a magistrate from his bed, reach the hospital, or obtain a blood sample once there."

13th ed., p. 360; at the end of Note 5, add:

Consider *United States v. Gray*, 669 F.3d 556 (5th Cir.2012) (resort to proctoscopy via search warrant, on information defendant concealing crack cocaine in his rectum, involving "slight" danger but a "demeaning and intrusive invasion," fails *Winston* "compelling need" test, as "there were other available avenues for obtaining this evidence, such as a cathartic or an enema").

13th ed., p. 360; in lieu of existing Note 6, insert:

6. Florence brought a § 1983 action claiming violation of his Fourth Amendment rights because, following his arrest on a database entry erroneously indicating there was still an outstanding bench warrant for his failure to appear at a court hearing two years earlier, he was thereafter held in two different county detention centers and in each case, prior to admission to the general jail population, was subjected to a strip search in which "he was required to lift his genitals, turn around, and cough in a squatting position." In FLORENCE v. BOARD OF CHOSEN FREEHOLDERS, 132 S.Ct. 1510 (2012), the Court, per Kennedy, J., concluded:

"The question here is whether undoubted security imperatives involved in jail supervision override the assertion that some detainees must be exempt from the more invasive search procedures at issue absent reasonable suspicion of a concealed weapon or other contraband. The Court has held that deference must be given to the officials in charge of the jail unless there is 'substantial evidence' demonstrating their response to the situation is exaggerated. Petitioner has not met this standard, and the record provides full justifications for the procedures used. * * *

"Petitioner acknowledges that correctional officials must be allowed to conduct an effective search during the intake process and that this will require at least some detainees to lift their genitals or cough in a squatting position. These procedures, similar to the ones upheld in *Bell*,[a] are designed to uncover contraband that can go undetected by a patdown, metal detector, and other less invasive searches. Petitioner maintains there is little benefit to conducting these more invasive steps on a new detainee who has not been arrested for a serious crime or for any offense involving a weapon or drugs. In his view these detainees should be exempt from this process unless they give officers a particular reason to suspect them of hiding contraband. It is

---

[a]   The reference is to *Bell v. Wolfish*, 13th ed., p. 272, fn. f.

reasonable, however, for correctional officials to conclude this standard would be unworkable. The record provides evidence that the seriousness of an offense is a poor predictor of who has contraband and that it would be difficult in practice to determine whether individual detainees fall within the proposed exemption.[b] * * *

"One of the central principles in *Atwater* [13th ed., p. 348] applies with equal force here. Officers who interact with those suspected of violating the law have an 'essential interest in readily administrable rules.'"

The next section of the opinion, joined by only four Justices, cautions: "This case does not require the Court to rule on the types of searches that would be reasonable in instances where, for example, a detainee will be held without assignment to the general jail population and without substantial contact with other detainees. * * * The circumstances before the Court * * * do not present the opportunity to consider a narrow exception of the sort Justice Alito describes, (concurring opinion), which might restrict whether an arrestee whose detention has not yet been reviewed by a magistrate or other judicial officer, and who can be held in available facilities removed from the general population, may be subjected to the types of searches at issue here."

The four dissenters objected that a reasonable suspicion standard had been endorsed by many "professional bodies," was applied by "many correctional facilities," was required by law "in at least 10 States" and by "at least seven Courts of Appeals," but yet "neither the majority's opinion nor the briefs set forth any clear example of an instance in which contraband was smuggled into the general jail population during intake that could not have been discovered if the jail was employing a reasonable suspicion standard."

13th ed., p. 362; after Note 8, add:

MARYLAND V. KING

569 U.S. ___, 133 S.Ct. 1958, 186 L.Ed.2d 1 (2013).

JUSTICE KENNEDY delivered the opinion of the Court. * * *

In 2009 Alonzo King was arrested in Wicomico County, Maryland, and charged with first- and second-degree assault for menacing a group of people with a shotgun. As part of a routine booking procedure for serious offenses [pursuant to the Md. DNA Collection Act], his DNA sample was taken by applying a cotton swab or filter paper—known as a buccal swab—to the inside of his cheeks. The DNA was found to match the DNA

---

[b] In elaboration of this point, the Court asserted: (1) "Experience shows that people arrested for minor offenses have tried to smuggle prohibited items into jail, sometimes by using their rectal cavities or genitals for the concealment"; (2) "Even if people arrested for a minor offense do not themselves wish to introduce contraband into a jail, they may be coerced into doing so by others"; and (3) "It also may be difficult * * * to classify inmates by their current and prior offenses before the intake search," as "officials there know so little about the people they admit at the outset."

taken from [a 2003] rape victim. King was tried and convicted for the rape. * * *

The Court of Appeals of Maryland, on review of King's rape conviction, ruled that the DNA taken when King was booked for the 2009 charge was an unlawful seizure because obtaining and using the cheek swab was an unreasonable search of the person. It set the rape conviction aside. This Court granted certiorari and now reverses the judgment of the Maryland court. * * *

The advent of DNA technology is one of the most significant scientific advancements of our era. * * * Since the first use of forensic DNA analysis to catch a rapist and murderer in England in 1986, law enforcement, the defense bar, and the courts have acknowledged DNA testing's "unparalleled ability both to exonerate the wrongly convicted and to identify the guilty. It has the potential to significantly improve both the criminal justice system and police investigative practices." * * *

The Act authorizes Maryland law enforcement authorities to collect DNA samples from "an individual who is charged with . . . a crime of violence or an attempt to commit a crime of violence; or . . . burglary or an attempt to commit burglary." Maryland law defines a crime of violence to include murder, rape, first-degree assault, kidnaping, arson, sexual assault, and a variety of other serious crimes. Once taken, a DNA sample may not be processed or placed in a database before the individual is arraigned (unless the individual consents). It is at this point that a judicial officer ensures that there is probable cause to detain the arrestee on a qualifying serious offense. If "all qualifying criminal charges are determined to be unsupported by probable cause . . . the DNA sample shall be immediately destroyed." DNA samples are also destroyed if "a criminal action begun against the individual . . . does not result in a conviction," "the conviction is finally reversed or vacated and no new trial is permitted," or "the individual is granted an unconditional pardon."

The Act also limits the information added to a DNA database and how it may be used. * * * No purpose other than identification is permissible * * *. Tests for familial matches are also prohibited. * * * The officers involved in taking and analyzing respondent's DNA sample complied with the Act in all respects. * * *

Respondent's identification as the rapist resulted in part through the operation of a national project to standardize collection and storage of DNA profiles. Authorized by Congress and supervised by the Federal Bureau of Investigation, the Combined DNA Index System (CODIS) connects DNA laboratories at the local, state, and national level. Since its authorization in 1994, the CODIS system has grown to include all 50 States and a number of federal agencies. * * *

All 50 States require the collection of DNA from felony convicts, and respondent does not dispute the validity of that practice. Twenty-eight States and the Federal Government have adopted laws similar to the Maryland Act authorizing the collection of DNA from some or all arrestees. Although those statutes vary in their particulars, such as what charges require a DNA sample, their similarity means that this case implicates more than the specific Maryland law. At issue is a standard, expanding technology already in widespread use throughout the Nation. * * *

A buccal swab is a far more gentle process than a venipuncture to draw blood. It involves but a light touch on the inside of the cheek; and although it can be deemed a search within the body of the arrestee, it requires no "surgical intrusions beneath the skin." The fact that an intrusion is negligible is of central relevance to determining reasonableness, although it is still a search as the law defines that term.

* * * In giving content to the inquiry whether an intrusion is reasonable, the Court has preferred "some quantum of individualized suspicion . . . [as] a prerequisite to a constitutional search or seizure. But the Fourth Amendment imposes no irreducible requirement of such suspicion."

In some circumstances, such as "[w]hen faced with special law enforcement needs, diminished expectations of privacy, minimal intrusions, or the like, the Court has found that certain general, or individual, circumstances may render a warrantless search or seizure reasonable." * * * The need for a warrant is perhaps least when the search involves no discretion that could properly be limited by the "interpo[lation of] a neutral magistrate between the citizen and the law enforcement officer."

The instant case can be addressed with this background. * * * The arrestee is already in valid police custody for a serious offense supported by probable cause. The DNA collection is not subject to the judgment of officers whose perspective might be "colored by their primary involvement in 'the often competitive enterprise of ferreting out crime.' " * * * Here, the search effected by the buccal swab of respondent falls within the category of cases this Court has analyzed by reference to the proposition that the "touchstone of the Fourth Amendment is reasonableness, not individualized suspicion."

Even if a warrant is not required, a search is not beyond Fourth Amendment scrutiny; for it must be reasonable in its scope and manner of execution. * * * This application of "traditional standards of reasonableness" requires a court to weigh "the promotion of legitimate governmental interests" against "the degree to which [the search] intrudes upon an individual's privacy." An assessment of reasonableness to determine the lawfulness of requiring this class of arrestees to provide a DNA sample is central to the instant case.

The legitimate government interest served by the Maryland DNA Collection Act is one that is well established: the need for law enforcement officers in a safe and accurate way to process and identify the persons and possessions they must take into custody. It is beyond dispute that "probable cause provides legal justification for arresting a person suspected of crime, and for a brief period of detention to take the administrative steps incident to arrest." Also uncontested is the "right on the part of the Government, always recognized under English and American law, to search the person of the accused when legally arrested." * * * Even in that context, the Court has been clear that individual suspicion is not necessary, because "[t]he constitutionality of a search incident to an arrest does not depend on whether there is any indication that the person arrested possesses weapons or evidence. The fact of a lawful arrest, standing alone, authorizes a search."

The "routine administrative procedure[s] at a police station house incident to booking and jailing the suspect" derive from different origins and have different constitutional justifications than, say, the search of a place * * * . The interests are further different when an individual is formally processed into police custody. * * * When probable cause exists to remove an individual from the normal channels of society and hold him in legal custody, DNA identification plays a critical role in serving those interests.

First, "[i]n every criminal case, it is known and must be known who has been arrested and who is being tried." An individual's identity is more than just his name or Social Security number, and the government's interest in identification goes beyond ensuring that the proper name is typed on the indictment. Identity has never been considered limited to the name on the arrestee's birth certificate. In fact, a name is of little value compared to the real interest in identification at stake when an individual is brought into custody. "It is a well recognized aspect of criminal conduct that the perpetrator will take unusual steps to conceal not only his conduct, but also his identity. * * * An 'arrestee may be carrying a false ID or lie about his identity,' and 'criminal history records . . . can be inaccurate or incomplete."

A suspect's criminal history is a critical part of his identity that officers should know when processing him for detention. It is a common occurrence that "[p]eople detained for minor offenses can turn out to be the most devious and dangerous criminals. * * * Police already seek this crucial identifying information. They use routine and accepted means as varied as comparing the suspect's booking photograph to sketch artists' depictions of persons of interest, showing his mugshot to potential witnesses, and of course making a computerized comparison of the arrestee's fingerprints against electronic databases of known criminals and unsolved crimes. In this respect the only difference between DNA analysis and the accepted use of fingerprint databases is the unparalleled accuracy DNA provides.

* * * A DNA profile is useful to the police because it gives them a form of identification to search the records already in their valid possession. In this respect the use of DNA for identification is no different than matching an arrestee's face to a wanted poster of a previously unidentified suspect; or matching tattoos to known gang symbols to reveal a criminal affiliation; or matching the arrestee's fingerprints to those recovered from a crime scene. * * *

Second, law enforcement officers bear a responsibility for ensuring that the custody of an arrestee does not create inordinate "risks for facility staff, for the existing detainee population, and for a new detainee." DNA identification can provide untainted information to those charged with detaining suspects and detaining the property of any felon. For these purposes officers must know the type of person whom they are detaining, and DNA allows them to make critical choices about how to proceed. * * *

Third, looking forward to future stages of criminal prosecution, "the Government has a substantial interest in ensuring that persons accused of crimes are available for trials." A person who is arrested for one offense but knows that he has yet to answer for some past crime may be more inclined to flee the instant charges, lest continued contact with the criminal justice system expose one or more other serious offenses. * * *

Fourth, an arrestee's past conduct is essential to an assessment of the danger he poses to the public, and this will inform a court's determination whether the individual should be released on bail. * * * Knowing that the defendant is wanted for a previous violent crime based on DNA identification is especially probative of the court's consideration of "the danger of the defendant to the alleged victim, another person, or the community."

This interest is not speculative. In considering laws to require collecting DNA from arrestees, government agencies around the Nation found evidence of numerous cases in which felony arrestees would have been identified as violent through DNA identification matching them to previous crimes but who later committed additional crimes because such identification was not used to detain them.

Present capabilities make it possible to complete a DNA identification that provides information essential to determining whether a detained suspect can be released pending trial. See, e.g., States Brief 18, n. 10 ("DNA identification database samples have been processed in as few as two days in California, although around 30 days has been average"). Regardless of when the initial bail decision is made, release is not appropriate until a further determination is made as to the person's identity in the sense not only of what his birth certificate states but also what other records and data disclose to give that identity more meaning in the whole context of who the person really is. * * * During this entire period, additional and supplemental data establishing more about the person's identity and background can provide critical information relevant to the conditions of release and whether to revisit an initial release determination. * * *

Even if an arrestee is released on bail, development of DNA identification revealing the defendant's unknown violent past can and should lead to the revocation of his conditional release. * * *

Finally, in the interests of justice, the identification of an arrestee as the perpetrator of some heinous crime may have the salutary effect of freeing a person wrongfully imprisoned for the same offense. "[P]rompt [DNA] testing . . . would speed up apprehension of criminals before they commit additional crimes, and prevent the grotesque detention of . . . innocent people." * * *

Perhaps the most direct historical analogue to the DNA technology used to identify respondent is the familiar practice of fingerprinting arrestees. From the advent of this technique, courts had no trouble determining that fingerprinting was a natural part of "the administrative steps incident to arrest." In the seminal case of *United States v. Kelly*, 55 F.2d 67 (C.A.2 1932), Judge Augustus Hand wrote that routine fingerprinting did not violate the Fourth Amendment precisely because it fit within the accepted means of processing an arrestee into custody:

> "Finger printing seems to be no more than an extension of methods of identification long used in dealing with persons under arrest for real or supposed violations of the criminal laws. It is known to be a very certain means devised by modern science to reach the desired end, and has become especially important in a time when increased population and vast aggregations of people in urban centers have rendered the notoriety of the individual in the community no longer a ready means of identification. * * *

> "We find no ground in reason or authority for interfering with a method of identifying persons charged with crime which has now become widely known and frequently practiced."

By the middle of the 20th century, it was considered "elementary that a person in lawful custody may be required to submit to photographing and fingerprinting as part of routine identification processes."

DNA identification is an advanced technique superior to fingerprinting in many ways, so much so that to insist on fingerprints as the norm would make little sense to either the forensic expert or a layperson. The additional intrusion upon the arrestee's privacy beyond that associated with fingerprinting is not significant, and DNA is a markedly more accurate form of identifying arrestees. A suspect who has changed his facial features to evade photographic identification or even one who has undertaken the more arduous task of altering his fingerprints cannot escape the revealing power of his DNA.

The respondent's primary objection to this analogy is that DNA identification is not as fast as fingerprinting, and so it should not be considered to be the 21st-century equivalent. But rapid analysis of fingerprints is itself of recent vintage. * * * The question of how long it takes to process identifying information obtained from a valid search goes only to the efficacy of the search for its purpose of prompt identification, not the constitutionality of the search. And the FBI has already begun testing devices that will enable police to process the DNA of arrestees within 90 minutes. * * *

By comparison to this substantial government interest and the unique effectiveness of DNA identification, the intrusion of a cheek swab to obtain a DNA sample is a minimal one. * * *

The reasonableness of any search must be considered in the context of the person's legitimate expectations of privacy. * * *

The expectations of privacy of an individual taken into police custody "necessarily [are] of a diminished scope." "[B]oth the person and the property in his immediate possession may be searched at the station house." *United States v. Edwards*, [13th ed., p. 359]. A search of the detainee's person when he is booked into custody may " 'involve a relatively extensive exploration,' " [*United States v.*] *Robinson*, [13th ed., p. 343], including "requir[ing] at least some detainees to lift their genitals or cough in a squatting position," *Florence* [*v. Board of Chosen Freeholders*], [Supp., p. 32]. * * *

The reasonableness inquiry here considers two other circumstances in which the Court has held that particularized suspicion is not categorically required: "diminished expectations of privacy [and] minimal intrusions." * * *

Here, by contrast to the approved standard procedures incident to any arrest detailed above, a buccal swab involves an even more brief and still minimal intrusion. * * * A brief intrusion of an arrestee's person is subject to the Fourth Amendment, but a swab of this nature does not increase the indignity already attendant to normal incidents of arrest. * * *

Finally, the Act provides statutory protections that guard against further invasion of privacy. As noted above, the Act requires that "[o]nly DNA records that directly relate to the identification of individuals shall be collected and stored." No purpose other than identification is permissible * * * .

In light of the context of a valid arrest supported by probable cause respondent's expectations of privacy were not offended by the minor intrusion of a brief swab of his cheeks. By contrast, that same context of arrest gives rise to significant state interests in identifying respondent not only so that the proper name can be attached to his charges but also so that the criminal justice system can make informed decisions concerning pretrial custody. Upon these considerations the Court concludes that DNA identification of arrestees is a reasonable search that can be considered part of a routine booking procedure. When officers make an arrest supported by probable cause to hold for a serious offense and they bring the suspect to the station to be detained in custody, taking and analyzing a cheek swab of the arrestee's DNA is, like fingerprinting and photographing, a legitimate police booking procedure that is reasonable under the Fourth Amendment. * * *

JUSTICE SCALIA, with whom JUSTICE GINSBURG, JUSTICE SOTOMAYOR, and JUSTICE KAGAN join, dissenting. * * *

Although there is a "closely guarded category of constitutionally permissible suspicionless searches," that has never included searches designed to serve "the normal need for law enforcement." Even the common name for suspicionless searches—"special needs" searches—itself reflects that they must be justified, always, by concerns "other than crime detection." * * *

So while the Court is correct to note that there are instances in which we have permitted searches without individualized suspicion, "[i]n none of these cases . . . did we indicate approval of a [search] whose primary purpose was to detect evidence of ordinary criminal wrongdoing." That limitation is crucial. It is only when a governmental purpose aside from crime-solving is at stake that we engage in the free-form "reasonableness" inquiry that the Court indulges at length today. To put it another way, both the legitimacy of the Court's method and the correctness of its outcome hinge entirely on the truth of a single proposition: that the primary purpose of these DNA searches is something other than simply discovering evidence of criminal wrongdoing. As I detail below, that proposition is wrong.

The Court alludes at several points to the fact that King was an arrestee, and arrestees may be validly searched incident to their arrest. But the Court does not really rest on this principle, and for good reason: The objects of a search incident to arrest must be either (1) weapons or evidence that might easily be destroyed, or (2) evidence relevant to the crime of arrest. Neither is the object of the search at issue here. * * *

Sensing (correctly) that it needs more, the Court elaborates at length the ways that the search here served the special purpose of "identifying" King. But that seems to me quite wrong—unless what one means by "identifying" someone is "searching for evidence that he has committed crimes unrelated to the crime of his arrest." At points the Court does appear to use "identifying" in that peculiar sense—claiming, for example, that knowing "an arrestee's past conduct is essential to an assessment of the danger he poses." If identifying someone means finding out what unsolved crimes he has committed, then identification is indistinguishable from the ordinary law-enforcement aims that have never been thought to justify a suspicionless search. Searching every lawfully stopped car, for example, might turn up information about unsolved crimes the driver had committed, but no one would say that such a search was aimed at "identifying" him, and no court would hold such a search lawful. I will therefore assume that the Court means that the DNA search at issue here was useful to "identify" King in the normal sense of that word * * * .

The portion of the Court's opinion that explains the identification rationale is strangely silent on the actual workings of the DNA search at issue here. To know those facts is to be instantly disabused of the notion that what happened had anything to do with identifying King.

[The dissent here notes a swab was taken from King on April 10 following his arrest on that day, but that King's DNA sample was not received by the State Police Forensic Services Division until April 23, where it sat until mailed to a testing lab on June 25, and the lab tests were not available until July 13, when they were entered into the state's DNA database, but it was not until August 4, nearly four months after King's arrest, that the sample forwarded to the FBI national database connected King with the rape.]

This places in a rather different light the Court's solemn declaration that the search here was necessary so that King could be identified at "every stage of the criminal process." * * *

In fact, if anything was "identified" at the moment that the DNA database returned a match, it was not King—his identity was already known. (The docket for the original criminal charges lists his full name, his race, his sex, his height, his weight, his date of birth, and his address.) Rather, what the August 4 match "identified" was *the previously-taken sample from the earlier crime.* That sample was genuinely mysterious to Maryland; the State knew that it had probably been left by the victim's attacker, but nothing else. King was not identified by his association with the sample; rather, the sample was identified by its association with

King. The Court effectively destroys its own "identification" theory when it acknowledges that the object of this search was "to see what [was] already known about [King]." King was who he was, and volumes of his biography could not make him any more or any less King. No minimally competent speaker of English would say, upon noticing a known arrestee's similarity "to a wanted poster of a previously unidentified suspect," that the *arrestee* had thereby been identified. It was the previously unidentified suspect who had been identified—just as, here, it was the previously unidentified rapist. * * *

So, to review: DNA testing does not even begin until after arraignment and bail decisions are already made. The samples sit in storage for months, and take weeks to test. When they are tested, they are checked against the Unsolved Crimes Collection—rather than the Convict and Arrestee Collection, which could be used to identify them. The Act forbids the Court's purpose (identification), but prescribes as its purpose what our suspicionless-search cases forbid ("official investigation into a crime"). Against all of that, it is safe to say that if the Court's identification theory is not wrong, there is no such thing as error.

The Court also attempts to bolster its identification theory with a series of inapposite analogies. * * *

It is on the fingerprinting of arrestees, however, that the Court relies most heavily. The Court does not actually say whether it believes that taking a person's fingerprints is a Fourth Amendment search, and our cases provide no ready answer to that question. Even assuming so, however, law enforcement's post-arrest use of fingerprints could not be more different from its post-arrest use of DNA. Fingerprints of arrestees are taken primarily to identify them (though that process sometimes solves crimes); the DNA of arrestees is taken to solve crimes (and nothing else). * * *

The Court also accepts uncritically the Government's representation at oral argument that it is developing devices that will be able to test DNA in mere minutes. [But the] issue before us is not whether DNA can some day be used for identification; nor even whether it can today be used for identification; but whether it *was used for identification here.*

* * * I cannot imagine what principle could possibly justify [the majority's "serious offense"] limitation, and the Court does not attempt to suggest any. If one believes that DNA will "identify" someone arrested for assault, he must believe that it will "identify" someone arrested for a traffic offense. This Court does not base its judgments on senseless distinctions. At the end of the day, *logic will out.* When there comes before us the taking of DNA from an arrestee for a traffic violation, the Court will predictably (and quite rightly) say, "We can find no significant difference between this case and *King.*" Make no mistake about it: As an

entirely predictable consequence of today's decision, your DNA can be taken and entered into a national DNA database if you are ever arrested, rightly or wrongly, and for whatever reason.

The most regrettable aspect of the suspicionless search that occurred here is that it proved to be quite unnecessary. All parties concede that it would have been entirely permissible, as far as the Fourth Amendment is concerned, for Maryland to take a sample of King's DNA as a consequence of his conviction for second-degree assault. So the ironic result of the Court's error is this: The only arrestees to whom the outcome here will ever make a difference are those who *have been acquitted* of the crime of arrest (so that their DNA could not have been taken upon conviction). In other words, this Act manages to burden uniquely the sole group for whom the Fourth Amendment's protections ought to be most jealously guarded: people who are innocent of the State's accusations.

Today's judgment will, to be sure, have the beneficial effect of solving more crimes; then again, so would the taking of DNA samples from anyone who flies on an airplane (surely the Transportation Security Administration needs to know the "identity" of the flying public), applies for a driver's license, or attends a public school. Perhaps the construction of such a genetic panopticon is wise. But I doubt that the proud men who wrote the charter of our liberties would have been so eager to open their mouths for royal inspection. * * *

NOTES AND QUESTIONS

1.   Consider SEARCHSZR § 5.4(c) (5th ed., 2013 Pocket Part): "What makes *King* so disappointing is that neither opinion comes to grips with the real issue in the case: whether on a balancing-of-interests analysis a standardized procedure—consisting of a suspicionless minimal search by way of a cheek swab to obtain DNA for the primary purpose of identifying the perpetrators of otherwise unsolved past and future crimes—may constitutionally be applied to all persons lawfully arrested and then held pursuant to a valid charge of a serious offense, in light of the reduced expectation of privacy of those detainees. The majority, instead claiming that 'identification' is the main objective of pre-conviction DNA testing, grounded its decision in a purported analogy to the photographing, fingerprinting and measuring of arrestees, and so never assessed the instant case in light of the one and only suspicionless-search/no-special-needs/balancing-of-interests precedent, *Samson v. California* [13th ed., p. 444]. The dissenters, seeming to deny the very existence of *Samson,* thus had no occasion to explain why, if under that case a person may be subjected to a suspicionless full police investigative search on the street because of his reduced expectation of privacy, attributable to the fact his parole status is 'akin to imprisonment,' it must be concluded that a lesser and standardized search of one during actual

incarceration violates the Fourth Amendment.[112.22] As a consequence, there is also lacking in both opinions any serious effort to assess what weight should be given, in a balancing-of-interests analysis, to the crime-solving objective of pre-conviction testing (which apparently is much less than is commonly assumed[112.23]).”

   2.   If, as the majority in *King* indicates, the pre-conviction DNA testing challenged in that case finds its constitutional justification in “significant state interests in identifying respondent,” does it follow that there are *constitutional* requirements relating to (i) precisely when an arrestee’s DNA sample may be processed or placed in a database, and (ii) destruction of DNA samples and removal of DNA profiles from databases in the event of nonconviction? Reconsider in this regard the provisions of the Maryland DNA Collection Act, described by the *King* majority but not encompassed within the Court’s holding, and consider also Note, 29 Ga.St.U.L.Rev. 1063, 1964 (2013) (“In the majority of states that take DNA samples upon arrest, DNA samples and profiles of individuals who are not ultimately convicted are not automatically destroyed; rather, the exonerated individuals must go through a lengthy process of requesting an expungement”); Note, 79 Geo.Wash.L.Rev. 1201, 1227 (2011) (“No such expungement procedure exists for an arrestee’s fingerprints—an arrestee who is ultimately not convicted has no way to affirmatively seek the destruction of her fingerprint records”); and FBI, Frequently Asked Questions (FAQs) on the CODIS Program and the National DNA Index System, http://www.fbi.gov/about-us/lab/biometric-analysis/codis/codis-and-ndis-fact-sheet (“Laboratories participating in the National DNA Index are required to expunge qualifying profiles from the National Index [in the case of] arrestees, if the participating laboratory receives a certified copy

---

   [112.22]   This is not to suggest that *Samson* itself is sound, as I have concluded otherwise elsewhere herein, * * *, but that only means the case should be repudiated, not ignored.

   [112.23]   Consider Garrett & Murphy, *Collecting DNA From Arrestees Won’t Solve More Crimes,*   http://host.madison.com/news/opinion/column/brandon-l-garrett-and-erin-murphy-collecting-dna-from-arrestees/article_05fc8ecf-2296-5797-ad25-d1e88f9d0501.html:

   “States like California, which vastly expanded DNA databanks to include arrestees, do not generate dramatically more matches between offenders and crime scenes than do states with much smaller databases, like New York or Illinois. That is because New York and Illinois, despite the smaller numbers of offenders in their databases, enter crime scene samples at rates comparable to California. Indeed, from 2010 to 2012, California halved the average number of offender profiles uploaded per month, but kept the number of samples from crime scenes constant. The result was an increase in database hits. The same dynamic played out in the United Kingdom. The lesson is clear: The police solve more crimes not by taking DNA from suspects who have never been convicted, but by collecting more evidence at crime scenes.

   “Even worse, taking DNA from a lot of arrestees slows the testing in active criminal investigations. After all, 12 million or more people are arrested each year. (According to one study, by age 23, nearly one-third of Americans have been arrested for an offense, not including minor traffic violations.) Backlogs created by arrestee DNA sampling means that rape kits and samples from convicted offenders sit in storage or go untested. This hurts innocent suspects, like Cody Davis, who was convicted in Florida because of a delay in testing evidence that later cleared him.”

   The dissent in *King*, however, does assert that absent the challenged procedure, there would be available at a later time, via presumably valid post-conviction DNA testing, the same information as to the same people, except for “those who *have been acquitted* of the crime of arrest.”

of a final court order documenting the charge has been dismissed, resulted in an acquittal or no charges have been brought within the applicable time period").

SECTION 6.   WARRANTLESS ENTRIES AND SEARCHES OF PREMISES

13th ed., p. 372; before Note 1, add:

0.1 Upon remand, the Kentucky supreme court concluded that "the sounds as described at the suppression hearing were indistinguishable from ordinary household sounds, and were consistent with the natural and reasonable result of a knock on the door. Nothing in the record suggests that the sounds officers heard were anything more than the occupants preparing to answer the door." *King v. Commonwealth*, 386 S.W.3d 119 (Ky.2012).

Under *King*, what should the result be on the facts of *United States v. Ramirez*, 676 F.3d 755 (8th Cir.2012)? Officers conducting surveillance at the bus station arrested two bus passengers carrying heroin in their shoes, and then learned those two had been traveling with a third person also carrying heroin, but that individual had already departed the station with two companions. By extraordinary good luck, police traced this group who, via three successive cab rides, had made their way indirectly to a certain motel and checked in. The desk clerk gave police a key card for the room the three had rented. No exigent circumstances existed at that point, for (as the court noted) there was "no evidence supporting the inference that these men knew the police were tracking them at all." An officer attempted to swipe the key card to gain entry into the room, but the card did not work. The officer then blocked the peep hole, knocked on the door, and announced "housekeeping." One of the men partially opened the door and, when the officer announced his presence and flashed his badge, attempted to push the door shut. The police then forced the door open with a battering ram, entered and searched and found heroin.

13th ed., p. 382; at the end of Note 3, add:

Consider that in *Stanton v. Sims*, 134 S.Ct. 3 (2013), a § 1983 case involving immediate hot pursuit, a unanimous Court, while expressing no view on whether the officer's conduct was unconstitutional, concluded the officer had improperly been denied qualified immunity, given that in *Welsh* there had been "no immediate or continuous pursuit of [Welsh] from the scene of a crime," and thus "nothing in the opinion establishes that the seriousness of the crime is equally important *in cases of hot pursuit*."

SECTION 7. WARRANTLESS SEIZURES AND SEARCHES OF VEHICLES AND CONTAINERS

13th ed., p. 388; in lieu of existing Note 4, insert:

4. In *United States v. Katzin,* 732 F.3d 187 (3d Cir.2013), the court held the automobile exception inapplicable to the attaching and monitoring of a GPS device under *United States v. Jones*, 13th ed., p. 279, because such action "is different: It creates a continuous police presence for the purpose of discovering evidence that may come into existence and/or be placed within the vehicle at some point in the future," and thus "extends the police intrusion well past the time it would normally take officers to enter a target vehicle and locate, extract, or examine the then-existing evidence."

13th ed., p. 406; before Note 2, add:

1A. There is post-*Gant* authority to the effect that even in an automobile context (and thus no less likely in other circumstances, see *State v. MacDicken*, 319 P.3d 31 (Wash.2014)) it is possible for the searched container to have such a close association with the arrestee's person that it is the search-of-person rule in *United States v. Robinson,* 13th ed., p. 343, rather than any application of or analogy to *Gant's* "time of the search" limitation that governs. Such was the conclusion reached in *State v. Byrd*, 310 P.3d 793 (Wash.2013), where the defendant was arrested while she was seated in a stopped vehicle. The arresting officer seized a purse from her lap and placed it on the ground before removing the defendant from the vehicle and securing her in a nearby patrol car—circumstances that surely would bar any reliance on the "possibility of access" branch of *Gant.* However, in response to the defendant's contention that once she was secured in the patrol car there was no risk that she could access any weapon or evidence in the purse, the court declared that there is a "distinction between searches of the arrestee's person and surroundings" and that the instant case fell within the former category. This was because "an article is 'immediately associated' with the arrestee's person and can be searched under *Robinson*, if the arrestee has actual possession of it at the time of a lawful custodial arrest." Pursuant to *Robinson*, the court asserted, "searches of the arrestee's person and personal effects do not require 'a case-by-case adjudication.'" The dissent in *Byrd* (albeit relying upon *state* constitutional law) argued that *Robinson* simply means that "[a]ny weapon or evidence secreted on the person of the arrestee is always accessible, so, a search of the person of the arrestee is always permissible," while with respect to search of "the area immediately around the arrestee" it must be shown "that the arrestee could reach the area to obtain a weapon or destroy evidence."

13th ed., p. 408; before Section 8, add:

RILEY V. CALIFORNIA
___ U.S. ___, 134 S.Ct. 2473, ___ L.Ed.2d ___ (2014).

CHIEF JUSTICE ROBERTS delivered the opinion of the Court.

These two cases raise a common question: whether the police may, without a warrant, search digital information on a cell phone seized from an individual who has been arrested. [In the first case, police searched Riley's person incident to his arrest on a weapons charge and seized a sophisticated cell phone of the "smart phone" variety found in his pocket. That officer found some evidence of gang activity, and a detective at the station later examined the phone more thoroughly and found photos and videos that were introduced into evidence at Riley's trial for a recent shooting. On appeal, that evidence was deemed to have been lawfully obtained in a valid search incident to arrest. In the second case, Wurie was arrested for a drug sale, and at the station a less sophisticated phone of the "flip phone" variety was found on his person. It was receiving multiple calls from a source identified as "my house," so the officer accessed the call log to determine the number, which led to issuance of a search warrant for Wurie's apartment. Evidence found therein was admitted at his trial, but on appeal that evidence was held to constitute the fruits of an illegal search of the phone.]

The two cases before us concern the reasonableness of a warrantless search incident to a lawful arrest. * * * Three related precedents set forth the rules governing such searches: [The Court here summarized the search-incident-to-arrest holdings re search of the person, premises and a vehicle in *United States v. Robinson* [13th ed., p. 343], *Chimel v. California* [13th ed., p. 363], and *Arizona v. Gant* [13th ed., p. 398], respectively.]

Absent more precise guidance from the founding era, we generally determine whether to exempt a given type of search from the warrant requirement "by assessing, on the one hand, the degree to which it intrudes upon an individual's privacy and, on the other, the degree to which it is needed for the promotion of legitimate governmental interests." Such a balancing of interests supported the search incident to arrest exception in *Robinson*, and a mechanical application of *Robinson* might well support the warrantless searches at issue here.

But while *Robinson*'s categorical rule strikes the appropriate balance in the context of physical objects, neither of its rationales has much force with respect to digital content on cell phones. On the government interest side, *Robinson* concluded that the two risks identified in *Chimel*—harm to officers and destruction of evidence—are present in all custodial arrests.

There are no comparable risks when the search is of digital data. In addition, *Robinson* regarded any privacy interests retained by an individual after arrest as significantly diminished by the fact of the arrest itself. Cell phones, however, place vast quantities of personal information literally in the hands of individuals. A search of the information on a cell phone bears little resemblance to the type of brief physical search considered in *Robinson*.

We therefore decline to extend *Robinson* to searches of data on cell phones, and hold instead that officers must generally secure a warrant before conducting such a search.

We first consider each *Chimel* concern in turn. In doing so, we do not overlook *Robinson*'s admonition that searches of a person incident to arrest, "while based upon the need to disarm and to discover evidence," are reasonable regardless of "the probability in a particular arrest situation that weapons or evidence would in fact be found." Rather than requiring the "case-by-case adjudication" that *Robinson* rejected, we ask instead whether application of the search incident to arrest doctrine to this particular category of effects would "untether the rule from the justifications underlying the *Chimel* exception," *Gant*.

Digital data stored on a cell phone cannot itself be used as a weapon to harm an arresting officer or to effectuate the arrestee's escape. Law enforcement officers remain free to examine the physical aspects of a phone to ensure that it will not be used as a weapon—say, to determine whether there is a razor blade hidden between the phone and its case. Once an officer has secured a phone and eliminated any potential physical threats, however, data on the phone can endanger no one.

Perhaps the same might have been said of the cigarette pack seized from Robinson's pocket. Once an officer gained control of the pack, it was unlikely that Robinson could have accessed the pack's contents. But unknown physical objects may always pose risks, no matter how slight, during the tense atmosphere of a custodial arrest. The officer in *Robinson* testified that he could not identify the objects in the cigarette pack but knew they were not cigarettes. Given that, a further search was a reasonable protective measure. No such unknowns exist with respect to digital data. * * *

The United States and California both suggest that a search of cell phone data might help ensure officer safety in more indirect ways, for example by alerting officers that confederates of the arrestee are headed to the scene. There is undoubtedly a strong government interest in warning officers about such possibilities, but neither the United States nor California offers evidence to suggest that their concerns are based on actual experience. * * * To the extent dangers to arresting officers may be implicated in a particular way in a particular case, they are better addressed through consideration of case-specific exceptions to the warrant requirement, such as the one for exigent circumstances.

The United States and California focus primarily on the second *Chimel* rationale: preventing the destruction of evidence.

Both Riley and Wurie concede that officers could have seized and secured their cell phones to prevent destruction of evidence while seeking a warrant. And once law enforcement officers have secured a cell phone, there is no longer any risk that the arrestee himself will be able to delete incriminating data from the phone.

The United States and California argue that information on a cell phone may nevertheless be vulnerable to two types of evidence destruction unique to digital data—remote wiping and data encryption. Remote wiping occurs when a phone, connected to a wireless network, receives a signal that erases stored data. This can happen when a third party sends a remote signal or when a phone is preprogrammed to delete data upon entering or leaving certain geographic areas (so-called "geofencing"). Encryption is a security feature that some modern cell phones use in addition to password protection. When such phones lock, data becomes protected by sophisticated encryption that renders a phone all but "unbreakable" unless police know the password.

As an initial matter, these broader concerns about the loss of evidence are distinct from *Chimel*'s focus on a defendant who responds to arrest by trying to conceal or destroy evidence within his reach. * * *

We have also been given little reason to believe that either problem is prevalent. * * *

In any event, as to remote wiping, law enforcement is not without specific means to address the threat. Remote wiping can be fully prevented by disconnecting a phone from the network. There are at least two simple ways to do this: First, law enforcement officers can turn the phone off or remove its battery. Second, if they are concerned about encryption or other potential problems, they can leave a phone powered on and place it in an enclosure that isolates the phone from radio waves. * * *

To the extent that law enforcement still has specific concerns about the potential loss of evidence in a particular case, there remain more targeted ways to address those concerns. If "the police are truly confronted with a 'now or never' situation,"—for example, circumstances suggesting that a defendant's phone will be the target of an imminent remote-wipe attempt—they may be able to rely on exigent circumstances to search the phone immediately. * * *

The search incident to arrest exception rests not only on the heightened government interests at stake in a volatile arrest situation, but also on an arrestee's reduced privacy interests upon being taken into police custody. *Robinson* focused primarily on the first of those rationales. But it also quoted with approval then-Judge Cardozo's account of the historical basis for the search incident to arrest exception: "Search of the person becomes lawful when grounds for arrest and accusation have been discovered, and the law is in the act of subjecting the body of the accused to its physical dominion." Put simply, a patdown of Robinson's clothing and an inspection of the cigarette pack found in his pocket constituted only minor additional intrusions compared to the substantial government authority exercised in taking Robinson into custody.

The fact that an arrestee has diminished privacy interests does not mean that the Fourth Amendment falls out of the picture entirely. * * * One such example, of course, is *Chimel*. *Chimel* refused to "characteriz[e] the invasion of privacy that results from a top-to-bottom search of a man's house as 'minor.' " * * *

Robinson is the only decision from this Court applying *Chimel* to a search of the contents of an item found on an arrestee's person. * * * Lower courts applying *Robinson* and *Chimel*, however, have approved searches of a variety of personal items carried by an arrestee.

The United States asserts that a search of all data stored on a cell phone is "materially indistinguishable" from searches of these sorts of physical items. That is like saying a ride on horseback is materially indistinguishable from a flight to the moon. Both are ways of getting from point A to point B, but little else justifies lumping them together. Modern cell phones, as a category, implicate privacy concerns far beyond those implicated by the search of a cigarette pack, a wallet, or a purse. A conclusion that inspecting the contents of an arrestee's pockets works no substantial additional intrusion on privacy beyond the arrest itself may make sense as applied to physical items, but any extension of that reasoning to digital data has to rest on its own bottom.

Cell phones differ in both a quantitative and a qualitative sense from other objects that might be kept on an arrestee's person. The term "cell phone" is itself misleading shorthand; many of these devices are in fact minicomputers that also happen to have the capacity to be used as a telephone. They could just as easily be called cameras, video players, rolodexes, calendars, tape recorders, libraries, diaries, albums, televisions, maps, or newspapers.

One of the most notable distinguishing features of modern cell phones is their immense storage capacity. Before cell phones, a search of a person was limited by physical realities and tended as a general matter to constitute only a narrow intrusion on privacy. * * *

But the possible intrusion on privacy is not physically limited in the same way when it comes to cell phones. The current top-selling smart phone has a standard capacity of 16 gigabytes (and is available with up to 64 gigabytes). Sixteen gigabytes translates to millions of pages of text, thousands of pictures, or hundreds of videos. * * * Even the most basic phones that sell for less than $20 might hold photographs, picture messages, text messages, Internet browsing history, a calendar, a thousand-entry phone book, and so on. * * *

The storage capacity of cell phones has several interrelated consequences for privacy. First, a cell phone collects in one place many distinct types of information—an address, a note, a prescription, a bank statement, a video—that reveal much more in combination than any isolated record. Second, a cell phone's capacity allows even just one type of information to convey far more than previously possible. The sum of an individual's private life can be reconstructed through a thousand photographs labeled with dates, locations, and descriptions; the same cannot be said of a photograph or two of loved ones tucked into a wallet. Third, the data on a phone can date back to the purchase of the phone, or even earlier. A person might carry in his pocket a slip of paper reminding him to call Mr. Jones; he would not carry a record of all his communications with Mr. Jones for the past several months, as would routinely be kept on a phone.[1]

Finally, there is an element of pervasiveness that characterizes cell phones but not physical records. Prior to the digital age, people did not typically carry a cache of sensitive personal information with them as they went about their day. Now it is the person who is not carrying a cell phone, with all that it contains, who is the exception. * * *

Although the data stored on a cell phone is distinguished from physical records by quantity alone, certain types of data are also qualitatively different. An Internet search and browsing history, for example, can be found on an Internet-enabled phone and could reveal an individual's private interests or concerns—perhaps a search for certain symptoms of disease, coupled with frequent visits to WebMD. Data on a cell phone can also reveal where a person has been. Historic location information is a standard feature on many smart phones and can reconstruct someone's specific movements down to the minute, not only around town but also within a particular building.

Mobile application software on a cell phone, or "apps," offer a range of tools for managing detailed information about all aspects of a person's life. * * * The average smart phone user has installed 33 apps, which together can form a revealing montage of the user's life.

---

[1] Because the United States and California agree that these cases involve searches incident to arrest, these cases do not implicate the question whether the collection or inspection of aggregated digital information amounts to a search under other circumstances.

In 1926, Learned Hand observed (in an opinion later quoted in *Chimel*) that it is "a totally different thing to search a man's pockets and use against him what they contain, from ransacking his house for everything which may incriminate him." If his pockets contain a cell phone, however, that is no longer true. Indeed, a cell phone search would typically expose to the government far more than the most exhaustive search of a house: A phone not only contains in digital form many sensitive records previously found in the home; it also contains a broad array of private information never found in a home in any form—unless the phone is.

To further complicate the scope of the privacy interests at stake, the data a user views on many modern cell phones may not in fact be stored on the device itself. * * *

The United States concedes that the search incident to arrest exception may not be stretched to cover a search of files accessed remotely—that is, a search of files stored in the cloud. Such a search would be like finding a key in a suspect's pocket and arguing that it allowed law enforcement to unlock and search a house. But officers searching a phone's data would not typically know whether the information they are viewing was stored locally at the time of the arrest or has been pulled from the cloud.

Apart from their arguments for a direct extension of *Robinson*, the United States and California offer various fallback options for permitting warrantless cell phone searches under certain circumstances. * * *

The United States first proposes that the *Gant* standard be imported from the vehicle context, allowing a warrantless search of an arrestee's cell phone whenever it is reasonable to believe that the phone contains evidence of the crime of arrest. But *Gant* relied on "circumstances unique to the vehicle context" to endorse a search solely for the purpose of gathering evidence.

At any rate, a *Gant* standard would prove no practical limit at all when it comes to cell phone searches. In the vehicle context, *Gant* generally protects against searches for evidence of past crimes. In the cell phone context, however, it is reasonable to expect that incriminating information will be found on a phone regardless of when the crime occurred. Similarly, in the vehicle context *Gant* restricts broad searches resulting from minor crimes such as traffic violations. That would not necessarily be true for cell phones. * * *

The United States also proposes a rule that would restrict the scope of a cell phone search to those areas of the phone where an officer reasonably believes that information relevant to the crime, the arrestee's identity, or officer safety will be discovered. This approach would again impose few meaningful constraints on officers. The proposed categories would sweep in a great deal of information, and officers would not always be able to discern in advance what information would be found where.

We also reject the United States' final suggestion that officers should always be able to search a phone's call log, as they did in Wurie's case. The Government relies on *Smith v. Maryland*, [13th ed., p. 510], which held that no warrant was required to use a pen register at telephone company premises to identify numbers dialed by a particular caller. The Court in that case, however, concluded that the use of a pen register was not a "search" at all under the Fourth Amendment. There is no dispute here that the officers engaged in a search of Wurie's cell phone. Moreover, call logs typically contain more than just phone numbers; they include any identifying information that an individual might add, such as the label "my house" in Wurie's case.

Finally, at oral argument California suggested a different limiting principle, under which officers could search cell phone data if they could have obtained the same information from a pre-digital counterpart. But the fact that a search in the pre-digital era could have turned up a photograph or two in a wallet does not justify a search of thousands of photos in a digital gallery. The fact that someone could have tucked a paper bank statement in a pocket does not justify a search of every bank statement from the last five years. And to make matters worse, such an analogue test would allow law enforcement to search a range of items contained on a phone, even though people would be unlikely to carry such a variety of information in physical form. * * *

In addition, an analogue test would launch courts on a difficult line-drawing expedition to determine which digital files are comparable to physical records. Is an e-mail equivalent to a letter? Is a voicemail equivalent to a phone message slip? It is not clear how officers could make these kinds of decisions before conducting a search, or how courts would apply the proposed rule after the fact. * * *

Our holding, of course, is not that the information on a cell phone is immune from search; it is instead that a warrant is generally required before such a search, even when a cell phone is seized incident to arrest. * * *

Moreover, even though the search incident to arrest exception does not apply to cell phones, other case-specific exceptions may still justify a warrantless search of a particular phone. "One well-recognized exception applies when ' "the exigencies of the situation" make the needs of law enforcement so compelling that [a] warrantless search is objectively reasonable under the Fourth Amendment.' " Such exigencies could include the need to prevent the imminent destruction of evidence in individual cases, to pursue a fleeing suspect, and to assist persons who are seriously injured or are threatened with imminent injury. * * *

In light of the availability of the exigent circumstances exception, there is no reason to believe that law enforcement officers will not be able to address some of the more extreme hypotheticals that have been suggested: a suspect texting an accomplice who, it is feared, is preparing to detonate a bomb, or a child abductor who may have information about the child's location on his cell phone. * * *[2]

JUSTICE ALITO, concurring in part and concurring in the judgment.

I agree with the Court that law enforcement officers, in conducting a lawful search incident to arrest, must generally obtain a warrant before searching information stored or accessible on a cell phone. I write separately to address two points.

First, I am not convinced at this time that the ancient rule on searches incident to arrest is based exclusively (or even primarily) on the need to protect the safety of arresting officers and the need to prevent the destruction of evidence. This rule antedates the adoption of the Fourth Amendment by at least a century. In *Weeks v. United States*, 232 U.S. 383 (1914), we held that the Fourth Amendment did not disturb this rule. * * *

[W]hen pre-*Weeks* authorities discussed the basis for the rule, what was mentioned was the need to obtain probative evidence. For example, an 1839 case stated that "it is clear, and beyond doubt, that . . . constables . . . are entitled, upon a lawful arrest by them of one charged with treason or felony, to take and detain property found in his possession which will form material evidence in his prosecution for that crime."

What ultimately convinces me that the rule is not closely linked to the need for officer safety and evidence preservation is that these rationales fail to explain the rule's well-recognized scope. It has long been accepted that written items found on the person of an arrestee may be examined and used at trial. But once these items are taken away from an arrestee (something that obviously must be done before the items are read), there is no risk that the arrestee will destroy them. Nor is there any risk that leaving these items unread will endanger the arresting officers. * * *

Despite my view on the point discussed above, I agree that we should not mechanically apply the rule used in the predigital era to the search of a cell phone. Many cell phones now in use are capable of storing and accessing a quantity of information, some highly personal, that no person

---

² In Wurie's case, for example, the dissenting First Circuit judge argued that exigent circumstances could have justified a search of Wurie's phone (discussing the repeated unanswered calls from "my house," the suspected location of a drug stash). But the majority concluded that the Government had not made an exigent circumstances argument. The Government acknowledges the same in this Court.

would ever have had on his person in hard-copy form. This calls for a new balancing of law enforcement and privacy interests.

The Court strikes this balance in favor of privacy interests with respect to all cell phones and all information found in them, and this approach leads to anomalies. For example, the Court's broad holding favors information in digital form over information in hard-copy form. Suppose that two suspects are arrested. Suspect number one has in his pocket a monthly bill for his land-line phone, and the bill lists an incriminating call to a long-distance number. He also has in his a wallet a few snapshots, and one of these is incriminating. Suspect number two has in his pocket a cell phone, the call log of which shows a call to the same incriminating number. In addition, a number of photos are stored in the memory of the cell phone, and one of these is incriminating. Under established law, the police may seize and examine the phone bill and the snapshots in the wallet without obtaining a warrant, but under the Court's holding today, the information stored in the cell phone is out.

While the Court's approach leads to anomalies, I do not see a workable alternative. Law enforcement officers need clear rules regarding searches incident to arrest, and it would take many cases and many years for the courts to develop more nuanced rules. And during that time, the nature of the electronic devices that ordinary Americans carry on their persons would continue to change.

This brings me to my second point. While I agree with the holding of the Court, I would reconsider the question presented here if either Congress or state legislatures, after assessing the legitimate needs of law enforcement and the privacy interests of cell phone owners, enact legislation that draws reasonable distinctions based on categories of information or perhaps other variables.

The regulation of electronic surveillance provides an instructive example. After this Court held that electronic surveillance constitutes a search even when no property interest is invaded, Congress responded by enacting Title III of the Omnibus Crime Control and Safe Streets Act of 1968. Since that time, electronic surveillance has been governed primarily, not by decisions of this Court, but by the statute, which authorizes but imposes detailed restrictions on electronic surveillance.

* * * Many forms of modern technology are making it easier and easier for both government and private entities to amass a wealth of information about the lives of ordinary Americans, and at the same time, many ordinary Americans are choosing to make public much information that was seldom revealed to outsiders just a few decades ago.

In light of these developments, it would be very unfortunate if privacy protection in the 21st century were left primarily to the federal courts using the blunt instrument of the Fourth Amendment.

Legislatures, elected by the people, are in a better position than we are to assess and respond to the changes that have already occurred and those that almost certainly will take place in the future.

NOTES AND QUESTIONS

1. Does *Riley,* concerning a search-of-the-person under *Robinson,* also apply to a container search made under *Acevedo,* 13th ed., p. 338? If so, considering that in *Riley* the Court characterized cell phones as "in fact minicomputers," would *Riley* determine the result in *Burgess,* 13th ed., p. 393?

2. Police noticed a van pull over to the curb in front of a 9-story apartment building, and saw a young girl alight and run into the building, after which the van made a U-turn and headed back the other direction. After a traffic stop, when the driver explained he was in a hurry to get home, police learned there was an outstanding warrant for the driver for distribution of child pornography, so they arrested the driver. In a valid search of the van under *Gant,* 13th ed., p. 398, police found a digital camera and a cell phone; they immediately searched both items and found photos dated that day constituting child pornography. Does *Riley* apply in the *Gant* search-of-vehicle context, and, if so, does it matter which branch of the *Gant* decision justified the initial car search? In any event, is the result the same as to the phone and camera, given the observation in *Riley* that cell phones "could just as easily be called cameras"?

SECTION 8. STOP AND FRISK

A. POLICE ACTION SHORT OF A SEIZURE

13th ed., p. 416; before Note 2, add:

1A. What if the investigating officer asks for and then holds the suspect's credentials? Compare *United States v. Tyler,* 512 F.3d 405 (7th Cir.2008) (defendant seized where officers "took his identification from him and retained it while they ran a warrant check"); with *State v. Martin,* 79 So.3d 951 (La.2011) (rejecting "*per se* rule" of several other jurisdictions that retention of identification creates a seizure, court concludes retention here during a "relatively brief" warrant check was not "so long that a reasonable person, having surrendered his identification in the first place * * * , would understand that he was no longer free to * * * go about his business").

B. GROUNDS FOR TEMPORARY SEIZURE FOR INVESTIGATION

13th ed., p. 420; after Note 2, add:

2A. If there is not a flyer or bulletin grounded in reasonable suspicion, as in *Hensley,* may a seizing officer who lacks facts constituting reasonable suspicion later justify his *Terry* stop on the aggregate of information known to the various officers working with him? Compare *United States v. Brown*, 621 F.3d 48 (1st Cir.2010) (proper to consider "the aggregate information available to all the officers involved in the investigation"); with *United States v. Massenburg*, 654 F.3d 480 (4th Cir.2011) ("Where officers working closely together have *not communicated* pertinent information, the acting officer weighs the costs and benefits of performing the search in total ignorance of the existence of that information—it is not known to her, so it cannot enter into the calculus. Therefore, for purposes of the exclusionary rule, that additional information must be irrelevant").

13th ed., p. 424; in lieu of existing Note 6, insert:

6. In NAVARETTE v. CALIFORNIA, 134 S.Ct. 1683 (2014), police stopped a pickup truck because it matched the description of a vehicle an anonymous[a] 911 caller recently reported had run her off the road; officers approaching the stopped vehicle smelled marijuana, searched the truck's bed, and found 30 pounds of marijuana. The lower court ruling upholding the stop was grounded in the proposition "that the danger exception postulated in *J.L.* applies when an anonymous tipster contemporaneously reports drunken or erratic driving on a public roadway and officers are able to corroborate significant innocent details of the tip, such as detailed descriptions of the vehicle and its location." The Supreme Court affirmed, 5–4, in an opinion (as the dissent put it) that "does not explicitly adopt such a departure from our normal Fourth Amendment requirement that anonymous tips must be corroborated" and "purports to adhere to our prior cases," such as *White* and *J.L.* As for the "initial question" in the instant case, "whether the 911 call was sufficiently reliable to credit the allegation" therein, the majority relied upon two propositions: (1) the anonymous caller, who "claimed eyewitness knowledge," "reported the incident soon after she was run off the road" (as indicated by the fact the police located the vehicle 19 miles away from the reported location roughly 18 minutes after the 911 call), and such a "contemporaneous report has long been treated as especially reliable," as is indicated by the "present sense impression" and "excited utterance" exceptions to the hearsay rule; and (2) "the caller's use of the 911 emergency system" is relevant, as such calls "can be recorded" and permit police "to verify important information about the caller," i.e., the caller's phone number and approximate location, and thus "a reasonable officer could conclude that a false tipster would think twice before using such a system." The dissenters, per Scalia, J., responded: (1) that for the majority's hearsay exceptions, it "is the immediacy that gives the statement some credibility," as "the declarant has not had time to dissemble or embellish," but there "is no such immediacy here," as between the purported event and the 911 call shortly thereafter there would have been "[p]lenty of time to dissemble or embellish," and also it is "unsettled" whether those exceptions apply absent other evidence of the alleged event or when the declarant's identity is unknown; and (2) "the ease of identifying 911 callers * * * proves absolutely nothing * * * unless the anonymous caller was *aware* of that fact," for it "is the tipster's *belief* in anonymity, not its *reality*, that will control his behavior."

The second issue in the case, as stated by the majority, was "whether the 911 caller's report of being run off the roadway created reasonable suspicion of an ongoing crime such as drunk driving as opposed to an isolated episode of past recklessness." As to this, the majority asserted: (3) that the alleged conduct, "running another car off the highway," "bears too great a resemblance to paradigmatic manifestations of drunk driving to be dismissed as the isolated example of recklessness," as such conduct "suggests lane-positioning problems, decreased vigilance, impaired judgment, or some combination of those recognized drunk driving cues"; (4) that petitioners' claim that the reported behavior could also be explained by, e.g., "an unruly child or other distraction," ignores the Court's consistent recognition that reasonable suspicion "need not rule out the possibility of innocent conduct," and (5) that the absence of "additional suspicious conduct" when the officers spotted the vehicle did not "dispel the reasonable suspicion of drunk driving," as it "is hardly surprising that the appearance of a marked police car would inspire more careful driving for a time." The dissenters responded: (3) that even assuming "a careless, reckless, or even intentional maneuver" by the driver of the truck, there is no basis for concluding that "reasonable suspicion of a *discrete instance* of irregular or hazardous driving generates a reasonable suspicion of *ongoing intoxicated driving*"; (4) that the caller's statement at most "conveys * * * that the truck did some apparently nontypical thing that forced the tipster off the roadway," so it may be that the truck "swerved to avoid an animal, a pothole, or a jaywalking pedestrian"; and (5) that while the police wisely "followed the truck for five minutes, presumably to see if it was being operated recklessly," during that interval the driver's conduct "was irreproachable," for which the majority's explanation is inadequate under the "traditional view that the dangers of intoxicated driving are the intoxicant's impairing effects on the body—effects that no mere act of the will can resist."

   [a] The caller actually identified herself by name, but because neither the caller nor the dispatcher who took the call was present at the suppression hearing, the prosecution did not introduce the recording of the call, and the prosecution and lower courts thereafter treated the tip as anonymous.

C. PERMISSIBLE EXTENT AND SCOPE OF TEMPORARY SEIZURE

13th ed., p. 432; before Note 9, add:

   8A. In *Arizona v. United States*, 132 S.Ct. 2492 (2012), the Court, 5–3, struck down most of Arizona's controversial immigration law on preemption grounds, but upheld without dissent the most hotly debated section, 2(B), which requires state officers to make a "reasonable attempt * * * to determine the immigration status" of any person they stop, detain, or arrest on some other legitimate basis if "reasonable suspicion exists that the person is an alien and is unlawfully present in the United States." The Court noted: "Three limits are built into the state provision. First, a detainee is presumed not to be an alien unlawfully present in the United States if he or she provides a valid Arizona driver's license or similar identification. Second, officers 'may not consider race, color or national origin . . . except to the extent permitted by the United States [and] Arizona Constitution[s].' Third, the provisions must be 'implemented in a manner consistent with federal law regulating immigration, protecting the civil rights of all persons and respecting the privileges and immunities of United States citizens.' * * *

"Some who support the challenge to § 2(B) argue that, in practice, state officers will be required to delay the release of some detainees for no reason other than to verify their immigration status. Detaining individuals solely to verify their immigration status would raise constitutional concerns. See, *e.g.,* *Arizona v. Johnson*, [13th ed., p. 429]; *Illinois v. Caballes*, [13th ed., p. 428]. * * *

"But § 2(B) could be read to avoid these concerns. To take one example, a person might be stopped for jaywalking in Tucson and be unable to produce identification. The first sentence of § 2(B) instructs officers to make a 'reasonable' attempt to verify his immigration status with ICE if there is reasonable suspicion that his presence in the United States is unlawful. The state courts may conclude that, unless the person continues to be suspected of some crime for which he may be detained by state officers, it would not be reasonable to prolong the stop for the immigration inquiry. * * *

"The nature and timing of this case counsel caution in evaluating the validity of § 2(B). The Federal Government has brought suit against a sovereign State to challenge the provision even before the law has gone into effect. There is a basic uncertainty about what the law means and how it will be enforced. At this stage, without the benefit of a definitive interpretation from the state courts, it would be inappropriate to assume § 2(B) will be construed in a way that creates a conflict with federal law. * * * This opinion does not foreclose other preemption and constitutional challenges to the law as interpreted and applied after it goes into effect."

E. PROTECTIVE SEARCH

13th ed., p. 434; at the end of Note 1, add:

If, in such an on-the-street situation, there are not grounds to frisk the companions, then what may the police do about them? Consider *United States v. Lewis,* 674 F.3d 1298 (11th Cir.2012). In "a 'high crime area' that is a 'hotbed' of drug and gun activity," two officers engaged in a consensual encounter with four men, asking whether any of them were carrying guns. One of them, McRae, answered in the affirmative, at which the officer ordered all four of the men to the ground for further investigation. Shortly thereafter, a gun was found near where one of the others, Lewis, was sitting, leading to his prosecution for unlawful possession of a firearm by an illegal alien. The court noted there was reasonable suspicion as to McRae, justifying a "brief stopping" of him to inquire whether he had "a valid concealed-weapons permit," but no "particularized reasonable suspicion concerning Lewis," so that the "central question [was] whether it was also reasonable under the circumstances for the officers to briefly detain all four individuals for reasons of safety." The court answered in the affirmative, relying upon "precedent from * * * the Supreme Court * * * establish[ing] that, for safety reasons, officers may in some circumstances, briefly detain individuals about whom they have no individualized reasonable suspicion of criminal activity in the course of conducting a valid *Terry* stop as to other related individuals." The court referred to *Maryland v. Wilson,* 13th ed., p. 361, fn. e, concluding that the "weighty" interest in officer safety justified ordering a passenger out of a vehicle even when only the driver is suspected of criminal activity, and *Brendlin v. California*, 13th ed., p. 417, stating it is "reasonable for passengers to expect that a police officer at the scene of a crime, arrest, or investigation will not let people move around in ways that could jeopardize his safety." The court then concluded that the detention of Lewis served "exactly the same safety purposes" as in the traffic stop cases, considering (i) "the admitted presence of * * * firearms," (ii) "the detention took place at night in a high crime area," and (iii) Lewis "was not some 'unrelated bystander,' * * * but rather 'an associate of [the] persons being investigated for criminal activities.'" A dissenting judge objected that the Supreme Court cases relied upon by the majority were distinguishable, as they were traffic stops where (as explained in *Arizona v. Johnson*) vehicle passengers are already lawfully seized, without reasonable suspicion as to them, incident to the stopping of the driver. Thus, the dissent concluded, what the police should have done in *Lewis* was "ask [those] men not suspected of any illegal activity to walk a safe distance away from the scene."

SECTION 9.   ADMINISTRATIVE INSPECTIONS AND REGULATORY SEARCHES: MORE ON BALANCING THE NEED AGAINST THE INVASION OF PRIVACY

13th ed., p. 441; at the end of Note 2, add:

Does *Riley v. California*, Supp., p. 47, have any significance as to *Arnold*, given that the Court in *Riley* characterized cell phones as "in fact minicomputers"?

Arnold was distinguished in *United States v. Cotterman*, 709 F.3d 952 (9th Cir.2013), on the ground that it permitted only "a quick look and unintrusive search of laptops," while the instant case involved a "forensic examination that comprehensively analyzed the hard drive of the computer." Given that "the uniquely sensitive nature of data on electronic devices carries with it a significant expectation of privacy[cc] and thus renders an exhaustive exploratory search more intrusive than with other forms of property," the court held that the Fourth Amendment "requires that officers make a commonsense differentiation between a manual review of files on an electronic device and application of computer software to analyze a hard drive, and utilize the latter only when they possess a 'particularized and objective basis for suspecting the person stopped of criminal activity.' "

cc In this regard, the court stressed three important considerations: (1) the "amount of private information carried by international travelers," given that the average laptop hard drive "can store over 200 million pages—the equivalent of five floors of a typical academic library"; (2) the "nature of the contents of electronic devices," which "contain the most intimate details of our lives: financial records, confidential business documents, medical records and private emails"; and (3) these "devices often retain sensitive and confidential information far beyond the perceived point of erasure," which "makes it impractical, if not impossible, for individuals to make meaningful decisions regarding what digital content to expose to the scrutiny that accompanies international travel."

13th ed., p. 442; at the end of the first paragraph of Note 4, add:

As for the more recent use of advanced imaging technology, it was upheld in *Electronic Privacy Information Center v. U.S. Dept. of Homeland Security*, 653 F.3d 1 (D.C.Cir.2011), stressing the AIT scanner's capability "of detecting * * * attempts to carry aboard airplanes explosives in liquid or powder form," and "the steps the TSA has already taken to protect passenger privacy, in particular distorting the image created using AIT and deleting it as soon as the passenger has been cleared," as well as allowing "any passenger [to] opt-out of AIT screening in favor of a patdown."

13th ed., p. 453; in lieu of existing Note 7, insert:

7.   Does the Supreme Court's decision in *Maryland v. King*, Supp., p. 33, settle any pre-existing uncertainty with regard to any and all post-conviction DNA testing, including of parolees and probationers?

SECTION 10.   CONSENT SEARCHES

A. THE NATURE OF "CONSENT"

13th ed., p. 459; at the end of Note 2, add:

Compare with *Boukater* the decisions in *United States v. Knope*, 655 F.3d 647 (7th Cir.2011) (where consent given after officer indicated that otherwise he would "try to" get search warrant, it is sufficient that "the expressed intention" was "genuine," in the sense that the officer "had a legitimate belief that she could obtain a warrant"); and *United States v. Hicks*, 650 F.3d 1058 (7th Cir.2011) (consent in response to threat to "obtain" a search warrant deemed valid, as "the ultimate question is the genuineness of the stated intent to get a warrant," depending on whether the officer "had a reasonable factual basis for probable cause," a test which "parallels the exclusionary rule's good faith exception" under *Leon*).

B. THIRD PARTY CONSENT

13th ed., p. 469; in lieu of the last paragraph of Note 3, insert:

What would the result have been in *Randolph* if the police had discovered evidence incriminating the *wife*? See *United States v. Rogers*, 661 F.3d 991 (8th Cir.2011). Should *Randolph* be deemed inapplicable to vehicle searches "because the social expectations for occupants of vehicles are unlike co-tenants in residences," as concluded in *State v. Copeland*, 399 S.W.3d 159 (Tex.Crim.App. 2013)?

4. *Randolph revisited.* In FERNANDEZ v. CALIFORNIA, 134 S.Ct. 1126 (2014), police saw a robbery suspect run into a building and then heard screams coming from one of the apartments therein. Roxanne Rojas, who appeared to be battered and bleeding, answered the door, and when officers indicated they wanted to conduct a protective sweep Fernandez came to the door and objected. Officers removed him from the apartment and placed him under arrest; he was then identified as the robber and taken to the station. About an hour later police returned to the apartment and obtained Rojas' consent to search, and items linking Fernandez to the robbery were found within; they were admitted at a trial resulting in his conviction, which was affirmed on an appeal subsequently affirmed by the Supreme Court (6–3) per Alito, J.

Fernandez relied upon dictum in *Randolph* suggesting that consent by one occupant might not be sufficient if "there is evidence that the police have removed the potentially objecting tenant from the entrance for the sake of avoiding a possible objection," to which the Court responded: "The *Randolph* dictum is best understood not to require an inquiry into the subjective intent of officers who detain or arrest a potential objector but instead to refer to situations in which the removal of the potential objector is not objectively reasonable," as "our Fourth Amendment cases 'have repeatedly rejected' a subjective approach. [O]nce it is recognized that the test is one of objective reasonableness, petitioner's argument collapses. He does not contest the fact that the police had reasonable grounds for removing him from the apartment so that they could speak with Rojas, an apparent victim of domestic violence, outside of petitioner's potentially intimidating presence. In fact, he does not even contest the existence of probable cause to place him under arrest. We therefore hold that an occupant who is absent due to a lawful detention or arrest stands in the same shoes as an occupant who is absent for any other reason."

Fernandez next argued "that his objection, made at the threshold of the premises that the police wanted to search, remained effective until he changed his mind and withdrew his objection," to which the Court first responded that this position could not be squared with the analysis in *Randolph*, as the "calculus of the hypothetical caller" discussed there "would likely be quite different if the objecting tenant was not standing at the door."[a] Moreover, such an approach "would produce a plethora of practical problems" (e.g., as to how long the objection could reasonably remain effective, how the objector's continuing "common authority" would be determined, and whether an effective objection could be made by one not present). The *Fernandez* majority thus concluded that *Randolph* "applies only where the objector is standing in the door saying 'stay out' when the officers propose to make a consent search."

Ginsburg, J., for the dissenters, objected: "The circumstances triggering 'the Fourth Amendment's traditional hostility to police entry into a home without a warrant' are at least as salient here as they were in *Randolph*. In both cases, '[t]he search at issue was a search solely for evidence'; '[t]he objecting party,' while on the premises, 'made his objection [to police entry] known clearly and directly to the officers seeking to enter the [residence]'; and 'the officers might easily have secured the premises and sought a warrant permitting them to enter.' Here, moreover, with the objector in custody, there was scant danger to persons on the premises, or risk that evidence might be destroyed or concealed, pending request for, and receipt of, a warrant." As for the majority's "practical problems" argument, the dissenters noted that "reading *Randolph* to require continuous physical presence poses administrative difficulties of its own. Does an occupant's refusal to consent lose force as soon as she absents herself from the doorstep, even if only for a moment? Are the police free to enter the instant after the objector leaves the door to retire for a nap, answer the phone, use the bathroom, or speak to another officer outside?"

The final paragraph of the *majority opinion* in *Fernandez* reads: "Denying someone in Rojas' position the right to allow the police to enter her home would also show disrespect for her independence. Having beaten Rojas, petitioner would bar her from controlling access to her own home until such time as he chose to relent. The Fourth Amendment does not give him that power." If that is so, then what if the police had obtained and acted upon Rojas' consent contemporaneously with his objection?

a   Scalia, J., concurring, took note of an argument by amicus that Fernandez "had a right under property law to exclude the police," which he said would make this "a more difficult case" except for the fact that the authorities cited "fail to establish that a guest would commit a trespass if one of two joint tenants invited the guest to enter and the other tenant forbade the guest to do so."

CHAPTER 8

NETWORK SURVEILLANCE

■ ■ ■

SECTION 1. THE FOURTH AMENDMENT

B. RIGHTS IN NON-CONTENT INFORMATION

13th ed., p. 515; after Note 2, add:

In 2013, it became publicly known that the United States Postal Service photographs the exterior of every item of postal mail—approximately 160 billion items per year. *See* Ron Nixon, *U.S. Postal Service Logging All Mail for Law Enforcement*, New York Times, July 3, 2013, at A1. Known as the Mail Isolation Control and Tracking program, the program photographs the outside of each item of mail and then stores copies of the images for an undetermined period of time. Government officials can then make requests to the postal service for retroactive mail covers enabling them to trace the path of letters that were sent. In other words, the post office copies everything and then discloses specific information to investigators pursuant to requests under the mail cover regulation.

Should the fact that the government can and does create images of the outside of every postal letter impact whether that information is protected by the Fourth Amendment?

13th ed., p. 518; after Note 6, add:

7. *Historical cell site location data.* Cellular phones send and receive signals through local cell towers that route communications. Whenever a cell phone is powered "on," the phone tries to contact local towers and establish a connection. In general, phones communicate with the nearest tower. Cellular phone providers generate records about which cell towers are connected to a particular phone whenever a communication to that phone begins and ends. For example, if a person makes a cell phone call at 2 pm and stays on the phone until 2:30 pm, the phone company will automatically generate a record of what cell tower was in communication with the phone at both 2 pm and 2:30 pm. Because people normally have their phones with them when communications are made, the records can be analyzed to determine the rough location of the phone's owner over time. These records are known as historical cell site data.

Lower courts have divided on whether and when historical cell site records are protected under the Fourth Amendment. Three different views have emerged.

On one hand, the Fifth Circuit and several district courts have held that cell site records are not protected under *Smith v. Maryland. See, e.g., In re Application of the United States of America for Historical Cell Site Data*, 724 F.3d 600 (5th Cir. 2013). Under this reasoning, cell site records are business records belonging to the phone company. Like the numbers dialed in *Smith*, the location records are voluntarily disclosed to the phone company to enable the phone company to place calls. As a result, they are unprotected under the Fourth Amendment just like the numbers dialed in *Smith*. The Fifth Circuit has explained:

> The cell service provider collects and stores historical cell site data for its own business purposes, perhaps to monitor or optimize service on its network or to accurately bill its customers for the segments of its network that they use. The Government does not require service providers to record this information or store it. The providers control what they record and how long these records are retained.

> In the case of such historical cell site information, the Government merely comes in after the fact and asks a provider to turn over records the provider has already created. Moreover, these are the providers' own records of transactions to which it is a party. The caller is not conveying location information to anyone other than his service provider. He is sending information so that the provider can perform the service for which he pays it: to connect his call. And the historical cell site information reveals his location information for addressing purposes, not the contents of his calls.

A second view, adopted by several district courts, is that the collection of many cell-site records at once constitutes a search because it amounts to long-term surveillance under the concurring opinions in *United States v. Jones*, [p. 279]. These courts have reasoned that when the government obtains cell site location records covering a long period of time, the collection of those records constitutes a collective Fourth Amendment search. *See, e.g., In re for an Order Authorizing the Release of Historical Cell-Site Information*, 809 F.Supp.2d 113 (E.D.N.Y. 2011) (warrant needed to obtain 113 days of location monitoring); *United States v. Powell*, 943 F.Supp.2d 759 (E.D. Mich. 2013) (warrant needed to obtain location information for 30–45 days).

A third view, adopted by the Eleventh Circuit, is that any collection of historical cell site records is a Fourth Amendment search because it has the potential to reveal private information. *See United States v. Davis*, ___ F.3d ___, 2014 WL 2599917 (11th Cir. 2014). Building on the concurring opinions in *Jones*, the Eleventh Circuit articulated a privacy theory of the Fourth Amendment by which government action becomes a search when it brings private acts into government view. According to the Eleventh Circuit, long-term GPS monitoring constitutes a search under the *Jones* concurrences because the location of a car is ordinarily public. It therefore takes time for GPS records of a car's location to accumulate into something private. In contrast, any acquisition of cell site data is a search because such data might reveal inherently private information:

> One's car, when it is not garaged in a private place, is visible to the public, and it is only the aggregation of many instances of the public seeing it that make it particularly invasive of privacy to secure GPS evidence of its location. As the circuit and some justices reasoned, the car owner can reasonably expect that although his individual movements may be observed, there will not be a "tiny constable" hiding in his vehicle to maintain a log of his movements.

> In contrast, even on a person's first visit to a gynecologist, a psychiatrist, a bookie, or a priest, one may assume that the visit is private if it was not conducted in a public way. One's cell phone, unlike an automobile, can accompany its owner anywhere. Thus, the exposure of the cell site location information can convert what would otherwise be a private event into a public one. When one's whereabouts are not public, then one may have a reasonable expectation of privacy in those whereabouts. Therefore, while it may be the case that even in light of the *Jones* opinion, GPS location information on an automobile would be protected only in the case of aggregated data, even one point of cell site location data can be within a reasonable expectation of privacy.

   8.   *Bulk acquisition of pen register information to identify terrorist activity: The National Security Agency's Section 215 telephony metadata program.* In *Smith v. Maryland*, the government obtained numbers dialed from a single telephone line in a single criminal case. Should a court rule differently if the government obtains numbers dialed from millions of telephone accounts all at once, as it has done under the NSA's telephony metadata program?

   Documents leaked by former NSA contractor Edward Snowden have disclosed that the federal government obtains non-content records from telephone service providers on a massive scale. The Foreign Intelligence Surveillance Court orders companies such as Verizon to turn over "all call detail records" of telephone calls inside the United States or between persons in the United States and persons abroad. *See* Glenn Greenwald, *NSA Collecting Phone Records of Millions of Verizon Customers Daily*, The Guardian, June 5, 2013. Employees at the NSA can then query the massive databases and try to identify terrorist activities.

   District courts have divided on whether such surveillance amounts to a Fourth Amendment search under *Smith v. Maryland*. Several courts have ruled that *Smith v. Maryland* continues to apply, and that the scale of the surveillance is irrelevant to the Fourth Amendment question. Under this view, the NSA's program cannot violate the Fourth Amendment because it does not 'search' anything. *See, e.g., American Civil Liberties Union v. Clapper*, 959 F.Supp.2d 724, 752 (S.D.N.Y. 2013) ("The collection of breathtaking amounts of information unprotected by the Fourth Amendment does not transform that sweep into a Fourth Amendment search."); *In re F.B.I. for an Order Requiring Production of Tangible Things*, 2013 WL 5741573 (For. Intell. Surv. Ct. 2013) ("[W]here one individual does not have a Fourth Amendment interest, grouping together a large number of similarly-situated individuals cannot result in a Fourth Amendment interest springing into existence *ex nihilo*.").

On the other hand, one judge has ruled that *Smith v. Maryland* does not apply to bulk surveillance conducted by the NSA. *See Klayman v. Obama*, 957 F.Supp.2d 1 (D.D.C. 2013). Under this view, bulk acquisition of pen register data is a Fourth Amendment search. Consider the court's analysis:

> When do present-day circumstances—the evolutions in the Government's surveillance capabilities, citizens' phone habits, and the relationship between the NSA and telecom companies—become so thoroughly unlike those considered by the Supreme Court thirty-four years ago that a precedent like *Smith* simply does not apply? The answer, unfortunately for the Government, is now.

> The Court in *Smith* was not confronted with the NSA's Bulk Telephony Metadata Program. Nor could the Court in 1979 have ever imagined how the citizens of 2013 would interact with their phones. For the many reasons discussed below, I am convinced that the surveillance program now before me is so different from a simple pen register that *Smith* is of little value in assessing whether the Bulk Telephony Metadata Program constitutes a Fourth Amendment search. To the contrary, for the following reasons, I believe that bulk telephony metadata collection and analysis almost certainly does violate a reasonable expectation of privacy.

> First, the pen register in *Smith* was operational for only a matter of days between March 6, 1976 and March 19, 1976, and there is no indication from the Court's opinion that it expected the Government to retain those limited phone records once the case was over. . . . This short-term, forward-looking (as opposed to historical), and highly-limited data collection is what the Supreme Court was assessing in *Smith*. The NSA telephony metadata program, on the other hand, involves the creation and maintenance of a historical database containing five years' worth of data. And I might add, there is the very real prospect that the program will go on for as long as America is combatting terrorism, which realistically could be forever!

> Second, the relationship between the police and the phone company in *Smith* is *nothing* compared to the relationship that has apparently evolved over the last seven years between the Government and telecom companies.

Third, the almost-Orwellian technology that enables the Government to store and analyze the phone metadata of every telephone user in the United States is unlike anything that could have been conceived in 1979.

Finally, and *most importantly,* not only is the Government's ability to collect, store, and analyze phone data greater now than it was in 1979, but the nature and quantity of the information contained in people's telephony metadata is much greater, as well.

Admittedly, what metadata *is* has not changed over time. As in *Smith*, the types of information at issue in this case are relatively limited: phone numbers dialed, date, time, and the like. But the ubiquity of phones has dramatically altered the *quantity* of information that is now available and, *more importantly*, what that information can tell the Government about people's lives.

Id. at 32–36 (emphasis in original).

9.   *Physically locating a computer that has connected to an open wireless network.* In some cases, the government may have reason to believe that a suspect is committing a crime over the Internet using another person's open wireless router. To find the suspect, agents can use computer software known as a "moocherhunter" program. Moocherhunter software allows anyone with a laptop and a directional antenna to find the general location of a computer connecting to a specific open wireless router. By moving the laptop around, and measuring the strength of the signal coming from the "mooching" computer, the software can be used to identify the physical location of the computer connecting to the wireless router.

In *United States v. Stanley*, ___ F.3d. ___, 2014 WL 2596012 (3d. Cir. 2014), the court considered whether a Fourth Amendment search occurred when the government used moocherhunter software to identify the physical location of a person using an open wireless router to commit a crime. In *Stanley*, the government learned that an Internet Protocol address associated with a private home was being used to distribute images of child pornography. Officers executed a warrant at the home but found nothing. The officers surmised that the computer distributing the illegal images was not inside the home. Instead, someone in the neighborhood was committing the offense by hopping on the home's wireless network that had been left open (that is, not password-protected). To find the wrongdoer, officers used the moocherhunter software and concluded that the wrongdoer was inside an apartment in a building across the street. Officers obtained a second search warrant to search the apartment, which belonged to Stanley. Inside Stanley's apartment, the officers found the computer that contained the distributed images.

The Third Circuit concluded that using the moocherhunter software to find Stanley's computer was not a search:

Stanley made no effort to confine his conduct to the interior of his home. In fact, his conduct—sharing child pornography with other Internet users via a stranger's Internet connection—was deliberately projected outside of his home, as it required interactions with persons and objects beyond the threshold of his residence.

In effect, Stanley opened his window and extended an invisible, virtual arm across the street to the Neighbor's router so that he could exploit his Internet connection. In so doing, Stanley deliberately ventured beyond the privacy protections of the home, and thus, beyond the safe harbor provided by *Kyllo*.

Stanley cannot avail himself of the privacy protections of his home merely because he initiated his transmission from there. Most importantly, while Stanley may have justifiably expected the path of his invisible radio waves to go undetected, society would not consider this expectation "legitimate" given the unauthorized nature of his transmission.

Here, the presence of Stanley's unauthorized signal was itself "wrongful." When Stanley deliberately connected to the Neighbor's unsecured wireless network, he essentially hijacked the Neighbor's router, forcing it to relay data to Comcast's modem and back to his computer, all without either the Neighbor's or Comcast's knowledge or consent. Stanley was, in effect, a virtual trespasser. As such, he can claim no "legitimate" expectation of privacy in the signal he used to effectuate this trespass—at least where, as here, the MoocherHunter revealed only the path of this signal and not its contents.

Id. at *4–*5.

SECTION 2. STATUTORY PRIVACY LAWS

D. THE STORED COMMUNICATIONS ACT

13th ed., p. 542; at the end of the chapter, add:

New Details Emerge About NSA Surveillance Practices

In June 2013, an NSA contractor named Edward Snowden began releasing classified documents he had obtained during his government employment to journalists at *The Guardian* and the *Washington Post*. The documents have provided new details about how the federal government has implemented the various FISA authorities.

According to the documents, the federal government has four different programs for collecting network information for national security purposes in bulk. Two programs concern metadata—that is, non-content addressing information. The program for telephone metadata is called MAINWAY, and the program for Internet metadata is called MARINA.

The two remaining programs operate on a much smaller scale and collect contents instead of metadata. One program, called NUCLEON, collects telephone contents in certain situations. The final program, called PRISM, collects Internet contents in certain situations. *See generally* Barton Gellman, *U.S. Surveillance Architecture Includes Collection of Revealing Internet, Phone Metadata*, Washington Post, June 15, 2013. So far, most of the details released about these four programs concern MAINWAY (the program that collects telephone metadata) and PRISM (the program that collects Internet contents).

The MAINWAY program to collect telephone metadata has used Section 215 of FISA. The government has obtained Section 215 orders that require telephone providers to provide the government with massive databases of all of their telephone metadata. *See* Glenn Greenwald, *NSA Collecting Phone Records of Millions of Verizon Customers Daily*, The Guardian, June 5, 2013. The FISA court judges have approved such procedures by interpreting the phrase "tangible things (including books, records, papers, documents and other items)" in 50 U.S.C. § 1861(a)(1) to include massive databases containing millions or even billions of records. The database can be queried when government agents have specific and articulable facts to believe that a particular selector will reveal foreign intelligence information. Before 2014, that determination was made within the executive branch. Starting in 2014, however, the FISA court began to approve each query of the database. *See* Order Granting the Government's Motion to Amend the Court's Primary Order Dated January 3, 2014, FISC Docket No. BR 14-01 (For. Intell. Surv. Ct. February 5, 2014).

The PRISM program appears to be a way of implementing § 702 of FISA, which permits the government to obtain wide-scale authority to conduct surveillance of individuals believed to be outside the United States. Some early reports about PRISM indicated that the NSA has direct access to the networks of major U.S. Internet companies including Microsoft, Yahoo, Google, Facebook, and AOL. However, later reports suggest that the NSA does not have direct access, and that the particular way that the government obtains PRISM materials varies for each provider. *See generally* Stephen Braun, Anne Flaherty, Jack Gillum & Matt Apuzzo, *Secret to Prism Program: Even Bigger Data Seizure*, Associated Press, June 15, 2013.

CHAPTER 9

POLICE INTERROGATION AND CONFESSIONS

■ ■ ■

SECTION 2. THE *MIRANDA* "REVOLUTION"

13th ed., p. 602; after the discussion of *Berkemer v. McCarty* in Note 6, add:

HOWES v. FIELDS, 132 S.Ct. 1181 (2012), underscored that "our decisions do not clearly establish that a prisoner is always in custody for purposes of *Miranda* whenever a prisoner is isolated from the general prison population and questioned about conduct [that occurred] outside the prison." The case arose as follows:

Fields, a Michigan state prisoner, was taken from his prison cell by a corrections officer to a conference room, where he was questioned by two sheriff's deputies about criminal activity he may have engaged in before being sent to prison. He was questioned for between five and seven hours. At no time was he given *Miranda* warnings or told that he did not have to speak with the deputies. However, he was told more than once that he was free to leave and return to his cell.

Although the deputies were armed, Fields remained free of restraints. The conference room was sometimes open and other time shut. Several times, Fields told the deputies he no longer wanted to talk to them, but he never asked to go back to his cell. Fields eventually confessed to engaging in sex with a 12-year-old boy. After he confessed, and the questioning concluded, he had to wait an additional 20 minutes for an escort back to his cell. He returned to his cell well after the hour he usually retired.

After his conviction, Fields sought federal habeas relief under the Antiterrorism and Effective Death Penalty Act of 1996 (AEDPA). The Sixth Circuit granted such relief, maintaining, as the Supreme Court described it, that the questioning of Fields in the conference room was "a 'custodial interrogation' within the meaning of *Miranda* because isolation from the general prison population combined with questioning about conduct occurring outside the prison makes any such interrogation custodial *per se*." A 6–3 majority, per Alito, J., joined by Roberts, C.J., and Scalia, Kennedy, Thomas and Kagan, J.J., reversed:

Contrary to the Sixth Circuit's ruling, *Miranda* did not hold that the "inherently compelling pressures" of custodial interrogation "are always present when a prisoner is taken aside and questioned about events outside the prison walls." Indeed, *Miranda* did not even establish that police questioning of a suspect at the station house is always custodial. See *Oregon v. Mathiason* [13th ed., p. 602].

"Not only does the categorical rule applied below go well beyond anything that is clearly established in our prior decisions, it is simply wrong. The three elements of that rule—(1) imprisonment, (2) questioning in private, and (3) questioning about events in the outside world—are not necessarily enough to create a custodial situation for *Miranda* purposes.

" * * * We held in *Maryland v. Shatzer* [13th ed., p. 637] that [the *Edwards* rule] does not apply when there is a sufficient break in custody between the suspect's invocation of the right to counsel and the initiation of subsequent questioning. And, what is significant for present purposes, we further held that a break in custody may occur while a suspect is serving a term in prison. If a break in custody can occur while a prisoner is serving an uninterrupted term of imprisonment, it must follow that imprisonment alone is not enough to create a custodial situation within the meaning of *Miranda*. * * *

"Because he was in prison, [respondent Fields] was not free to leave the conference room by himself and to make his own way through the facility to his cell. Instead, he was escorted to the conference room and, when he ultimately decided to end the interview, he had to wait about 20 minutes for a corrections officer to arrive and escort him to his cell. But he would have been subject to this same restraint even if he had been taken to the conference room for some reason other than police questioning; under no circumstances could he have reasonably expected to be able to roam free. And while respondent testified that he 'was told * * * if I did not want to cooperate, I needed to go back to my cell,' these words did not coerce cooperation by threatening harsher conditions. * * * Returning to his cell would merely have returned him to his usual environment. See *Shatzer*, supra.

"Taking into account all of the circumstances of the questioning—including especially the undisputed fact that respondent was told that he was free to end the questioning and to return to his cell—we hold that respondent was not in custody within the meaning of *Miranda*."

Ginsburg, J., joined by Breyer and Sotomayor, concurred in part and dissented in part. Given the Court's rulings on what counts as "custody" for *Miranda* purposes, she agreed that "the law is not 'clearly established' in respondent Field's favor." But she disagreed with the Court's determination that Fields was not in custody for *Miranda* purposes: "Were the case here on direct review, I would vote to hold that *Miranda* precludes the State's introduction of Fields's confession as evidence against him." Justice Ginsburg continued:

"Fields, serving time for disorderly conduct, was of course '[i]n custody,' but not 'for purposes of *Miranda*,' the Court concludes. I would not train, as the Court does, on the question of whether there can be custody within custody. Instead, I would ask, as *Miranda* put it, whether Fields was subjected to 'incommunicado interrogation * * * in a police-dominated atmosphere,' whether his 'freedom of action [was] curtailed in any significant way.' Those should be the key questions, and to each I would answer 'yes.' * * *

"Critical to the Court's judgment is 'the undisputed fact that [Fields] was told that he was free to end the questioning and return to his cell. Never mind the facts suggesting that Fields's submission to the overnight interview was anything but voluntary. Was Fields 'held for interrogation'? Brought to, and left alone with, the gun-bearing deputies, he surely was in my judgment."

" * * * Today, for people already in prison, the Court finds it adequate for the police to say: 'You are free to terminate this interrogation and return to your cell.' Such a statement is no substitute for one ensuring that an individual is aware of his rights."

13th ed., p. 640; at the end of Justice Scalia's majority opinion in *Maryland v. Shatzer*, add new footnote a:

ᵃ In *Howes v. Fields*, discussed at Supp., p. 73, Justice Alito, writing for a 6–3 majority, observed that in granting federal habeas relief, the U.S. Court of Appeals for the Sixth Circuit had relied on the "categorical rule" that the questioning of a prisoner "is always custodial when the prisoner is removed from the general prison population and questioned about events that occurred outside the prison." "On the contrary," commented Justice Alito, "we have repeatedly declined to adopt any categorical rule with respect to whether the questioning of a prison inmate is custodial."

Justice Alito also observed that the Sixth Circuit "purported to find support for its *per se* rule in *Shatzer*, relying on our statement that '[n]o one questions that *Shatzer* was in custody for *Miranda* purposes'" when he was interrogated. "But this statement," continued Alito, "means only that the issue of custody was not contested before us. It strains credibility to read the statement as constituting an 'unambiguous conclusion' or 'finding' by this Court that *Shatzer* was in custody.'"

13th ed., p. 659; after Note 5, add:

6. For strong criticism of *Berghuis v. Thompkins*, see Erwin Chemerinsky, *The Roberts Court and Criminal Procedure at Age Five*, 43 Tex.Tech.L.Rev. 13, 18–21 (2010); Joshua Dressler & Alan C. Michaels, *Understanding Criminal Procedure* 467, 471–72 (6th ed. 2013); Yale Kamisar, *The Rise, Decline, and Fall (?) of Miranda*, 87 Wash.L.Rev. 965, 1008–21 (2012).

13ᵗʰ ed., p. 659; after Note 23, add:

23A. *When suspects are not in custody, and therefore not given any* **Miranda** *warnings, do they have a "right to remain silent"? If they do, must they expressly invoke this right*?

SALINAS V. TEXAS
___ U.S. ___, 133 S.Ct. 2174, 186 L.Ed.2d 376 (2013).

JUSTICE ALITO announced the judgment of the Court and delivered an opinion in which THE CHIEF JUSTICE and JUSTICE KENNEDY join.

[The police asked defendant to come to the police station to clear himself as a suspect in a murder case. When the defendant arrived at the station, he was not in custody; he was free to leave at that time. As a result, he was not given any *Miranda* warnings.

[Defendant was asked a number of questions and answered them. Then he was asked whether the shotgun from his home would match the shells recovered at the scene of the murder. At this point, defendant declined to answer. Instead, he looked down at the floor, shuffled his feet, bit his bottom lip, and clenched his hands in his lap. After a few moments of silence, the defendant answered other questions.

[During the prosecutor's closing argument, he used the defendant's reaction when questioned earlier as evidence of his guilt. He pointed out to the jury that the defendant had remained silent when asked about the shotgun. The prosecutor told the jury that an innocent person would not have reacted the same way. Instead, an innocent person would have denied that he was involved. He would have said: "I wasn't there." But Salinas "didn't respond that way."

[The Court noted that it granted certiorari to resolve a division of authority in the lower courts over whether the prosecution may use a defendant's assertion of the privilege against self-incrimination during noncustodial police questioning of a suspect as part of its case in chief. However, because the defendant never did invoke the privilege during the police questioning of him, the Court found it "unnecessary to reach that question."]

The privilege against self-incrimination "is an exception to the general rule that the Government has the right to everyone's testimony." To prevent the privilege from shielding information not properly within its scope, we have long held that a witness who "desires the protection of the privilege * * * must claim it" at the time relies on it. *Minnesota v. Murphy*, 13th ed., p. 603, fn. b.[1]

That requirement ensures that the Government is put on notice when a witness intends to rely on the privilege so that it may either argue

---

[1] Murphy, a probationer, arranged to meet with his probation officer as she had requested. He then admitted he had committed serious crimes a number of years earlier. A 6–3 majority, per White, J., concluded that Murphy could not claim the "in custody" exception to the general rule that the privilege against self-incrimination is not self-executing: "[A]ny compulsion [Murphy] might have felt from the possibility that terminating the meeting would have led to revocation of probation was not comparable to the pressure on a suspect who is painfully aware that he literally cannot escape a persistent custodial interrogation."

that the testimony sought could not be self-incriminating or cure any potential self-incrimination through a grant of immunity. * * *

We have previously recognized two exceptions to the requirement that witnesses invoke the privilege, but neither applies here. First, we held in *Griffin v. California* (1965) [13th ed., p. 1450], that a criminal defendant need not take the stand and assert the privilege at his own trial. That exception reflects the fact that a criminal defendant has an "absolute right not to testify." [Because the defendant] had no comparable unqualified right during his interview with the police, his silence falls outside the *Griffin* exception.

Second, we have held that a witness' failure to invoke the privilege must be excused where governmental coercion makes his forfeiture of the privilege involuntary. Thus, in *Miranda*, we said that a suspect who is subjected to the "inherently compelling pressures" of an unwarned custodial interrogation need not invoke the privilege.

[However, as the defendant] himself acknowledges, he agreed to accompany the officers to the station and "was free to leave at any time during the interview." * * * We have before us no allegation that [the defendant's] failure to assert the privilege was involuntary, and it would have been a simple matter for him to say that he was not answering the officer's question on Fifth Amendment grounds. Because he failed to do so, the prosecution's use of his noncustodial silence did not violate the Fifth Amendment. * * *

Our cases establish that a defendant normally does not invoke the privilege by remaining silent. * * * We have also repeatedly held that the express invocation requirement applies when an official has reason to suspect that the answer to his question would incriminate the witness. Thus, in *Murphy*, supra, we held that the defendant's self-incriminating answers to his probation officer were properly admitted at trial because he failed to invoke the privilege. In reaching that conclusion, we rejected the notion "that a witness must 'put the Government on notice' by formally availing himself of the privilege only when he alone 'is reasonably aware of the incriminating tendency of the questions.'"

[The defendant] does not dispute the vitality of either of those lines of precedent but instead argues that we should adopt an exception for cases at their intersection. [Defendant] would have us hold that although neither a witness' silence nor official suspicions are enough to excuse the express invocation requirement, the invocation requirement does not apply where a witness is silent in the face of official suspicions. [Such a view] would do little to protect those genuinely relying on the Fifth Amendment privilege while placing a needless new burden on society's interest in the admission of evidence that is protective of a defendant's guilt.

[The defendant's] proposed exception would also be very difficult to reconcile with *Berghuis v. Thompkins*. There, we held in the closely related context of post-*Miranda* silence that a defendant failed to invoke the privilege when he refused to respond to police questioning for 2 hours and 45 minutes. If the extended custodial silence in that case did not invoke the privilege, then surely the momentary silence in this case did not do so either.

[The dissent attempts] to distinguish *Berghuis* by observing that it did not concern the admissibility of the defendant's silence but instead involved the admissibility of his subsequent statements. But regardless of whether prosecutors seek to use silence or a confession that follows, the logic of *Berghuis* applies with equal force: A suspect who stands mute has not done enough to put police on notice that he is relying on his Fifth Amendment privilege.

[Defendant and the dissent also maintain that] reliance on the Fifth Amendment privilege is the most likely explanation for silence in a case such as this one. But whatever the most probable explanation, such silence is "insolubly ambiguous." See *Doyle v. Ohio* [13th ed., p. 918] * * * . [Defendant] alone knew why he did not answer the officer's question, and it was therefore his "burden [to] make a timely assertion of the privilege."

[Defendant suggests] that it would be unfair to require a suspect unschooled in the particulars of legal doctrine to do anything more than remain silent in order to invoke his "right to remain silent." [But] popular misconceptions notwithstanding, the Fifth Amendment guarantees that no one may be "compelled in any criminal case to be a witness against himself"; it does not establish an unqualified "right to remain silent." A witness' constitutional right to refuse to answer questions depends on his reason for doing so, and courts need to know those reasons to evaluate the merits of a Fifth Amendment claim. * * *

Finally, we are not persuaded by [defendant's] arguments that applying the usual express invocation requirement where a witness is silent during a noncustodial police interview will prove unworkable in practice. * * * Notably, [defendant's] approach would produce its own line-drawing problems, as this case vividly illustrates. When the interviewing officer asked [the defendant] if his shotgun would match the shell casings found at the crime scene, [the defendant] made movements that suggested surprise and anxiety. At precisely what point such reactions transform "silence" into expressive conduct would be a difficult and recurring question that our decision allows us to avoid.

[Defendant] worries that officers could unduly pressure suspects into talking by telling them that their silence could be used in a future prosecution. But as [defendant] himself concedes, police officers "have done nothing wrong" when they "accurately state the law." We found no constitutional infirmity in government officials telling the defendant in *Murphy* that he was required to speak truthfully to his parole officer, and we see no greater danger in the interview tactics [the defendant] identifies.

JUSTICE THOMAS, with whom JUSTICE SCALIA joins, concurring in the judgment.

* * * In my view, Salinas' claim would fail even if he had invoked the privilege because the prosecutor's comments regarding his precustodial silence did not compel him to give self-incriminating testimony.

In *Griffin v. California*, this Court held that the Fifth Amendment prohibits a prosecutor or judge from commenting on a defendant's failure to testify. * * * Salinas argues that we should extend *Griffin*'s no-adverse inference rule to a defendant's silence during a precustodial interview. I have previously explained that [*Griffin*] "lacks foundation in the Constitution's text, history, or logic" and should not be extended. I adhere to that view today. * * *

At the time of the founding, English and American courts strongly encouraged defendants to give unsworn statements and drew adverse inference when they failed to do so. Given *Griffin*'s indefensible foundation, I would not extend it to a defendant's silence during a precustodial interview. * * *

JUSTICE BREYER, with whom JUSTICE GINSBURG, JUSTICE SOTOMAYOR, and JUSTICE KAGAN join, dissenting.

In my view the Fifth Amendment here prohibits the prosecution from commenting on the petitioner's silence in response to police questioning. And I dissent from the Court's contrary conclusion. * * *

* * * To permit a prosecutor to comment on a defendant's constitutionally protected silence would put that defendant in an impossible predicament. He must either answer the question or remain silent. If he answers the question, he may well reveal, for example, prejudicial facts, disreputable associates, or suspicious circumstances— even if he is innocent. * * * If he remains silent, the prosecutor may well use that silence to suggest a consciousness of guilt. And if the defendant then takes the witness stand in order to explain either his speech or his silence, the prosecution may introduce, say for impeachment purposes, a prior conviction that the law would otherwise make inadmissible. Thus, where the Fifth Amendment is at issue, to allow comment on silence directly or indirectly can compel an individual to act as "a witness against himself"—very much what the Fifth Amendment forbids. * * * And that is similarly so whether the questioned individual, as part of his decision to remain silent, invokes the Fifth Amendment explicitly or implicitly,

through words, through deeds, or through reference to surrounding circumstances.

It is consequently not surprising that this Court, more than half a century ago, explained that "no ritualistic formula is necessary in order to invoke the privilege." Thus, a prosecutor may not comment on a defendant's failure to testify at trial—even if neither the defendant nor anyone else ever mentions a Fifth Amendment right not to do so. Circumstances, not a defendant's statement, tie the defendant's silence to the right. Similarly, a prosecutor may not comment on the fact that a defendant in custody, *after* receiving *Miranda* warnings, "stood mute"—regardless of whether he "claimed his privilege" in so many words. Again, it is not any explicit statement but, instead, the defendant's deeds (silence) and circumstances (receipt of the warnings) that tie together silence and constitutional right. Most lower courts have so construed the law, even where the defendant, having received *Miranda* warnings, answers some questions while remaining silent as to others.

The cases in which this Court has insisted that a defendant expressly mention the Fifth Amendment by name in order to rely on its privilege to protect silence are cases where (1) the circumstances surrounding the silence (unlike the present case) did not give rise to an inference that the defendant intended, by his silence, to exercise his Fifth Amendment rights; *and* (2) the questioner greeted by the silence (again unlike the present case) had a special need to know whether the defendant sought to rely on the protections of the Fifth Amendment. [In] such cases, the government needs to know the basis for refusing to answer "so that it may either argue that the testimony sought could not be self-incriminating or cure any potential self-incrimination through a grant of immunity." * * *

Perhaps most illustrative is *Jenkins v. Anderson*, 447 U.S. 231 (1980), a case upon which the plurality relies, and upon which the Texas Court of Criminal Appeals relied almost exclusively. Jenkins killed someone, and was not arrested until he turned himself in two weeks later. On cross-examination at his trial, Jenkins claimed that his killing was in self-defense after being attacked. The prosecutor then asked why he did not report the alleged attack, and in closing argument suggested that Jenkins' failure to do so cast doubt on his claim to have acted in self-defense. We explained that this unusual form of "prearrest silence" was not constitutionally protected from use at trial. Perhaps even more aptly, Justice Stevens' concurrence noted that "the privilege against compulsory self incrimination is simply irrelevant" in such circumstances. How would anyone have known that Jenkins, while failing to report an attack, was relying on the Fifth Amendment? And how would the government have had any way of determining whether his claim was valid? In *Jenkins*, no one had any reason to connect silence to the Fifth Amendment; and the government had no opportunity to contest any alleged connection.

Still further afield from today's case are *Murphy* and *Garner*, neither of which involved silence at all. Rather, in both cases, a defendant had earlier *answered* questions posed by the government—in *Murphy*, by speaking with a probation officer, and in *Garner*, by completing a tax return. [See] *Garner* v. *United States*, 424 U.S. 648 (1976). At the time of providing answers, neither circumstances nor deeds nor words suggested reliance on the Fifth Amendment: Murphy simply answered questions posed by his probation officer; Garner simply filled out a tax return. They did not argue that their selfincriminating statements had been "compelled" in violation of the Fifth Amendment until later, at trial. The Court held that those statements were *not* compelled. The circumstances indicated that the defendants had affirmatively chosen to speak and to write.

Thus, we have two sets of cases: One where express invocation of the Fifth Amendment was not required to tie one's silence to its protections, and another where something like express invocation was required, because circumstances demanded some explanation for the silence (or the statements) in order to indicate that the Fifth Amendment was at issue.

There is also a third set of cases, cases that may well fit into the second category but where the Court has held that the Fifth Amendment both applies and does not require express invocation *despite* ambiguous circumstances. The Court in those cases has made clear that an individual, when silent, need not expressly invoke the Fifth Amendment if there are "inherently compelling pressures" not to do so. *Miranda*. Thus, in *Garrity* v. *New Jersey* [13th ed., p. 710], the Court held that no explicit assertion of the Fifth Amendment was required where, in the course of an investigation, such assertion would, by law, have cost police officers their jobs. Similarly, this Court did not require explicit assertion in response to a grand jury subpoena where that assertion would have cost two architects their public contracts or a political official his job. *Lefkowitz* v. *Turley*, 414 U.S. 70, 75–76 (1973); *Lefkowitz* v. *Cunningham* [13th ed., p. 674]. * * *

The plurality refers to one additional case, namely *Berghuis* v. *Thompkins*. But that case is here beside the point. In *Berghuis*, the defendant was in custody, he had been informed of his *Miranda* rights, and he was subsequently silent in the face of 2 hours and 45 minutes of questioning before he offered any substantive answers. The Court held that he had waived his Fifth Amendment rights in respect to his *later speech*. The Court said nothing at all about a prosecutor's right to comment on his preceding silence and no prosecutor sought to do so. Indeed, how could a prosecutor lawfully have tried to do so, given this

Court's statement in *Miranda* itself that a prosecutor cannot comment on the fact that, after receiving *Miranda* warnings, the suspect "stood mute"?

We end where we began. "[N]o ritualistic formula is necessary in order to invoke the privilege." Much depends on the circumstances of the particular case, the most important circumstances being: (1) whether one can fairly infer that the individual being questioned is invoking the Amendment's protection; (2) if that is unclear, whether it is particularly important for the questioner to know whether the individual is doing so; and (3) even if it is, whether, in any event, there is a good reason for excusing the individual from referring to the Fifth Amendment, such as inherent penalization simply by answering.

Applying these principles to the present case, I would hold that Salinas need not have expressly invoked the Fifth Amendment. The context was that of a criminal investigation. Police told Salinas that and made clear that he was a suspect. His interrogation took place at the police station. Salinas was not represented by counsel. The relevant question—about whether the shotgun from Salinas' home would incriminate him—amounted to a switch in subject matter. And it was obvious that the new question sought to ferret out whether Salinas was guilty of murder.

These circumstances give rise to a reasonable inference that Salinas' silence derived from an exercise of his Fifth Amendment rights. This Court has recognized repeatedly that many, indeed most, Americans are aware that they have a constitutional right not to incriminate themselves by answering questions posed by the police during an interrogation conducted in order to figure out the perpetrator of a crime. See *Dickerson v. United States* [set forth in 13th ed., p. 677]. The nature of the surroundings, the switch of topic, the particular question—all suggested that the right we have and generally *know* we have was at issue at the critical moment here. Salinas, not being represented by counsel, would not likely have used the precise words "Fifth Amendment" to invoke his rights because he would not likely have been aware of technical legal requirements, such as a need to identify the Fifth Amendment by name.

At the same time, the need to categorize Salinas' silence as based on the Fifth Amendment is supported here by the presence, in full force, of the predicament I discussed earlier, namely that of not forcing Salinas to choose between incrimination through speech and incrimination through silence. That need is also supported by the absence of any special reason that the police had to know, with certainty, whether Salinas was, in fact, relying on the Fifth Amendment—such as whether to doubt that there really was a risk of self-incrimination, or whether to grant immunity. Given these circumstances, Salinas' silence was "sufficient to put the [government] on notice of an apparent claim of the privilege." That being so, for reasons similar to those given in *Griffin*, the Fifth Amendment bars the evidence of silence admitted against Salinas and mentioned by the prosecutor.

I recognize that other cases may arise where facts and circumstances surrounding an individual's silence present a closer question. The critical question—whether those circumstances give rise to a fair inference that the silence rests on the Fifth Amendment—will not always prove easy to administer. But that consideration does not support the plurality's rule-based approach here, for the administrative problems accompanying the plurality's approach are even worse.

The plurality says that a suspect must "expressly invoke the privilege against self-incrimination." But does it really mean that the suspect must use the exact words "Fifth Amendment"? How can an individual who is not a lawyer know that these particular words are legally magic? Nor does the Solicitor General help when he adds that the suspect may "mak[e] the claim 'in any language that [the questioner] may reasonably be expected to understand as an attempt to invoke the privilege.'" What counts as "making the claim"? Suppose the individual says, "Let's discuss something else," or "I'm not sure I want to answer that"; or suppose he just gets up and leaves the room. * * * How is simple silence in the present context any different?

The basic problem for the plurality is that an effort to have a simple, clear "explicit statement" rule poses a serious obstacle to those who, like Salinas, seek to assert their basic Fifth Amendment right to remain silent, for they are likely unaware of any such linguistic detail. At the same time, acknowledging that our case law does not require use of specific words leaves the plurality without the administrative benefits it might hope to find in requiring that detail.

Far better, in my view, to pose the relevant question directly: Can one fairly infer from an individual's silence and surrounding circumstances an exercise of the Fifth Amendment's privilege? The need for simplicity, the constitutional importance of applying the Fifth Amendment to those who seek its protection, and this Court's case law all suggest that this is the right question to ask here. And the answer to that question in the circumstances of today's case is clearly: yes.

For these reasons, I believe that the Fifth Amendment prohibits a prosecutor from commenting on Salinas's silence. I respectfully dissent from the Court's contrary conclusion.

13th ed., p. 675; after Note 31, add:

31A.   *Avoiding Miranda.* According to American officials, a Libyan suspected of playing a major role in the deadly attack on the U.S. Mission in

Benghazi is talking freely with American interrogators aboard a Navy Ship in the Mediterranean Sea. See Michael Schmidt, et al., *Trial Secondary as U.S. Questions a Libyan Suspect*, N.Y. Times, June 20, 2014, p. 1.

Interrogators began questioning the suspect, Ahmed Aber Khattala, on the U.S.S. New York shortly after he was taken into custody. After several days of questioning, the suspect still had not been given the *Miranda* warnings. The interrogation demonstrates how the F.B.I. has become comfortable concentrating on gathering intelligence when questioning those suspected of terrorism rather than seeking evidence admissible in court.

The authorities want to transport the suspect on the Navy ship because they want to build rapport with him. Moreover, putting the suspect on a plane would involve taking him to a foreign country, which could involve legal and diplomatic entanglements.

According to the federal rules of criminal procedure, a person taken into custody—even a suspect arrested overseas—must be brought before a magistrate judge for an initial hearing without "unnecessary delay." That usually means 48 hours. But a violation of the presentment rule is usually limited. The penalty for the violation is unlikely to be dismissal of the charges.

13th ed., p. 688; after Note 6, add:

6A. *Support from law enforcement officials.* As pointed out in Sherry F. Colb, *Interrogation as a Thermometer of Public Fear* (review of 2012 book, *Confessions of Guilt*, by George Thomas III & Richard Leo), 11 Ohio State J.Crim.L. 231 242 n. 51 (2013), in the *Dickerson* case "[f]ormer Attorney General Griffin Bell and other law enforcement officers filed an amicus brief arguing that *Miranda* 'promotes effective law enforcement by providing a bright line rule for police officers to follow.'"

CHAPTER 10

LINEUPS, SHOWUPS AND OTHER PRE-TRIAL IDENTIFICATION PROCEDURES

■ ■ ■

SECTION 1.*WADE* AND *GILBERT*: CONSTITUTIONAL CONCERN ABOUT THE DANGERS INVOLVED IN EYEWITNESS IDENTIFICATIONS

13th ed., p. 767; after Note 4, add:

    4A. ***A partial-exclusion approach.*** Although courtroom identifications are highly suggestive (the defendant is sitting at counsel's table waiting to be identified), they are not highly regulated by the courts. Consider Brandon L. Garrett, *Eyewitnesses and Exclusion*, 65 Vand. L. Rev. 451, 461 (2012): "Courts generally reject arguments that in-court identifications are inherently suggestive. . . . Judges may view the courtroom identification as pure theater or a witness demonstration, but . . . they also seem to think that the presence of counsel and the solemnity of testimony under oath in a courtroom makes the courtroom identification more, not less, reliable." Professor Garrett takes issue with that approach, noting that "[t]oday courts almost always allow courtroom identifications, but they sometimes bar prior identifications. Instead, courts should per se exclude courtroom identifications if there was a prior identification, but they should sometimes admit out-of-court identifications. The result will encourage greater attention to procedures used out-of-court, when the eyewitness's memory was most fresh, reliable, and accurate." Id. at 457. Do you agree?

SECTION 3. DUE PROCESS LIMITATIONS

13th ed., p. 786; after Note 5, add:

    6. ***Conflating the due process and Sixth Amendment inquiries.*** The vast majority of state courts has borrowed the "independent source" doctrine from the *Wade-Gilbert* line of Sixth Amendment right-to-counsel cases and held that an in-court identification is permissible despite an inadmissible out-of-court identification by the same eyewitness provided that the court finds that there is an "independent source"—i.e., a source other than the prior, inadmissible out-of-court identification—for the in-court identification. See Garrett, supra (collecting cases). Professor Garrett has argued that this approach "has it backwards:"

"[T]he Pennsylvania Supreme Court asked 'whether there exists a basis for identification which is independent of the allegedly suggestive showup.' How could there be such a basis? The same eyewitness is testifying at trial with a memory affected by the showup. Similarly, a South Carolina appellate court noted that '[t]he in-court identification is admissible if based on information independent of the out-of-court procedure.' What 'information' does that eyewitness have that is 'independent' where nothing has transpired except that the eyewitness is now confronted with the same person in a courtroom setting?"

Garrett, supra at 456, 478. As Professor Garrett explains, "[i]n the eyewitness context, neither time nor unrelated events can 'dissipate the taint.' . . . The very idea that a courtroom identification could be seen as 'independent' is anomalous [because, in] the courtroom, the eyewitness cannot access a memory of what happened that is 'independent' of the suggestive lineups that came before." Garrett, *supra* at 484–85; see also id. at 487 (noting that several state and federal courts "cite to other evidence in the case as another 'independent' basis for allowing the in-court identification;" if there is sufficient other evidence of guilt, that will "help to show that [the in-court identification] was reliable or 'independent' of any suggestive police conduct").

SECTION 4. SOCIAL SCIENCE RESEARCH OF IDENTIFICATION PROCEDURES AND THE NEED FOR REFORM

13th ed., p. 787; at the end of the first paragraph of Note 2, add:

Social science research demonstrates that young children and the elderly are more susceptible to having their memories of an event distorted by misinformation after the fact, as are "people who have lower cognitive abilities" and "persons with certain personality characteristics, such as being high in cooperativeness." Gary L. Wells & Elizabeth Loftus, *Eyewitness Memory for People and Events, Handbook of Psychology, Forensic Psychology*, vol. 11, ch. 25, p. 621 (2013). Should a different legal standard apply when determining how reliable these individuals' identifications are after a suggestive procedure?

CHAPTER 11

GRAND JURY INVESTIGATIONS

■ ■ ■

SECTION 5. SELF-INCRIMINATION AND THE COMPELLED PRODUCTION OF DOCUMENTS

B. THE ACT-OF-PRODUCTION DOCTRINE

13th ed., p. 878; after Note 6, add:

6A. *Encryption.* In IN RE GRAND JURY SUBPOENA DUCES TECUM DATED MARCH 25, 2011, 670 F.3d 1335 (11th Cir. 2012), law enforcement officers, in the course of a child pornography investigation, seized, pursuant to a search warrant, two laptops and 5 external hard drives belonging to Doe. After FBI forensic examiners were unable to access certain portions of the hard drives because of encryption, a federal grand jury issued a subpoena duces tecum requiring Doe "to produce the 'unencrypted contents' of the digital media [i.e. the hard drives] and 'any and all containers or folders thereon.'" After Doe asserted the self-incrimination privilege, the district court, at the prosecution's request, granted Doe "limited-act-of-production immunity." The immunity order prohibited the "use of Doe's act of production of the unencrypted contents of the hard drives," but did not extend "to the Government's 'derivative use' of the decrypted contents of the drives as evidence * * * in a criminal prosecution." Challenging the immunity as insufficient, Doe refused to comply with subpoena, and was held in civil contempt. On appeal, the Eleventh Circuit (per Tjoflat, J.) reversed. The district court, it concluded, erred first "in concluding that Doe's act of decryption and production would not constitute testimony," and second, in limiting the immunity. As to the first error, the Eleventh Circuit reasoned:

"The Supreme Court has marked out two ways in which an act of production is not testimonial. First, the Fifth Amendment privilege is not triggered where the Government merely compels some physical act, i.e., where the individual is not called upon to make use of the contents of his or her mind. The most famous example is the key to the lock of a strongbox containing documents. * * * Second, under the 'forgone conclusion' doctrine, an act of production is not testimonial—even if the act conveys a fact regarding the existence or location, possession, or authenticity of the subpoenaed materials—if the Government can show with 'reasonable particularity' that, at the time it sought to compel the act of production, it already knew of the materials, thereby making any testimonial aspect a 'foregone conclusion.' * * *

"[As to the first alternative], the decryption and production of the hard drives would require the use of the contents of Doe's mind. * * * [It] would be tantamount to testimony by Doe of his knowledge of the existence and location of potentially incriminating files; of his possession, control, and access to the encrypted portions of the drives; and of his capability to decrypt the files. We are unpersuaded by the Government's derivation of the key/combination analogy in arguing that Doe's production of the unencrypted files would be nothing more than a physical non-testimonial transfer. The Government attempts to avoid the analogy by arguing that it does not seek the combination or the key, but rather the contents. This argument badly misses the mark. In *Fisher* * * * and again in *Hubbell*, the Government never sought the 'key' or the 'combination' to the safe for its own sake; rather, the Government sought the files being withheld, just as the Government does here. Requiring Doe to use a decryption password is most certainly more akin to requiring the production of a combination because both demand the use of the contents of the mind, and the production is accompanied by the implied factual statements noted above that could prove to be incriminatory.

"Moving to the second point, the question becomes whether the purported testimony was a 'forgone conclusion.' We think not. Nothing in the record before us reveals that the Government knew whether any files exist or the location of those files on the hard drives; what's more, nothing in the record illustrates that the Government knew with reasonable particularity that Doe was even capable of accessing the encrypted portions of the drives. * * *

"[T]he Government points to [forensic expert's] McCrohan's testimony [at the contempt show-cause hearing]. * * * But McCrohan's testimony simply does not stretch as far as the Government wishes it would. As an initial matter, McCrohan admitted on cross-examination that he had no idea whether there was data on the encrypted devices. Responding to a question from Doe as to whether the random characters definitely indicated that encrypted data is present or instead could have indicated blank space, McCrohan conceded, 'Well, you would see random characters, but you wouldn't know necessarily whether it was blank.' Moreover, when pressed to answer why investigators believed data may be hidden, McCrohan replied, 'The scope of my examination didn't go that far,' and, 'We couldn't get into them, so we can't make that call.' * * *

"To be fair, the Government has shown that the combined storage space of the drives *could* contain files that number well into the millions. And the Government has also shown that the drives are encrypted. The Government has not shown, however, that the drives actually contain any files, nor has it shown which of the twenty million files the drives are capable of holding may prove useful. The Government has emphasized at every stage of the proceedings in this case that the forensic analysis showed random characters.

But random characters are not files; because the True Crypt program displays random characters if there are files *and* if there is empty space, we simply do not know what, if anything, was hidden based on the facts before us. It is not enough for the Government to argue that the encrypted drives are *capable* of storing vast amounts of data. * * * In short, the Government physically possesses the media devices, but it does not know what if anything is held on the encrypted drives. Along the same lines, we are not persuaded by the suggestion that simply because the devices were encrypted necessarily means that Doe was trying to hide something. Just as a vault is capable of storing mountains of incriminating documents or anything at all.

"In sum, we think this case is far closer to the *Hubbell* end of the spectrum than it is to the *Fisher* end. * * * Here, the Government has not shown that it possessed even a remotely similar knowledge [to that in *Fisher*] as to the *files* on the hard drives. Case law from the Supreme Court does not demand that the Government identify exactly the documents it seeks, but it does require some specificity in its requests—categorical requests for documents the Government anticipates are likely to exist simply will not suffice.

"The Government tries to analogize this case to *In re Boucher*, 2009 WL 424718 (D. Vt. Feb. 19, 2009). The facts of the *Boucher* appear to be somewhat similar to the facts of this case, but we do not find the Government's analogy persuasive. Like this case, in *Boucher* the Government sought to compel a suspect to produce an unencrypted version of a drive on his laptop. Previously, the Government had reviewed portions of the encrypted drive with the suspect but was unable to reopen the drive once it was closed. During this initial viewing, * * * after observing images of the animated child pornography on the unencrypted portions of the hard drive, a Special Agent from the Immigration and Custom's Enforcement (ICE) with experience and special training in recognizing child pornography was called. The ICE agent examined the computer and saw a file labeled '2yo getting raped during diaper change,' but was unable to open it. After the suspect navigated to the encrypted portion of the hard drive, the ICE agent located and examined several videos or images that appeared to be child pornography. The district court concluded that the 'foregone conclusion' doctrine applied under those facts because any testimonial value derived from the act of production was already known to the Government and therefore added nothing to its case. * * *

"The Government correctly notes that *Boucher* did not turn on the fact that the Government knew the contents of the file. *Fisher* and *Hubbell* though, still require knowledge *that the files exist*. Thus, while in *Boucher* it was irrelevant that the Government know what was contained in the file '2yo getting raped during diaper change,' it was crucial that the Government knew that there existed a file under such a name.[27] That is simply not the

---

[27] It is because of the Government's lack of knowledge in this case that we can easily distinguish another recent decision, *United States v. Fricosu*, 841 F.Supp.2d 1232 (D. Colo.2012). In *Fricosu*, the Government, after seizing a laptop computer suspected of containing

case here. We find no support in the record for the conclusion that the Government, at the time it sought to compel production, knew to any degree of particularity what, if anything, was hidden behind the encrypted wall.[28]"

Turning to the immunity order, the Eleventh Circuit concluded that, since the act-of-production was protected by the Fifth Amendment, use-and-derivate immunity was required. Accordingly, the Government could not provide immunity "only for the act of production, and then seek to introduce the contents of the production, regardless of whether those contents are characterized as non-testimonial evidence, because doing so would allow the use of evidence *derived* from the original testimonial statement. * * * The government's [contrary view] in essence asks us to revisit the 'manna from heaven theory' * * * [which *Hubbell*] definitively foreclosed * * *."

---

incrimination information, was unable to access certain encrypted portions of the computer. * * * The court [there] concluded that no testimony was associated with the compelled production of the unencrypted contents of the laptop computer. In reaching this conclusion, the court heavily relied upon a tape recording of a phone call introduced by the Government between *Fricosu* and another individual, where the defendant admitted, "[The content at issue] was on my laptop." * * *

    [28] To be clear, the Government does not have to show that it knows specific file names. Knowledge of a file name, like the Government had in *Boucher*, would be an easy way for the Government to carry its burden of showing that the existence of the files it seeks is a "foregone conclusion." That said, if the Government is unaware of a particular file name, it still must show with some reasonable particularity that it seeks a certain file and is aware, based on other information, that (1) the file exists in some specified location, (2) the file is possessed by the target of the subpoena, and (3) the file is authentic. * * *

CHAPTER 12

THE SCOPE OF THE EXCLUSIONARY RULES

■ ■ ■

SECTION 1. "STANDING" TO OBJECT TO THE ADMISSION OF EVIDENCE

B. THE CURRENT APPROACH

13th ed., p. 887; after first Note, add:

A Question About "Standing" in United States v. Jones

In the recent case of *United States v. Jones* (2012), set forth in 13th ed., p. 279, the majority's holding was expressly limited to instances in which the requisite "trespass" was to "a target's vehicle," and the Court dropped a footnote at that point noting that the vehicle in question "was registered to Jones's wife," although Jones "was the exclusive driver" and thus "had at least the property rights of a bailee." The Court declined to further consider Jones' status, noting that the lower court (utilizing a privacy theory, not a trespass theory) had determined Jones had standing. Since under the approach of the *Jones* majority it is the fact that the "Government physically occupied private property" that counts, does this mean that the standing issue is to be determined only as of the date of installation of the GPS device, so that, as the concurring Justices observe, "if the GPS device had been installed before respondent's wife gave him the keys, respondent would have no claim for trespass—and presumably, no Fourth Amendment claim either"?

PART 3

THE COMMENCEMENT OF FORMAL PROCEEDINGS

■ ■ ■

CHAPTER 13

PRETRIAL RELEASE

■ ■ ■

SECTION 1. THE RIGHT TO BAIL; PRETRIAL RELEASE PROCEDURES

13th ed., p. 941; before Note 7, add:

Consider *Fields v. Henry County*, 701 F.3d 180 (6th Cir.2012), where Fields was arrested for misdemeanor domestic assault, denied any post-booking bail because of a county 12-hour hold policy that, under state law, did not apply in the instant case, and then appeared the next morning before a judge, who set Fields' bail at $5,000 by using a bond schedule. As for the delay, the court stated: "The Eighth Amendment's protections address the amount of bail, not the timing. There is no constitutional right to speedy bail." As for any "procedural due process claim" regarding the delay, the court responded it would necessitate a "liberty interest" created by state law, not the case here because Fields had no "right to be released earlier than he was." Regarding the judicial use of a bond schedule, the court rejected Fields' contention "that he was entitled to a 'particularized examination' before having his bond set," as "nothing in the Eighth Amendment requires a particular type of 'process' or examination." Rather, use of a bond schedule violates the Eighth Amendment only if the amount specified for a particular offense is "grossly disproportional to the gravity of that offense," which Fields did not allege.

SECTION 2. PREVENTIVE DETENTION

13th ed., p. 957; after the phrase "fair likelihood" on line 2, add new footnote a:

[a] Actually, as for the extent of this burden, there is considerable variation among the states, which have selected from among the following possibilities, ranging from least to most demanding: fair likelihood, preponderance of the evidence, substantial showing or substantial evidence, clear and convincing, and evidence which viewed in the light most favorable to the state would suffice to sustain a jury's guilty verdict. See *Fry v. State*, 990 N.E.2d 429 (Ind.2013), assessing the various approaches.

13th ed., p. 958; before Note 4, add:

3A. Consider *Lopez-Valenzuela v. County of Maricopa*, 719 F.3d 1054 (9th Cir. 2013), concerning a recently-added provision to the Arizona Constitution commanding that bail not be set for "serious felony offenses as prescribed by the legislature if the person charged has entered or remained in the United States illegally and if the proof is evident or the presumption great as to the present charge." Apparently no discretion was left to the judge to grant bail; and the underlying concern was not with dangerousness of the defendant but rather the defendant's risk of flight. The court held (1) that under *Salerno* this provision did not violate substantive due process, for (a) the legislature did "not express a clear punitive intent," and (b) the provision was not "excessive in relation to its legitimate alternative purpose," notwithstanding *Salerno*'s requirement that there be an "individualized determination of dangerousness," because the provision at issue in the instant case "seeks to target flight risk rather than dangerousness"; (2) that Arizona's choice of a probable cause standard as to defendant's situation as an illegal alien, as compared with the "clear preponderance" standard upheld in *Salerno*, "does not amount to a procedural due process violation"; and (3) that for the above-stated reasons it could not be said that the Arizona provision "is arbitrary and unreasonable in violation of the Eighth Amendment."

CHAPTER 14

THE DECISION WHETHER TO PROSECUTE

■ ■ ■

SECTION 3. CHALLENGING THE PROSECUTOR'S DISCRETION

B. THE DECISION TO PROSECUTE

13th ed., p. 998; before Note 6, add:

If, as the dissent in *Pettitt* asserts, the statute appears to mandate "full enforcement," is that the end of the matter? Consider *State v. Rice,* 279 P.3d 849 (Wash.2012), where Rice objected that her conviction of kidnapping with "special allegations," i.e., sexual motivation and juvenile victim, which increased her sentence, was invalid because state statutes mandated that a prosecutor file such special allegations whenever there is sufficient evidence to support them. The court concluded that the statutes in question "are directory rather than mandatory" because they "do not attach any legal consequences to a prosecutor's noncompliance," but emphasized that such an interpretation of the statutes (which used the word "shall") was supported by the fact that the statutes "would be unconstitutional if they were mandatory." Specifically, the court stated "that a prosecutor's broad charging discretion"— "necessarily * * * broader than a mere consideration of sufficiency of evidence and likelihood of conviction" and "including the authority to be merciful and to seek individualized justice"—is part of the inherent authority granted to prosecuting attorneys as executive officers under the Washington State Constitution.

D. SELECTION OF THE CHARGE

13th ed., p. 1009; before Note 7, add:

6A. What would be the proper application of *Goodwin* on these facts, from *United States v. LaDeau,* 734 F.3d 561 (6th Cir.2013)? LaDeau was indicted on a single count of possessing child pornography, punishable by a sentence range of zero to ten years' imprisonment. LaDeau moved pretrial to suppress evidence that he had any such materials in his possession; the motion was granted, which "eviscerated the government's possession case" and "eliminated its ability to prosecute the charge alleged in the first indictment." This left the government with three charging options: (1) conspiracy to possess child pornography, in violation of 18 U.S.C.

§ 2252A(b)(2), punishable by zero to ten years; (2) conspiracy to receive child pornography, in violation of 18 U.S.C. § 2252A(b)(2), punishable by five to twenty years; or (3) conspiracy to receive or possess child pornography, in violation of the general conspiracy statute, 18 U.S.C. § 371, punishable by zero to five years. The government opted for the second alternative, "based on evidence that had been in the government's possession since before the initial indictment."

CHAPTER 16

GRAND JURY REVIEW

■ ■ ■

SECTION 3. CHALLENGES TO THE EVIDENCE BEFORE THE GRAND JURY

13th ed., p. 1061; before Note 6, add:

5A. _Extended consequences._ As the Court explained in _Kaley v. United_ States, 134 S.Ct. 1090 (2013), the _Costello_ analysis leads to treating the grand jury indictment as a "conclusively determining * * * probable cause" for purposes beyond enabling the prosecution. At issue in _Kaley_ was the application of a federal money laundering provision authorizing the issuance of a pre-trial asset restraint (a "freeze order") precluding transfer of assets that would be subject to forfeiture upon conviction. _United States v. Monsanto_, 491 U.S. 600 (1989), a companion case to _Caplin & Drysdale Chartered v. United States_ (13th ed., Note 5, p. 129), held that such a restraint did not violate due process or the Sixth Amendment (assuming that the asset-freeze would prevent the defendant from retaining counsel of choice), provided there is "probable cause to think (1) that the defendant has committed an offense permitting forfeiture, and (2) that the property at issue has the requisite connection to that crime." _Monsanto_, as noted, in _Kaley_, "declined to consider whether Due Process requires a hearing to establish either or both of those aspects of forfeitability." Subsequently, "lower courts generally provided a hearing to any indicted defendant seeking to lift an asset restraint to pay for a lawyer * * *. They uniformly allowed the defendant to litigate the second issue stated above [probable cause as to whether the assets are sufficiently related to the crime to be subject to forfeiture], * * * [but] divided over extending the hearing to the first issue [probable cause as to the crime]." In _Kaley_, the indicted defendants sought only to challenge probable cause as to the crime, seeking to show "that the case against them was 'baseless.'" The federal lower courts held that a hearing on that issue was not available since the grand jury indictment conclusively established the needed probable cause. Describing the only issue before it as "whether an indicted defendant has a constitutional right to contest the grand jury's prior determination of that matter," a divided Supreme Court (6-3) affirmed. The Court majority, per Kagan, J., reasoned in part:

"This Court has often recognized the grand jury's singular role in finding the probable cause necessary to initiate a prosecution for a serious crime.

See, e.g., *Costello v. United States.* '[A]n indictment fair upon its face, and returned by a 'properly constituted grand jury,' we have explained, 'conclusively determines the existence of probable cause to believe the defendant perpetrated the offense alleged.' *Gerstein v. Pugh* [13th ed., Note 11, p. 340]. And 'conclusively' has meant, case in and case out, just that. * * * The grand jury gets to say—without any review, oversight, or second-guessing—whether probable cause exists to think that a person committed a crime. * * *

"And that inviolable grand jury finding, we have decided, may do more than commence a criminal proceeding (with all the economic, reputational, and personal harm that entails); the determination may also serve the purpose of immediately depriving the accused of her freedom. If the person charged is not yet in custody, an indictment triggers 'issuance of an arrest warrant without further inquiry' into the case's strength. Alternatively, if the person was arrested without a warrant, an indictment eliminates her Fourth Amendment right to a prompt judicial assessment of probable cause to support any detention. See *Gerstein* [fn.d., p. 341]. In either situation, this Court—relying on the grand jury's 'historical role of protecting individuals from unjust persecution'—has 'let [that body's] judgment substitute for that of a neutral and detached magistrate.'

"The same result follows when, as here, an infringement on the defendant's property depends on a showing of probable cause that she committed a crime. If judicial review of the grand jury's probable cause determination is not warranted (as we have so often held) to put a defendant on trial or place her in custody, then neither is it needed to freeze her property. The grand jury that is good enough—reliable enough, protective enough—to inflict those other grave consequences through its probable cause findings must be adequate to impose this one too. Indeed, *Monsanto* already noted the absence of any reason to hold property seizures to different rules: As described earlier, the Court partly based its adoption of the probable cause standard on the incongruity of subjecting an asset freeze to any stricter requirements than apply to an arrest or ensuing detention."

Dissenting in *Kaley*, Chief Justice Roberts, joined by Justices Breyer and Sotomayor, argued that the majority was giving insufficient weight to the fair trial implications of a "denial of counsel of choice" by viewing "syllogistic-type reasoning [as] effectively resolv[ing] the case." Allowing the defendant to challenge the probable cause needed for the freeze need not be viewed as "relitigating the grand jury finding." While "the grand jury decides whether a defendant should be required to stand trial, the judge decides pretrial matters," and the validity of the freeze order was a pretrial matter. Thus, the dissent noted, although the grand jury indictment identifies the property that is subject to forfeiture, there was agreement that the trial court must grant a hearing allowing the defendant to challenge "the grand jury's probable cause finding as to traceability." Responding, the majority distinguished the judicial determination of that issue, noting that (1) "the tracing of assets is a technical matter far removed from the grand jury's core competence and traditional function," and (2) "a judge's finding that the assets are not traceable to the crime charged in no way casts doubt on the prosecution itself."[a] The dissent replied, in turn, that "nothing in [*Monsanto*] or the indictment * * * justifies treating one grand jury finding differently from another."

---

[a] The majority viewed the dissent's position as opening the door to "strange and destructive consequences" via "inconsistent findings" by the judge and grand jury as to probable cause supporting the charges. While the dissent argued that the findings would not be inconsistent because the evidence the prosecutor presented in the freeze-order hearing would not necessarily be the same as that presented to the grand jury, the majority viewed that likely difference as part of the administrative difficulty posed. Because the hearing would be held "well before the rules of criminal procedure—or principles of due process—would otherwise require [disclosure]," the prosecutor ("particularly in organized crime and drug trafficking prosecutions, in which forfeiture questions often arise") would face a dilemma—provide a "sneak preview which might not just aid the defendant's preparations but also facilitate witness tampering or jeopardize witness safety" or "hold back some of its evidence" and thereby risk a negative ruling that "would diminish the likelihood of ultimately recovering stolen asserts to which the public is entitled." Moreover, "any defense counsel worth his salt—whatever the merits of the case—would put the prosecutor to * * * [that] choice."

CHAPTER 17

THE CHARGING INSTRUMENT

■ ■ ■

SECTION 2. APPLYING THE BASIC PLEADING STANDARDS

13th ed., p. 1109; after Note 4, add:

4A. *The Rule 12 Amendment.* In 2006, following the lower court extension of *Cotton* to essential-elements defects generally (see Note 5 infra), the Department of Justice urged the Judicial Conference to consider deleting the reference to "fails * * * to state an offense" in the noticed-at-any-time proviso in Rule 12(b). That objection had been placed alongside the "fails to invoke the court's jurisdiction" objection, but *Cotton* had clearly established that the "failure to state an offense" was not a jurisdictional defect. After extensive discussion in the Criminal Rules Advisory Committee and the Judicial Conference Committee on Rules (including consideration of three different amendment proposals and public comments from various sources), the Judicial Conference adopted a proposal that was later approved by the Supreme Court. That proposal, set forth in Supp., Appendix D, will take effect on December 1, 2014 unless Congress acts to the contrary. Under the new Rule 12(b)(3)(B) provision, objections that must be made before trial continue to include "a defect in the indictment or information," and the list of encompassed defects includes "failure to state an offense." In accord with this change, Rule 12(b)(2) on objections that may be made "at any time while the case is pending" now refers only to the "motion that the court lacks jurisdiction." Under the new Rule 12(c)(3), a court "may consider * * * [an untimely] motion, objection or request [including a failure-to-state-an-offense objection] if the party shows good cause." As to the content of "good cause," at least where the untimely objection is first raised after conviction, see the discussion in *Davis v. United States*, 13th ed., Note 4, p. 1583.

CHAPTER 19

JOINDER AND SEVERANCE

■ ■ ■

SECTION 2.   FAILURE TO JOIN
RELATED OFFENSES

13th ed., p. 1149; at the end of Note 1, add:

As for option (2), at least one court has declined to go that route on the ground that "[m]ultiple punishments that result from a single prosecution do not subject a defendant to the evils attendant upon successful prosecutions," namely, "the 'embarrassment, expense and ordeal' of repetitive trials, 'compelling [the accused] to live in a continuing state of anxiety and insecurity,' and creating 'a risk of conviction through sheer governmental perseverance.'" *Ex parte Chaddock*, 369 S.W.3d 880 (Tex.Crim.App.2012). A concurring opinion in *Chaddock* suggested the "two different meanings" objection in *Dixon* should not be taken too seriously given Justice Scalia's view that the multiple punishment issue should be considered under the due process clause rather than the double jeopardy clause.

13th ed., p. 1159; at the end of Note 2, add:

Compare *Joya v. United States*, 53 A.3d 309 (D.C.2012): "We do not think the dictum in *Johnson* can fairly be read to mean that it can never be appropriate to apply collateral estoppel when the government has not sought to initiate successive prosecution. [W]e think the better reasoning is that it can, and that a defendant's waiver of double-jeopardy protection through a successful motion for severance does not amount to a waiver of the principle that the government may not re-litigate an issue resolved in a prior trial."

CHAPTER 20

SPEEDY TRIAL AND OTHER
SPEEDY DISPOSITION

■ ■ ■

SECTION 1. SPEEDY TRIAL

13th ed., p. 1185; before Note 2, add:

In *Boyer v. Louisiana*, 133 S.Ct. 1702 (2013), cert. had been granted to decide whether a delay caused by a State's failure to fund counsel for an indigent's defense should weigh against the State in determining whether there was a deprivation of defendant's Sixth Amendment right to a speedy trial. The writ was dismissed, per curiam, as improvidently granted; three concurring Justices explained this was because the record did not support the state court's assertion most of the 7-year delay was attributable to a "funding crisis." The other four Justices opted to "defer to" the state court's "factual determination," and then concluded that a "State's failure to provide adequate funding for an indigent's defense that prevents a case from going to trial is no different" than the "overcrowded courts" cited in *Barker* or the "systemic breakdown" mentioned in *Brillon*.

PART 4

THE ADVERSARY SYSTEM AND THE DETERMINATION OF GUILT OR INNOCENCE

• • •

Part 4

THE ADVERSARY SYSTEM AND THE DETERMINATION OF GUILT OR INNOCENCE

CHAPTER 22

GUILTY PLEAS

■ ■ ■

SECTION 1. SOME VIEWS OF NEGOTIATED PLEAS

B. THE PROBLEM OF DISPARITY

13th ed., p. 1273; at the end of Note 2, add:

Compare the recent view of two Justices, Note 6B, Supp., p. 14.

SECTION 2. REJECTED, KEPT AND BROKEN BARGAINS; UNREALIZED EXPECTATIONS

13th ed., p. 1286; after *Gibson* in Note 4, add:

But consider *Crider v. State*, 984 N.E.2d 618 (Ind.2013) (express waiver of right to appeal illegal sentence invalid here, where "the plea agreement did not provide for an illegal sentence," as "when entering a contract with the prosecutor, a defendant is entitled to presume that [the] trial court will order performance of the contract in compliance with the law," but "where a plea agreement provides for the illegality later challenged, a waiver contained therein will be upheld" because "the defendant benefitted from the plea").

13th ed., p. 1287; at the end of Note 4, add:

What then of other plea agreement terms that limit what the defense attorney can do? Consider, for example, *State v. Hess*, 23 A.3d 373 (N.J.2011), holding that provisions in a plea agreement that would restrict "the right of counsel to argue for a lesser sentence, or to argue against an aggravating factor or for a mitigating factor, or how the factors should be balanced," are "void," as they "would deprive defendants of the needed advocacy of their attorneys and deny our courts the needed insight to administer justice."

13th ed., p. 1287; at the end of Note 5, add:

If the defendant accepts such a plea bargain, should he later be able to have his guilty plea nullified because the accepted punishment is not authorized by law, given the offense to which he pled guilty? Compare *State v. Setters*, 25 P.3d 893 (Mont.2001) (plea bargain that defendant would plead guilty to lesser offense of tampering with public records in exchange for dismissal of theft charge, but defendant to be responsible for restitution for latter offense, as determined at sentencing, invalid, as law does not permit restitution for the tampering offense); with *In re Flatt-Moore*, 959 N.E.2d 241 (Ind.2012) (defendant may "consent to a sentence that would be otherwise unauthorized to gain benefits in a plea agreement," and thus, regarding the unaccepted first plea offer in this case, that a Class C felony check fraud charge be reduced to a Class A misdemeanor if the defendant were to "pay his victim in excess of what the Restitution Statute may have allowed," it "would not necessarily render the agreement illegal or otherwise improper"). (But the prosecutor in *Flatt-Moore* went too far; see Supp., p. 126–127.)

13th ed., p. 1287; at the end of footnote f, add:

Still another position is that taken in *Hurlow v. United States*, 726 F.3d 958 (7th Cir.2013), namely, that it is "an attorney's ineffectiveness with regard to the plea agreement as a whole, and not just the specific waiver provision at issue, [that] renders the waiver unenforceable," which covered the instant case given defendant's allegation "that his decision to plead guilty resulted from counsel's ineffectiveness" in "fail[ing] to inform him that a challenge to the search was possible."

13th ed., p. 1287; at the end of footnote h, add:

However, "a violation of a professional rule of discipline does not equate to a constitutional violation" of a guilty plea defendant's rights. *Cooper v. State*, S.W.3d 148 (Mo.2011).

13th ed., p. 1292; after Note 7, add:

8.   Regarding the Fed.R.Crim.P. 11(c) prohibition upon judicial participation in plea discussions, in *United States v. Davila*, 133 S.Ct. 2139 (2013), the Court concluded that since this prohibition "was adopted as a prophylactic measure, not one impelled by the Due Process Clause or any other constitutional requirement," it follows that "pre-plea exhortations to admit guilt," just as with "[p]lea colloquy requirements [that] come into play *after* a defendant has agreed to plead guilty," are subject to Fed.R.Crim.P. 11(h), declaring that a "variance from the requirements of this rule is harmless error if it does not affect substantial rights."

13th ed., p. 1297; at the end of Note 9, add:

May a so-called "hammer clause" provision in the plea agreement be enforced, such as that for a specified breach by the defendant (a) he is to receive a sentence above the statutory maximum, *McClanahan v. Commonwealth*, 308 S.W.3d 694 (Ky.2010), (b) the trial judge's sentencing discretion is totally abrogated, *Knox v. Commonwealth*, 361 S.W.3d 891 (Ky.2012), or (c) the trial judge's discretion regarding defendant's effort to withdraw his guilty plea is totally abrogated, *Prater v. Commonwealth*, 421 S.W.3d 380 (Ky.2014)?

13th ed., p. 1300; before Note 14, add:

13A.   Compare *United States v. Purser*, 747 F.3d 284 (5th Cir.2014), where defendant pled guilty to a conspiracy charge pursuant to a plea agreement in which the government promised to recommend only a 4-level increase with respect to a specific provision in the Sentencing Guidelines. The government instead recommended a 6-level increase, but before sentencing withdrew that recommendation in order to comply with the plea agreement; while the probation officer's final presentence report nonetheless included a proposed 6-level increase, the judge at sentencing declined to make such an increase, and instead provided for a 4-level increase to "eliminate any possible objection that the Government has breached the plea agreement." The defendant, in seeking to appeal other aspects of his sentence despite the fact the plea bargain also included an appeal waiver, claimed the plea waiver was void because of the government's breach. The court of appeals acknowledged it had "previously read *Santobello* to foreclose a harmlessness inquiry," but then noted the Supreme Court opined in *Puckett* [13th ed., p. 1554] that "*some* breaches may be curable upon timely objection–for example, where the prosecution simply forgot its commitment and is willing to adhere to the [plea] agreement." The court in *Purser* then concluded:

"* * * Cure and harmless error stand on different footing from each other. Cure, unlike harmless error, is the removal of legal defect or correction of legal error; that is, performance of the contract. Simply put, with a cure of breach, the government abides by the plea agreement, while harmless error excuses a lapse of government performance. * * * Here, the Government cured its breach by withdrawing its objection and arguing the application of the lesser enhancement, both prior to and at sentencing, and the district court subsequently acted consistently with the plea agreement."

SECTION 3. PROFESSIONAL RESPONSIBILITY; THE ROLE OF PROSECUTOR AND DEFENSE COUNSEL

13th ed., p. 1308; in lieu of Note 3, insert:

MISSOURI V. FRYE
___ U.S. ___, 132 S.Ct. 1399, 182 L.Ed.2d 379 (2012).

JUSTICE KENNEDY delivered the opinion of the Court.

[Frye was charged with driving with a revoked license after three prior convictions of that offense, a felony punishable by up to four years. In a letter to Frye's counsel, the prosecutor extended a choice of two plea bargains, the most lenient being reduction of the charge to a misdemeanor and recommendation of a 90-day sentence. Frye's attorney never advised him of the offers, and after their expiration (and after Frye had once again been arrested for the same offense) Frye pled guilty without any underlying plea agreement and was sentenced to three years in prison. At a later post-conviction hearing, Frye testified he would have entered a guilty plea to the misdemeanor had he known of the offer. On appeal, the state court held that Frye's counsel's performance was deficient and that Frye had been prejudiced.]

It is well settled that the right to the effective assistance of counsel applies to certain steps before trial. The "Sixth Amendment guarantees a defendant the right to have counsel present at all 'critical' stages of the criminal proceedings." Critical stages include arraignments, postindictment interrogations, postindictment lineups, and the entry of a guilty plea.

With respect to the right to effective counsel in plea negotiations, a proper beginning point is to discuss two cases from this Court considering the role of counsel in advising a client about a plea offer and an ensuing guilty plea: *Hill v. Lockhart*, [13th ed., p. 1345, fn. b]; and *Padilla v. Kentucky*, [13th ed., p. 1315].

Hill established that claims of ineffective assistance of counsel in the plea bargain context are governed by the two-part test set forth in *Strickland* [13th ed., p. 137]. * * *

In *Hill*, the decision turned on the second part of the *Strickland* test. There, a defendant who had entered a guilty plea claimed his counsel had misinformed him of the amount of time he would have to serve before he became eligible for parole. But the defendant had not alleged that, even if adequate advice and assistance had been given, he would have elected to plead not guilty and proceed to trial. Thus, the Court found that no prejudice from the inadequate advice had been shown or alleged.

In *Padilla*, the Court again discussed the duties of counsel in advising a client with respect to a plea offer that leads to a guilty plea. * * * The Court made clear that "the negotiation of a plea bargain is a critical phase of litigation for purposes of the Sixth Amendment right to effective assistance of counsel."[a]

In the case now before the Court the State, as petitioner, points out that the legal question presented is different from that in *Hill* and *Padilla*. In those cases the claim was that the prisoner's plea of guilty was invalid because counsel had provided incorrect advice pertinent to the plea. In the instant case, by contrast, the guilty plea that was accepted, and the plea proceedings concerning it in court, were all based on accurate advice and information from counsel. The challenge is not to the advice pertaining to the plea that was accepted but rather to the course of legal representation that preceded it with respect to other potential pleas and plea offers.

---

[a] Is this so without regard to *when* the negotiation occurs? Reconsider Ch. 4, § 1 B, and compare *United States v. Moody*, 206 F.3d 609 (6th Cir.2000) (Sixth Amendment right to counsel does not attach during pre-arrest, pre-indictment negotiation, as " 'critical stages' of criminal proceedings begin only with the initiation of formal criminal proceedings"); with *United States v. Wilson*, 719 F.Supp.2d 1260 (D.Or.2010) ("To conclude that petitioner had no right to counsel in evaluating the government's plea offer simply because the government had not yet obtained a formal indictment would elevate form over substance, and undermine the reliability of the pre-indictment plea negotiation process").

To give further support to its contention that the instant case is in a category different from what the Court considered in *Hill* and *Padilla*, the State urges that there is no right to a plea offer or a plea bargain in any event. See *Weatherford v. Bursey*, [13th ed., p. 1322]. It claims Frye therefore was not deprived of any legal benefit to which he was entitled. Under this view, any wrongful or mistaken action of counsel with respect to earlier plea offers is beside the point.

The State is correct to point out that *Hill* and *Padilla* concerned whether there was ineffective assistance leading to acceptance of a plea offer, a process involving a formal court appearance with the defendant and all counsel present. Before a guilty plea is entered the defendant's understanding of the plea and its consequences can be established on the record. This affords the State substantial protection against later claims that the plea was the result of inadequate advice. At the plea entry proceedings the trial court and all counsel have the opportunity to establish on the record that the defendant understands the process that led to any offer, the advantages and disadvantages of accepting it, and the sentencing consequences or possibilities that will ensue once a conviction is entered based upon the plea. *Hill* and *Padilla* both illustrate that, nevertheless, there may be instances when claims of ineffective assistance can arise after the conviction is entered. Still, the State, and the trial court itself, have had a substantial opportunity to guard against this contingency by establishing at the plea entry proceeding that the defendant has been given proper advice or, if the advice received appears to have been inadequate, to remedy that deficiency before the plea is accepted and the conviction entered.

When a plea offer has lapsed or been rejected, however, no formal court proceedings are involved. This underscores that the plea-bargaining process is often in flux, with no clear standards or timelines and with no judicial supervision of the discussions between prosecution and defense. Indeed, discussions between client and defense counsel are privileged. So the prosecution has little or no notice if something may be amiss and perhaps no capacity to intervene in any event. And, as noted, the State insists there is no right to receive a plea offer. For all these reasons, the State contends, it is unfair to subject it to the consequences of defense counsel's inadequacies, especially when the opportunities for a full and fair trial, or, as here, for a later guilty plea albeit on less favorable terms, are preserved.

The State's contentions are neither illogical nor without some persuasive force, yet they do not suffice to overcome a simple reality. Ninety-seven percent of federal convictions and ninety-four percent of state convictions are the result of guilty pleas. The reality is that plea bargains have become so central to the administration of the criminal justice system that defense counsel have responsibilities in the plea bargain process, responsibilities that must be met to render the adequate assistance of counsel that the Sixth Amendment requires in the criminal process at critical stages. Because ours "is for the most part a system of pleas, not a system of trials," it is insufficient simply to point to the guarantee of a fair trial as a backstop that inoculates any errors in the pretrial process. * * * See also Barkow, *Separation of Powers and the Criminal Law*, 58 Stan. L.Rev. 989, 1034 (2006) ("[Defendants] who do take their case to trial and lose receive longer sentences than even Congress or the prosecutor might think appropriate, because the longer sentences exist on the books largely for bargaining purposes. This often results in individuals who accept a plea bargain receiving shorter sentences than other individuals who are less morally culpable but take a chance and go to trial"). In today's criminal justice system, therefore, the negotiation of a plea bargain, rather than the unfolding of a trial, is almost always the critical point for a defendant. * * *

The inquiry then becomes how to define the duty and responsibilities of defense counsel in the plea bargain process. This is a difficult question. "The art of negotiation is at least as nuanced as the art of trial advocacy and it presents questions farther removed from immediate judicial supervision." Bargaining is, by its nature, defined to a substantial degree by personal style. The alternative courses and tactics in negotiation are so individual that it may be neither prudent nor practicable to try to elaborate or define detailed standards for the proper discharge of defense counsel's participation in the process.

This case presents neither the necessity nor the occasion to define the duties of defense counsel in those respects, however. Here the question is whether defense counsel has the duty to communicate the terms of a formal offer to accept a plea on terms and conditions that may result in a lesser sentence, a conviction on lesser charges, or both.

This Court now holds that, as a general rule, defense counsel has the duty to communicate formal offers from the prosecution to accept a plea on terms and conditions that may be favorable to the accused. Any exceptions to that rule need not be explored here, for the offer was a formal one with a fixed expiration date. When defense counsel allowed the offer to expire without advising the defendant or allowing him to consider it, defense counsel did not render the effective assistance the Constitution requires.

Though the standard for counsel's performance is not determined solely by reference to codified standards of professional practice, these standards can be important guides. The American Bar Association recommends defense counsel "promptly communicate and explain to the defendant all plea offers made by the prosecuting attorney," ABA Standards for Criminal Justice, Pleas of Guilty 14–3.2(a) (3d ed.1999), and this standard has been adopted by numerous state and federal courts over the last 30 years. The standard for prompt communication and consultation is also set out in state bar professional standards for attorneys.

The prosecution and the trial courts may adopt some measures to help ensure against late, frivolous, or fabricated claims after a later, less advantageous plea offer has been accepted or after a trial leading to conviction with resulting harsh consequences. First, the fact of a formal offer means that its terms and its processing can be documented so that what took place in the negotiation process becomes more clear if some later inquiry turns on the conduct of earlier pretrial negotiations. Second, States may elect to follow rules that all offers must be in writing, again to ensure against later misunderstandings or fabricated charges. Third, formal offers can be made part of the record at any subsequent plea proceeding or before a trial on the merits, all to ensure that a defendant has been fully advised before those further proceedings commence. * * *

Here defense counsel did not communicate the formal offers to the defendant. As a result of that deficient performance, the offers lapsed. Under *Strickland*, the question then becomes what, if any, prejudice resulted from the breach of duty.

To show prejudice from ineffective assistance of counsel where a plea offer has lapsed or been rejected because of counsel's deficient performance, defendants must demonstrate a reasonable probability they would have accepted the earlier plea offer had they been afforded effective assistance of counsel. Defendants must also demonstrate a reasonable probability the plea would have been entered without the prosecution canceling it or the trial court refusing to accept it, if they had the authority to exercise that discretion under state law. To establish prejudice in this instance, it is necessary to show a reasonable probability that the end result of the criminal process would have been more favorable by reason of a plea to a lesser charge or a sentence of less prison time. * * *

In order to complete a showing of *Strickland* prejudice, defendants who have shown a reasonable probability they would have accepted the earlier plea offer must also show that, if the prosecution had the discretion to cancel it or if the trial court had the discretion to refuse to accept it, there is a reasonable probability neither the prosecution nor the trial court would have prevented the offer from being accepted or implemented. This further showing is of particular importance because a defendant has no right to be offered a plea, nor a federal right that the judge accept it. In at least some States, including Missouri, it appears the prosecution has some discretion to cancel a plea agreement to which the defendant has agreed. The Federal Rules, some state rules including in

Missouri, and this Court's precedents give trial courts some leeway to accept or reject plea agreements. It can be assumed that in most jurisdictions prosecutors and judges are familiar with the boundaries of acceptable plea bargains and sentences. So in most instances it should not be difficult to make an objective assessment as to whether or not a particular fact or intervening circumstance would suffice, in the normal course, to cause prosecutorial withdrawal or judicial nonapproval of a plea bargain. The determination that there is or is not a reasonable probability that the outcome of the proceeding would have been different absent counsel's errors can be conducted within that framework. * * *

There appears to be a reasonable probability Frye would have accepted the prosecutor's original offer of a plea bargain if the offer had been communicated to him, because he pleaded guilty to a more serious charge, with no promise of a sentencing recommendation from the prosecutor. It may be that in some cases defendants must show more than just a guilty plea to a charge or sentence harsher than the original offer. For example, revelations between plea offers about the strength of the prosecution's case may make a late decision to plead guilty insufficient to demonstrate, without further evidence, that the defendant would have pleaded guilty to an earlier, more generous plea offer if his counsel had reported it to him. Here, however, that is not the case. * * *

The Court of Appeals failed, however, to require Frye to show that the first plea offer, if accepted by Frye, would have been adhered to by the prosecution and accepted by the trial court. Whether the prosecution and trial court are required to do so is a matter of state law, and it is not the place of this Court to settle those matters. * * *

We remand for the Missouri Court of Appeals to consider these state-law questions, because they bear on the federal question of *Strickland* prejudice. If, as the Missouri court stated here, the prosecutor could have canceled the plea agreement, and if Frye fails to show a reasonable probability the prosecutor would have adhered to the agreement, there is no *Strickland* prejudice. Likewise, if the trial court could have refused to accept the plea agreement, and if Frye fails to show a reasonable probability the trial court would have accepted the plea, there is no *Strickland* prejudice. In this case, given Frye's new offense for driving without a license on December 30, 2007, there is reason to doubt that the prosecution would have adhered to the agreement or that the trial court would have accepted it at the January 4, 2008, hearing, unless they were required by state law to do so. * * *

JUSTICE SCALIA, with whom THE CHIEF JUSTICE, JUSTICE THOMAS, and JUSTICE ALITO join, dissenting. * * *

The Court announces its holding that "as a general rule, defense counsel has the duty to communicate formal offers from the prosecution" as though that resolves a disputed point; in reality, however, neither the State nor the Solicitor General argued that counsel's performance here was adequate. The only issue was whether the inadequacy deprived Frye of his constitutional right to a fair trial. In other cases, however, it will not be so clear that counsel's plea-bargaining skills, which must now meet a constitutional minimum, are adequate. "[H]ow to define the duty and responsibilities of defense counsel in the plea bargain process," the Court acknowledges, "is a difficult question," since "[b]argaining is, by its nature, defined to a substantial degree by personal style." Indeed. What if an attorney's "personal style" is to establish a reputation as a hard bargainer by, for example, advising clients to proceed to trial rather than accept anything but the most favorable plea offers? It seems inconceivable that a lawyer could compromise his client's constitutional rights so that he can secure better deals for other clients in the future; does a hard-bargaining "personal style" now violate the Sixth Amendment? The Court ignores such difficulties, however, since "[t]his case presents neither the necessity nor the occasion to define the duties of defense counsel in those respects." Perhaps not. But it does present the necessity of confronting the serious difficulties that will be created by constitutionalization of the plea-bargaining process. It will not do simply to announce that they will be solved in the sweet by-and-by.

While the inadequacy of counsel's performance in this case is clear enough, whether it was prejudicial (in the sense that the Court's new version of *Strickland* requires) is not. The Court's description of how that question is to be answered on remand is alone enough to show how unwise it is to constitutionalize the plea-bargaining process. Prejudice is to be determined, the Court tells us, by a process of retrospective crystal-ball gazing posing as legal analysis. First of all, of course, we must estimate whether the defendant would have accepted the earlier plea bargain. Here that seems an easy question, but as the Court acknowledges, it will not always be. Next, since Missouri, like other States, permits accepted plea offers to be withdrawn by the prosecution (a reality which alone should suffice, one would think, to demonstrate that Frye had no entitlement to the plea bargain), we must estimate whether the prosecution would have withdrawn the plea offer. And finally, we must estimate whether the trial court would have approved the plea agreement. These last two estimations may seem easy in the present case, since Frye committed a new infraction before the hearing at which the agreement would have been presented; but they assuredly will not be easy in the mine run of cases.

The Court says "[i]t can be assumed that in most jurisdictions prosecutors and judges are familiar with the boundaries of acceptable plea bargains and sentences." Assuredly it can, just as it can be assumed that the sun rises in the west; but I know of no basis for the assumption.

Virtually no cases deal with the standards for a prosecutor's withdrawal from a plea agreement beyond stating the general rule that a prosecutor may withdraw any time prior to, but not after, the entry of a guilty plea or other action constituting detrimental reliance on the defendant's part. And cases addressing trial courts' authority to accept or reject plea agreements almost universally observe that a trial court enjoys broad discretion in this regard. Of course after today's opinions there will be cases galore, so the Court's assumption would better be cast as an optimistic prediction of the certainty that will emerge, many years hence, from our newly created constitutional field of plea-bargaining law. Whatever the "boundaries" ultimately devised (if that were possible), a vast amount of discretion will still remain, and it is extraordinary to make a defendant's constitutional rights depend upon a series of retrospective mind-readings as to how that discretion, in prosecutors and trial judges, would have been exercised.

The plea-bargaining process is a subject worthy of regulation, since it is the means by which most criminal convictions are obtained. It happens not to be, however, a subject covered by the Sixth Amendment, which is concerned not with the fairness of bargaining but with the fairness of conviction. * * * A legislature could solve the problems presented by these cases in a much more precise and efficient manner. It might begin, for example, by penalizing the attorneys who made such grievous errors. That type of sub-constitutional remedy is not available to the Court, which is limited to penalizing (almost) everyone else by reversing valid convictions or sentences. Because that result is inconsistent with the Sixth Amendment and decades of our precedent, I respectfully dissent.

The companion case of LAFLER v. COOPER, 132 S.Ct. 1376 (2012), also 5–4 on similar analysis, involved a situation in which the favorable plea offer *was* "reported to the client but, on advice of counsel, was rejected," after which there "was a full and fair trial before a jury," resulting in a guilty verdict and "a sentence harsher than that offered in the rejected plea bargain." The conceded ineffective assistance was telling defendant Cooper that he could not be convicted at trial of assault with intent to murder because the victim had been shot below the waist. The Court, per Justice Kennedy, on the matter of prejudice, rejected the contention that a "fair trial wipes clean any deficient performance by defense counsel during plea bargaining," as such a claim "ignores the reality that criminal justice today is for the most part a system of pleas, not a system of trials."[b] Prejudice was shown here, the majority in *Cooper* concluded, because (i) "but for counsel's deficient performance there is a

---

[b] See Note 6A, Supp., p. 9, for excerpts from the majority and dissenting opinions in *Cooper* regarding this issue.

reasonable probability [respondent] and the trial court would have accepted the guilty plea" and (ii) "as a result of not accepting the plea and being convicted at trial, respondent received a minimum sentence 3 ½ times greater than he would have received under the plea."

The *Cooper* majority then turned to "the question of what constitutes an appropriate remedy" when, as in *Cooper* and *Frye*, "a defendant shows ineffective assistance of counsel has caused the rejection of a plea," thereby "leading to a trial [or different plea] and a more severe sentence" (a matter on which lower courts were divided[c]):

"Sixth Amendment remedies should be 'tailored to the injury suffered from the constitutional violation and should not unnecessarily infringe on competing interests.' Thus, a remedy must 'neutralize the taint' of a constitutional violation, while at the same time not grant a windfall to the defendant or needlessly squander the considerable resources the State properly invested in the criminal prosecution.

"The specific injury suffered by defendants who decline a plea offer as a result of ineffective assistance of counsel and then receive a greater sentence as a result of trial can come in at least one of two forms. In some cases, the sole advantage a defendant would have received under the plea is a lesser sentence. This is typically the case when the charges that would have been admitted as part of the plea bargain are the same as the charges the defendant was convicted of after trial. In this situation the court may conduct an evidentiary hearing to determine whether the defendant has shown a reasonable probability that but for counsel's errors he would have accepted the plea. If the showing is made, the court may exercise discretion in determining whether the defendant should receive the term of imprisonment the government offered in the plea, the sentence he received at trial, or something in between.

"In some situations it may be that resentencing alone will not be full redress for the constitutional injury. If, for example, an offer was for a guilty plea to a count or counts less serious than the ones for which a defendant was convicted after trial, or if a mandatory sentence confines a judge's sentencing discretion after trial, a resentencing based on the conviction at trial may not suffice. In these circumstances, the proper exercise of discretion to remedy the constitutional injury may be to require the prosecution to reoffer the plea proposal. Once this has

---

c   In *Frye*, the state court deemed it sufficient to "undo" the subsequent conviction, after which the defendant would be allowed "either to insist on a trial or to plead guilty to any offense the prosecutor deemed it appropriate to charge," while in *Cooper* the federal district court on habeas ordered "specific performance of [respondent's] original plea agreement." A third view, as in *State v. Greuber*, 165 P.3d 1185 (Utah 2007), was that *neither* is "an appropriate remedy for the claimed harm": the *Frye* approach is wrong because "a new trial does not remedy the lost opportunity to plead," while the *Cooper* approach is wrong because under "the doctrine of separation of powers" a court lacks the power to order renewal of the plea offer "in the absence of prosecutorial misconduct."

occurred, the judge can then exercise discretion in deciding whether to vacate the conviction from trial and accept the plea or leave the conviction undisturbed.

"In implementing a remedy in both of these situations, the trial court must weigh various factors; and the boundaries of proper discretion need not be defined here. Principles elaborated over time in decisions of state and federal courts, and in statutes and rules, will serve to give more complete guidance as to the factors that should bear upon the exercise of the judge's discretion. At this point, however, it suffices to note two considerations that are of relevance.

"First, a court may take account of a defendant's earlier expressed willingness, or unwillingness, to accept responsibility for his or her actions. Second, it is not necessary here to decide as a constitutional rule that a judge is required to prescind (that is to say disregard) any information concerning the crime that was discovered after the plea offer was made. The time continuum makes it difficult to restore the defendant and the prosecution to the precise positions they occupied prior to the rejection of the plea offer, but that baseline can be consulted in finding a remedy that does not require the prosecution to incur the expense of conducting a new trial.

"Petitioner argues that implementing a remedy here will open the floodgates to litigation by defendants seeking to unsettle their convictions. Petitioner's concern is misplaced. Courts have recognized claims of this sort for over 30 years, and yet there is no indication that the system is overwhelmed by these types of suits or that defendants are receiving windfalls as a result of strategically timed *Strickland* claims. In addition, the 'prosecution and the trial courts may adopt some measures to help ensure against late, frivolous, or fabricated claims after a later, less advantageous plea offer has been accepted or after a trial leading to conviction.' *Frye*. This, too, will help ensure against meritless claims. * * *

"As a remedy, the District Court ordered specific performance of the original plea agreement. The correct remedy in these circumstances, however, is to order the State to reoffer the plea agreement. Presuming respondent accepts the offer, the state trial court can then exercise its discretion in determining whether to vacate the convictions and resentence respondent pursuant to the plea agreement, to vacate only some of the convictions and resentence respondent accordingly, or to leave the convictions and sentence from trial undisturbed."

The four *Cooper* dissenters (also dissenting in *Frye*) were critical of the majority's remedy analysis. Scalia, J., speaking for three of them, stated:

"Why, one might ask, require a 'reoffer' of the plea agreement, and its acceptance by the defendant? If the district court finds (as a necessary element, supposedly, of *Strickland* prejudice) that Cooper would have accepted the original offer, and would thereby have avoided trial and conviction, why not skip the reoffer-and-reacceptance minuet and simply leave it to the discretion of the state trial court what the remedy shall be? The answer, of course, is camouflage. Trial courts, after all, regularly accept or reject plea agreements, so there seems to be nothing extraordinary about their accepting or rejecting the new one mandated by today's decision. But the acceptance or rejection of a plea agreement that has no status whatever under the United States Constitution is worlds apart from what this is: 'discretionary' specification of a remedy for an unconstitutional criminal conviction.

"To be sure, the Court asserts that there are 'factors' which bear upon (and presumably limit) exercise of this discretion—factors that it is not prepared to specify in full, much less assign some determinative weight. 'Principles elaborated over time in decisions of state and federal courts, and in statutes and rules' will (in the Court's rosy view) sort all that out. I find it extraordinary that 'statutes and rules' can specify the remedy for a criminal defendant's unconstitutional conviction. Or that the remedy for an unconstitutional conviction should ever be subject at all to a trial judge's discretion. Or, finally, that the remedy could ever include no remedy at all.

"I suspect that the Court's squeamishness in fashioning a remedy, and the incoherence of what it comes up with, is attributable to its realization, deep down, that there is no real constitutional violation here anyway. The defendant has been fairly tried, lawfully convicted, and properly sentenced, and any 'remedy' provided for this will do nothing but undo the just results of a fair adversarial process."

Alito, J., dissenting, who agreed with the criticisms in the Scalia dissent quoted above, added: "The Court, for its part, finds it unnecessary to define 'the boundaries of proper discretion' in today's opinion. In my view, requiring the prosecution to renew an old plea offer would represent an abuse of discretion in at least two circumstances: first, when important new information about a defendant's culpability comes to light after the offer is rejected, and, second, when the rejection of the plea offer results in a substantial expenditure of scarce prosecutorial or judicial resources."

In *Burt v. Titlow*, infra, the federal court of appeals, upon finding ineffective assistance by counsel Toca, remanded with instructions that the prosecution must reoffer the original plea agreement to Titlow, and that the state court should "consul[t]" the plea agreement and "fashion" a remedy for the violation of Titlow's Sixth Amendment rights. While the Supreme Court found no such violation, Ginsburg, J., doubted that Toca had acted reasonably, but then explained her concurrence: "Nevertheless, one thing is crystal clear. The prosecutor's agreement to the plea bargain hinged entirely on Titlow's willingness to testify at [Rogers's] trial. Once Titlow reneged on that half of the deal, the bargain failed. Absent an extant bargain, there was nothing to renew. In short, the prosecutor could not be ordered to 'renew' a plea proposal never offered in the first place. With the plea offer no longer alive, Titlow was convicted after a trial free from reversible error."

13th ed., p. 1312; at the end of Note 5, add:

Consider the foregoing questions, as well as the *Rogers* and *Purdy* positions, in light of *Burt v. Titlow*, 134 S.Ct. 10 (2013). Titlow and Rogers were charged with the murder of Rogers' husband. After explaining that the state's evidence could support a conviction for first-degree murder, Titlow's attorney negotiated a manslaughter plea and 7–15 year sentence in exchange for an agreement that Titlow would testify against Rogers, but three days before Rogers's trial Titlow's new counsel, Toca, demanded a lower minimum sentence and, when the prosecutor refused, advised Titlow to withdraw the guilty plea, which Titlow did. Rogers was acquitted, but Titlow was then convicted of second-degree murder and sentenced to 20–40 years. Upon Titlow's appeal, claiming ineffective assistance of counsel, the state appellate court rejected the claim, concluding Toca's actions were reasonable in light of his client's protestations of innocence. On federal habeas review, the court of appeals ruled that the factual predicate of the state court's decision—that the plea withdrawal was based on Titlow's assertion of innocence—was an unreasonable interpretation of the factual record. The Supreme Court reversed; taking into account the "doubly deferential" standard of review applicable on federal habeas per *Cullen v. Pinholster*, 13th ed., p. 1611, the Court concluded that the record supported the state court's finding that Toca advised withdrawal of the plea only after Titlow's proclamation of innocence. In the course of reaching that conclusion, the Court, per Alito, J., noted that the state court "correctly recognized that there is nothing inconsistent about a defendant's asserting innocence on the one hand and refusing to plead guilty to manslaughter accompanied by higher-than-normal punishment on the other. Indeed, a defendant convinced of his or her own innocence may have a particularly optimistic view of the likelihood of acquittal, and therefore be more likely to drive a hard bargain with the prosecution before pleading guilty. * * * Although a defendant's proclamation of innocence does not relieve counsel of his normal responsibilities under *Strickland*, it may affect the advice counsel gives."

Sotomayor, J., concurring, elaborated on that last statement as follows: "The first part of that statement bears emphasis: Regardless of whether a defendant asserts her innocence (or admits her guilt), her counsel must 'make an independent examination of the facts, circumstances, pleadings and laws involved and then . . . offer his informed opinion as to what plea should be entered.' *Von Moltke v. Gillies*, 332 U.S. 708, 721 (1948) (plurality opinion). A defendant possesses " 'the ultimate authority' " to determine her plea. *Florida v. Nixon*, 543 U.S. 175 (2004). But a lawyer must abide by his client's decision in this respect only after having provided the client with competent and fully informed advice, including an analysis of the risks that the client would face in proceeding to trial. Given our recognition that 'a defendant's proclamation of innocence does not relieve counsel of his normal responsibilities,' our further observation that such a proclamation 'may affect the advice counsel gives,' states only the obvious: that a lawyer's advice will always reflect the objectives of the representation, as determined by the adequately informed client."

13th ed., p. 1313; in Note 6, replace all through "Would it make" with:

In *Frye*, would it have made

13th ed., p. 1314; in Note 8, replace the first five words with:

Does it follow from *Frye*

13th ed., p. 1316; before Note 12, add:

What would be the correct result in the following two situations, as to defendant's arguments based upon (i) the traditional direct/collateral consequences distinction and (ii) *Padilla*,[d] where in each instance defendant sought to overturn his guilty plea because of his lack of awareness of a consequence about which his counsel did not advise him? *Commonwealth v. Abraham*, 62 A.3d 343 (Pa.2012), where the Public Employee Pension Forfeiture Act mandated that defendant, a 67-year-old retiree, forfeit all of his lifetime pension of $1,500 per month—where defendant lost on both (i) and (ii). *People v. Hughes,* 983 N.E.2d 439 (Ill.2012), where the Attorney General opted to file a petition to have defendant committed under the Sexually Violent Persons Commitment Act, potentially resulting in defendant's confinement for life—where defendant lost on (i) but prevailed on (ii).

Regarding the matter of prejudice, what if, as in *United States v. Akinsade*, 686 F.3d 248 (4th Cir.2012), defense counsel, re the government's plea offer, erroneously told defendant "he could not be deported based on the single offense" and defendant—now facing mandatory deportation—thereafter pled guilty, and in the rule 11 colloquy the district court said that "if you are not a citizen, you could be deported."

[d] Putting aside the fact that in *Chaidez v. United States*, Supp., p. 154, *Padilla* was held to announce a new rule and thus not to be retroactive.

13th ed., p. 1317; delete Note 14

13th ed., p. 1320; in the middle of the page, correct the cross-reference:

See Note 4, p. 1336.

13th ed., p. 1324; in lieu of the existing second paragraph of Note 3, insert:

Consider also *State v. Huebler*, 275 P.3d 91 (Nev.2012), noting that "courts have split as to whether the Court's decision [in *Ruiz*] also encompasses exculpatory information," and concluding:

"In our opinion, the considerations that led to the decision in *Ruiz* do not lead to the same conclusion when it comes to material exculpatory information. While the value of impeachment information may depend on innumerable variables that primarily come into play at trial and therefore arguably make it less than critical information in entering a guilty plea, the same cannot be said of exculpatory information, which is special not just in relation to the fairness of a trial but also in relation to whether a guilty plea is valid and accurate. For this reason, the due-process calculus also weighs in favor of the added safeguard of requiring the State to disclose material exculpatory information before the defendant enters a guilty plea.

" * * * We therefore hold that a defendant may challenge the validity of a guilty plea based on the prosecution's failure to disclose material exculpatory information before entry of the plea. * * *

"The guilty-plea context, however, requires a different approach to the prejudice component of a *Brady* violation. Prejudice for purposes of a *Brady* violation requires a showing that the withheld evidence is 'material.' Normally, evidence is material if it 'creates a reasonable doubt.' That standard of materiality is not helpful in the guilty-plea context because the defendant has admitted guilt. In fashioning a materiality test in that context, we also must be mindful that guilty pleas are presumptively valid and that the defendant therefore bears a heavy burden when challenging the validity of a guilty plea.

"Other courts considering this issue have applied a standard of materiality that is based on the relevance of the withheld evidence to the defendant's decision to plead guilty: 'whether there is a reasonable probability that but for the failure to disclose the *Brady* material, the defendant would have refused to plead and would have gone to trial.' "

13th ed., p. 1329; after the first paragraph of Note 3, add:

There are limits, however, as to how far the prosecutor may go in accommodating the victim, as illustrated by *In re Flatt-Moore*, 959 N.E.2d 241 (Ind.2012), involving a professional misconduct charge against a prosecutor. One "JH" was charged with Class C felony check fraud because of insufficient funds checks totaling $68,956.91, given to "Big Rivers" as payment for agricultural products. After consultation with Big Rivers' attorney, the prosecutor offered JH a plea agreement whereby JH would be convicted of a Class A misdemeanor "on the condition that [he] agree to whatever terms and amounts Big River was demanding." That demand was for $108,501.60 by a specified date, to cover the three checks, plus a purported billing error, attorneys' fees and interest. JH accepted, but the plea agreement was thereafter withdrawn when JH failed to pay the full amount by the specified date. In finding that the prosecutor "engaged in attorney misconduct by surrendering her prosecutorial discretion in plea negotiations entirely to the pecuniary demands of the victim of the crime," the court commented:

"This is not to suggest that prosecutor may not allow crime victims to have substantial and meaningful input into plea agreements offered to the offenders at whose hands they suffered. But by giving Big Rivers unfettered veto power in the plea negotiations leading up to the First Plea Offer, Respondent entirely gave up her prosecutorial discretion to enter into what would otherwise be a fair and just resolution of the charges. If a prosecutor puts the conditions for resolving similar crimes entirely in the hands of the victims, defendants whose victims are unreasonable or vindictive cannot receive the same consideration as defendants whose victims are reasonable in their demands. At the very least, such a practice gives the appearance that resolution of criminal charges could turn on the whims of victims rather than the equities of each case."

SECTION 4. RECEIVING THE DEFENDANT'S PLEA; PLEA WITHDRAWAL

C. DETERMINING GUILTY PLEA IS UNDERSTANDINGLY MADE

13th ed., p. 1334; at the end of Note 4, add:

Quite different from the *Boykin* rights is another set of rights—those relating to the legitimate bases for taking an appeal—that are waived (or, more precisely, forfeited) by virtue of a plea of guilty. See 13th ed., p. 1343 infra. But judges receiving guilty pleas are under no obligation to warn guilty plea defendants of that fact. As noted in *United States v. Avila*, 733 F.3d 1258 (10th Cir.2013), the Federal "Rules do not explicitly require that the court inform a defendant that an unconditional guilty plea may limit the defendant's ability to appeal," a situation the court found "troubling." But *Avila* had to do with a judge's *mis*advice regarding the extent of a guilty plea defendant's right to appeal. The judge told defendant that if he was convicted at trial he would have the right to an "appeal," and that if he were to plead guilty and the plea was accepted, then he would "still have the right to an appeal," thus telling the defendant in effect that he "would have the same unlimited right to appeal following the entry of his plea as he would after a trial." The court held that if during a plea colloquy the court "chooses to advise the defendant concerning his right to appeal following the entry of the plea, the court must ensure that the defendant understands that his right to appeal may be limited by an unconditional guilty plea." Because that was not done in the instant case, the defendant was entitled to withdraw his guilty plea.

CHAPTER 23

TRIAL BY JURY

■ ■ ■

SECTION 1. RIGHT TO JURY TRIAL

13th ed., p. 1351; in the text of Note 1, after footnote c, add:

Fines well in excess of $5000 do not necessarily trigger the jury right. Typical is the reasoning in *United States v. Dugan*, 667 F.3d 84 (2d Cir.2011). There the court upheld a misdemeanor conviction, without a jury, under 18 U.S.C. § 248(a), which punishes physical obstruction of a reproductive health facility with up to six months' imprisonment and a $10,000 fine. "Because offenses carrying prison sentences of six months or less are presumed to be petty, in order to overcome this presumption, Dugan would have to demonstrate that the $10,000 monetary penalty is 'so severe' as to 'reflect a legislative determination that the offense in question is a 'serious' one.' *Blanton*. While Dugan is correct that the $10,000 maximum fine is $5,000 more than the maximum monetary penalty enumerated in the statutory definition of 'petty offense,' the Supreme Court has never adopted this statutory definition as defining the contours of the constitutional right to a jury trial, and we cannot agree that the additional $5,000 is 'so severe' as to transform this otherwise petty offense into a serious one."

13th ed., p. 1379; at the end of Note b, add:

One commentator has observed that the *McCollum* decision makes sense if one considers that preventing the exclusion of black jurors and the acquittals of white defendants charged with brutality against blacks were key aims of Reconstruction Amendments and legislation. James Forman, Jr., *Juries and Race in the Nineteenth Century*, 113 Yale L.J. 895 (2004). But *McCollum* has not been limited to peremptory strikes excluding those who are members of minority racial groups.

CHAPTER 25

THE CRIMINAL TRIAL

■ ■ ■

SECTION 2. CONFRONTATION AND TESTIMONIAL HEARSAY

13th ed., p. 1449; after Note 1, add:

Then in *Williams v. Illinois*, 132 S.Ct. 2221 (2012), the Court splintered over whether the Confrontation Clause was violated when an expert testified about a DNA analysis that she did not conduct. No rationale commanded a majority. In a plurality opinion, the four justices who dissented in *Bullcoming* decided that the statements in the DNA analyst's report discussed by the expert witness in *Williams* were not testimonial. The plurality reasoned that the report (1) was not offered for its truth but instead as a basis for the opinion of the expert witness; (2) was "not inherently inculpatory"; and (3) was "produced before any suspect was identified." All five other justices expressly rejected this reasoning. Four of the five—Justices Kagan, Sotomayor, Scalia, and Ginsburg—found the case indistinguishable from *Bullcoming* and concluded that introduction of the report through the expert witness denied Williams his right to cross examine the DNA analyst under the Confrontation Clause. Justice Thomas, however, delivered a separate opinion, which, when combined with the plurality opinion of the *Bullcoming* dissenters, provided the fifth vote for *rejecting* the defendant's confrontation clause claim.

Applying the rationale he had articulated in his concurring opinion in *Bryant*, Justice Thomas reasoned that the DNA report referenced by the expert witness in her testimony against Williams was not "testimonial" because it lacked sufficient indicia of solemnity. "[T]he scope of the confrontation right is properly limited to extrajudicial statements similar in solemnity to the Marian examination practices that the Confrontation Clause was designed to prevent," he explained. "By certifying the truth of the analyst's representations, the unsworn *Bullcoming* report bore 'a "striking resemblance," ' to the Marian practice in which magistrates examined witnesses, typically on oath, and 'certif[ied] the results to the court.' "And, he continued, "in *Melendez-Diaz,* we observed that 'certificates' are functionally identical to live, in-court testimony, doing precisely what a witness does on direct examination.' Cellmark's report is marked by no such indicia of solemnity." Justice Thomas's Sixth Amendment test, although it provided the deciding vote in *Williams*, has yet to be endorsed by any other justice.

SECTION 3. RIGHTS TO REMAIN SILENT AND TO TESTIFY

13th ed., p. 1453; at the end of the next to last paragraph in Note 1, add:

"Griffin is impossible to square with the text of the Fifth Amendment," Justices Thomas and Scalia have also argued. "A defendant is not 'compelled . . . to be a witness against himself' simply because a jury has been told that it may draw an adverse inference from his silence." *Salinas v. Texas*, 133 S.Ct. 2174 (2013) (Thomas, J., concurring, joined by Scalia, J.), see Supp., p. 76.

CHAPTER 26

REPROSECUTION AND THE BAN AGAINST DOUBLE JEOPARDY

■ ■ ■

SECTION 1. REPROSECUTION AFTER A MISTRIAL

A. MISTRIAL OVER THE OBJECTION OF DEFENDANT

13th ed., p. 1469; at the end of Note 1, add:

The rule in *Crist* is a bright line. The defendant is put in jeopardy at the moment the jury is sworn, regardless of whether there is any actual risk of conviction. *Martinez v. Illinois*, 134 S.Ct. 2070 (2014).

13th ed., p. 1474; in lieu of existing Note 1, insert:

1. Explaining in *Lett* why the state court's decision finding manifest necessity was a reasonable application of clearly established federal law under the habeas statute, the Court stated it had never held that a trial judge must make particular findings or take any particular alternative steps prior to declaring a mistrial based on jury deadlock. Two years later, in *Blueford v. Arkansas*, 132 S.Ct. 2044 (2012), the Court made the same point again, this time when upholding, on direct appeal, a state decision finding manifest necessity for mistrial after a jury reported that it had voted unanimously against murder but was deadlocked on lesser charges. Rejecting the defendant's argument that the trial judge "should have taken 'some action,' whether through partial verdict forms or other means, to allow the jury to give effect to [its votes rejecting murder charges], and then considered a mistrial only as to the remaining charges," the Court once again stated, "We have never required a trial court, before declaring a mistrial because of a hung jury, to consider any particular means of breaking the impasse—let alone to consider giving the jury new options for a verdict." The Court continued, "As permitted under Arkansas law, the jury's options in this case were limited to two: either convict on one of the offenses, or acquit on all. * * * the trial court did not abuse its discretion by refusing to add another option—that of acquitting on some offenses but not others."

In situations where mistrial is based on something other than deadlock, the Court's statement in *Washington* that the record must demonstrate that "the trial judge acted responsibly and deliberately, and accorded careful

133

consideration to respondent's interest in having the trial concluded in a single proceeding," continues to suggest that trial judges must consider alternatives to mistrial as part of the manifest necessity analysis. *See e.g., United States v. Fisher*, 624 F.3d 713 (5th Cir.2010) (no manifest necessity for mistrial after scheduling conflict prevented critical government witnesses from testifying when judge did not consider reasonable alternatives); *Smith v. Brown*, 105 A.D.3d 965, 962 N.Y.S.2d 713 (2013) (no manifest necessity once juror dismissed, noting alternatives to mistrial included defendant's consent to proceed with 11 jurors and curative instructions); *Morris v. Livote*, 105 A.D.3d 43, 962 N.Y.S.2d 59 (2013) (no manifest necessity for mistrial after "blatant, intentional misconduct" of defense counsel in eliciting prejudicial information on cross examination, when "more specific curative instructions or a poll of the jurors to ascertain whether they could render an impartial verdict would have been appropriate"); *Day v. Haskell*, 799 N.W.2d 355 (N.D.2011) (no manifest necessity after defendant left alone in the courtroom with the jurors and the bailiff, when judge failed to consider alternatives to mistrial such as curing instructions).

SECTION 2.   REPROSECUTION FOLLOWING AN ACQUITTAL

13th ed., p. 1489; at the end of Note 2, add:

One recurring situation is a trial court's decision to enter judgment of acquittal because the government failed to introduce sufficient evidence of a fact that turns out not to be an element of the offense. As the Court explained in *Evans v. Michigan*, 133 S.Ct. 1069 (2013), "There is no question the trial court's ruling was wrong; it was predicated upon a clear misunderstanding of what facts the State needed to prove under State law. But that is of no moment. *Martin Linen, Sanabria*, [*Arizona v. Rumsey*, 467 U.S. 203 (1984)], *Smalis*, and *Smith* all instruct that an acquittal due to insufficient evidence precludes retrial, whether the court's evaluation of the evidence was 'correct or not,' and regardless of whether the court's decision flowed from an incorrect antecedent ruling of law." "This case, like our previous ones, involves an antecedent legal error that led to an acquittal because the State failed to prove some fact it was not actually required to prove." "It should make no difference whether the court employs the formality of directing the jury to return an acquittal or whether the court enters an acquittal itself."

13th ed., p. 1489; after the first sentence of Note 3, add:

The Court in *Evans v. Michigan*, 133 S.Ct. 1069 (2013), reviewed the difference: "an 'acquittal' includes 'a ruling by the court that the evidence is insufficient to convict,' a 'factual finding [that] necessarily establish[es] the criminal defendant's lack of criminal culpability,' and any other 'rulin[g] which relate[s] to the ultimate question of guilt or innocence.' *Scott*. These sorts of substantive rulings stand apart from procedural rulings that may also terminate a case midtrial, which we generally refer to as dismissals or mistrials. Procedural dismissals include rulings on questions that 'are unrelated to factual guilt or innocence,' but 'which serve other purposes,' including 'a legal judgment that a defendant, although criminally culpable, may not be punished' because of some problem like an error with the indictment." Continued the Court, "The distinction drawn in *Scott* has stood the test of time, and we expect courts will continue to have little 'difficulty in distinguishing between those rulings which relate to the ultimate question of guilt or innocence and those which serve other purposes.' "

In *Martinez v. Illinois*, 134 S.Ct. 2020 (2014), after the jury was selected and sworn, the prosecution was unable to produce two of its witnesses. The state declared it was "not participating" in the trial and would produce no evidence, and the defendant moved for directed verdict of acquittal, which the trial judge granted. Because the court "acted on its view that the prosecution had failed to prove its case," the Court explained, this was a "textbook acquittal," not a dismissal. The trial judge, the Court observed, told the prosecution on the day of trial that it could "move to dismiss [its] case" before the jury was sworn, but the state declined to accept that invitation, missing its chance to avoid the double jeopardy bar. The Court added that jeopardy had attached, "even if the trial court had chosen to dismiss the case or declare a mistrial rather than granting Martinez's motion for a directed verdict, the Double Jeopardy Clause probably would still bar his retrial," noting that "precisely this scenario" took place in *Downum*.

13th ed., p. 1489; at the end of Note 3, add:

Responding to the argument that the acquittal rule allows a defendant to reap a "windfall" from the trial court's unreviewable error, the Court in *Evans* stated, "sovereigns are hardly powerless to prevent this sort of situation * * * . Nothing obligates a jurisdiction to afford its trial courts the power to grant a midtrial acquittal, and at least two States [Nevada and Louisiana] disallow the practice. Many jurisdictions, including the federal system, allow or encourage their courts to defer consideration of a motion to acquit until after the jury returns a verdict, which mitigates double jeopardy concerns. See Fed. Rule Crim. Proc. 29(b). And for cases such as this, in which a trial court's interpretation of the relevant criminal statute is likely to prove dispositive, we see no reason why jurisdictions could not provide for mandatory or expedited interlocutory appeals if they wished to prevent misguided acquittals from being entered. But having chosen to vest its courts with the power to grant midtrial acquittals, the State must bear the corresponding risk that some acquittals will be granted in error."

13th ed., p. 1489; after the first paragraph of Note 4, add:

In *Evans*, a similar argument was raised with the same result. The Court explained, "even if the Government is correct that Evans could have challenged [before trial] the charging document on the same legal theory he used to challenge the sufficiency of the evidence, it matters that he made only the latter motion, a motion that necessarily may not be made until trial is underway. Evans cannot be penalized for requesting from the court a ruling on the merits of the State's case, as the Michigan Rules entitled him to do; whether he could have also brought a distinct procedural objection earlier on is beside the point."

CHAPTER 27

SENTENCING

■ ■ ■

SECTION 1. INTRODUCTION TO SENTENCING

B. TYPES OF SENTENCES

13th ed., p. 1506; at the end of Section B, add:

"Forfeitures," the Court has reasoned, "help to ensure that crime does not pay: They at once punish wrongdoing, deter future illegality, and 'lessen the economic power' of criminal enterprises." *Kaley v. United States*, 134 S. Ct. 1090 (2014).

SECTION 3. CONSTITUTIONAL LIMITS ON SENTENCING PROCEDURE

A. INFORMATION CONSIDERED IN SETTING THE SENTENCE

13th ed., p. 1516; before the last paragraph of Note 1, add:

In a later case, the Court noted that "there are reasonable arguments that the logic of *Mitchell* does not apply" in a capital sentencing proceeding that follows a guilty plea in which the defendant admitted "every relevant fact on which [the state] bore the burden of proof." In such a case the state "could not have shifted to respondent its 'burden of proving facts relevant to the crime.' " *White v. Woodall*, 134 S.Ct. 1697 (2014). The Court also rejected the argument that the holdings of *Mitchell* and *Estelle v. Smith* necessarily require a blanket no-inference instruction (see *Carter v. Kentucky*, 13th ed., p. 1452 n. 6) during the penalty phase of a capital case. It noted that "it is not uncommon for a constitutional rule to apply somewhat differently at the penalty phase than it does at the guilt phase" and that "*Mitchell* itself suggests that some inferences from silence regarding remorse might be permissible."

13th ed., p. 1517; for the last two sentences at the end of Note 2, substitute:

Since *Williams*, the Court has upheld against double jeopardy challenges the practice of using uncharged and even acquitted conduct to justify a higher sentence within the range authorized for the offense of conviction. *See, e.g.,*

United States v. Booker, p. 1531, Note 6, where the Court stated: "In *Witte v. United States,* 515 U.S. 389 (1995), we held that the Double Jeopardy Clause did not bar a prosecution for conduct that had provided the basis for an enhancement of the defendant's sentence in a prior case. We concluded that 'consideration of information about the defendant's character and conduct at sentencing does not result in "punishment" for any offense other than the one of which the defendant was convicted.' Rather, the defendant is 'punished only for the fact that the present offense was carried out in a manner that warrants increased punishment. . . .' *United States v. Watts,* 519 U.S. 148 (1997) *(per curiam)* (quoting *Witte*). In *Watts,* relying on *Witte,* we held that the Double Jeopardy Clause permitted a court to consider acquitted conduct in sentencing a defendant under the Guidelines." Since *Booker,* every circuit to have considered the question has held that acquitted conduct may be used in setting a sentence, so long as it is proved by a preponderance standard.

When very broad statutory sentencing ranges with high ceilings permit judges to choose severe sentences based on uncharged or acquitted conduct, critics continue to argue that this allows prosecutors "to achieve an indirect conviction" for the other criminal conduct "at the sentencing hearing, where [defendants] lack the procedural protections of trial." Recent Case, 125 Harv. L. Rev. 1860, 1867 (2013) (discussing *United States v. Fitch,* 659 F.3d 788 (9th Cir. 2011), which upheld sentence of nearly 22 years for fraud based on judicial finding at sentencing that defendant had murdered his wife as part of the fraudulent scheme). If you agree, what are the possible ways to address this problem?

As for the use of prior *convictions* in sentencing, see the discussion of *Almendarez-Torres v. United States,* 523 U.S. 224 (1998), pp. 1522–23.

D. JURY TRIAL AND BURDEN OF PROOF

13th ed., p. 1526; at the end of Note 3, delete footnote e and add:

Eleven years later, in ALLEYNE v. UNITED STATES, 133 S.Ct. 2151 (2013), the position of the dissenting justices in *Harris* prevailed. The Court overruled *Harris* and *McMillan* and held that permitting judges to determine facts that trigger mandatory minimum sentences "cannot be reconciled with our reasoning in *Apprendi.*" Alleyne had been convicted of violating 18 U.S.C. § 924(c)(1)(A), which provided a sentence of "not less than 5 years" for anyone who "uses or carries a firearm" in relation to a "crime of violence," and "not less than 7 years" "if the firearm is brandished." The jury that convicted Alleyne indicated on the verdict form that he had "[u]sed or carried a firearm during and in relation to a crime of violence," but did not indicate a finding that the firearm was "[b]randished." The presentence report recommended a 7-year sentence and Alleyne objected, arguing that the jury did not find brandishing beyond a reasonable doubt and that he was subject only to the five-year mandatory minimum. Relying on *Harris,* the judge overruled the objection, found Alleyne had brandished the firearm, and imposed a sentence of seven years, which was upheld on appeal.

Writing for the Court, Justice Thomas traced the "linkage of facts with particular sentence ranges (defined by both the minimum and the maximum)" at common law, and "a well-established practice of including in the indictment, and submitting to the jury, every fact that was a basis for imposing or increasing punishment * * *." This rule, he explained, allowed the defendant to predict the judgment, if convicted. "Consistent with common-law and early American practice, *Apprendi* concluded that any 'facts that increase the prescribed range of penalties to which a criminal defendant is exposed' are elements of the crime. * * * While *Harris* limited *Apprendi* to facts increasing the statutory maximum, the principle applied in *Apprendi* applies with equal force to facts increasing the mandatory minimum."

"It is indisputable that a fact triggering a mandatory minimum alters the prescribed range of sentences to which a criminal defendant is exposed. * * * And because the legally prescribed range *is* the penalty affixed to the crime, * * * it follows that a fact increasing either end of the range produces a new penalty and constitutes an ingredient of the offense. * * * It is impossible to dissociate the floor of a sentencing range from the penalty affixed to the crime. * * * Moreover, it is impossible to dispute that facts increasing the legally prescribed floor *aggravate* the punishment. * * * Elevating the low-end of a sentencing range heightens the loss of liberty associated with the crime: the defendant's 'expected punishment has increased as a result of the narrowed range' and 'the prosecution is empowered, by invoking the mandatory minimum, to require the judge to impose a higher punishment than he might wish.'). * * * This reality demonstrates that the core crime and the fact triggering the mandatory minimum sentence together constitute a new, aggravated crime, each element of which must be submitted to the jury.[2]"

"Defining facts that increase a mandatory statutory minimum to be part of the substantive offense enables the defendant to predict the legally applicable penalty from the face of the indictment. * * * It also preserves the historic role of the jury as an intermediary between the State and criminal defendants. * * * As noted, the essential Sixth Amendment inquiry is whether a fact is an element of the crime. When a finding of fact alters the legally prescribed punishment so as to aggravate it, the fact necessarily forms a constituent part of a new offense and must be submitted to the jury. It is no answer to say that the defendant could have received the same sentence with or without that fact. It is obvious, for example, that a defendant could not be convicted and sentenced for assault, if the jury only finds the facts for

---

[2] Juries must find any facts that increase either the statutory maximum or minimum because the Sixth Amendment applies where a finding of fact both alters the legally prescribed range *and* does so in a way that aggravates the penalty. Importantly, this is distinct from factfinding used to guide judicial discretion in selecting a punishment "within limits fixed by law." *Williams v. New York*, 337 U.S. 241, 246 (1949). While such findings of fact may lead judges to select sentences that are more severe than the ones they would have selected without those facts, the Sixth Amendment does not govern that element of sentencing.

larceny, even if the punishments prescribed for each crime are identical. One reason is that each crime has different elements and a defendant can be convicted only if the jury has found each element of the crime of conviction.

Similarly, because the fact of brandishing aggravates the legally prescribed range of allowable sentences, it constitutes an element of a separate, aggravated offense that must be found by the jury, regardless of what sentence the defendant *might* have received if a different range had been applicable. Indeed, if a judge were to find a fact that increased the statutory maximum sentence, such a finding would violate the Sixth Amendment, even if the defendant ultimately received a sentence falling within the original sentencing range (*i.e.,* the range applicable without that aggravating fact). * * * The essential point is that the aggravating fact produced a higher range, which, in turn, conclusively indicates that the fact is an element of a distinct and aggravated crime. It must, therefore, be submitted to the jury and found beyond a reasonable doubt." * * * "Our ruling today does not mean that any fact that influences judicial discretion must be found by a jury. We have long recognized that broad sentencing discretion, informed by judicial factfinding, does not violate the Sixth Amendment. * * * [E]stablishing what punishment is available by law and setting a specific punishment within the bounds that the law has prescribed are two different things.' *Apprendi*, at 519 (THOMAS, J., concurring). Our decision today is wholly consistent with the broad discretion of judges to select a sentence within the range authorized bylaw."

As to stare decisis and the overruling of *Harris*, Justice Thomas added, "The force of *stare decisis* is at its nadir in cases concerning procedural rules that implicate fundamental constitutional protections," "Because *Harris* is irreconcilable with the reasoning of *Apprendi* and the original meaning of the Sixth Amendment, we follow the latter."[e]

"The judge, rather than the jury, found brandishing, thus violating petitioner's Sixth Amendment rights," the Court concluded. "Accordingly, we vacate the Sixth Circuit's judgment with respect to Alleyne's sentence on the § 924(c)(1)(A) conviction and remand the case for resentencing consistent with the jury's verdict."

Justice Breyer concurred, explaining that it seemed "highly anomalous to read *Apprendi* as insisting that juries find sentencing facts that *permit* a judge to impose a higher sentence while not insisting that juries find sentencing facts that *require* a judge to impose a higher sentence." Although he said "I continue to disagree with *Apprendi*," he joined the majority, explaining "the time has come to end this anomaly"

Chief Justice Roberts wrote in dissent, joined by Justices Scalia and Kennedy. "Our holdings that a judge may not sentence a defendant to more

---

[e]   Justice Sotomayor, joined by Justices Ginsburg and Kagan, defended the Court's decision to overrule *McMillan* and *Harris*, stating those cases had been "thoroughly undermined by intervening decisions" and that "no significant reliance interests are at stake that might justify adhering to their result."

than the jury has authorized properly preserve the jury right as a guard against judicial overreaching." In this case, he noted "The jury's verdict authorized the judge to impose the precise sentence he imposed for the precise factual reason he imposed it," and the Sixth Amendment "demands nothing more." Criticizing the lack of historical evidence for the Court's position, Chief Justice Roberts also argued that the "question here is about the power of judges, not juries. Under the rule in place until today, a legislature could tell judges that certain facts carried certain weight, and require the judge to devise a sentence based on that weight—so long as the sentence remained within the range authorized by the jury. Now, in the name of the jury right that formed a barrier between the defendant and the State, the majority has erected a barrier between judges and legislatures, establishing that discretionary sentencing is the domain of judges. Legislatures must keep their respectful distance."

"I find this new rule impossible to square with the historical understanding of the jury right as a defense *from* judges, not a defense *of* judges. . . . Just as the Sixth Amendment 'limits judicial power only to the extent that the claimed judicial power infringes on the province of the jury,' *Blakely*, 542 U. S., at 308, so too it limits *legislative* power only to the extent *that* power infringes on the province of the jury. Because the claimed infringement here is on the province of the judge, not the jury, the jury right has no work to do."

Justice Alito dissented separately, arguing that "If the Court is of a mind to reconsider existing precedent, a prime candidate should be *Apprendi.*" He questioned both the historical analysis in that "dubious" case and the illogic of accepting discretionary sentencing under its rationale. Finally, he observed, that "if *Harris* is not entitled to *stare decisis* weight, then neither is the Court's opinion in this case. After all, only four Members of the Court think that the Court's holding is the correct reading of the Constitution."

13th ed., p. 1533; in lieu of existing Notes 7 and 8, insert:

7. *The principles behind the Apprendi rule—treating range-raising facts as elements.* Notice that the problem addressed in these cases is not that judges rather than juries are selecting sentences, nor that judges, when setting sentences, are considering facts not proven as part of the conviction. The Court has never backed off its conclusion that there is no Sixth Amendment right to a jury's determination of punishment *within* the range authorized for the offense.[i] And the Court continues to support judicial fact-finding at sentencing under the relaxed procedures authorized more than fifty years ago in *Williams,* p. 1510. Instead, the Court has concluded that no

---

[i] E.g., Spaziano v. Florida, 468 U.S. 447 (1984). Only a handful of states authorize jury sentencing, and most of these only when a defendant opts for a jury trial. In at least some of these states, because jurors are given little or no access to information about average sentences, sentencing guidelines, parole, or probation, their sentences tend to be more severe than those imposed by judges. King & Noble, *Jury Sentencing in Practice—A Three-State Study*, 57 Vand. L. Rev. 885 (2004).

matter how a legislature may label facts that it has specified as triggering a higher range of punishment, those facts must be treated like elements of the offense and proven to a jury beyond a reasonable doubt.

As a matter of constitutional interpretation, is this range-raising standard for differentiating between elements and sentencing facts *preferable* to the tests advanced by those who have objected to the *Apprendi* rule? These tests include requiring proof beyond a reasonable doubt to a jury when a statute was "tailored to permit the * * * finding to be a tail which was the dog of the substantive offense" (*McMillan*, Note 1, p. 1520); allowing a legislature to define what is sentencing factor and what is element "within constraints of fairness" (*Booker*, Breyer's dissent, above); limiting trial protections to facts that are related to the offense, while allowing judges to find facts related to the offender (Berman, *Conceptualizing Booker*, 38 Ariz. St. L.J. 38 (2008)); and adopting a sliding scale of procedural protections for sentencing rather than an approach that provides some facts with "full-blown trial protections" and others "almost none"? (Berman & Bibas, *Making Sentencing Sensible*, 4 Ohio St. J.Crim.L. 37 (2006)).

8. ***Legislative options.*** If a legislature chooses to structure judicial sentencing discretion, what options does it have? In addition to the advisory guidelines system that a majority of the Court created in *Booker*, Justice Breyer, in his dissenting opinion in *Apprendi*, listed four other options—1) single, mandatory sentences for each crime; 2) indeterminate sentences (subject to discretionary release by paroling authorities) chosen by judges within broad statutory sentence ranges; 3) guidelines systems with aggravating facts proven to juries; or 4) inverted guidelines—"attaching astronomically high sentences to each crime, followed by long lists of mitigating facts, [to be found by judges] which, for the most part, would consist of the absence of aggravating facts." If options 2 and 4 above are permissible, what constitutional values are preserved by the Court's rule in *Apprendi, Blakely, and Alleyne*? Does the rule provide better notice of potential punishment to the accused? Is the rule merely "formalism" (see the dissenting opinion of Justice O'Connor in *Apprendi*, at p. 1529)? Reconsider Justice Steven's response to this claim in footnote 16 of his majority opinion in *Apprendi,* and footnote 19 of Justice Scalia's opinion in *Blakely*.

So far, a small number of states affected by *Blakely* have opted for new legislation retaining mandatory guidelines and requiring enhancements to be proven to a jury, Justice Breyer's option number 3, above, but in these states the number of enhancements per crime are few and only a small number of cases per year involve contested enhancements. Other states where enhancing facts are more plentiful or invoked more frequently have switched to advisory guidelines. *E.g.* Tenn. Code Ann. § 40–35–210(c) (2006).

13th ed., p. 1536; after Note 11, add:

12. ***Fines, restitution, forfeiture.*** In *Ice,* the Court suggested that the *Apprendi* rule had been extended far enough. It stated, "the potential

intrusion of *Apprendi*'s rule into other state initiatives on sentencing choices or accoutrements—for example, permitting trial judges to find facts about the offense's nature or the defendant's character in determining the length of supervised release, required attendance at drug rehabilitation programs or terms of community service, and the imposition of fines and restitution— would cut the rule loose from its moorings." In 2012, a different majority of the Court in *Southern Union v. United States*, 132 S.Ct. 2344 (2012), dismissed this warning as dicta and "not binding." After reviewing "ample historical evidence" from the 19th Century "showing that juries routinely found facts that set the maximum amounts of fines, the Court held 'that rule of *Apprendi* applies to the imposition of criminal fines.'" Apart from the *Ice* dicta dismissed in *Southern Union*, the Court has yet to address facts concerning the amount of loss that are required for fixing restitution as part of a sentence, and has said nothing about facts concerning the relationship between crime and asset that are required for forfeiting an asset as part of a sentence. Lower courts have refused to apply *Apprendi* in these contexts, but it is possible that will change with the Court's affirmation of *Apprendi*'s vitality and scope in *Southern Union*.

PART 5

APPEALS, POST-CONVICTION REVIEW

■ ■ ■

CHAPTER 28

APPEALS

■ ■ ■

SECTION 4. REVIEW FOR CLAIMS NOT RAISED ON TIME

13th ed., p. 1553; in lieu of existing Note 3b, insert:

b.   That is plain—at the time the error is reviewed on appeal.
Speaking to the second factor, the *Olano* Court noted that the error must be "plain," which is "synonymous with 'clear' or equivalently 'obvious.'" But the error need not be obvious or clear to the trial judge, explained Justice Breyer writing for the Court in *Henderson v. United States,* 133 S.Ct. 1121 (2013). "[P]lain-error review is not a grading system for trial judges. It has broader purposes, including in part allowing courts of appeals better to identify those instances in which the application of a new rule of law to cases on appeal will meet the demands of fairness and judicial integrity." The "plain" requirement is met not only where an unobjected-to decision of a trial judge "was *plainly incorrect* at the time it was made" but also "where an error is 'plain' even if the trial judge's decision was plainly *correct* at the time when it was made but subsequently becomes incorrect based on a change in law," *Johnson,* and "where the law is unsettled at the time of error but plain at the time of review." Rejecting the "practical importance" of any increased incentive for parties to avoid objecting in hopes of better law by the time of appeal, the Court reasoned "counsel normally has other good reasons for calling a trial court's attention to potential error—for example, it is normally to the advantage of counsel and his client to get the error speedily corrected. And, even where that is not so, counsel cannot rely upon the 'plain error' rule to make up for a failure to object at trial. After all, that rule will help only if (1) the law changes in the defendant's favor, (2) the change comes after trial but before the appeal is decided, (3) the error affected the defendant's 'substantial rights,' and (4) the error 'seriously affect[ed] the fairness, integrity or public reputation of judicial proceedings.' If there is a lawyer who would deliberately forgo objection *now* because he perceives some slightly expanded chance to argue for 'plain error' *later,* we suspect that, like the unicorn, he finds his home in the imagination, not the courtroom."

In dissent, Justice Scalia, joined by Justices Thomas and Alito, argued the Court's decision contradicted the text of Rule 52, and also added: "Where a criminal case always has been, or has at trial been shown to be, a sure loser with the jury, it makes entire sense to stand silent while the court makes a mistake that may be the basis for undoing the conviction. The happy-happy thought that counsel will not 'deliberately forgo objection' is not a delusion that this Court has hitherto indulged, worrying as it has (in an opinion joined by the author of today's opinion) about counsel's ' "sandbagging the court' " by 'remaining silent about his objection and belatedly raising the error only if the case does not conclude in his favor.' *Puckett.* . . . In any event, sandbagging is not the only evil to be feared. What is to be feared even more is a lessening of counsel's diligent efforts to identify uncertain points of law and bring them (or rather the defendant's version of them) to the court's attention, *so that error will never occur."*

CHAPTER 29

POST-CONVICTION REVIEW: FEDERAL HABEAS CORPUS

■ ■ ■

SECTION 1. THE BASIC STRUCTURE OF FEDERAL HABEAS CORPUS RELIEF

13th ed., p. 1573; before Note 5, add:

c. Consequences of failure to appoint state post-conviction counsel for federal habeas review. The Court in *Martinez v. Ryan,* 132 S.Ct. 1309 (2012), declined to address directly whether or not the Constitution required states to provide counsel in collateral proceedings. But in what it termed an "equitable ruling" concerning the scope of federal habeas review, the Court assumed that some states would continue to decline to provide counsel in postconviction proceedings, and held that a state's failure to appoint counsel for prisoners filing their first state post-conviction petitions would not be cost free. Prior to the *Martinez* ruling, in order to secure federal habeas review of a claim not raised properly in state post-conviction proceedings, a petitioner had to demonstrate either innocence, or else "cause" for default attributable to something "external" to the defense, such as state interference. After *Martinez,* federal habeas review of one particular claim—a claim of ineffective assistance of *trial* counsel—is no longer foreclosed by the failure to adequately raise that claim in an initial state collateral proceeding, if the petitioner did not have effective legal representation at the time. See Note 1, par. a, infra, discussing *Martinez.*

SECTION 3. LATE OR SUCCESSIVE PETITIONS

13th ed., p. 1581; at the end of Note 1, add:

Noting that "[s]ensitivity to the injustice of incarcerating an innocent individual should not abate when the impediment is AEDPA's statute of limitations," the Court in *McQuiggin v. Perkins*, 133 S.Ct. 1924 (2013), held that a petitioner who does not qualify for equitable tolling may nevertheless avoid the statutory time bar if he convinces "the district court that, in light of the new evidence, no juror, acting reasonably, would have voted to find him guilty beyond a reasonable doubt." The timing of the petition, the Court held "is a factor bearing on the 'reliability of th[e] evidence' purporting to show actual innocence." Although the majority thought it reasonable to assume that "Congress would want a limitations period to yield when what is at stake is a State's incarceration of an individual for a crime, it has become clear, no reasonable person would find he committed," four dissenting justices concluded otherwise, calling the Court's ruling "a pure judicial override of the statute Congress enacted."

SECTION 4.   CLAIMS FORECLOSED BY PROCEDURAL DEFAULT

13th ed., p. 1587; in lieu of existing paragraph *a* of Note 1, insert:

 a.   Ineffective assistance as cause. Since *Sykes*, the Court has recognized that the failure of defense counsel to raise a claim of constitutional error, when that failure amounts to a violation of the Sixth Amendment's right to the effective assistance of counsel, will constitute "cause" for default. For example, a federal habeas court will consider the merits of a jury selection claim that a state court refused to reach because it was raised late, if the petitioner can show that his attorney's failure to raise the jury selection claim was itself a violation of *Strickland*, and that he pursued the *Strickland* violation in state court. *See Edwards v. Carpenter*, 529 U.S. 446 (2000).

 This rule was explained and applied by the Court in *Coleman v. Thompson*, 501 U.S. 722, 753–55 (1991). Coleman, who was later executed, lost his chance at federal habeas review of several claims after when the state court held they were untimely—his lawyer missed the deadline for appealing his state post-conviction decision by three days. The Supreme Court in rejecting his attempt to establish "cause and prejudice" for the default noted that " 'the existence of cause for a procedural default must ordinarily turn on whether the prisoner can show that some objective factor external to the defense impeded counsel's efforts to comply with the State's procedural rule.' For example, 'a showing that the factual or legal basis for a claim was not reasonably available to counsel, . . . or that 'some interference by officials' . . . made compliance impracticable, would constitute cause under this standard.' " Continued the Court, "Where a petitioner defaults a claim as a result of the denial of the right to effective assistance of counsel, the State, which is responsible for the denial as a constitutional matter, must bear the cost of any resulting default and the harm to state interests that federal habeas review entails. . . . In the absence of a constitutional violation, the petitioner bears the risk in federal habeas for all attorney errors made in the course of the representation." Because Coleman had no constitutional right to counsel for his state collateral appeal, his counsel's mistake, however egregious, did not itself amount to a violation of any constitutional right. Accordingly, there was no "cause" to excuse the default of his claims. Reiterated the Court in *Coleman*: "[C]ounsel's ineffectiveness will constitute cause only if it is an independent constitutional violation."

The Court has not interpreted the Constitution to mandate that states provide counsel during post-conviction proceedings, but many states require that some constitutional claims be raised at that stage and not on direct appeal.[1] Until 2012, this meant that under *Coleman,* absent a showing of actual innocence, see Note 3, 13th ed. p. 1591, a prisoner would receive no federal review of such a claim if his failure to raise it properly in state court was the result of the absence or incompetence of state post-conviction counsel. The Court qualified this rule in *Martinez v. Ryan*, 132 S.Ct. 1309 (2012). In *Martinez,* the Court held that the absence of effective assistance during *initial review* collateral proceedings may establish cause for a prisoner's default of one specific claim—the ineffective assistance of trial counsel—if state law requires prisoners to raise that claim in that collateral proceeding. Writing for a seven-justice majority, Justice Kennedy explained that "where * * * the initial-review collateral proceeding is the first designated proceeding for a prisoner to raise a claim of ineffective assistance at trial, the collateral proceeding is in many ways the equivalent of a prisoner's direct appeal as to the ineffective-assistance claim. * * * To present a claim of ineffective assistance at trial in accordance with the State's procedures, [a claim that often requires investigative work, an understanding of trial strategy, and information outside the trial record], * * * a prisoner likely needs an effective attorney." The Court concluded that "when a State requires a prisoner to raise an ineffective assistance of counsel claim in a collateral proceeding, a prisoner may establish cause for a default of an ineffective assistance claim in two circumstances. The first is where the state courts did not appoint counsel in the initial-review collateral proceeding for a claim of ineffective assistance at trial. The second is where appointed counsel in the initial-review collateral proceeding, where the claim should have been raised, was ineffective under the standards of *Strickland.* To overcome the default, a prisoner must also demonstrate that the underlying ineffective-assistance-of-counsel claim is a substantial one, which is to say that the prisoner must demonstrate that the claim has some merit. Cf. *Miller-El v. Cockrell*, 537 U.S. 322 (2003) (describing standards for certificates of appealability to issue)."

The *Martinez* Court was careful to note that this was an "equitable ruling" not a "constitutional" one. A constitutional ruling would have (1)

---

[1]   In *Massaro v. United States*, 538 U.S. 500 (2003), the Court explained why this rule makes sense: The trial court, in which collateral proceedings are filed, the Court reasoned, is "the forum best suited to developing the facts necessary to determining the adequacy of representation during an entire trial. The court may take testimony from witnesses * * * and from the counsel alleged to have rendered the deficient performance." When presented to the trial court in a post-conviction proceeding, rather than on appeal, the claim "often will be ruled upon by the same * * * judge who presided at trial, [who] should have an advantageous perspective for determining the effectiveness of counsel's conduct and whether any deficiencies were prejudicial." Were defendants required to raise ineffectiveness claims on direct appeal, the Court explained, "trial counsel [would] be unwilling to help appellate counsel familiarize himself with a record for the purpose of understanding how it reflects trial counsel's own incompetence," and "[a]ppellate courts would waste time and resources attempting to address some claims that were meritless and other claims that, though colorable, would be handled more efficiently if addressed in the first instance" by the trial court. See 13th ed., p. 134, Note 7.

created "a free-standing constitutional claim to raise"; (2) "require[d] the appointment of counsel in initial-review collateral proceedings"; (3) "impose[d] the same system of appointing counsel in every State"; and (4) "require[d] a reversal in all state collateral cases on direct review from state courts if the States' system of appointing counsel did not conform to the constitutional rule." Instead, the equitable ruling "permits a State to elect between appointing counsel in initial-review collateral proceedings or not asserting a procedural default and raising a defense on the merits in federal habeas proceedings," and does not affect direct review of state collateral cases. The ineffectiveness of a postconviction attorney is not a "ground for relief," it "merely allows a federal court to consider the merits of a claim that otherwise would have been procedurally defaulted."

The Court also stated that its ruling "does not concern attorney errors in other kinds of proceedings, including appeals from initial-review collateral proceedings," as was the case in *Coleman,* "second or successive collateral proceedings, and petitions for discretionary review in a State's appellate courts." The "limited nature" of the ruling, the Court added, "reflects the importance of the right to the effective assistance of trial counsel," and "addresses only the constitutional claims presented in this case, where the State barred the defendant from raising the claims on direct appeal."

Justice Scalia, joined by Justice Thomas, dissented. He criticized the Court's ruling as essentially forcing states to appoint counsel in post-conviction proceedings, ignoring "the very reason for a procedural-default rule: the comity and respect that federal courts must accord state-court judgments." He argued that the Court had abandoned the "North Star of our excuse-for-cause jurisprudence," namely that attorney error can be cause when it amounts to a factor "external to the petitioner." Lawyer errors are not external unless they amount to "constitutionally ineffective" assistance "imputed to the State (for the State has failed to comply with the constitutional requirement to provide effective counsel)," he reasoned. He also mocked the Court's effort to limit the ruling to ineffective assistance of trial counsel claims, predicting that it will be extended to other claims where a state post-conviction proceeding is the first opportunity to receive review, such as ineffective assistance of *appellate* counsel claims, *Brady* claims, and claims based on newly discovered evidence. By inviting litigation about the effectiveness of post-conviction and trial counsel in all federal habeas cases, he argued, the ruling will "squander[ ] state taxpayers' money" without making much difference in non-capital cases, and will defer execution in every capital case for several more years.

It did not take the Court long to begin to expand the *Martinez* exception, as the dissenters predicted. The very next term in *Trevino v. Thaler,* 133 S.Ct. 1911 (2013), the Court applied the *Martinez* equitable exception to a capital case in Texas, where state law did not "require" petitioners to wait until collateral review to claim ineffective assistance of trial counsel. The Court concluded that the *Martinez* holding applies "where, as here, state procedural framework, by reason of its design and operation, makes it highly unlikely in a typical case that a defendant will have a meaningful opportunity to raise a claim of ineffective assistance of trial counsel on direct appeal." In Texas, the Court reasoned, it is "virtually impossible" for counsel to adequately present this claim on appeal because the trial court record often lacks the necessary facts. Nor are motions for new trial an adequate substitute—such motions must be filed before counsel has an opportunity to review even the trial record. In addition, "Texas courts in effect have directed defendants to raise claims of ineffective assistance of trial counsel on collateral, rather than on direct, review," resulting in only a "comparatively small number of cases in which a defendant has used the motion-for-a-new-trial mechanism to expand the record on appeal and then received a hearing on his ineffective-assistance-of-trial counsel claim on direct appeal."

Assume you are a legislator in a state where the "state procedural framework . . . makes it highly unlikely in a typical case that a defendant will have a meaningful opportunity to raise a claim of ineffective assistance of trial counsel on direct appeal," a phrase that appears to describe the situation in the vast majority of states. How would you evaluate the relative costs and benefits of the following: 1) amending state law to permit meaningful review of ineffective assistance of trial counsel claims on direct appeal, with remand for evidentiary hearings as necessary, 2) providing a statutory right to counsel for petitioners in their initial state post-conviction proceedings; or 3) making no changes to state law and when petitioners raise defaulted ineffective assistance of trial counsel claims in federal habeas proceedings, defending those criminal judgments either by showing that that the claims are not "substantial" under *Martinez*, or by showing that the claims fail on the merits?

For an empirically based argument that states will likely choose the third option, see King, *Enforcing Effective Assistance After* Martinez, 122 Yale L. J. 2428 (2013): "State judges know that strategies far less expensive than hearings and counsel are available to help deflect later attacks in federal habeas," such as "[i]ssuing an alternative ruling on the merits," with or without an affidavit from the petitioner's trial counsel. Moreover, "[m]ost noncapital cases receiving federal habeas relief have been, and will continue to be, cheap to fix. New trial orders are uncommon. A large portion of [ineffective assistance of trial counsel] claims themselves seek only a sentence reduction or an opportunity to appeal. Even relief for a *Lafler* or *Frye* claim only requires amending the judgment to reflect the foregone deal, not a new trial." In states where "judges must enlist appointed counsel from the same pool of attorneys available to represent defendants before conviction or on direct appeal, and pay them from the same funds . . . adding more representation responsibilities in postconviction proceedings is a likely nonstarter. . . . Even if state judges decided to safeguard their convictions against federal review by appointing counsel in postconviction cases, they could safely restrict this strategy to only those petitioners challenging their *convictions* (not their sentences), after a trial (not a plea), and who are serving particularly lengthy sentences. The *Martinez* dissenters' prediction that states will have no choice but to provide counsel in every case is absurd."

Compare Primus, *Effective Trial Counsel after* Martinez v. Ryan: *Focusing on the Adequacy of State Procedures*, 122 Yale L. J. 2604 (2013) (arguing that to avoid the procedural default defense, petitioners should pursue arguments that state procedures for raising ineffectiveness claims are systematically inadequate, and also stating "it is possible that refusing to give state prisoners reasonable opportunities to raise ineffective-assistance-of-trial-counsel claims will push the Supreme Court to recognize the constitutional right to postconviction counsel that it failed to recognize in [*Martinez*]. Alternatively, it might encourage the Court to look to other equitable doctrines to give states more of an incentive to provide defendants with a realistic chance to contend that their Sixth Amendment rights were violated.").

SECTION 5. RETROACTIVITY—WHICH LAW APPLIES?

13th ed., p. 1602; at the end of Note 2, add:

Nevertheless, the Court observed later, quoting *Banks,* " 'the mere existence of a dissent,' like the existence of conflicting authority in state or lower federal courts, does not establish that a rule is new." *Chaidez v. United States*, 133 S.Ct. 1103 (2013).

The Court in *Chaidez* explained that "when all we do is apply a general standard to the kind of factual circumstances it was meant to address, we will rarely state a new rule for *Teague* purposes." For example, "garden-variety applications of the test in *Strickland*," such as *Rompilla* p. 168, and *Wiggins,* p. 167, the Court stated, "do not produce new rules." But *Padilla v. Kentucky*, p. 1315, did not apply *Strickland*'s general standard to yet another factual situation, the Court concluded in *Chaidez*. *Padilla* decided the separate threshold question whether *Strickland* applied at all. "Before *Padilla*, we had declined to decide whether the Sixth Amendment had any relevance to a lawyer's advice about matters not part of a criminal proceeding," said the Court. *Padilla* announced a new rule because it held that advice about deportation was not "categorically removed" from the scope of the Sixth Amendment right to counsel just because it involved only a "collateral consequence" of a conviction.

SECTION 6.   STANDARDS FOR REVIEWING STATE COURT INTERPRETATIONS AND APPLICATIONS OF FEDERAL LAW

A. CONTRARY DECISIONS AND UNREASONABLE APPLICATIONS

13th ed., p. 1607; before the last sentence of Part II, add new footnote a:

a   The Court in *Johnson v. Williams*, 133 S.Ct. 1088 (2013), held that the presumption that a federal claim was adjudicated on the merits should apply not only when a state court did not address any of the defendant's claims, as in *Richter*, but also when the state court addresses some but not all of a defendant's claims. The Court then went on to emphasize "while the *Richter* presumption is a strong one that may be rebutted only in unusual circumstances, it is not irrebuttable." If the state court denies the defendant's claim under a state standard that is either "quite different" or "less protective" than the federal constitutional standard, or "a provision of the Federal Constitution or a federal precedent was simply mentioned in passing in a footnote or was buried in a string cite," the Court explained, "the presumption that the federal claim was adjudicated on the merits may be rebutted—either by the habeas petitioner (for the purpose of showing that the claim should be considered by the federal court *de novo*) or by the State (for the purpose of showing that the federal claim should be regarded as procedurally defaulted)." The Court noted two circumstances that would constitute adequate rebuttal. First, "when a defendant does so little to raise his claim that he fails to ' "fairly present" ' it in 'each appropriate state court,' * * * the *Richter* presumption is fully rebutted." Second, "[w]hen the evidence leads very clearly to the conclusion that a federal claim was inadvertently overlooked in state court, § 2254(d) entitles the prisoner to an unencumbered opportunity to make his case before a federal judge." After reviewing the state court's opinion and Williams' litigation strategy, the Court found that he had not rebutted the presumption, and concluded it was "exceedingly unlikely that the California Court of Appeal overlooked Williams' federal claim."

13th ed., p. 1610; after Note 1, add:

1a.   *Refusing to extend a holding is not unreasonable.* The Court rejected a so-called "unreasonable-refusal-to-extend rule," in *White v. Woodall*, 134 S.Ct. 1697 (2014). "Section 2254(d)(1)," the Court explained, "provides a remedy for instances in which a state court unreasonably applies this Court's precedent; it does not require state courts to extend that precedent or license federal courts to treat the failure to do so as error. Thus, 'if a habeas court must extend a rationale before it can apply to the facts at hand,' then by definition the rationale was not "clearly established at the time of the state-court decision.' AEDPA's carefully constructed framework 'would be undermined if habeas courts introduced rules not clearly established under the guise of extensions to existing law.' * * * This is not to say that § 2254(d)(1) requires an ' "identical factual pattern before a legal rule must be applied." ' To the contrary, state courts must reasonably apply the rules 'squarely established' by this Court's holdings to the facts of each case. * * * The critical point is that relief is available under § 2254(d)(1)'s unreasonable-application clause if, and only if, it is so obvious that a clearly established rule applies to a given set of facts that there could be no 'fairminded disagreement' on the question."

1b. *State court as the "principle forum" for constitutional challenges; the "parity" debate.* The Court in *Burt v. Titlow*, 134 S.Ct. 10 (2013), reiterated (without dissent): "AEDPA recognizes a foundational principle of our federal system: State courts are adequate forums for the vindication of federal rights. * * * 'state courts have the solemn responsibility equally with the federal courts to safeguard constitutional rights,' and this Court has refused to sanction any decision that would 'reflec[t] negatively upon [a] state court's ability to do so.' * * * Especially where a case involves such a common claim as ineffective assistance of counsel under *Strickland*—a claim state courts have now adjudicated in countless criminal cases for nearly 30 years—'there is no intrinsic reason why the fact that a man is a federal judge should make him more competent, or conscientious, or learned . . . than his neighbor in the state courthouse.' " [quoting *Stone v. Powell*, 428 U. S. 465, 494, n. 35 (1976), [13th ed. p 1576]).

A different view of state courts was expressed by Justice Brennan dissenting in *Stone v. Powell*: "State judges popularly elected may have difficulty resisting popular pressures not experienced by federal judges given lifetime tenure designed to immunize them from such influences," he wrote. Others continue to echo such concerns: Carol S. & Steiker & Jordan M. Steiker, *Part II: Report to the Ali Concerning Capital Punishment*, 89 Tex. L. Rev. 367, 392 (2010): "Almost 90% of state judges face some kind of popular election. . . . Despite the fact that there is good reason to have confidence in the personal integrity of the individual men and women who comprise the elected judiciary, several statistical studies suggest that, in the aggregate, judicial behavior in criminal cases generally and capital cases in particular appears to be influenced by election cycles." See also Hon. Lynn Adelman & Jon Deitrich, *Why Habeas Review of State Court Convictions is More Important than Ever*, 24 Fed. Sent. R. 292, 294 (2012) ("habeas review by life-tenured federal judges remains the only viable means of protecting the constitutional rights of the criminally accused in states with an elected judiciary"); Burt Neuborne, *The Myth of Parity*, 90 Harv.L.Rev. 1105 (1977). Should federal habeas law vary depending upon whether a state's judiciary is appointed or elected? For the latest on judicial selection in the states, see www.ajs.org.

13th ed., p. 1611; before Section B, add:

5. *When is a decision "contrary to" clearly established Supreme Court precedent?* Section 2254(d) also authorizes habeas relief for claims rejected on the merits in state court if the state court decision is "contrary to" clearly established Supreme Court precedent. Concurring in *Williams v. Taylor*, 529 U.S. 362, 405–07 (2000), Justice O'Connor, writing for the Court, explained that to fall within the "contrary to" clause, "the state court's decision must be substantially different from the relevant precedent of this Court." She continued:

"A state-court decision will certainly be contrary to our clearly established precedent if the state court applies a rule that contradicts the governing law set forth in our cases. Take, for example, our decision in *Strickland*. . . . If a state court were to reject a prisoner's claim of ineffective assistance of counsel on the grounds that the prisoner had not established by a preponderance of the evidence that the result of his criminal proceeding would have been different, that decision would be 'diametrically different,' 'opposite in character or nature,' and 'mutually opposed' to our clearly established precedent because we held in *Strickland* that the prisoner need only demonstrate a 'reasonable probability that . . . the result of the proceeding would have been different.' A state-court decision will also be contrary to this Court's clearly established precedent if the state court confronts a set of facts that are materially indistinguishable from a decision of this Court and nevertheless arrives at a result different from our precedent. Accordingly, in either of these two scenarios, a federal court will be unconstrained by § 2254(d)(1) because the state-court decision falls within that provision's 'contrary to' clause.

"On the other hand, a run-of-the-mill state-court decision applying the correct legal rule from our cases to the facts of a prisoner's case would not fit comfortably within § 2254(d)(1)'s 'contrary to' clause. Assume, for example, that a state-court decision on a prisoner's ineffective-assistance claim correctly identifies *Strickland* as the controlling legal authority and, applying that framework, rejects the prisoner's claim. Quite clearly, the state-court decision would be in accord with our decision in *Strickland* as to the legal prerequisites for establishing an ineffective-assistance claim, even assuming the federal court considering the prisoner's habeas application might reach a different result applying the *Strickland* framework itself. It is difficult, however, to describe such a run-of-the-mill state-court decision as 'diametrically different' from, 'opposite in character or nature' from, or 'mutually opposed' to *Strickland,* our clearly established precedent. Although the state-court decision may be contrary to the federal court's conception of how *Strickland* ought to be applied in that particular case, the decision is not 'mutually opposed' to *Strickland* itself.

"Justice Stevens would instead construe § 2254(d)(1)'s 'contrary to' clause to encompass such a routine state-court decision. That construction, however, saps the 'unreasonable application' clause of any meaning. If a federal habeas court can, under the 'contrary to' clause, issue the writ whenever it concludes that the state court's *application* of clearly established federal law was incorrect, the 'unreasonable application' clause becomes a nullity."

The latest application of this standard came in *Lafler v. Cooper* [also discussed in this Supp., p. 9 and Supp., p. 157]. The state court decision rejecting Cooper's ineffective assistance of counsel claim read:

"To establish ineffective assistance, the defendant must demonstrate that his counsel's performance fell below an objective standard of reasonableness and that counsel's representation so prejudiced the defendant that he was deprived of a fair trial. With respect to the prejudice aspect of the test, the defendant must demonstrate a reasonable probability that, but for counsel's errors, the result of the proceedings would have been different, and that the attendant proceedings were fundamentally unfair and unreliable.

"Defendant challenges the trial court's finding after a . . . hearing that defense counsel provided effective assistance to defendant during the plea bargaining process. He contends that defense counsel failed to convey the benefits of the plea offer to him and ignored his desire to plead guilty, and that these failures led him to reject a plea offer that he now wishes to accept. However, the record shows that defendant knowingly and intelligently rejected two plea offers and chose to go to trial. The record fails to support defendant's contentions that defense counsel's representation was ineffective because he rejected a defense based on [a] claim of self-defense and because he did not obtain a more favorable plea bargain for defendant."

Writing for the five-justice majority in *Lafler v. Cooper*, Justice Kennedy did not consider whether this state court decision was an unreasonable application of clearly established federal law, but instead found that it was "contrary to" *Strickland*. He explained:

"The Michigan Court of Appeals identified respondent's [ineffective assistance] claim but failed to apply *Strickland* to assess it. Rather than applying *Strickland*, the state court simply found that respondent's rejection of the plea was knowing and voluntary. . . . An inquiry into whether the rejection of a plea is knowing and voluntary, however, is not the correct means by which to address a claim of ineffective assistance of counsel. . . . After stating the incorrect standard, moreover, the state court then made an irrelevant observation about counsel's performance at trial and mischaracterized respondent's claim as a complaint that his attorney did not obtain a more favorable plea bargain. By failing to apply Strickland to assess the claim respondent raised, the state court's adjudication was contrary to clearly established federal law. And in that circumstance the federal courts in this habeas action can determine the principles necessary to grant relief."

The four dissenting justices in *Lafler v. Cooper* thought that the state court had indeed applied the *Strickland* test, and that relief must be denied because the state court's application was not unreasonable. The dissenters noted that the Supreme Court had never before held that a person could establish "prejudice" if plea negotiations ultimately resulted in a fair trial:

The first paragraph [of the state court's analysis], far from ignoring *Strickland*, recites its standard with a good deal more accuracy than the Court's opinion. The second paragraph, which is presumably an application of the standard recited in the first, says that 'defendant knowingly and intelligently rejected two plea offers and chose to go to trial.' This can be regarded as a denial that there was anything 'fundamentally unfair' about

Cooper's conviction and sentence, so that no *Strickland* prejudice had been shown. On the other hand, the entire second paragraph can be regarded as a contention that Cooper's claims of inadequate representation were unsupported by the record. The state court's analysis was admittedly not a model of clarity, but federal habeas corpus is a 'guard against extreme malfunctions in the state criminal justice systems,' not a license to penalize a state court for its opinion-writing technique. *Harrington v. Richter* [13th Edition, p. 1605] . . . Since it is ambiguous whether the state court's holding was based on a lack of prejudice or rather the court's factual determination that there had been no deficient performance, to provide relief under AEDPA this Court must conclude that both holdings would have been unreasonable applications of clearly established law. See *Premo v. Moore*, [13th Edition, Note 2, p. 1310]. The first is impossible of doing, since this Court has never held that a defendant in Cooper's position can establish Strickland prejudice. The Sixth Circuit thus violated AEDPA in granting habeas relief, and the Court now does the same."

Did the *Lafler v. Cooper* Court modify the interpretation of the "contrary to" standard in *Williams*? Consider one author's reaction to the Court's decision:

"*Lafler*'s 'contrary to' analysis leaves the daunting 'unreasonable application' standard of *Richter* in place—both decisions were authored by Justice Kennedy, and the [*Lafler*] Court carefully avoided discussion of the 'unreasonable application' standard. But the decision in *Lafler* appears to have loosened the 'contrary to' standard a notch for future cases, encouraging petitioners to argue that the state court never applied the correct federal precedent (even when that precedent is cited or described), instead of arguing than that the court's application of federal law was unreasonable. The combination of *Lafler* and *Richter* also suggests that when reviewing state court criminal opinions, 'less is more'—a summary state denial will not be disturbed unless all possible (hypothetical) applications would have been unreasonable, while a merits decision accompanied by an ambiguously phrased rationale that could be construed as failing to apply the correct rule is vulnerable to attack." Nancy King, *Lafler v. Cooper* and AEDPA, 122 YALE L.J. ONLINE 35 (2012), http://www.yalelawjournal.org/forum/lafler-v-cooper-and-aedpa.

APPENDIX A

SELECTED PROVISIONS OF THE UNITED STATES CONSTITUTION

■ ■ ■

Section 9.   * * *

[2] The privilege of the Writ of Habeas Corpus shall not be suspended, unless when in Cases of Rebellion or Invasion the public Safety may require it.

[3] No Bill of Attainder or ex post facto Law shall be passed.

ARTICLE III

Section 1.   The judicial Power of the United States, shall be vested in one supreme Court, and in such inferior Courts as the Congress may from time to time ordain and establish. The Judges, both of the supreme and inferior Courts, shall hold their Offices during good Behaviour, and shall, at stated Times, receive for their Services a Compensation, which shall not be diminished during their Continuance in Office.

Section 2.   [1] The judicial Power shall extend to all Cases, in Law and Equity, arising under this Constitution, the Laws of the United States, and Treaties made, or which shall be made, under their Authority;—to all Cases affecting Ambassadors, other public Ministers and Consuls;—to all Cases of admiralty and maritime Jurisdiction;—to Controversies to which the United States shall be a Party;—to Controversies between two or more States;—between a State and Citizens of another State;—between Citizens of different States;—between Citizens of the same State claiming Lands under the Grants of different States, and between a State, or the Citizens thereof, and foreign States, Citizens or Subjects.

[3] The trial of all Crimes, except in Cases of Impeachment, shall be by Jury; and such Trial shall be held in the State where the said Crimes shall have been committed; but when not committed within any State, the Trial shall be at such Place or Places as the Congress may by Law have directed.

Section 3.   [1] Treason against the United States, shall consist only in levying War against them, or, in adhering to their Enemies, giving them Aid and Comfort. No Person shall be convicted of Treason unless on the Testimony of two Witnesses to the same overt Act, or on Confession in open Court.

[2] The Congress shall have Power to declare the Punishment of Treason, but no Attainder of Treason shall work Corruption of Blood, or Forfeiture except during the Life of the Person attainted.

ARTICLE IV

Section 2.   [1] The Citizens of each State shall be entitled to all Privileges and Immunities of Citizens in the several States.

[2] A Person charged in any State with Treason, Felony, or other Crime, who shall flee from Justice, and be found in another State, shall on demand of the executive Authority of the State from which he fled, be delivered up, to be removed to the State having Jurisdiction of the Crime.

ARTICLE VI

[2] This Constitution, and the Laws of the United States which shall be made in Pursuance thereof; and all Treaties made, or which shall be made, under the Authority of the United States, shall be the supreme Law.

AMENDMENT I [1791]

Congress shall make no law respecting an establishment of religion, or prohibiting the free exercise thereof; or abridging the freedom of speech, or of the press; or the right of the people peaceably to assemble, and to petition the Government for a redress of grievances.

AMENDMENT II [1791]

A well regulated Militia, being necessary to the security of a free State, the right of the people to keep and bear Arms, shall not be infringed.

AMENDMENT III [1791]

No Soldier shall, in time of peace be quartered in any house, without the consent of the Owner, nor in time of war, but in a manner to be prescribed by law.

AMENDMENT IV [1791]

The right of the people to be secure in their persons, houses, papers, and effects, against unreasonable searches and seizures, shall not be violated, and no Warrants shall issue, but upon probable cause, supported by Oath or affirmation, and particularly describing the place to be searched, and the persons or things to be seized.

Amendment V [1791]

No person shall be held to answer for a capital, or otherwise infamous crime, unless on a presentment or indictment of a Grand Jury, except in cases arising in the land or naval forces, or in the Militia, when in actual service in time of War or public danger; nor shall any person be subject for the same offence to be twice put in jeopardy of life or limb; nor shall be compelled in any criminal case to be a witness against himself, nor be deprived of life, liberty, or property, without due process of law; nor shall private property be taken for public use, without just compensation.

Amendment VI [1791]

In all criminal prosecutions, the accused shall enjoy the right to a speedy and public trial, by an impartial jury of the State and district wherein the crime shall have been committed, which district shall have been previously ascertained by law, and to be informed of the nature and cause of the accusation; to be confronted with the witnesses against him; to have compulsory process for obtaining witnesses in his favor, and to have the Assistance of Counsel for his defence.

Amendment VII [1791]

In Suits at common law, where the value in controversy shall exceed twenty dollars, the right of trial by jury shall be preserved, and no fact tried by jury, shall be otherwise re-examined in any Court of the United States, than according to the rules of the common law.

Amendment VIII [1791]

Excessive bail shall not be required, nor excessive fines imposed, nor cruel and unusual punishments inflicted.

Amendment IX [1791]

The enumeration in the Constitution, of certain rights, shall not be construed to deny or disparage others retained by the people.

Amendment X [1791]

The powers not delegated to the United States by the Constitution, nor prohibited by it to the States, are reserved to the States respectively, or to the people.

Amendment XIII [1865]

Section 1.   Neither slavery nor involuntary servitude, except as a punishment for crime whereof the party shall have been duly convicted, shall exist within the United States, or any place subject to their jurisdiction.

Section 2. Congress shall have power to enforce this article by appropriate legislation.

AMENDMENT XIV [1868]

Section 1. All persons born or naturalized in the United States, and subject to the jurisdiction thereof, are citizens of the United States and of the State wherein they reside. No State shall make or enforce any law which shall abridge the privileges or immunities of citizens of the United States; nor shall any State deprive any person of life, liberty, or property, without due process of law; nor deny to any person within its jurisdiction the equal protection of the laws.

Section 5. The Congress shall have power to enforce, by appropriate legislation, the provisions of the article.

AMENDMENT XV [1870]

Section 1. The right of citizens of the United States to vote shall not be denied or abridged by the United States or by any State on account of race, color, or previous condition of servitude.

Section 2. The Congress shall have power to enforce this article by appropriate legislation.

APPENDIX B

SELECTED FEDERAL STATUTORY PROVISIONS

■ ■ ■

Analysis

WIRE AND ELECTRONIC COMMUNICATIONS INTERCEPTION AND INTERCEPTION OF ORAL COMMUNICATIONS

(18 U.S.C. §§ 2510–2511, 2515–2518, 2520–2521).

§ 2510. Definitions

As used in this chapter

(1) "wire communication means any aural transfer made in whole or in part through the use of facilities for the transmission of communications by the aid of wire, cable, or other like connection between the point of origin and the point of reception (including the use of such connection in a switching station) furnished or operated by any person engaged in providing or operating such facilities for the transmission of interstate or foreign communications or communications affecting interstate or foreign commerce;

(2) "oral communication" means any oral communication uttered by a person exhibiting an expectation that such communication is not subject to interception under circumstances justifying such expectation, but such term does not include any electronic communication;

(3) "State" means any State of the United States, the District of Columbia, the Commonwealth of Puerto Rico, and any territory or possession of the United States;

(4) "intercept" means the aural or other acquisition of the contents of any wire, electronic, or oral communication through the use of any electronic, mechanical, or other device.

(5) "electronic, mechanical, or other device" means any device or apparatus which can be used to intercept a wire, oral, or electronic communication other than—

(a) any telephone or telegraph instrument, equipment or facility, or any component thereof, (i) furnished to the subscriber or user by a provider of wire or electronic communication service in the ordinary course of its business and being used by the subscriber or user in the ordinary course of its business or furnished by such subscriber or user for connection to the facilities of such service and used in the ordinary course of its business; or (ii) being used by a provider of wire or electronic communication service in the ordinary course of its business, or by an investigative or law enforcement officer in the ordinary course of his duties;

(b) a hearing aid or similar device being used to correct subnormal hearing to not better than normal;

(6) "person" means any employee, or agent of the United States or any State or political subdivision thereof, and any individual, partnership, association, joint stock company, trust, or corporation;

(7) "Investigative or law enforcement officer" means any officer of the United States or of a State or political subdivision thereof, who is empowered by law to conduct investigations of or to make arrests for offenses enumerated in this chapter, and any attorney authorized by law to prosecute or participate in the prosecution of such offenses;

(8) "contents", when used with respect to any wire, oral, or electronic communication, includes any information concerning the substance, purport, or meaning of that communication;

(9) "Judge of competent jurisdiction" means—

(a) a judge of a United States district court or a United States court of appeals; and

(b) a judge of any court of general criminal jurisdiction of a State who is authorized by a statute of that State to enter orders authorizing interceptions of wire, oral, or electronic communications;

(10) "communication common carrier" has the meaning given that term in section 3 of the Communications Act of 1934;

(11) "aggrieved person" means a person who was a party to any intercepted wire, oral, or electronic communication or a person against whom the interception was directed;

(12) "electronic communication" means any transfer of signs, signals, writing, images, sounds, data, or intelligence of any nature transmitted in whole or in part by a wire, radio, electromagnetic, photoelectronic or photooptical system that affects interstate or foreign commerce, but does not include—

(A) any wire or oral communication;

(B) any communication made through a tone-only paging device;

(C) any communication from a tracking device (as defined in section 3117 of this title); or

(D) electronic funds transfer information stored by a financial institution in a communications system used for the electronic storage and transfer of funds;

(13) "user" means any person or entity who—

(A) uses an electronic communication service; and

(B) is duly authorized by the provider of such service to engage in such use;

(14) "electronic communications system" means any wire, radio, electromagnetic, photooptical or photoelectronic facilities for the transmission of wire or electronic communications, and any computer facilities or related electronic equipment for the electronic storage of such communications;

(15) "electronic communication service" means any service which provides to users thereof the ability to send or receive wire or electronic communications;

(16) "readily accessible to the general public" means, with respect to a radio communication, that such communication is not—

(A) scrambled or encrypted;

(B) transmitted using modulation techniques whose essential parameters have been withheld from the public with the intention of preserving the privacy of such communication;

(C) carried on a subcarrier or other signal subsidiary to a radio transmission;

(D) transmitted over a communication system provided by a common carrier, unless the communication is a tone only paging system communication; or

(E) transmitted on frequencies allocated under part 25, subpart D, E, or F of part 74, or part 94 of the Rules of the Federal Communications Commission, unless, in the case of a communication transmitted on a frequency allocated under part 74 that is not exclusively allocated to broadcast auxiliary services, the communication is a two-way voice communication by radio;

(17) "electronic storage" means—

(A) any temporary, intermediate storage of a wire or electronic communication incidental to the electronic transmission thereof; and

(B) any storage of such communication by an electronic communication service for purposes of backup protection of such communication;

(18) "aural transfer" means a transfer containing the human voice at any point between and including the point of origin and the point of reception;

(19) "foreign intelligence information", for purposes of section 2517(6) of this title, means—

(A) information, whether or not concerning a United States person, that relates to the ability of the United States to protect against—

(i) actual or potential attack or other grave hostile acts of a foreign power or an agent of a foreign power;

(ii) sabotage or international terrorism by a foreign power or an agent of a foreign power; or

(iii) clandestine intelligence activities by an intelligence service or network of a foreign power or by an agent of a foreign power; or

(B) information, whether or not concerning a United States person, with respect to a foreign power or foreign territory that relates to—

(i) the national defense or the security of the United States; or

(ii) the conduct of the foreign affairs of the United States;

(20) "protected computer" has the meaning set forth in section 1030; and

(21) "computer trespasser"—

(A) means a person who accesses a protected computer without authorization and thus has no reasonable expectation of privacy in any communication transmitted to, through, or from the protected computer; and

(B) does not include a person known by the owner or operator of the protected computer to have an existing contractual relationship with the owner or operator of the protected computer for access to all or part of the protected computer.

§ 2511. Interception and disclosure of wire, oral, or electronic communications prohibited

(1) Except as otherwise specifically provided in this chapter any person who—

(a) intentionally intercepts, endeavors to intercept, or procures any other person to intercept or endeavor to intercept, any wire, oral, or electronic communication;

(b) intentionally uses, endeavors to use, or procures any other person to use or endeavor to use any electronic, mechanical, or other device to intercept any oral communication when—

(i) such device is affixed to, or otherwise transmits a signal through, a wire, cable, or other like connection used in wire communication; or

(ii) such device transmits communications by radio, or interferes with the transmission of such communication; or

(iii) such person knows, or has reason to know, that such device or any component thereof has been sent through the mail or transported in interstate or foreign commerce; or

(iv) such use or endeavor to use (A) takes place on the premises of any business or other commercial establishment the operations of which affect interstate or foreign commerce; or (B) obtains or is for the purpose of obtaining information relating to the operations of any business or other commercial establishment the operations of which affect interstate or foreign commerce; or

(v) such person acts in the District of Columbia, the Commonwealth of Puerto Rico, or any territory or possession of the United States;

(c) intentionally discloses, or endeavors to disclose, to any other person the contents of any wire, oral, or electronic communication, knowing or having reason to know that the information was obtained through the interception of a wire, oral, or electronic communication in violation of this subsection;

(d) intentionally uses, or endeavors to use, the contents of any wire, oral, or electronic communication, knowing or having reason to know that the information was obtained through the interception of a wire, oral, or electronic communication in violation of this subsection; or

(e)(i) intentionally discloses, or endeavors to disclose, to any other person the contents of any wire, oral, or electronic communication, intercepted by means authorized by sections 2511(2)(a)(ii), 2511(2)(b)–(c), 2511(2)(e), 2516, and 2518 of this chapter, (ii) knowing or having reason to know that the information was obtained through the interception of such a communication in connection with a criminal investigation, (iii) having obtained or received the information in connection with a criminal investigation, and (iv) with intent to improperly obstruct, impede, or interfere with a duly authorized criminal investigation,

shall be punished as provided in subsection (4) or shall be subject to suit as provided in subsection (5).

(2)(a)(i) It shall not be unlawful under this chapter for an operator of a switchboard, or an officer, employee, or agent of a provider of wire or electronic communication service, whose facilities are used in the transmission of a wire or electronic communication, to intercept, disclose, or use that communication in the normal course of his employment while engaged in any activity which is a necessary incident to the rendition of his service or to the protection of the rights or property of the provider of that service, except that a provider of wire communication service to the public shall not utilize service observing or random monitoring except for mechanical or service quality control checks.

(ii) Notwithstanding any other law, providers of wire or electronic communication service, their officers, employees, and agents, landlords, custodians, or other persons, are authorized to provide information, facilities, or technical assistance to persons authorized by law to intercept wire, oral, or electronic communications or to conduct electronic surveillance, as defined in section 101 of the Foreign Intelligence Surveillance Act of 1978, if such provider, its officers, employees, or agents, landlord, custodian, or other specified person, has been provided with—

(A) a court order directing such assistance or a court order pursuant to section 704 of the Foreign Intelligence Surveillance Act of 1978 signed by the authorizing judge, or

(B) a certification in writing by a person specified in section 2518(7) of this title or the Attorney General of the United States that no warrant or court order is required by law, that all statutory requirements have been met, and that the specified assistance is required,

setting forth the period of time during which the provision of the information, facilities, or technical assistance is authorized and specifying the information, facilities, or technical assistance required. No provider of wire or electronic communication service, officer, employee, or agent thereof, or landlord, custodian, or other specified person shall disclose the existence of any interception or surveillance or the device used to accomplish the interception or surveillance with respect to which the person has been furnished a court order or certification under this chapter, except as may otherwise be required by legal process and then only after prior notification to the Attorney General or to the principal prosecuting attorney of a State or any political subdivision of a State, as may be appropriate. Any such disclosure, shall render such person liable for the civil damages provided for in section 2520. No cause of action shall lie in any court against any provider of wire or electronic communication service, its officers, employees, or agents, landlord, custodian, or other specified person for providing information, facilities, or assistance in accordance with the terms of a court order, statutory authorization, or certification under this chapter.

(iii) If a certification under subparagraph (ii)(B) for assistance to obtain foreign intelligence information is based on statutory authority, the certification shall identify the specific statutory provision and shall certify that the statutory requirements have been met.

(b) It shall not be unlawful under this chapter for an officer, employee, or agent of the Federal Communications Commission, in the normal course of his employment and in discharge of the monitoring responsibilities exercised by the Commission in the enforcement of chapter 5 of title 47 of the United States Code, to intercept a wire or electronic communication, or oral communication transmitted by radio, or to disclose or use the information thereby obtained.

(c) It shall not be unlawful under this chapter for a person acting under color of law to intercept a wire, oral, or electronic communication, where such person is a party to the communication or one of the parties to the communication has given prior consent to such interception.

(d) It shall not be unlawful under this chapter for a person not acting under color of law to intercept a wire, oral, or electronic communication where such person is a party to the communication or where one of the parties to the communication has given prior consent to such interception unless such communication is intercepted for the purpose of committing any criminal or tortious act in violation of the Constitution or laws of the United States or of any State.

(e) Notwithstanding any other provision of this title or section 705 or 706 of the Communications Act of 1934, it shall not be unlawful for an officer, employee, or agent of the United States in the normal course of his official duty to conduct electronic surveillance, as defined in section 101 of the Foreign Intelligence Surveillance Act of 1978, as authorized by that Act.

(f) Nothing contained in this chapter or chapter 121 or 206 of this title, or section 705 of the Communications Act of 1934, shall be deemed to affect the acquisition by the United States Government of foreign intelligence information from international or foreign communications, or foreign intelligence activities conducted in accordance with otherwise applicable Federal law involving a foreign electronic communications system, utilizing a means other than electronic surveillance as defined in section 101 of the Foreign Intelligence Surveillance Act of 1978, and procedures in this chapter or chapter 121 and the Foreign Intelligence Surveillance Act of 1978 shall be the exclusive means by which electronic surveillance, as defined in section 101 of such Act, and the interception of domestic wire, oral, and electronic communications may be conducted.

(g) It shall not be unlawful under this chapter or chapter 121 of this title for any person—

(i) to intercept or access an electronic communication made through an electronic communication system that is configured so that such electronic communication is readily accessible to the general public;

(ii) to intercept any radio communication which is transmitted—

(I) by any station for the use of the general public, or that relates to ships, aircraft, vehicles, or persons in distress;

(II) by any governmental, law enforcement, civil defense, private land mobile, or public safety communications system, including police and fire, readily accessible to the general public;

(III) by a station operating on an authorized frequency within the bands allocated to the amateur, citizens band, or general mobile radio services; or

(IV) by any marine or aeronautical communications system;

(iii) to engage in any conduct which—

(I) is prohibited by section 633 of the Communications Act of 1934; or

(II) is excepted from the application of section 705(a) of the Communications Act of 1934 by section 705(b) of that Act;

(iv) to intercept any wire or electronic communication the transmission of which is causing harmful interference to any lawfully operating station or consumer electronic equipment, to the extent necessary to identify the source of such interference; or

(v) for other users of the same frequency to intercept any radio communication made through a system that utilizes frequencies monitored by individuals engaged in the provision or the use of such system, if such communication is not scrambled or encrypted.

(h) It shall not be unlawful under this chapter—

(i) to use a pen register or a trap and trace device (as those terms are defined for the purposes of chapter 206 (relating to pen registers and trap and trace devices) of this title); or

(ii) for a provider of electronic communication service to record the fact that a wire or electronic communication was initiated or completed in order to protect such provider, another provider furnishing service toward the completion of the wire or electronic communication, or a user of that service, from fraudulent, unlawful or abusive use of such service.

(i) It shall not be unlawful under this chapter for a person acting under color of law to intercept the wire or electronic communications of a computer trespasser transmitted to, through, or from the protected computer, if—

(I) the owner or operator of the protected computer authorizes the interception of the computer trespasser's communications on the protected computer;

(II) the person acting under color of law is lawfully engaged in an investigation;

(III) the person acting under color of law has reasonable grounds to believe that the contents of the computer trespasser's communications will be relevant to the investigation; and

(IV) such interception does not acquire communications other than those transmitted to or from the computer trespasser.

(3)(a) Except as provided in paragraph (b) of this subsection, a person or entity providing an electronic communication service to the public shall not intentionally divulge the contents of any communication (other than one to such person or entity, or an agent thereof) while in transmission on that service to any person or entity other than an addressee or intended recipient of such communication or an agent of such addressee or intended recipient.

(b) A person or entity providing electronic communication service to the public may divulge the contents of any such communication—

(i) as otherwise authorized in section 2511(2)(a) or 2517 of this title;

(ii) with the lawful consent of the originator or any addressee or intended recipient of such communication;

(iii) to a person employed or authorized, or whose facilities are used, to forward such communication to its destination; or

(iv) which were inadvertently obtained by the service provider and which appear to pertain to the commission of a crime, if such divulgence is made to a law enforcement agency.

(4)(a) Except as provided in paragraph (b) of this subsection or in subsection (5), whoever violates subsection (1) of this section shall be fined under this title or imprisoned not more than five years, or both.

(b) Conduct otherwise an offense under this subsection that consists of or relates to the interception of a satellite transmission that is not encrypted or scrambled and that is transmitted—

(i) to a broadcasting station for purposes of retransmission to the general public; or

(ii) as an audio subcarrier intended for redistribution to facilities open to the public, but not including data transmissions or telephone calls,

is not an offense under this subsection unless the conduct is for the purposes of direct or indirect commercial advantage or private financial gain.

[(c) Redesignated (b)]

(5)(a)(i) If the communication is—

(A) a private satellite video communication that is not scrambled or encrypted and the conduct in violation of this chapter is the private viewing of that communication and is not for a tortious or illegal purpose or for purposes of direct or indirect commercial advantage or private commercial gain; or

(B) a radio communication that is transmitted on frequencies allocated under subpart D of part 74 of the rules of the Federal Communications Commission that is not scrambled or encrypted and the conduct in violation of this chapter is not for a tortious or illegal purpose or for purposes of direct or indirect commercial advantage or private commercial gain,

then the person who engages in such conduct shall be subject to suit by the Federal Government in a court of competent jurisdiction.

(ii) In an action under this subsection—

(A) if the violation of this chapter is a first offense for the person under paragraph (a) of subsection (4) and such person has not been found liable in a civil action under section 2520 of this title, the Federal Government shall be entitled to appropriate injunctive relief; and

(B) if the violation of this chapter is a second or subsequent offense under paragraph (a) of subsection (4) or such person has been found liable in any prior civil action under section 2520, the person shall be subject to a mandatory $500 civil fine.

(b) The court may use any means within its authority to enforce an injunction issued under paragraph (ii)(A), and shall impose a civil fine of not less than $500 for each violation of such an injunction.

§ 2515. Prohibition of use as evidence of intercepted wire or oral communications

Whenever any wire or oral communication has been intercepted, no part of the contents of such communication and no evidence derived therefrom may be received in evidence in any trial, hearing, or other proceeding in or before any court, grand jury, department, officer, agency, regulatory body, legislative committee, or other authority of the United States, a State, or a political subdivision thereof if the disclosure of that information would be in violation of this chapter.

§ 2516. Authorization for interception of wire, oral, or electronic communications

(1) The Attorney General, Deputy Attorney General, Associate Attorney General, or any Assistant Attorney General, any acting Assistant Attorney General, or any Deputy Assistant Attorney General or acting Deputy Assistant Attorney General in the Criminal Division or National Security Division specially designated by the Attorney General, may authorize an application to a Federal judge of competent jurisdiction for, and such judge may grant in conformity with section 2518 of this chapter an order authorizing or approving the interception of wire or oral communications by the Federal Bureau of Investigation, or a Federal agency having responsibility for the investigation of the offense as to which the application is made, when such interception may provide or has provided evidence of—

(a) any offense punishable by death or by imprisonment for more than one year under sections 2122 and 2274 through 2277 of title 42 of the United States Code (relating to the enforcement of the Atomic Energy Act of 1954), section 2284 of title 42 of the United States Code (relating to sabotage of nuclear facilities or fuel), or under the following chapters of this title: chapter 10 (relating to biological weapons), chapter 37 (relating to espionage), chapter 55 (relating to kidnapping), chapter 90 (relating to protection of trade secrets), chapter 105 (relating to sabotage), chapter 115 (relating to treason), chapter 102 (relating to riots), chapter 65 (relating to malicious mischief), chapter 111 (relating to destruction of vessels), or chapter 81 (relating to piracy);

(b) a violation of section 186 or section 501(c) of title 29, United States Code (dealing with restrictions on payments and loans to labor organizations), or any offense which involves murder, kidnapping, robbery, or extortion, and which is punishable under this title;

(c) any offense which is punishable under the following sections of this title: section 37 (relating to violence at international airports), section 43 (relating to animal enterprise terrorism), section 81 (arson within special maritime and territorial jurisdiction), section 201 (bribery of public officials and witnesses), section 215 (relating to bribery of bank officials), section 224 (bribery in sporting contests), subsection (d), (e), (f), (g), (h), or (i) of section 844 (unlawful use of explosives), section 1032 (relating to concealment of assets), section 1084 (transmission of wagering information), section 751 (relating to escape), section 832 (relating to nuclear and weapons of mass destruction threats), section 842 (relating to explosive materials), section 930 (relating to possession of weapons in Federal facilities), section 1014 (relating to loans and credit applications generally; renewals and discounts), section 1114 (relating to officers and employees of the United States), section 1116 (relating to protection of foreign officials), sections 1503, 1512, and 1513 (influencing or injuring an officer, juror, or witness generally), section 1510 (obstruction of criminal investigations), section 1511 (obstruction of State or local law enforcement), section 1591 (sex trafficking of children by force, fraud, or coercion), section 1751 (Presidential and Presidential staff assassination, kidnapping, and assault), section 1951 (interference with commerce by threats or violence), section 1952 (interstate and foreign travel or transportation in aid of racketeering enterprises), section 1958 (relating to use of interstate commerce facilities in the commission of murder for hire), section 1959 (relating to violent crimes in aid of racketeering activity), section 1954 (offer, acceptance, or solicitation to influence operations of employee benefit plan), section 1955 (prohibition of business enterprises of gambling), section 1956 (laundering of monetary instruments), section 1957 (relating to engaging in monetary transactions in property derived from specified unlawful activity), section 659 (theft from interstate shipment), section 664 (embezzlement from pension and welfare funds), section 1343 (fraud by wire, radio, or television), section 1344 (relating to bank fraud), section 1992 (relating to terrorist attacks against mass transportation), sections 2251 and 2252 (sexual exploitation of children), section 2251A (selling or buying of children), section 2252A (relating to material constituting or containing child pornography), section 1466A (relating to child obscenity), section 2260 (production of sexually explicit depictions of a minor for importation into the United States), sections 2421, 2422, 2423, and 2425 (relating to transportation for illegal sexual activity and related crimes), sections 2312, 2313, 2314, and 2315 (interstate transportation of stolen property), section 2321 (relating to trafficking in certain motor vehicles or motor vehicle parts), section 2340A (relating to torture), section 1203 (relating to hostage taking), section 1029 (relating to fraud and related activity in connection with access devices), section 3146 (relating to penalty for failure to appear), section 3521(b)(3) (relating to witness relocation and assistance), section 32 (relating to destruction of aircraft or aircraft facilities), section 38 (relating to aircraft parts fraud), section 1963 (violations with respect to racketeer influenced and corrupt organizations), section 115 (relating to threatening or retaliating against a Federal official), section 1341 (relating to mail fraud), a felony violation of section 1030 (relating to computer fraud and abuse), section 351 (violations with respect to congressional, Cabinet, or Supreme Court assassinations, kidnapping, and assault), section 831 (relating to prohibited transactions involving nuclear materials), section 33 (relating to destruction of motor vehicles or motor vehicle facilities), section 175 (relating to biological weapons), section 175c (relating to variola virus), section 956 (conspiracy to harm persons or property overseas), a felony violation of section 1028 (relating to production of false identification documentation), section 1425 (relating to the procurement of citizenship or nationalization unlawfully), section 1426 (relating to the reproduction of naturalization or citizenship papers), section 1427 (relating to the sale of naturalization or citizenship papers), section 1541 (relating to passport issuance without authority), section 1542 (relating to false statements in passport applications), section 1543 (relating to forgery or false use of passports), section 1544 (relating to misuse of passports), or section 1546 (relating to fraud and misuse of visas, permits, and other documents), section 555 (relating to construction or use of international border tunnels);

(d) any offense involving counterfeiting punishable under section 471, 472, or 473 of this title;

(e) any offense involving fraud connected with a case under title 11 or the manufacture, importation, receiving, concealment, buying, selling, or otherwise dealing in narcotic drugs, marihuana, or other dangerous drugs, punishable under any law of the United States;

(f) any offense including extortionate credit transactions under sections 892, 893, or 894 of this title;

(g) a violation of section 5322 of title 31, United States Code (dealing with the reporting of currency transactions), or section 5324 of title 31, United States Code (relating to structuring transactions to evade reporting requirement prohibited);

(h) any felony violation of sections 2511 and 2512 (relating to interception and disclosure of certain communications and to certain intercepting devices) of this title;

(i) any felony violation of chapter 71 (relating to obscenity) of this title;

(j) any violation of section 60123(b) (relating to destruction of a natural gas pipeline), section 46502 (relating to aircraft piracy), the second sentence of section 46504 (relating to assault on a flight crew with dangerous weapon), or section 46505(b)(3) or (c) (relating to explosive or incendiary devices, or endangerment of human life, by means of weapons on aircraft) of title 49;

(k) any criminal violation of section 2778 of title 22 (relating to the Arms Export Control Act);

(l) the location of any fugitive from justice from an offense described in this section;

(m) a violation of section 274, 277, or 278 of the Immigration and Nationality Act (8 U.S.C. 1324, 1327, or 1328) (relating to the smuggling of aliens);

(n) any felony violation of sections 922 and 924 of title 18, United States Code (relating to firearms);

(o) any violation of section 5861 of the Internal Revenue Code of 1986 (relating to firearms);

(p) a felony violation of section 1028 (relating to production of false identification documents), section 1542 (relating to false statements in passport applications), section 1546 (relating to fraud and misuse of visas, permits, and other documents), section 1028A (relating to aggravated identity theft) of this title or a violation of section 274, 277, or 278 of the Immigration and Nationality Act (relating to the smuggling of aliens);

(q) any criminal violation of section 229 (relating to chemical weapons) or section 2332, 2332a, 2332b, 2332d, 2332f, 2332g, 2332h, 2339, 2339A, 2339B, 2339C, or 2339D of this title (related to terrorism);

(r) any criminal violation of section 1 (relating to illegal restraints of trade or commerce), 2 (relating to illegal monopolizing of trade or commerce), or 3 (relating to illegal restraints of trade or commerce in territories or the District of Columbia) of the Sherman Act (15 U.S.C. 1, 2, 3);

(s) any violation of section 670 (relating to theft of medical products); or

(t) any conspiracy to commit any offense described in any subparagraph of this paragraph.

(2) The principal prosecuting attorney of any State, or the principal prosecuting attorney of any political subdivision thereof, if such attorney is authorized by a statute of that State to make application to a State court judge of competent jurisdiction for an order authorizing or approving the interception of wire, oral, or electronic communications, may apply to such judge for, and such judge may grant in conformity with section 2518 of this chapter and with the applicable State statute an order authorizing, or approving the interception of wire, oral, or electronic communications by investigative or law enforcement officers having responsibility for the investigation of the offense as to which the application is made, when such interception may provide or has provided evidence of the commission of the offense of murder, kidnapping, gambling, robbery, bribery, extortion, or dealing in narcotic drugs, marihuana or other dangerous drugs, or other crime dangerous to life, limb, or property, and punishable by imprisonment for more than one year, designated in any applicable State statute authorizing such interception, or any conspiracy to commit any of the foregoing offenses.

(3) Any attorney for the Government (as such term is defined for the purposes of the Federal Rules of Criminal Procedure) may authorize an application to a Federal judge of competent jurisdiction for, and such judge may grant, in conformity with section 2518 of this title, an order authorizing or approving the interception of electronic communications by an investigative or law enforcement officer having responsibility for the investigation of the offense as to which the application is made, when such interception may provide or has provided evidence of any Federal felony.

§ 2517. Authorization for disclosure and use of intercepted wire, oral, or electronic communications

(1) Any investigative or law enforcement officer who, by any means authorized by this chapter, has obtained knowledge of the contents of any wire, oral, or electronic communication, or evidence derived therefrom, may disclose such contents to another investigative or law enforcement officer to the extent that such disclosure is appropriate to the proper performance of the official duties of the officer making or receiving the disclosure.

(2) Any investigative or law enforcement officer who, by any means authorized by this chapter, has obtained knowledge of the contents of any wire, oral, or electronic communication or evidence derived therefrom may use such contents to the extent such use is appropriate to the proper performance of his official duties.

(3) Any person who has received, by any means authorized by this chapter, any information concerning a wire, oral, or electronic communication, or evidence derived therefrom intercepted in accordance with the provisions of this chapter may disclose the contents of that communication or such derivative evidence while giving testimony under oath or affirmation in any proceeding held under the authority of the United States or of any State or political subdivision thereof.

(4) No otherwise privileged wire, oral, or electronic communication intercepted in accordance with, or in violation of, the provisions of this chapter shall lose its privileged character.

(5) When an investigative or law enforcement officer, while engaged in intercepting wire, oral, or electronic communications in the manner authorized herein, intercepts wire, oral, or electronic communications relating to offenses other than those specified in the order of authorization or approval, the contents thereof, and evidence derived therefrom, may be disclosed or used as provided in subsections (1) and (2) of this section. Such contents and any evidence derived therefrom may be used under subsection (3) of this section when authorized or approved by a judge of competent jurisdiction where such judge finds on subsequent application that the contents were otherwise intercepted in accordance with the provisions of this chapter. Such application shall be made as soon as practicable.

(6) Any investigative or law enforcement officer, or attorney for the Government, who by any means authorized by this chapter, has obtained knowledge of the contents of any wire, oral, or electronic communication, or evidence derived therefrom, may disclose such contents to any other Federal law enforcement, intelligence, protective, immigration, national defense, or national security official to the extent that such contents include foreign intelligence or counterintelligence (as defined in section 3

of the National Security Act of 1947 (50 U.S.C. 401a)), or foreign intelligence information (as defined in subsection (19) of section 2510 of this title), to assist the official who is to receive that information in the performance of his official duties. Any Federal official who receives information pursuant to this provision may use that information only as necessary in the conduct of that person's official duties subject to any limitations on the unauthorized disclosure of such information.

(7) Any investigative or law enforcement officer, or other Federal official in carrying out official duties as such Federal official, who by any means authorized by this chapter, has obtained knowledge of the contents of any wire, oral, or electronic communication, or evidence derived therefrom, may disclose such contents or derivative evidence to a foreign investigative or law enforcement officer to the extent that such disclosure is appropriate to the proper performance of the official duties of the officer making or receiving the disclosure, and foreign investigative or law enforcement officers may use or disclose such contents or derivative evidence to the extent such use or disclosure is appropriate to the proper performance of their official duties.

(8) Any investigative or law enforcement officer, or other Federal official in carrying out official duties as such Federal official, who by any means authorized by this chapter, has obtained knowledge of the contents of any wire, oral, or electronic communication, or evidence derived therefrom, may disclose such contents or derivative evidence to any appropriate Federal, State, local, or foreign government official to the extent that such contents or derivative evidence reveals a threat of actual or potential attack or other grave hostile acts of a foreign power or an agent of a foreign power, domestic or international sabotage, domestic or international terrorism, or clandestine intelligence gathering activities by an intelligence service or network of a foreign power or by an agent of a foreign power, within the United States or elsewhere, for the purpose of preventing or responding to such a threat. Any official who receives information pursuant to this provision may use that information only as necessary in the conduct of that person's official duties subject to any limitations on the unauthorized disclosure of such information, and any State, local, or foreign official who receives information pursuant to this provision may use that information only consistent with such guidelines as the Attorney General and Director of Central Intelligence shall jointly issue.

§ 2518. Procedure for interception of wire, oral, or electronic communications

(1) Each application for an order authorizing or approving the interception of a wire, oral, or electronic communication under this chapter shall be made in writing upon oath or affirmation to a judge of

competent jurisdiction and shall state the applicant's authority to make such application. Each application shall include the following information:

(a) the identity of the investigative or law enforcement officer making the application, and the officer authorizing the application;

(b) a full and complete statement of the facts and circumstances relied upon by the applicant, to justify his belief that an order should be issued, including (i) details as to the particular offense that has been, is being, or is about to be committed, (ii) except as provided in subsection (11), a particular description of the nature and location of the facilities from which or the place where the communication is to be intercepted, (iii) a particular description of the type of communications sought to be intercepted, (iv) the identity of the person, if known, committing the offense and whose communications are to be intercepted;

(c) a full and complete statement as to whether or not other investigative procedures have been tried and failed or why they reasonably appear to be unlikely to succeed if tried or to be too dangerous;

(d) a statement of the period of time for which the interception is required to be maintained. If the nature of the investigation is such that the authorization for interception should not automatically terminate when the described type of communication has been first obtained, a particular description of facts establishing probable cause to believe that additional communications of the same type will occur thereafter;

(e) a full and complete statement of the facts concerning all previous applications known to the individual authorizing and making the application, made to any judge for authorization to intercept, or for approval of interceptions of, wire, oral, or electronic communications involving any of the same persons, facilities or places specified in the application, and the action taken by the judge on each such application; and

(f) where the application is for the extension of an order, a statement setting forth the results thus far obtained from the interception, or a reasonable explanation of the failure to obtain such results.

(2) The judge may require the applicant to furnish additional testimony or documentary evidence in support of the application.

(3) Upon such application the judge may enter an ex parte order, as requested or as modified, authorizing or approving interception of wire,

oral, or electronic communications within the territorial jurisdiction of the court in which the judge is sitting (and outside that jurisdiction but within the United States in the case of a mobile interception device authorized by a Federal court within such jurisdiction), if the judge determines on the basis of the facts submitted by the applicant that—

    (a) there is probable cause for belief that an individual is committing, has committed, or is about to commit a particular offense enumerated in section 2516 of this chapter;

    (b) there is probable cause for belief that particular communications concerning that offense will be obtained through such interception;

    (c) normal investigative procedures have been tried and have failed or reasonably appear to be unlikely to succeed if tried or to be too dangerous;

    (d) except as provided in subsection (11), there is probable cause for belief that the facilities from which, or the place where, the wire, oral, or electronic communications are to be intercepted are being used, or are about to be used, in connection with the commission of such offense, or are leased to, listed in the name of, or commonly used by such person.

(4) Each order authorizing or approving the interception of any wire, oral, or electronic communication under this chapter shall specify—

    (a) the identity of the person, if known, whose communications are to be intercepted;

    (b) the nature and location of the communications facilities as to which, or the place where, authority to intercept is granted;

    (c) a particular description of the type of communication sought to be intercepted, and a statement of the particular offense to which it relates;

    (d) the identity of the agency authorized to intercept the communications, and of the person authorizing the application; and

    (e) the period of time during which such interception is authorized, including a statement as to whether or not the interception shall automatically terminate when the described communication has been first obtained.

An order authorizing the interception of a wire, oral, or electronic communication under this chapter shall, upon request of the applicant, direct that a provider of wire or electronic communication service, landlord, custodian or other person shall furnish the applicant forthwith all information, facilities, and technical assistance necessary to accomplish the interception unobtrusively and with a minimum of interference with the services that such service provider, landlord, custodian, or person is according the person whose communications are to be intercepted. Any provider of wire or electronic communication service, landlord, custodian or other person furnishing such facilities or technical assistance shall be compensated therefor by the applicant for reasonable expenses incurred in providing such facilities or assistance. Pursuant to section 2522 of this chapter, an order may also be issued to enforce the assistance capability and capacity requirements under the Communications Assistance for Law Enforcement Act.

(5) No order entered under this section may authorize or approve the interception of any wire, oral, or electronic communication for any period longer than is necessary to achieve the objective of the authorization, nor in any event longer than thirty days. Such thirty-day period begins on the earlier of the day on which the investigative or law enforcement officer first begins to conduct an interception under the order or ten days after the order is entered. Extensions of an order may be granted, but only upon application for an extension made in accordance with subsection (1) of this section and the court making the findings required by subsection (3) of this section. The period of extension shall be no longer than the authorizing judge deems necessary to achieve the purposes for which it was granted and in no event for longer than thirty days. Every order and extension thereof shall contain a provision that the authorization to intercept shall be executed as soon as practicable, shall be conducted in such a way as to minimize the interception of communications not otherwise subject to interception under this chapter, and must terminate upon attainment of the authorized objective, or in any event in thirty days. In the event the intercepted communication is in a code or foreign language, and an expert in that foreign language or code is not reasonably available during the interception period, minimization may be accomplished as soon as practicable after such interception. An interception under this chapter may be conducted in whole or in part by Government personnel, or by an individual operating under a contract with the Government, acting under the supervision of an investigative or law enforcement officer authorized to conduct the interception.

(6) Whenever an order authorizing interception is entered pursuant to this chapter, the order may require reports to be made to the judge who issued the order showing what progress has been made toward achievement of the authorized objective and the need for continued interception. Such reports shall be made at such intervals as the judge may require.

(7) Notwithstanding any other provision of this chapter, any investigative or law enforcement officer, specially designated by the Attorney General, the Deputy Attorney General, the Associate Attorney

General, or by the principal prosecuting attorney of any State or subdivision thereof acting pursuant to a statute of that State, who reasonably determines that—

(a) an emergency situation exists that involves—

(i) immediate danger of death or serious physical injury to any person,

(ii) conspiratorial activities threatening the national security interest, or

(iii) conspiratorial activities characteristic of organized crime,

that requires a wire, oral, or electronic communication to be intercepted before an order authorizing such interception can, with due diligence, be obtained, and

(b) there are grounds upon which an order could be entered under this chapter to authorize such interception,

may intercept such wire, oral, or electronic communication if an application for an order approving the interception is made in accordance with this section within forty-eight hours after the interception has occurred, or begins to occur. In the absence of an order, such interception shall immediately terminate when the communication sought is obtained or when the application for the order is denied, whichever is earlier. In the event such application for approval is denied, or in any other case where the interception is terminated without an order having been issued, the contents of any wire, oral, or electronic communication intercepted shall be treated as having been obtained in violation of this chapter, and an inventory shall be served as provided for in subsection (d) of this section on the person named in the application.

(8) (a) The contents of any wire, oral, or electronic communication intercepted by any means authorized by this chapter shall, if possible, be recorded on tape or wire or other comparable device. The recording of the contents of any wire, oral, or electronic communication under this subsection shall be done in such a way as will protect the recording from editing or other alterations. Immediately upon the expiration of the period of the order, or extensions thereof, such recordings shall be made available to the judge issuing such order and sealed under his directions. Custody of the recordings shall be wherever the judge orders. They shall not be destroyed except upon an order of the issuing or denying judge and in any event shall be kept for ten years. Duplicate recordings may be made for use or disclosure pursuant to the provisions of subsections (1) and (2) of section 2517 of this chapter for investigations. The presence of the seal provided for by this subsection, or a satisfactory explanation for the absence thereof, shall be a prerequisite for the use or disclosure of the

contents of any wire, oral, or electronic communication or evidence derived therefrom under subsection (3) of section 2517.

(b) Applications made and orders granted under this chapter shall be sealed by the judge. Custody of the applications and orders shall be wherever the judge directs. Such applications and orders shall be disclosed only upon a showing of good cause before a judge of competent jurisdiction and shall not be destroyed except on order of the issuing or denying judge, and in any event shall be kept for ten years.

(c) Any violation of the provisions of this subsection may be punished as contempt of the issuing or denying judge.

(d) Within a reasonable time but not later than ninety days after the filing of an application for an order of approval under section 2518(7)(b) which is denied or the termination of the period of an order or extensions thereof, the issuing or denying judge shall cause to be served, on the persons named in the order or the application, and such other parties to intercepted communications as the judge may determine in his discretion that is in the interest of justice, an inventory which shall include notice of—

(1) the fact of the entry of the order or the application;

(2) the date of the entry and the period of authorized, approved or disapproved interception, or the denial of the application; and

(3) the fact that during the period wire, oral, or electronic communications were or were not intercepted.

The judge, upon the filing of a motion, may in his discretion make available to such person or his counsel for inspection such portions of the intercepted communications, applications and orders as the judge determines to be in the interest of justice. On an ex parte showing of good cause to a judge of competent jurisdiction the serving of the inventory required by this subsection may be postponed.

(9) The contents of any wire, oral, or electronic communication intercepted pursuant to this chapter or evidence derived therefrom shall not be received in evidence or otherwise disclosed in any trial, hearing, or other proceeding in a Federal or State court unless each party, not less than ten days before the trial, hearing, or proceeding, has been furnished with a copy of the court order, and accompanying application, under which the interception was authorized or approved. This ten-day period may be waived by the judge if he finds that it was not possible to furnish the party with the above information ten days before the trial, hearing, or proceeding and that the party will not be prejudiced by the delay in receiving such information.

(10)(a) Any aggrieved person in any trial, hearing, or proceeding in or before any court, department, officer, agency, regulatory body, or other authority of the United States, a State, or a political subdivision thereof, may move to suppress the contents of any wire or oral communication intercepted pursuant to this chapter, or evidence derived therefrom, on the grounds that—

(i) the communication was unlawfully intercepted;

(ii) the order of authorization or approval under which it was intercepted is insufficient on its face; or

(iii) the interception was not made in conformity with the order of authorization or approval.

Such motion shall be made before the trial, hearing, or proceeding unless there was no opportunity to make such motion or the person was not aware of the grounds of the motion. If the motion is granted, the contents of the intercepted wire or oral communication, or evidence derived therefrom, shall be treated as having been obtained in violation of this chapter. The judge, upon the filing of such motion by the aggrieved person, may in his discretion make available to the aggrieved person or his counsel for inspection such portions of the intercepted communication or evidence derived therefrom as the judge determines to be in the interests of justice.

(b) In addition to any other right to appeal, the United States shall have the right to appeal from an order granting a motion to suppress made under paragraph (a) of this subsection, or the denial of an application for an order of approval, if the United States attorney shall certify to the judge or other official granting such motion or denying such application that the appeal is not taken for purposes of delay. Such appeal shall be taken within thirty days after the date the order was entered and shall be diligently prosecuted.

(c) The remedies and sanctions described in this chapter with respect to the interception of electronic communications are the only judicial remedies and sanctions for nonconstitutional violations of this chapter involving such communications.

(11) The requirements of subsections (1)(b)(ii) and (3)(d) of this section relating to the specification of the facilities from which, or the place where, the communication is to be intercepted do not apply if—

(a) in the case of an application with respect to the interception of an oral communication—

(i) the application is by a Federal investigative or law enforcement officer and is approved by the Attorney General, the Deputy Attorney General, the Associate

Attorney General, an Assistant Attorney General, or an acting Assistant Attorney General;

(ii) the application contains a full and complete statement as to why such specification is not practical and identifies the person committing the offense and whose communications are to be intercepted; and

(iii) the judge finds that such specification is not practical; and

(b) in the case of an application with respect to a wire or electronic communication—

(i) the application is by a Federal investigative or law enforcement officer and is approved by the Attorney General, the Deputy Attorney General, the Associate Attorney General, an Assistant Attorney General, or an acting Assistant Attorney General;

(ii) the application identifies the person believed to be committing the offense and whose communications are to be intercepted and the applicant makes a showing that there is probable cause to believe that the person's actions could have the effect of thwarting interception from a specified facility;

(iii) the judge finds that such showing has been adequately made; and

(iv) the order authorizing or approving the interception is limited to interception only for such time as it is reasonable to presume that the person identified in the application is or was reasonably proximate to the instrument through which such communication will be or was transmitted.

(12) An interception of a communication under an order with respect to which the requirements of subsections (1)(b)(ii) and (3)(d) of this section do not apply by reason of subsection (11)(a) shall not begin until the place where the communication is to be intercepted is ascertained by the person implementing the interception order. A provider of wire or electronic communications service that has received an order as provided for in subsection (11)(b) may move the court to modify or quash the order on the ground that its assistance with respect to the interception cannot be performed in a timely or reasonable fashion. The court, upon notice to the government, shall decide such a motion expeditiously.

§ 2520. Recovery of civil damages authorized

(a) In general.—Except as provided in section 2511(2)(a)(ii), any person whose wire, oral, or electronic communication is intercepted, disclosed, or intentionally used in violation of this chapter may in a civil action recover from the person or entity, other than the United States, which engaged in that violation such relief as may be appropriate.

(b) Relief.—In an action under this section, appropriate relief includes—

(1) such preliminary and other equitable or declaratory relief as may be appropriate;

(2) damages under subsection (c) and punitive damages in appropriate cases; and

(3) a reasonable attorney's fee and other litigation costs reasonably incurred.

(c) Computation of damages.—(1) In an action under this section, if the conduct in violation of this chapter is the private viewing of a private satellite video communication that is not scrambled or encrypted or if the communication is a radio communication that is transmitted on frequencies allocated under subpart D of part 74 of the rules of the Federal Communications Commission that is not scrambled or encrypted and the conduct is not for a tortious or illegal purpose or for purposes of direct or indirect commercial advantage or private commercial gain, then the court shall assess damages as follows:

(A) If the person who engaged in that conduct has not previously been enjoined under section 2511(5) and has not been found liable in a prior civil action under this section, the court shall assess the greater of the sum of actual damages suffered by the plaintiff, or statutory damages of not less than $50 and not more than $500.

(B) If, on one prior occasion, the person who engaged in that conduct has been enjoined under section 2511(5) or has been found liable in a civil action under this section, the court shall assess the greater of the sum of actual damages suffered by the plaintiff, or statutory damages of not less than $100 and not more than $1000.

(2) In any other action under this section, the court may assess as damages whichever is the greater of—

(A) the sum of the actual damages suffered by the plaintiff and any profits made by the violator as a result of the violation; or

(B) statutory damages of whichever is the greater of $100 a day for each day of violation or $10,000.

(d) Defense.—A good faith reliance on—

(1) a court warrant or order, a grand jury subpoena, a legislative authorization, or a statutory authorization;

(2) a request of an investigative or law enforcement officer under section 2518(7) of this title; or

(3) a good faith determination that section 2511(3) or 2511(2)(i) of this title permitted the conduct complained of;

is a complete defense against any civil or criminal action brought under this chapter or any other law.

(e) Limitation.—A civil action under this section may not be commenced later than two years after the date upon which the claimant first has a reasonable opportunity to discover the violation.

(f) Administrative discipline.—If a court or appropriate department or agency determines that the United States or any of its departments or agencies has violated any provision of this chapter, and the court or appropriate department or agency finds that the circumstances surrounding the violation raise serious questions about whether or not an officer or employee of the United States acted willfully or intentionally with respect to the violation, the department or agency shall, upon receipt of a true and correct copy of the decision and findings of the court or appropriate department or agency promptly initiate a proceeding to determine whether disciplinary action against the officer or employee is warranted. If the head of the department or agency involved determines that disciplinary action is not warranted, he or she shall notify the Inspector General with jurisdiction over the department or agency concerned and shall provide the Inspector General with the reasons for such determination.

(g) Improper disclosure is violation.—Any willful disclosure or use by an investigative or law enforcement officer or governmental entity of information beyond the extent permitted by section 2517 is a violation of this chapter for purposes of section 2520(a).

§ 2521. Injunction against illegal interception

Whenever it shall appear that any person is engaged or is about to engage in any act which constitutes or will constitute a felony violation of this chapter, the Attorney General may initiate a civil action in a district court of the United States to enjoin such violation. The court shall proceed as soon as practicable to the hearing and determination of such an action, and may, at any time before final determination, enter such a restraining order or prohibition, or take such other action, as is warranted to prevent a continuing and substantial injury to the United States or to any person or class of persons for whose protection the action is brought. A proceeding under this section is governed by the Federal Rules of Civil Procedure, except that, if an indictment has been returned against the respondent, discovery is governed by the Federal Rules of Criminal Procedure.

STORED WIRE AND ELECTRONIC COMMUNICATIONS AND TRANSACTIONAL RECORDS ACCESS

§ 2702. Voluntary disclosure of customer communications or records

(a) Prohibitions.—Except as provided in subsection (b) or (c)—

(1) a person or entity providing an electronic communication service to the public shall not knowingly divulge to any person or entity the contents of a communication while in electronic storage by that service; and

(2) a person or entity providing remote computing service to the public shall not knowingly divulge to any person or entity the contents of any communication which is carried or maintained on that service—

(A) on behalf of, and received by means of electronic transmission from (or created by means of computer processing of communications received by means of electronic transmission from), a subscriber or customer of such service;

(B) solely for the purpose of providing storage or computer processing services to such subscriber or customer, if the provider is not authorized to access the contents of any such communications for purposes of providing any services other than storage or computer processing; and

(3) a provider of remote computing service or electronic communication service to the public shall not knowingly divulge a record or other information pertaining to a subscriber to or customer of such service (not including the contents of communications covered by paragraph (1) or (2)) to any governmental entity.

(b) Exceptions for disclosure of communications.—A provider described in subsection (a) may divulge the contents of a communication—

(1) to an addressee or intended recipient of such communication or an agent of such addressee or intended recipient;

(2) as otherwise authorized in section 2517, 2511(2)(a), or 2703 of this title;

(3) with the lawful consent of the originator or an addressee or intended recipient of such communication, or the subscriber in the case of remote computing service;

(4) to a person employed or authorized or whose facilities are used to forward such communication to its destination;

(5) as may be necessarily incident to the rendition of the service or to the protection of the rights or property of the provider of that service;

(6) to the National Center for Missing and Exploited Children, in connection with a report submitted thereto under section 2258A;

(7) to a law enforcement agency—

    (A) if the contents—

        (i) were inadvertently obtained by the service provider; and

        (ii) appear to pertain to the commission of a crime;
    or

    [(B) Repealed. Pub.L. 108–21, Title V, § 508(b)(1)(A), Apr. 30, 2003, 117 Stat. 684]

    [(C) Repealed. Pub.L. 107–296, Title II, § 225(d)(1)(C), Nov. 25, 2002, 116 Stat. 2157]

(8) to a governmental entity, if the provider, in good faith, believes that an emergency involving danger of death or serious physical injury to any person requires disclosure without delay of communications relating to the emergency.

(c) Exceptions for disclosure of customer records.—A provider described in subsection (a) may divulge a record or other information pertaining to a subscriber to or customer of such service (not including the contents of communications covered by subsection (a)(1) or (a)(2))—

(1) as otherwise authorized in section 2703;

(2) with the lawful consent of the customer or subscriber;

(3) as may be necessarily incident to the rendition of the service or to the protection of the rights or property of the provider of that service;

(4) to a governmental entity, if the provider, in good faith, believes that an emergency involving danger of death or serious physical injury to any person requires disclosure without delay of information relating to the emergency;

(5) to the National Center for Missing and Exploited Children, in connection with a report submitted thereto under section 2258A; or

(6) to any person other than a governmental entity.

(d) Reporting of emergency disclosures.—On an annual basis, the Attorney General shall submit to the Committee on the Judiciary of the House of Representatives and the Committee on the Judiciary of the Senate a report containing—

(1) the number of accounts from which the Department of Justice has received voluntary disclosures under subsection (b)(8); and

(2) a summary of the basis for disclosure in those instances where—

(A) voluntary disclosures under subsection (b)(8) were made to the Department of Justice; and

(B) the investigation pertaining to those disclosures was closed without the filing of criminal charges.

§ 2703. Required disclosure of customer communications or records

(a) Contents of wire or electronic communications in electronic storage.—A governmental entity may require the disclosure by a provider of electronic communication service of the contents of a wire or electronic communication, that is in electronic storage in an electronic communications system for one hundred and eighty days or less, only pursuant to a warrant issued using the procedures described in the Federal Rules of Criminal Procedure (or, in the case of a State court, issued using State warrant procedures) by a court of competent jurisdiction. A governmental entity may require the disclosure by a provider of electronic communications services of the contents of a wire or electronic communication that has been in electronic storage in an electronic communications system for more than one hundred and eighty days by the means available under subsection (b) of this section.

(b) Contents of wire or electronic communications in a remote computing service.—(1) A governmental entity may require a provider of remote computing service to disclose the contents of any wire or electronic communication to which this paragraph is made applicable by paragraph (2) of this subsection—

(A) without required notice to the subscriber or customer, if the governmental entity obtains a warrant issued using the procedures described in the Federal Rules of Criminal Procedure (or, in the case of a State court, issued using State warrant procedures) by a court of competent jurisdiction; or

(B) with prior notice from the governmental entity to the subscriber or customer if the governmental entity—

(i) uses an administrative subpoena authorized by a Federal or State statute or a Federal or State grand jury or trial subpoena; or

(ii) obtains a court order for such disclosure under subsection (d) of this section;

except that delayed notice may be given pursuant to section 2705 of this title.

(2) Paragraph (1) is applicable with respect to any wire or electronic communication that is held or maintained on that service—

(A) on behalf of, and received by means of electronic transmission from (or created by means of computer processing of communications received by means of electronic transmission from), a subscriber or customer of such remote computing service; and

(B) solely for the purpose of providing storage or computer processing services to such subscriber or customer, if the provider is not authorized to access the contents of any such communications for purposes of providing any services other than storage or computer processing.

(c) Records concerning electronic communication service or remote computing service.—(1) A governmental entity may require a provider of electronic communication service or remote computing service to disclose a record or other information pertaining to a subscriber to or customer of such service (not including the contents of communications) only when the governmental entity—

(A) obtains a warrant issued using the procedures described in the Federal Rules of Criminal Procedure (or, in the case of a State court, issued using State warrant procedures) by a court of competent jurisdiction;

(B) obtains a court order for such disclosure under subsection (d) of this section;

(C) has the consent of the subscriber or customer to such disclosure;

(D) submits a formal written request relevant to a law enforcement investigation concerning telemarketing fraud for the name, address, and place of business of a subscriber or customer of such provider, which subscriber or customer is engaged in telemarketing (as such term is defined in section 2325 of this title); or

(E) seeks information under paragraph (2).

(2) A provider of electronic communication service or remote computing service shall disclose to a governmental entity the—

(A) name;

(B) address;

(C) local and long distance telephone connection records, or records of session times and durations;

(D) length of service (including start date) and types of service utilized;

(E) telephone or instrument number or other subscriber number or identity, including any temporarily assigned network address; and

(F) means and source of payment for such service (including any credit card or bank account number),

of a subscriber to or customer of such service when the governmental entity uses an administrative subpoena authorized by a Federal or State statute or a Federal or State grand jury or trial subpoena or any means available under paragraph (1).

(3) A governmental entity receiving records or information under this subsection is not required to provide notice to a subscriber or customer.

(d) Requirements for court order.—A court order for disclosure under subsection (b) or (c) may be issued by any court that is a court of competent jurisdiction and shall issue only if the governmental entity offers specific and articulable facts showing that there are reasonable grounds to believe that the contents of a wire or electronic communication, or the records or other information sought, are relevant and material to an ongoing criminal investigation. In the case of a State governmental authority, such a court order shall not issue if prohibited by the law of such State. A court issuing an order pursuant to this section, on a motion made promptly by the service provider, may quash or modify such order, if the information or records requested are unusually voluminous in nature or compliance with such order otherwise would cause an undue burden on such provider.

(e) No cause of action against a provider disclosing information under this chapter.—No cause of action shall lie in any court against any provider of wire or electronic communication service, its officers, employees, agents, or other specified persons for providing information, facilities, or assistance in accordance with the terms of a court order, warrant, subpoena, statutory authorization, or certification under this chapter.

(f) Requirement to preserve evidence.—

(1) In general.—A provider of wire or electronic communication services or a remote computing service, upon the request of a governmental entity, shall take all necessary steps to preserve records and other evidence in its possession pending the issuance of a court order or other process.

(2) Period of retention.—Records referred to in paragraph (1) shall be retained for a period of 90 days, which shall be extended for an additional 90-day period upon a renewed request by the governmental entity.

(g) Presence of officer not required.—Notwithstanding section 3105 of this title, the presence of an officer shall not be required for service or execution of a search warrant issued in accordance with this chapter requiring disclosure by a provider of electronic communications service or remote computing service of the contents of communications or records or other information pertaining to a subscriber to or customer of such service.

§ 2707. Civil action

(a) Cause of action.—Except as provided in section 2703(e), any provider of electronic communication service, subscriber, or other person aggrieved by any violation of this chapter in which the conduct constituting the violation is engaged in with a knowing or intentional state of mind may, in a civil action, recover from the person or entity, other than the United States, which engaged in that violation such relief as may be appropriate.

(b) Relief.—In a civil action under this section, appropriate relief includes—

(1) such preliminary and other equitable or declaratory relief as may be appropriate;

(2) damages under subsection (c); and

(3) a reasonable attorney's fee and other litigation costs reasonably incurred.

(c) Damages.—The court may assess as damages in a civil action under this section the sum of the actual damages suffered by the plaintiff and any profits made by the violator as a result of the violation, but in no case shall a person entitled to recover receive less than the sum of $1,000. If the violation is willful or intentional, the court may assess punitive damages. In the case of a successful action to enforce liability under this section, the court may assess the costs of the action, together with reasonable attorney fees determined by the court.

(d) Administrative discipline.—If a court or appropriate department or agency determines that the United States or any of its departments or agencies has violated any provision of this chapter, and the court or appropriate department or agency finds that the circumstances surrounding the violation raise serious questions about whether or not an officer or employee of the United States acted willfully or intentionally with respect to the violation, the department or agency shall, upon receipt of a true and correct copy of the decision and findings of the court or appropriate department or agency promptly initiate a proceeding to determine whether disciplinary action against the officer or employee is warranted. If the head of the department or agency involved determines that disciplinary action is not warranted, he or she shall notify the Inspector General with jurisdiction over the department or agency concerned and shall provide the Inspector General with the reasons for such determination.

(e) Defense.—A good faith reliance on—

(1) a court warrant or order, a grand jury subpoena, a legislative authorization, or a statutory authorization (including a request of a governmental entity under section 2703(f) of this title);

(2) a request of an investigative or law enforcement officer under section 2518(7) of this title; or

(3) a good faith determination that section 2511(3) of this title permitted the conduct complained of is a complete defense to any civil or criminal action brought under this chapter or any other law.

(f) Limitation.—A civil action under this section may not be commenced later than two years after the date upon which the claimant first discovered or had a reasonable opportunity to discover the violation.

(g) Improper disclosure.—Any willful disclosure of a "record", as that term is defined in section 552a(a) of title 5, United States Code, obtained by an investigative or law enforcement officer, or a governmental entity, pursuant to section 2703 of this title, or from a device installed pursuant to section 3123 or 3125 of this title, that is not a disclosure made in the proper performance of the official functions of the officer or governmental entity making the disclosure, is a violation of this chapter. This provision shall not apply to information previously lawfully disclosed (prior to the commencement of any civil or administrative proceeding under this chapter) to the public by a Federal, State, or local governmental entity or by the plaintiff in a civil action under this chapter.

§ 2708. Exclusivity of remedies

The remedies and sanctions described in this chapter are the only judicial remedies and sanctions for nonconstitutional violations of this chapter.

SEARCHES AND SEIZURES

(18 U.S.C. §§ 3103a, 3105, 3109).

§ 3103a. Additional grounds for issuing warrant

(a) In general.—In addition to the grounds for issuing a warrant in section 3103 of this title, a warrant may be issued to search for and seize any property that constitutes evidence of a criminal offense in violation of the laws of the United States.

(b) Delay.—With respect to the issuance of any warrant or court order under this section, or any other rule of law, to search for and seize any property or material that constitutes evidence of a criminal offense in violation of the laws of the United States, any notice required, or that may be required, to be given may be delayed if—

(1) the court finds reasonable cause to believe that providing immediate notification of the execution of the warrant may have an adverse result (as defined in section 2705, except if the adverse results consist only of unduly delaying a trial);

(2) the warrant prohibits the seizure of any tangible property, any wire or electronic communication (as defined in section 2510), or, except as expressly provided in chapter 121, any stored wire or electronic information, except where the court finds reasonable necessity for the seizure; and

(3) the warrant provides for the giving of such notice within a reasonable period not to exceed 30 days after the date of its execution, or on a later date certain if the facts of the case justify a longer period of delay.

(c) Extensions of delay.—Any period of delay authorized by this section may be extended by the court for good cause shown, subject to the condition that extensions should only be granted upon an updated showing of the need for further delay and that each additional delay should be limited to periods of 90 days or less, unless the facts of the case justify a longer period of delay.

(d) Reports.—

(1) Report by judge.—Not later than 30 days after the expiration of a warrant authorizing delayed notice (including any extension thereof) entered under this section, or the denial of such warrant (or request for extension), the issuing or denying judge shall report to the Administrative Office of the United States Courts—

(A) the fact that a warrant was applied for;

(B) the fact that the warrant or any extension thereof was granted as applied for, was modified, or was denied;

(C) the period of delay in the giving of notice authorized by the warrant, and the number and duration of any extensions; and

(D) the offense specified in the warrant or application.

(2) Report by administrative office of the United States courts.—Beginning with the fiscal year ending September 30, 2007, the Director of the Administrative Office of the United States Courts shall transmit to Congress annually a full and complete report summarizing the data required to be filed with the Administrative Office by paragraph (1), including the number of applications for warrants and extensions of warrants authorizing delayed notice, and the number of such warrants and extensions granted or denied during the preceding fiscal year.

(3) Regulations.—The Director of the Administrative Office of the United States Courts, in consultation with the Attorney General, is authorized to issue binding regulations dealing with the content and form of the reports required to be filed under paragraph (1).

§ 3105. Persons authorized to serve search warrant

A search warrant may in all cases be served by any of the officers mentioned in its direction or by an officer authorized by law to serve such warrant, but by no other person, except in aid of the officer on his requiring it, he being present and acting in its execution.

§ 3109. Breaking doors or windows for entry or exit

The officer may break open any outer or inner door or window of a house, or any part of a house, or anything therein, to execute a search warrant, if, after notice of his authority and purpose, he is refused admittance or when necessary to liberate himself or a person aiding him in the execution of the warrant.

BAIL REFORM ACT OF 1984

(18 U.S.C. §§ 3141–3150).

§ 3141. Release and detention authority generally

(a) Pending trial.—A judicial officer authorized to order the arrest of a person under section 3041 of this title before whom an arrested person is brought shall order that such person be released or detained, pending judicial proceedings, under this chapter.

(b) Pending sentence or appeal.—A judicial officer of a court of original jurisdiction over an offense, or a judicial officer of a Federal appellate court, shall order that, pending imposition or execution of sentence, or pending appeal of conviction or sentence, a person be released or detained under this chapter.

§ 3142. Release or detention of a defendant pending trial

(a) In general.—Upon the appearance before a judicial officer of a person charged with an offense, the judicial officer shall issue an order that, pending trial, the person be—

(1) released on personal recognizance or upon execution of an unsecured appearance bond, under subsection (b) of this section;

(2) released on a condition or combination of conditions under subsection (c) of this section;

(3) temporarily detained to permit revocation of conditional release, deportation, or exclusion under subsection (d) of this section; or

(4) detained under subsection (e) of this section.

(b) Release on personal recognizance or unsecured appearance bond.—The judicial officer shall order the pretrial release of the person on personal recognizance, or upon execution of an unsecured appearance bond in an amount specified by the court, subject to the condition that the person not commit a Federal, State, or local crime during the period of release and subject to the condition that the person cooperate in the collection of a DNA sample from the person if the collection of such a sample is authorized pursuant to section 3 of the DNA Analysis Backlog Elimination Act of 2000 (42 U.S.C. 14135a), unless the judicial officer determines that such release will not reasonably assure the appearance of the person as required or will endanger the safety of any other person or the community.

(c) Release on conditions.—(1) If the judicial officer determines that the release described in subsection (b) of this section will not reasonably assure the appearance of the person as required or will endanger the safety of any other person or the community, such judicial officer shall order the pretrial release of the person—

(A) subject to the condition that the person not commit a Federal, State, or local crime during the period of release and subject to the condition that the person cooperate in the collection of a DNA sample from the person if the collection of such a sample is authorized pursuant to section 3 of the DNA Analysis Backlog Elimination Act of 2000 (42 U.S.C. 14135a); and

(B) subject to the least restrictive further condition, or combination of conditions, that such judicial officer determines will reasonably assure the appearance of the person as required and the safety of any other person and the community, which may include the condition that the person—

(i) remain in the custody of a designated person, who agrees to assume supervision and to report any violation of a release condition to the court, if the designated person is able reasonably to assure the judicial officer that the person will appear as required and will not pose a danger to the safety of any other person or the community;

(ii) maintain employment, or, if unemployed, actively seek employment;

(iii) maintain or commence an educational program;

(iv) abide by specified restrictions on personal associations, place of abode, or travel;

(v) avoid all contact with an alleged victim of the crime and with a potential witness who may testify concerning the offense;

(vi) report on a regular basis to a designated law enforcement agency, pretrial services agency, or other agency;

(vii) comply with a specified curfew;

(viii) refrain from possessing a firearm, destructive device, or other dangerous weapon;

(ix) refrain from excessive use of alcohol, or any use of a narcotic drug or other controlled substance, as defined in section 102 of the Controlled Substances Act (21 U.S.C. 802), without a prescription by a licensed medical practitioner;

(x) undergo available medical, psychological, or psychiatric treatment, including treatment for drug or alcohol dependency, and remain in a specified institution if required for that purpose;

(xi) execute an agreement to forfeit upon failing to appear as required, property of a sufficient unencumbered value, including money, as is reasonably necessary to assure the appearance of the person as required, and shall provide the court with proof of ownership and the value of the property along with information regarding existing encumbrances as the judicial office may require;

(xii) execute a bail bond with solvent sureties; who will execute an agreement to forfeit in such amount as is reasonably necessary to assure appearance of the person as required and shall provide the court with information regarding the value of the assets and liabilities of the surety if other than an approved surety and the nature and extent of encumbrances against the surety's property; such surety shall have a net worth which shall have sufficient unencumbered value to pay the amount of the bail bond;

(xiii) return to custody for specified hours following release for employment, schooling, or other limited purposes; and

(xiv) satisfy any other condition that is reasonably necessary to assure the appearance of the person as required and to assure the safety of any other person and the community.

In any case that involves a minor victim under section 1201, 1591, 2241, 2242, 2244(a)(1), 2245, 2251, 2251A, 2252(a)(1), 2252(a)(2), 2252(a)(3), 2252A(a)(1), 2252A(a)(2), 2252A(a)(3), 2252A(a)(4), 2260, 2421, 2422, 2423, or 2425 of this title, or a failure to register offense under section 2250 of this title, any release order shall contain, at a minimum, a condition of electronic monitoring and each of the conditions specified at subparagraphs (iv), (v), (vi), (vii), and (viii).

(2) The judicial officer may not impose a financial condition that results in the pretrial detention of the person.

(3) The judicial officer may at any time amend the order to impose additional or different conditions of release.

(d) Temporary detention to permit revocation of conditional release, deportation, or exclusion.—If the judicial officer determines that—

(1) such person—

(A) is, and was at the time the offense was committed, on—

(i) release pending trial for a felony under Federal, State, or local law;

(ii) release pending imposition or execution of sentence, appeal of sentence or conviction, or completion of sentence, for any offense under Federal, State, or local law; or

(iii) probation or parole for any offense under Federal, State, or local law; or

(B) is not a citizen of the United States or lawfully admitted for permanent residence, as defined in section 101(a)(20) of the Immigration and Nationality Act (8 U.S.C. 1101(a)(20)); and

(2) such person may flee or pose a danger to any other person or the community;

such judicial officer shall order the detention of such person, for a period of not more than ten days, excluding Saturdays, Sundays, and holidays, and direct the attorney for the Government to notify the appropriate court, probation or parole official, or State or local law enforcement official, or the appropriate official of the Immigration and Naturalization Service. If the official fails or declines to take such person into custody during that period, such person shall be treated in accordance with the other provisions of this section, notwithstanding the applicability of other provisions of law governing release pending trial or deportation or exclusion proceedings. If temporary detention is sought under paragraph (1)(B) of this subsection, such person has the burden of proving to the court such person's United States citizenship or lawful admission for permanent residence.

(e) Detention.—

(1) If, after a hearing pursuant to the provisions of subsection (f) of this section, the judicial officer finds that no condition or combination of conditions will reasonably assure the appearance of the person as required and the safety of any other person and the community, such judicial officer shall order the detention of the person before trial.

(2) In a case described in subsection (f)(1) of this section, a rebuttable presumption arises that no condition or combination of conditions will reasonably assure the safety of any other person and the community if such judicial officer finds that—

(A) the person has been convicted of a Federal offense that is described in subsection (f)(1) of this section, or of a State or local offense that would have been an offense described in subsection (f)(1) of this section if a circumstance giving rise to Federal jurisdiction had existed;

(B) the offense described in subparagraph (A) of this subsection was committed while the person was on release pending trial for a Federal, State, or local offense; and

(C) a period of not more than five years has elapsed since the date of conviction, or the release of the person from imprisonment, for the offense described in subparagraph (A) of this subsection, whichever is later.

(3) Subject to rebuttal by the person, it shall be presumed that no condition or combination of conditions will reasonably assure the appearance of the person as required and the safety of the community if the judicial officer finds that there is probable cause to believe that the person committed—

(A) an offense for which a maximum term of imprisonment of ten years or more is prescribed in the Controlled Substances Act (21 U.S.C. 801 et seq.), the Controlled Substances Import and Export Act (21 U.S.C. 951 et seq.), or chapter 705 of title 46;

(B) an offense under section 924(c), 956(a), or 2332b of this title;

(C) an offense listed in section 2332b(g)(5)(B) of title 18, United States Code, for which a maximum term of imprisonment of 10 years or more is prescribed;

(D) an offense under chapter 77 of this title for which a maximum term of imprisonment of 20 years or more is prescribed; or

(E) an offense involving a minor victim under section 1201, 1591, 2241, 2242, 2244(a)(1), 2245, 2251, 2251A, 2252(a)(1), 2252(a)(2), 2252(a)(3), 2252A(a)(1), 2252A(a)(2), 2252A(a)(3), 2252A(a)(4), 2260, 2421, 2422, 2423, or 2425 of this title.

(f) Detention hearing.—The judicial officer shall hold a hearing to determine whether any condition or combination of conditions set forth in subsection (c) of this section will reasonably assure the appearance of such person as required and the safety of any other person and the community—

(1) upon motion of the attorney for the Government, in a case that involves—

(A) a crime of violence*, a violation of section 1591, or an offense listed in section 2332b(g)(5)(B) for which a maximum term of imprisonment of 10 years or more is prescribed;

(B) an offense for which the maximum sentence is life imprisonment or death;

(C) an offense for which a maximum term of imprisonment of ten years or more is prescribed in the Controlled Substances Act (21 U.S.C. 801 et seq.), the Controlled Substances Import and Export Act (21 U.S.C. 951 et seq.), or chapter 705 of title 46

(D) any felony if such person has been convicted of two or more offenses described in subparagraphs (A) through (C) of this paragraph, or two or more State or local offenses that would have been offenses described in subparagraphs (A) through (C) of this paragraph if a circumstance giving rise to Federal jurisdiction had existed, or a combination of such offenses; or

(E) any felony that is not otherwise a crime of violence that involves a minor victim or that involves the possession or use of a firearm or destructive device (as those terms are defined in section 921), or any other dangerous weapon, or involves a failure to register under section 2250 of title 18, United States Code; or

(2) Upon motion of the attorney for the Government or upon the judicial officer's own motion, in a case that involves—

(A) a serious risk that such person will flee; or

(B) a serious risk that such person will obstruct or attempt to obstruct justice, or threaten, injure, or intimidate, or attempt to threaten, injure, or intimidate, a prospective witness or juror.

The hearing shall be held immediately upon the person's first appearance before the judicial officer unless that person, or the attorney for the Government, seeks a continuance. Except for good cause, a continuance on motion of such person may not exceed five days (not including any intermediate Saturday, Sunday, or legal holiday), and a continuance on

---

* The phrase "crime of violence" is defined in 18 U.S.C. § 3156(a)(4) as meaning: "(A) an offense that has an element of the offense the use, attempted use, or threatened use of physical force against the person or property of another, or (B) any other offense that is a felony and that, by its nature, involves a substantial risk that physical force against the person or property of another may be used in the course of committing the offense."

motion of the attorney for the Government may not exceed three days (not including any intermediate Saturday, Sunday, or legal holiday). During a continuance, such person shall be detained, and the judicial officer, on motion of the attorney for the Government or sua sponte, may order that, while in custody, a person who appears to be a narcotics addict receive a medical examination to determine whether such person is an addict. At the hearing, such person has the right to be represented by counsel, and, if financially unable to obtain adequate representation, to have counsel appointed. The person shall be afforded an opportunity to testify, to present witnesses, to cross-examine witnesses who appear at the hearing, and to present information by proffer or otherwise. The rules concerning admissibility of evidence in criminal trials do not apply to the presentation and consideration of information at the hearing. The facts the judicial officer uses to support a finding pursuant to subsection (e) that no condition or combination of conditions will reasonably assure the safety of any other person and the community shall be supported by clear and convincing evidence. The person may be detained pending completion of the hearing. The hearing may be reopened, before or after a determination by the judicial officer, at any time before trial if the judicial officer finds that information exists that was not known to the movant at the time of the hearing and that has a material bearing on the issue whether there are conditions of release that will reasonably assure the appearance of such person as required and the safety of any other person and the community.

(g) Factors to be considered.—The judicial officer shall, in determining whether there are conditions of release that will reasonably assure the appearance of the person as required and the safety of any other person and the community, take into account the available information concerning—

   (1) the nature and circumstances of the offense charged, including whether the offense is a crime of violence, a violation of section 1591, a Federal crime of terrorism, or involves a minor victim or a controlled substance, firearm, explosive, or destructive device;

   (2) the weight of the evidence against the person;

   (3) the history and characteristics of the person, including—

      (A) the person's character, physical and mental condition, family ties, employment, financial resources, length of residence in the community, community ties, past conduct, history relating to drug or alcohol abuse, criminal history, and record concerning appearance at court proceedings; and

(B) whether, at the time of the current offense or arrest, the person was on probation, on parole, or on other release pending trial, sentencing, appeal, or completion of sentence for an offense under Federal, State, or local law; and

(4) the nature and seriousness of the danger to any person or the community that would be posed by the person's release. In considering the conditions of release described in subsection (c)(1)(B)(xi) or (c)(1)(B)(xii) of this section, the judicial officer may upon his own motion, or shall upon the motion of the Government, conduct an inquiry into the source of the property to be designated for potential forfeiture or offered as collateral to secure a bond, and shall decline to accept the designation, or the use as collateral, of property that, because of its source, will not reasonably assure the appearance of the person as required.

(h) Contents of release order.—In a release order issued under subsection (b) or (c) of this section, the judicial officer shall—

(1) include a written statement that sets forth all the conditions to which the release is subject, in a manner sufficiently clear and specific to serve as a guide for the person's conduct; and

(2) advise the person of—

(A) the penalties for violating a condition of release, including the penalties for committing an offense while on pretrial release;

(B) the consequences of violating a condition of release, including the immediate issuance of a warrant for the person's arrest; and

(C) sections 1503 of this title (relating to intimidation of witnesses, jurors, and officers of the court), 1510 (relating to obstruction of criminal investigations), 1512 (tampering with a witness, victim, or an informant), and 1513 (retaliating against a witness, victim, or an informant).

(i) Contents of detention order.—In a detention order issued under subsection (e) of this section, the judicial officer shall—

(1) include written findings of fact and a written statement of the reasons for the detention;

(2) direct that the person be committed to the custody of the Attorney General for confinement in a corrections facility separate, to the extent practicable, from persons awaiting or serving sentences or being held in custody pending appeal;

(3) direct that the person be afforded reasonable opportunity for private consultation with counsel; and

(4) direct that, on order of a court of the United States or on request of an attorney for the Government, the person in charge of the corrections facility in which the person is confined deliver the person to a United States marshal for the purpose of an appearance in connection with a court proceeding.

The judicial officer may, by subsequent order, permit the temporary release of the person, in the custody of a United States marshal or another appropriate person, to the extent that the judicial officer determines such release to be necessary for preparation of the person's defense or for another compelling reason.

(j) Presumption of innocence.—Nothing in this section shall be construed as modifying or limiting the presumption of innocence.

§ 3143. Release or detention of a defendant pending sentence or appeal

(a) Release or detention pending sentence.—(1) Except as provided in paragraph (2), the judicial officer shall order that a person who has been found guilty of an offense and who is awaiting imposition or execution of sentence, other than a person for whom the applicable guideline promulgated pursuant to 28 U.S.C. 994 does not recommend a term of imprisonment, be detained, unless the judicial officer finds by clear and convincing evidence that the person is not likely to flee or pose a danger to the safety of any other person or the community if released under section 3142(b) or (c). If the judicial officer makes such a finding, such judicial officer shall order the release of the person in accordance with section 3142(b) or (c).

(2) The judicial officer shall order that a person who has been found guilty of an offense in a case described in subparagraph (A), (B), or (C) of subsection (f)(1) of section 3142 and is awaiting imposition or execution of sentence be detained unless—

(A)(i) the judicial officer finds there is a substantial likelihood that a motion for acquittal or new trial will be granted; or

(ii) an attorney for the Government has recommended that no sentence of imprisonment be imposed on the person; and

(B) the judicial officer finds by clear and convincing evidence that the person is not likely to flee or pose a danger to any other person or the community.

(b) Release or detention pending appeal by the defendant.— (1) Except as provided in paragraph (2), the judicial officer shall order that a person who has been found guilty of an offense and sentenced to a term of imprisonment, and who has filed an appeal or a petition for a writ of certiorari, be detained, unless the judicial officer finds—

(A) by clear and convincing evidence that the person is not likely to flee or pose a danger to the safety of any other person or the community if released under section 3142(b) or (c) of this title; and

(B) that the appeal is not for the purpose of delay and raises a substantial question of law or fact likely to result in—

(i) reversal,

(ii) an order for a new trial,

(iii) a sentence that does not include a term of imprisonment, or

(iv) a reduced sentence to a term of imprisonment less than the total of the time already served plus the expected duration of the appeal process.

If the judicial officer makes such findings, such judicial officer shall order the release of the person in accordance with section 3142(b) or (c) of this title, except that in the circumstance described in subparagraph (B)(iv) of this paragraph, the judicial officer shall order the detention terminated at the expiration of the likely reduced sentence.

(2) The judicial officer shall order that a person who has been found guilty of an offense in a case described in subparagraph (A), (B), or (C) of subsection (f)(1) of section 3142 and sentenced to a term of imprisonment, and who has filed an appeal or a petition for a writ of certiorari, be detained.

(c) Release or detention pending appeal by the government.—The judicial officer shall treat a defendant in a case in which an appeal has been taken by the United States under section 3731 of this title, in accordance with section 3142 of this title, unless the defendant is otherwise subject to a release or detention order.

Except as provided in subsection (b) of this section, the judicial officer, in a case in which an appeal has been taken by the United States under section 3742, shall—

(1) if the person has been sentenced to a term of imprisonment, order that person detained; and

(2) in any other circumstance, release or detain the person under section 3142.

§ 3144. Release or detention of a material witness

If it appears from an affidavit filed by a party that the testimony of a person is material in a criminal proceeding, and if it is shown that it may become impracticable to secure the presence of the person by subpoena, a judicial officer may order the arrest of the person and treat the person in accordance with the provisions of section 3142 of this title. No material witness may be detained because of inability to comply with any condition of release if the testimony of such witness can adequately be secured by deposition, and if further detention is not necessary to prevent a failure of justice. Release of a material witness may be delayed for a reasonable period of time until the deposition of the witness can be taken pursuant to the Federal Rules of Criminal Procedure.

§ 3145. Review and appeal of a release or detention order

(a) Review of a release order.—If a person is ordered released by a magistrate judge, or by a person other than a judge of a court having original jurisdiction over the offense and other than a Federal appellate court—

    (1) the attorney for the Government may file, with the court having original jurisdiction over the offense, a motion for revocation of the order or amendment of the conditions of release; and

    (2) the person may file, with the court having original jurisdiction over the offense, a motion for amendment of the conditions of release.

The motion shall be determined promptly.

(b) Review of a detention order.—If a person is ordered detained by a magistrate judge, or by a person other than a judge of a court having original jurisdiction over the offense and other than a Federal appellate court, the person may file, with the court having original jurisdiction over the offense, a motion for revocation or amendment of the order. The motion shall be determined promptly.

(c) Appeal from a release or detention order.—An appeal from a release or detention order, or from a decision denying revocation or amendment of such an order, is governed by the provisions of section 1291 of title 28 and section 3731 of this title. The appeal shall be determined promptly. A person subject to detention pursuant to section 3143(a)(2) or (b)(2), and who meets the conditions of release set forth in section 3143(a)(1) or (b)(1), may be ordered released, under appropriate conditions, by the judicial officer, if it is clearly shown that there are exceptional reasons why such person's detention would not be appropriate.

§ 3146. Penalty for failure to appear

(a) Offense.—Whoever, having been released under this chapter knowingly—

(1) fails to appear before a court as required by the conditions of release; or

(2) fails to surrender for service of sentence pursuant to a court order;

shall be punished as provided in subsection (b) of this section.

(b) Punishment.—(1) The punishment for an offense under this section is—

(A) if the person was released in connection with a charge of, or while awaiting sentence, surrender for service of sentence, or appeal or certiorari after conviction for—

(i) an offense punishable by death, life imprisonment, or imprisonment for a term of 15 years or more, a fine under this title or imprisonment for not more than ten years, or both;

(ii) an offense punishable by imprisonment for a term of five years or more, a fine under this title or imprisonment for not more than five years, or both;

(iii) any other felony, a fine under this title or imprisonment for not more than two years, or both; or

(iv) a misdemeanor, a fine under this title or imprisonment for not more than one year, or both; and

(B) if the person was released for appearance as a material witness, a fine under this chapter or imprisonment for not more than one year, or both.

(2) A term of imprisonment imposed under this section shall be consecutive to the sentence of imprisonment for any other offense.

(c) Affirmative defense.—It is an affirmative defense to a prosecution under this section that uncontrollable circumstances prevented the person from appearing or surrendering, and that the person did not contribute to the creation of such circumstances in reckless disregard of the requirement to appear or surrender, and that the person appeared or surrendered as soon as such circumstances ceased to exist.

(d) Declaration of forfeiture.—If a person fails to appear before a court as required, and the person executed an appearance bond pursuant to section 3142(b) of this title or is subject to the release condition set forth in clause (xi) or (xii) of section 3142(c)(1)(B) of this title, the judicial officer may, regardless of whether the person has been charged with an offense under this section, declare any property designated pursuant to that section to be forfeited to the United States.

§ 3147. Penalty for an offense committed while on release

A person convicted of an offense committed while released under this chapter shall be sentenced, in addition to the sentence prescribed for the offense to—

(1) a term of imprisonment of not more than ten years if the offense is a felony; or

(2) a term of imprisonment of not more than one year if the offense is a misdemeanor.

A term of imprisonment imposed under this section shall be consecutive to any other sentence of imprisonment.

§ 3148. Sanctions for violation of a release condition

(a) Available sanctions.—A person who has been released under section 3142 of this title, and who has violated a condition of his release, is subject to a revocation of release, an order of detention, and a prosecution for contempt of court.

(b) Revocation of release.—The attorney for the Government may initiate a proceeding for revocation of an order of release by filing a motion with the district court. A judicial officer may issue a warrant for the arrest of a person charged with violating a condition of release, and the person shall be brought before a judicial officer in the district in which such person's arrest was ordered for a proceeding in accordance with this section. To the extent practicable, a person charged with violating the condition of release that such person not commit a Federal, State, or local crime during the period of release, shall be brought before the judicial officer who ordered the release and whose order is alleged to have been violated. The judicial officer shall enter an order of revocation and detention if, after a hearing, the judicial officer—

(1) finds that there is—

(A) probable cause to believe that the person has committed a Federal, State, or local crime while on release; or

(B) clear and convincing evidence that the person has violated any other condition of release; and

(2) finds that—

(A) based on the factors set forth in section 3142(g) of this title, there is no condition or combination of conditions of release that will assure that the person will not flee or pose a danger to the safety of any other person or the community; or

(B) the person is unlikely to abide by any condition or combination of conditions of release.

If there is probable cause to believe that, while on release, the person committed a Federal, State, or local felony, a rebuttable presumption arises that no condition or combination of conditions will assure that the person will not pose a danger to the safety of any other person or the community. If the judicial officer finds that there are conditions of release that will assure that the person will not flee or pose a danger to the safety of any other person or the community, and that the person will abide by such conditions, the judicial officer shall treat the person in accordance with the provisions of section 3142 of this title and may amend the conditions of release accordingly.

(c) Prosecution for contempt.—The judicial officer may commence a prosecution for contempt, under section 401 of this title, if the person has violated a condition of release.

§ 3149. Surrender of an offender by a surety

A person charged with an offense, who is released upon the execution of an appearance bond with a surety, may be arrested by the surety, and if so arrested, shall be delivered promptly to a United States marshal and brought before a judicial officer. The judicial officer shall determine in accordance with the provisions of section 3148(b) whether to revoke the release of the person, and may absolve the surety of responsibility to pay all or part of the bond in accordance with the provisions of Rule 46 of the Federal Rules of Criminal Procedure. The person so committed shall be held in official detention until released pursuant to this chapter or another provision of law.

§ 3150. Applicability to a case removed from a State court

The provisions of this chapter apply to a criminal case removed to a Federal court from a State court.

SPEEDY TRIAL ACT OF 1974 (AS AMENDED)

(18 U.S.C. §§ 3161–3162, 3164).

§ 3161. Time limits and exclusions

(a) In any case involving a defendant charged with an offense, the appropriate judicial officer, at the earliest practicable time, shall, after consultation with the counsel for the defendant and the attorney for the Government, set the case for trial on a day certain, or list it for trial on a weekly or other short-term trial calendar at a place within the judicial district, so as to assure a speedy trial.

(b) Any information or indictment charging an individual with the commission of an offense shall be filed within thirty days from the date on which such individual was arrested or served with a summons in connection with such charges. If an individual has been charged with a felony in a district in which no grand jury has been in session during such thirty-day period, the period of time for filing of the indictment shall be extended an additional thirty days.

(c)(1) In any case in which a plea of not guilty is entered, the trial of a defendant charged in an information or indictment with the commission of an offense shall commence within seventy days from the filing date (and making public) of the information or indictment, or from the date the defendant has appeared before a judicial officer of the court in which such charge is pending, whichever date last occurs. If a defendant consents in writing to be tried before a magistrate judge on a complaint, the trial shall commence within seventy days from the date of such consent.

(2) Unless the defendant consents in writing to the contrary, the trial shall not commence less than thirty days from the date on which the defendant first appears through counsel or expressly waives counsel and elects to proceed pro se.

(d)(1) If any indictment or information is dismissed upon motion of the defendant, or any charge contained in a complaint filed against an individual is dismissed or otherwise dropped, and thereafter a complaint is filed against such defendant or individual charging him with the same offense or an offense based on the same conduct or arising from the same criminal episode, or an information or indictment is filed charging such defendant with the same offense or an offense based on the same conduct or arising from the same criminal episode, the provisions of subsections (b) and (c) of this section shall be applicable with respect to such subsequent complaint, indictment, or information, as the case may be.

(2) If the defendant is to be tried upon an indictment or information dismissed by a trial court and reinstated following an appeal, the trial shall commence within seventy days from the date the action occasioning the trial becomes final, except that the court retrying the case may extend the period for trial not to exceed one hundred and eighty days from the date the action occasioning the trial becomes final if the unavailability of witnesses or other factors resulting from the passage of time shall make trial within seventy days impractical. The periods of delay enumerated in section 3161(h) are excluded in computing the time limitations specified in this section. The sanctions of section 3162 apply to this subsection.

(e) If the defendant is to be tried again following a declaration by the trial judge of a mistrial or following an order of such judge for a new trial, the trial shall commence within seventy days from the date the action occasioning the retrial becomes final. If the defendant is to be tried again following an appeal or a collateral attack, the trial shall commence within seventy days from the date the action occasioning the retrial becomes final, except that the court retrying the case may extend the period for retrial not to exceed one hundred and eighty days from the date the action occasioning the retrial becomes final if unavailability of witnesses or other factors resulting from passage of time shall make trial within seventy days impractical. The periods of delay enumerated in section 3161(h) are excluded in computing the time limitations specified in this section. The sanctions of section 3162 apply to this subsection.

(f) Notwithstanding the provisions of subsection (b) of this section, for the first twelve-calendar-month period following the effective date of this section as set forth in section 3163(a) of this chapter the time limit imposed with respect to the period between arrest and indictment by subsection (b) of this section shall be sixty days, for the second such twelve-month period such time limit shall be forty-five days and for the third such period such time limit shall be thirty-five days.

(g) Notwithstanding the provisions of subsection (c) of this section, for the first twelve-calendar-month period following the effective date of this section as set forth in section 3163(b) of this chapter, the time limit with respect to the period between arraignment and trial imposed by subsection (c) of this section shall be one hundred and eighty days, for the second such twelve-month period such time limit shall be one hundred and twenty days, and for the third such period such time limit with respect to the period between arraignment and trial shall be eighty days.

(h) The following periods of delay shall be excluded in computing the time within which an information or an indictment must be filed, or in computing the time within which the trial of any such offense must commence:

(1) Any period of delay resulting from other proceedings concerning the defendant, including but not limited to—

(A) delay resulting from any proceeding, including any examinations, to determine the mental competency or physical capacity of the defendant;

(B) delay resulting from trial with respect to other charges against the defendant;

(C) delay resulting from any interlocutory appeal;

(D) delay resulting from any pretrial motion, from the filing of the motion through the conclusion of the hearing on, or other prompt disposition of, such motion;

(E) delay resulting from any proceeding relating to the transfer of a case or the removal of any defendant from another district under the Federal Rules of Criminal Procedure;

(F) delay resulting from transportation of any defendant from another district, or to and from places of examination or hospitalization, except that any time consumed in excess of ten days from the date an order of removal or an order directing such transportation, and the defendant's arrival at the destination shall be presumed to be unreasonable;

(G) delay resulting from consideration by the court of a proposed plea agreement to be entered into by the defendant and the attorney for the Government; and

(H) delay reasonably attributable to any period, not to exceed thirty days, during which any proceeding concerning the defendant is actually under advisement by the court.

(2) Any period of delay during which prosecution is deferred by the attorney for the Government pursuant to written agreement with the defendant, with the approval of the court, for the purpose of allowing the defendant to demonstrate his good conduct.

(3)(A) Any period of delay resulting from the absence or unavailability of the defendant or an essential witness.

(B) For purposes of subparagraph (A) of this paragraph, a defendant or an essential witness shall be considered absent when his whereabouts are unknown and, in addition, he is attempting to avoid apprehension or prosecution or his whereabouts cannot be determined by due diligence. For purposes of such subparagraph, a defendant or an essential witness shall be considered unavailable whenever his whereabouts are known but his presence for trial cannot be obtained by due diligence or he resists appearing at or being returned for trial.

(4) Any period of delay resulting from the fact that the defendant is mentally incompetent or physically unable to stand trial.

(5) If the information or indictment is dismissed upon motion of the attorney for the Government and thereafter a charge is filed against the defendant for the same offense, or any offense required to be joined with that offense, any period of delay from the date the charge was dismissed to the date the time limitation would commence to run as to the subsequent charge had there been no previous charge.

(6) A reasonable period of delay when the defendant is joined for trial with a codefendant as to whom the time for trial has not run and no motion for severance has been granted.

(7)(A) Any period of delay resulting from a continuance granted by any judge on his own motion or at the request of the defendant or his counsel or at the request of the attorney for the Government, if the judge granted such continuance on the basis of his findings that the ends of justice served by taking such action outweigh the best interest of the public and the defendant in a speedy trial. No such period of delay resulting from a continuance granted by the court in accordance with this paragraph shall be excludable under this subsection unless the court sets forth, in the record of the case, either orally or in writing, its reasons for finding that the ends of justice served by the granting of such continuance outweigh the best interests of the public and the defendant in a speedy trial.

(B) The factors, among others, which a judge shall consider in determining whether to grant a continuance under subparagraph (A) of this paragraph in any case are as follows:

(i) Whether the failure to grant such a continuance in the proceeding would be likely to make a continuation of such proceeding impossible, or result in a miscarriage of justice.

(ii) Whether the case is so unusual or so complex, due to the number of defendants, the nature of the prosecution, or the existence of novel questions of fact or law, that it is unreasonable to expect adequate preparation for pretrial proceedings or for the trial itself within the time limits established by this section.

(iii) Whether, in a case in which arrest precedes indictment, delay in the filing of the indictment is caused because the arrest occurs at a time such that it is unreasonable to expect return and filing of the indictment within the period specified in section 3161(b), or because the facts upon which the grand jury must base its determination are unusual or complex.

(iv) Whether the failure to grant such a continuance in a case which, taken as a whole, is not so unusual or so complex as to fall within clause (ii), would deny the defendant reasonable time to obtain counsel, would unreasonably deny the defendant or the Government continuity of counsel, or would deny counsel for the defendant or the attorney for the Government the reasonable time necessary for effective preparation, taking into account the exercise of due diligence.

(C) No continuance under subparagraph (A) of this paragraph shall be granted because of general congestion of the court's calendar, or lack of diligent preparation or failure to obtain available witnesses on the part of the attorney for the Government.

(8) Any period of delay, not to exceed one year, ordered by a district court upon an application of a party and a finding by a preponderance of the evidence that an official request, as defined in section 3292 of this title, has been made for evidence of any such offense and that it reasonably appears, or reasonably appeared at the time the request was made, that such evidence is, or was, in such foreign country.

(i) If trial did not commence within the time limitation specified in section 3161 because the defendant had entered a plea of guilty or nolo contendere subsequently withdrawn to any or all charges in an indictment or information, the defendant shall be deemed indicted with respect to all charges therein contained within the meaning of section 3161, on the day the order permitting withdrawal of the plea becomes final.

(j)(1) If the attorney for the Government knows that a person charged with an offense is serving a term of imprisonment in any penal institution, he shall promptly—

(A) undertake to obtain the presence of the prisoner for trial; or

(B) cause a detainer to be filed with the person having custody of the prisoner and request him to so advise the prisoner and to advise the prisoner of his right to demand trial.

(2) If the person having custody of such prisoner receives a detainer, he shall promptly advise the prisoner of the charge and of the prisoner's right to demand trial. If at any time thereafter the prisoner informs the person having custody that he does demand trial, such person shall cause notice to that effect to be sent promptly to the attorney for the Government who caused the detainer to be filed.

(3) Upon receipt of such notice, the attorney for the Government shall promptly seek to obtain the presence of the prisoner for trial.

(4) When the person having custody of the prisoner receives from the attorney for the Government a properly supported request for temporary custody of such prisoner for trial, the prisoner shall be made available to that attorney for the Government (subject, in cases of interjurisdictional

transfer, to any right of the prisoner to contest the legality of his delivery).

(k)(1) If the defendant is absent (as defined by subsection (h)(3)) on the day set for trial, and the defendant's subsequent appearance before the court on a bench warrant or other process or surrender to the court occurs more than 21 days after the day set for trial, the defendant shall be deemed to have first appeared before a judicial officer of the court in which the information or indictment is pending within the meaning of subsection (c) on the date of the defendant's subsequent appearance before the court.

(2) If the defendant is absent (as defined by subsection (h)(3)) on the day set for trial, and the defendant's subsequent appearance before the court on a bench warrant or other process or surrender to the court occurs not more than 21 days after the day set for trial, the time limit required by subsection (c), as extended by subsection (h), shall be further extended by 21 days.

§ 3162. Sanctions

(a)(1) If, in the case of any individual against whom a complaint is filed charging such individual with an offense, no indictment or information is filed within the time limit required by section 3161(b) as extended by section 3161(h) of this chapter, such charge against that individual contained in such complaint shall be dismissed or otherwise dropped. In determining whether to dismiss the case with or without prejudice, the court shall consider, among others, each of the following factors: the seriousness of the offense; the facts and circumstances of the case which led to the dismissal; and the impact of a reprosecution on the administration of this chapter and on the administration of justice.

(2) If a defendant is not brought to trial within the time limit required by section 3161(c) as extended by section 3161(h), the information or indictment shall be dismissed on motion of the defendant. The defendant shall have the burden of proof of supporting such motion but the Government shall have the burden of going forward with the evidence in connection with any exclusion of time under subparagraph 3161(h) (3). In determining whether to dismiss the case with or without prejudice, the court shall consider, among others, each of the following factors: the seriousness of the offense; the facts and circumstances of the case which led to the dismissal; and the impact of a reprosecution on the administration of this chapter and on the administration of justice. Failure of the defendant to move for dismissal prior to trial or entry of a plea of guilty or nolo contendere shall constitute a waiver of the right to dismissal under this section.

(b) In any case in which counsel for the defendant or the attorney for the Government (1) knowingly allows the case to be set for trial without disclosing the fact that a necessary witness would be unavailable for trial; (2) files a motion solely for the purpose of delay which he knows is totally frivolous and without merit; (3) makes a statement for the purpose of obtaining a continuance which he knows to be false and which is material to the granting of a continuance; or (4) otherwise willfully fails to proceed to trial without justification consistent with section 3161 of this chapter, the court may punish any such counsel or attorney, as follows:

(A) in the case of an appointed defense counsel, by reducing the amount of compensation that otherwise would have been paid to such counsel pursuant to section 3006A of this title in an amount not to exceed 25 per centum thereof;

(B) in the case of a counsel retained in connection with the defense of a defendant, by imposing on such counsel a fine of not to exceed 25 per centum of the compensation to which he is entitled in connection with his defense of such defendant;

(C) by imposing on any attorney for the Government a fine of not to exceed $250;

(D) by denying any such counsel or attorney for the Government the right to practice before the court considering such case for a period of not to exceed ninety days; or

(E) by filing a report with an appropriate disciplinary committee.

The authority to punish provided for by this subsection shall be in addition to any other authority or power available to such court.

(c) The court shall follow procedures established in the Federal Rules of Criminal Procedure in punishing any counsel or attorney for the Government pursuant to this section.

§ 3164.   Persons detained or designated as being of high risk

(a) The trial or other disposition of cases involving—

(1) a detained person who is being held in detention solely because he is awaiting trial, and

(2) a released person who is awaiting trial and has been designated by the attorney for the Government as being of high risk,

shall be accorded priority.

(b) The trial of any person described in subsection (a) (1) or (a) (2) of this section shall commence not later than ninety days following the beginning of such continuous detention or designation of high risk by the attorney for the Government. The periods of delay enumerated in section

3161(h) are excluded in computing the time limitation specified in this section.

(c) Failure to commence trial of a detainee as specified in subsection (b), through no fault of the accused or his counsel, or failure to commence trial of a designated releasee as specified in subsection (b), through no fault of the attorney for the Government, shall result in the automatic review by the court of the conditions of release. No detainee, as defined in subsection (a), shall be held in custody pending trial after the expiration of such ninety-day period required for the commencement of his trial. A designated releasee, as defined in subsection (a), who is found by the court to have intentionally delayed the trial of his case shall be subject to an order of the court modifying his nonfinancial conditions of release under this title to insure that he shall appear at trial as required.

JENCKS ACT

(18 U.S.C. § 3500).

§ 3500. Demands for production of statements and reports of witnesses

(a) In any criminal prosecution brought by the United States, no statement or report in the possession of the United States which was made by a Government witness or prospective Government witness (other than the defendant) shall be the subject of subpena, discovery, or inspection until said witness has testified on direct examination in the trial of the case.

(b) After a witness called by the United States has testified on direct examination, the court shall, on motion of the defendant, order the United States to produce any statement (as hereinafter defined) of the witness in the possession of the United States which relates to the subject matter as to which the witness has testified. If the entire contents of any such statement relate to the subject matter of the testimony of the witness, the court shall order it to be delivered directly to the defendant for his examination and use.

(c) If the United States claims that any statement ordered to be produced under this section contains matter which does not relate to the subject matter of the testimony of the witness, the court shall order the United States to deliver such statement for the inspection of the court in camera. Upon such delivery the court shall excise the portions of such statement which do not relate to the subject matter of the testimony of the witness. With such material excised, the court shall then direct delivery of such statement to the defendant for his use. If, pursuant to such procedure, any portion of such statement is withheld from the defendant and the defendant objects to such withholding, and the trial is continued to an adjudication of the guilt of the defendant, the entire text of such statement shall be preserved by the United States and, in the event the defendant appeals, shall be made available to the appellate court for the purpose of determining the correctness of the ruling of the trial judge. Whenever any statement is delivered to a defendant pursuant to this section, the court in its discretion, upon application of said defendant, may recess proceedings in the trial for such time as it may determine to be reasonably required for the examination of such statement by said defendant and his preparation for its use in the trial.

(d) If the United States elects not to comply with an order of the court under subsection (b) or (c) hereof to deliver to the defendant any such statement, or such portion thereof as the court may direct, the court shall strike from the record the testimony of the witness, and the trial shall proceed unless the court in its discretion shall determine that the interests of justice require that a mistrial be declared.

(e) The term "statement", as used in subsections (b), (c), and (d) of this section in relation to any witness called by the United States, means—

(1) a written statement made by said witness and signed or otherwise adopted or approved by him;

(2) a stenographic, mechanical, electrical, or other recording, or a transcription thereof, which is a substantially verbatim recital of an oral statement made by said witness and recorded contemporaneously with the making of such oral statement; or

(3) a statement, however taken or recorded, or a transcription thereof, if any, made by said witness to a grand jury.

LITIGATION CONCERNING SOURCES OF EVIDENCE

(18 U.S.C. § 3504).

§ 3504. Litigation concerning sources of evidence

(a) In any trial, hearing, or other proceeding in or before any court, grand jury, department, officer, agency, regulatory body, or other authority of the United States—

(1) upon a claim by a party aggrieved that evidence is inadmissible because it is the primary product of an unlawful act or because it was obtained by the exploitation of an unlawful act, the opponent of the claim shall affirm or deny the occurrence of the alleged unlawful act;

(2) disclosure of information for a determination if evidence is inadmissible because it is the primary product of an unlawful act occurring prior to June 19, 1968, or because it was obtained by the exploitation of an unlawful act occurring prior to June 19, 1968, shall not be required unless such information may be relevant to a pending claim of such inadmissibility; and

(3) no claim shall be considered that evidence of an event is inadmissible on the ground that such evidence was obtained by the exploitation of an unlawful act occurring prior to June 19, 1968, if such event occurred more than five years after such allegedly unlawful act.

(b) As used in this section "unlawful act" means any act the use of any electronic, mechanical, or other device (as defined in section 2510(5) of this title) in violation of the Constitution or laws of the United States or any regulation or standard promulgated pursuant thereto.

CRIMINAL APPEALS ACT OF 1970 (AS AMENDED)

(18 U.S.C. § 3731).

§ 3731. Appeal by United States

In a criminal case an appeal by the United States shall lie to a court of appeals from a decision, judgment, or order of a district court dismissing an indictment or information or granting a new trial after verdict or judgment, as to any one or more counts, or any part thereof, except that no appeal shall lie where the double jeopardy clause of the United States Constitution prohibits further prosecution.

An appeal by the United States shall lie to a court of appeals from a decision or order of a district court suppressing or excluding evidence or requiring the return of seized property in a criminal proceeding, not made after the defendant has been put in jeopardy and before the verdict or finding on an indictment or information, if the United States attorney certifies to the district court that the appeal is not taken for purpose of delay and that the evidence is a substantial proof of a fact material in the proceeding.

An appeal by the United States shall lie to a court of appeals from a decision or order, entered by a district court of the United States, granting the release of a person charged with or convicted of an offense, or denying a motion for revocation of, or modification of the conditions of, a decision or order granting release.

The appeal in all such cases shall be taken within thirty days after the decision, judgment or order has been rendered and shall be diligently prosecuted.

The provisions of this section shall be liberally construed to effectuate its purposes.

CRIME VICTIMS' RIGHTS

(18 U.S.C. § 3771).

§ 3771. Crime victims' rights

(a) Rights of crime victims.—A crime victim has the following rights:

(1) The right to be reasonably protected from the accused.

(2) The right to reasonable, accurate, and timely notice of any public court proceeding, or any parole proceeding, involving the crime or of any release or escape of the accused.

(3) The right not to be excluded from any such public court proceeding, unless the court, after receiving clear and convincing evidence, determines that testimony by the victim would be materially altered if the victim heard other testimony at that proceeding.

(4) The right to be reasonably heard at any public proceeding in the district court involving release, plea, sentencing, or any parole proceeding.

(5) The reasonable right to confer with the attorney for the Government in the case.

(6) The right to full and timely restitution as provided in law.

(7) The right to proceedings free from unreasonable delay.

(8) The right to be treated with fairness and with respect for the victim's dignity and privacy.

(b) Rights afforded.—

(1) In general.—

In any court proceeding involving an offense against a crime victim, the court shall ensure that the crime victim is afforded the rights described in subsection (a). Before making a determination described in subsection (a)(3), the court shall make every effort to permit the fullest attendance possible by the victim and shall consider reasonable alternatives to the exclusion of the victim from the criminal proceeding. The reasons for any decision denying relief under this chapter shall be clearly stated on the record.

(2) Habeas corpus proceedings.—

(A) In general.—In a Federal habeas corpus proceeding arising out of a State conviction, the court shall ensure that a crime victim is afforded the rights described in paragraphs (3), (4), (7), and (8) of subsection (a).

(B) Enforcement.—

(i) In general.—These rights may be enforced by the crime victim or the crime victim's lawful representative in the manner described in paragraphs (1) and (3) of subsection (d).

(ii) Multiple victims.—In a case involving multiple victims, subsection (d)(2) shall also apply.

(C) Limitation.—This paragraph relates to the duties of a court in relation to the rights of a crime victim in Federal habeas corpus proceedings arising out of a State conviction, and does not give rise to any obligation or requirement applicable to personnel of any agency of the Executive Branch of the Federal Government.

(D) Definition.—For purposes of this paragraph, the term "crime victim" means the person against whom the State offense is committed or, if that person is killed or incapacitated, that person's family member or other lawful representative.

(c) Best efforts to accord rights.—

(1) Government.—Officers and employees of the Department of Justice and other departments and agencies of the United States engaged in the detection, investigation, or prosecution of crime shall make their best efforts to see that crime victims are notified of, and accorded, the rights described in subsection (a).

(2) Advice of attorney.—The prosecutor shall advise the crime victim that the crime victim can seek the advice of an attorney with respect to the rights described in subsection (a).

(3) Notice.—Notice of release otherwise required pursuant to this chapter shall not be given if such notice may endanger the safety of any person.

(d) Enforcement and limitations.—

(1) Rights.—The crime victim or the crime victim's lawful representative, and the attorney for the Government may assert the rights described in subsection (a). A person accused of the crime may not obtain any form of relief under this chapter.

(2) Multiple crime victims.—In a case where the court finds that the number of crime victims makes it impracticable to accord all of the crime victims the rights described in subsection (a), the court shall fashion a reasonable procedure to give effect to this chapter that does not unduly complicate or prolong the proceedings.

(3) Motion for relief and writ of mandamus.—The rights described in subsection (a) shall be asserted in the district court in which a defendant is being prosecuted for the crime or, if no prosecution is underway, in the district court in the district in which the crime occurred. The district court shall take up and decide any motion asserting a victim's right forthwith. If the district court denies the relief sought, the movant may petition the court of appeals for a writ of mandamus. The court of appeals may issue the writ on the order of a single judge pursuant to circuit rule or the Federal Rules of Appellate Procedure. The court of appeals shall take up and decide such application forthwith within 72 hours after the petition has been filed. In no event shall proceedings be stayed or subject to a continuance of more than five days for purposes of enforcing this chapter. If the court of appeals denies the relief sought, the reasons for the denial shall be clearly stated on the record in a written opinion.

(4) Error.—In any appeal in a criminal case, the Government may assert as error the district court's denial of any crime victim's right in the proceeding to which the appeal relates.

(5) Limitation on relief.—In no case shall a failure to afford a right under this chapter provide grounds for a new trial. A victim may make a motion to re-open a plea or sentence only if—

(A) the victim has asserted the right to be heard before or during the proceeding at issue and such right was denied;

(B) the victim petitions the court of appeals for a writ of mandamus within 14 days; and

(C) in the case of a plea, the accused has not pled to the highest offense charged.

This paragraph does not affect the victim's right to restitution as provided in title 18, United States Code.

(6) No cause of action.—Nothing in this chapter shall be construed to authorize a cause of action for damages or to create, to enlarge, or to imply any duty or obligation to any victim or other person for the breach of which the United States or any of its officers or employees could be held liable in damages. Nothing

in this chapter shall be construed to impair the prosecutorial discretion of the Attorney General or any officer under his direction.

(e) Definitions.—For the purposes of this chapter, the term "crime victim" means a person directly and proximately harmed as a result of the commission of a Federal offense or an offense in the District of Columbia. In the case of a crime victim who is under 18 years of age, incompetent, incapacitated, or deceased, the legal guardians of the crime victim or the representatives of the crime victim's estate, family members, or any other persons appointed as suitable by the court, may assume the crime victim's rights under this chapter, but in no event shall the defendant be named as such guardian or representative.

(f) Procedures to promote compliance.—

(1) Regulations.—Not later than 1 year after the date of enactment of this chapter, the Attorney General of the United States shall promulgate regulations to enforce the rights of crime victims and to ensure compliance by responsible officials with the obligations described in law respecting crime victims.

(2) Contents.—The regulations promulgated under paragraph (1) shall—

(A) designate an administrative authority within the Department of Justice to receive and investigate complaints relating to the provision or violation of the rights of a crime victim;

(B) require a course of training for employees and offices of the Department of Justice that fail to comply with provisions of Federal law pertaining to the treatment of crime victims, and otherwise assist such employees and offices in responding more effectively to the needs of crime victims;

(C) contain disciplinary sanctions, including suspension or termination from employment, for employees of the Department of Justice who willfully or wantonly fail to comply with provisions of Federal law pertaining to the treatment of crime victims; and

(D) provide that the Attorney General, or the designee of the Attorney General, shall be the final arbiter of the complaint, and that there shall be no judicial review of the final decision of the Attorney General by a complainant.

JURY SELECTION AND SERVICE ACT OF 1968 (AS AMENDED)

(28 U.S.C. §§ 1861–1863, 1865–1867).

§ 1861. Declaration of policy

It is the policy of the United States that all litigants in Federal courts entitled to trial by jury shall have the right to grand and petit juries selected at random from a fair cross section of the community in the district or division wherein the court convenes. It is further the policy of the United States that all citizens shall have the opportunity to be considered for service on grand and petit juries in the district courts of the United States, and shall have an obligation to serve as jurors when summoned for that purpose.

§ 1862. Discrimination prohibited

No citizen shall be excluded from service as a grand or petit juror in the district courts of the United States or in the Court of International Trade on account of race, color, religion, sex, national origin, or economic status.

§ 1863. Plan for random jury selection

(a) Each United States district court shall devise and place into operation a written plan for random selection of grand and petit jurors that shall be designed to achieve the objectives of sections 1861 and 1862 of this title, and that shall otherwise comply with the provisions of this title. The plan shall be placed into operation after approval by a reviewing panel consisting of the members of the judicial council of the circuit and either the chief judge of the district whose plan is being reviewed or such other active district judge of that district as the chief judge of the district may designate. The panel shall examine the plan to ascertain that it complies with the provisions of this title. If the reviewing panel finds that the plan does not comply, the panel shall state the particulars in which the plan fails to comply and direct the district court to present within a reasonable time an alternative plan remedying the defect or defects. Separate plans may be adopted for each division or combination of divisions within a judicial district. The district court may modify a plan at any time and it shall modify the plan when so directed by the reviewing panel. The district court shall promptly notify the panel, the Administrative Office of the United States Courts, and the Attorney General of the United States, of the initial adoption and future modifications of the plan by filing copies therewith. Modifications of the plan made at the instance of the district court shall become effective after approval by the panel. Each district court shall submit a report on the jury selection process within its jurisdiction to the Administrative Office of the United States Courts in such form and at such times as the Judicial

Conference of the United States may specify. The Judicial Conference of the United States may, from time to time, adopt rules and regulations governing the provisions and the operation of the plans formulated under this title.

(b) Among other things, such plan shall—

(1) either establish a jury commission, or authorize the clerk of the court, to manage the jury selection process. If the plan establishes a jury commission, the district court shall appoint one citizen to serve with the clerk of the court as the jury commission: *Provided, however*, That the plan for the District of Columbia may establish a jury commission consisting of three citizens. The citizen jury commissioner shall not belong to the same political party as the clerk serving with him. The clerk or the jury commission, as the case may be, shall act under the supervision and control of the chief judge of the district court or such other judge of the district court as the plan may provide. Each jury commissioner shall, during his tenure in office, reside in the judicial district or division for which he is appointed. Each citizen jury commissioner shall receive compensation to be fixed by the district court plan at a rate not to exceed $50 per day for each day necessarily employed in the performance of his duties, plus reimbursement for travel, subsistence, and other necessary expenses incurred by him in the performance of such duties. The Judicial Conference of the United States may establish standards for allowance of travel, subsistence, and other necessary expenses incurred by jury commissioners.

(2) specify whether the names of prospective jurors shall be selected from the voter registration lists or the lists of actual voters of the political subdivisions within the district or division. The plan shall prescribe some other source or sources of names in addition to voter lists where necessary to foster the policy and protect the rights secured by sections 1861 and 1862 of this title. The plan for the District of Columbia may require the names of prospective jurors to be selected from the city directory rather than from voter lists. The plans for the districts of Puerto Rico and the Canal Zone may prescribe some other source or sources of names of prospective jurors in lieu of voter lists, the use of which shall be consistent with the policies declared and rights secured by sections 1861 and 1862 of this title. The plan for the district of Massachusetts may require the names of prospective jurors to be selected from the resident list provided for in chapter 234A, Massachusetts General Laws, or comparable authority, rather than from voter lists.

(3) specify detailed procedures to be followed by the jury commission or clerk in selecting names from the sources specified in paragraph (2) of this subsection. These procedures shall be designed to ensure the random selection of a fair cross section of the persons residing in the community in the district or division wherein the court convenes. They shall ensure that names of persons residing in each of the counties, parishes, or similar political subdivisions within the judicial district or division are placed in a master jury wheel; and shall ensure that each county, parish, or similar political subdivision within the district or division is substantially proportionally represented in the master jury wheel for that judicial district, division, or combination of divisions. For the purposes of determining proportional representation in the master jury wheel, either the number of actual voters at the last general election in each county, parish, or similar political subdivision, or the number of registered voters if registration of voters is uniformly required throughout the district or division, may be used.

(4) provide for a master jury wheel (or a device similar in purpose and function) into which the names of those randomly selected shall be placed. The plan shall fix a minimum number of names to be placed initially in the master jury wheel, which shall be at least one-half of 1 per centum of the total number of persons on the lists used as a source of names for the district or division; but if this number of names is believed to be cumbersome and unnecessary, the plan may fix a smaller number of names to be placed in the master wheel, but in no event less than one thousand. The chief judge of the district court, or such other district court judge as the plan may provide, may order additional names to be placed in the master jury wheel from time to time as necessary. The plan shall provide for periodic emptying and refilling of the master jury wheel at specified times, the interval for which shall not exceed four years.

(5)(A) except as provided in subparagraph (B), specify those groups of persons or occupational classes whose members shall, on individual request therefor, be excused from jury service. Such groups or classes shall be excused only if the district court finds, and the plan states, that jury service by such class or group would entail undue hardship or extreme inconvenience to the members thereof, and excuse of members thereof would not be inconsistent with sections 1861 and 1862 of this title.

(B) specify that volunteer safety personnel, upon individual request, shall be excused from jury service. For purposes of this subparagraph, the term "volunteer safety personnel" means individuals serving a public agency (as defined in section 1203(6) of title I of the Omnibus Crime Control and Safe Streets Act of 1968) in an official capacity, without compensation, as firefighters or members of a rescue squad or ambulance crew.

(6) specify that the following persons are barred from jury service on the ground that they are exempt: (A) members in active service in the Armed Forces of the United States; (B) members of the fire or police departments of any State, the District of Columbia, any territory or possession of the United States, or any subdivision of a State, the District of Columbia, or such territory or possession; (C) public officers in the executive, legislative, or judicial branches of the Government of the United States, or of any State, the District of Columbia, any territory or possession of the United States, or any subdivision of a State, the District of Columbia, or such territory or possession, who are actively engaged in the performance of official duties.

(7) fix the time when the names drawn from the qualified jury wheel shall be disclosed to parties and to the public. If the plan permits these names to be made public, it may nevertheless permit the chief judge of the district court, or such other district court judge as the plan may provide, to keep these names confidential in any case where the interests of justice so require.

(8) specify the procedures to be followed by the clerk or jury commission in assigning persons whose names have been drawn from the qualified jury wheel to grand and petit jury panels.

(c) The initial plan shall be devised by each district court and transmitted to the reviewing panel specified in subsection (a) of this section within one hundred and twenty days of the date of enactment of the Jury Selection and Service Act of 1968. The panel shall approve or direct the modification of each plan so submitted within sixty days thereafter. Each plan or modification made at the direction of the panel shall become effective after approval at such time thereafter as the panel directs, in no event to exceed ninety days from the date of approval. Modifications made at the instance of the district court under subsection (a) of this section shall be effective at such time thereafter as the panel directs, in no event to exceed ninety days from the date of modification.

(d) State, local, and Federal officials having custody, possession, or control of voter registration lists, lists of actual voters, or other appropriate records shall make such lists and records available to the jury commission or clerks for inspection, reproduction, and copying at all reasonable times as the commission or clerk may deem necessary and proper for the performance of duties under this title. The district courts shall have jurisdiction upon application by the Attorney General of the United States to compel compliance with this subsection by appropriate process.

§ 1865. Qualifications for jury service

(a) The chief judge of the district court, or such other district court judge as the plan may provide, on his initiative or upon recommendation of the clerk or jury commission, or the clerk under supervision of the court if the court's jury selection plan so authorizes, shall determine solely on the basis of information provided on the juror qualification form and other competent evidence whether a person is unqualified for, or exempt, or to be excused from jury service. The clerk shall enter such determination in the space provided on the juror qualification form and in any alphabetical list of names drawn from the master jury wheel. If a person did not appear in response to a summons, such fact shall be noted on said list.

(b) In making such determination the chief judge of the district court, or such other district court judge as the plan may provide, or the clerk if the court's jury selection plan so provides, shall deem any person qualified to serve on grand and petit juries in the district court unless he—

(1) is not a citizen of the United States eighteen years old who has resided for a period of one year within the judicial district;

(2) is unable to read, write, and understand the English language with a degree of proficiency sufficient to fill out satisfactorily the juror qualification form;

(3) is unable to speak the English language;

(4) is incapable, by reason of mental or physical infirmity, to render satisfactory jury service; or

(5) has a charge pending against him for the commission of, or has been convicted in a State or Federal court of record of, a crime punishable by imprisonment for more than one year and his civil rights have not been restored.

§ 1866. Selection and summoning of jury panels

(a) The jury commission, or in the absence thereof the clerk, shall maintain a qualified jury wheel and shall place in such wheel names of all persons drawn from the master jury wheel who are determined to be qualified as jurors and not exempt or excused pursuant to the district court plan. From time to time, the jury commission or the clerk shall draw at random from the qualified jury wheel such number of names of persons as may be required for assignment to grand and petit jury panels.

The clerk or jury commission shall post a general notice for public review in the clerk's office and on the court's website explaining the process by which names are periodically and randomly drawn. The jury commission or the clerk shall prepare a separate list of names of persons assigned to each grand and petit jury panel.

(b) When the court orders a grand or petit jury to be drawn, the clerk or jury commission or their duly designated deputies shall issue summonses for the required number of jurors.

Each person drawn for jury service may be served personally, or by registered, certified, or first-class mail addressed to such person at his usual residence or business address.

If such service is made personally, the summons shall be delivered by the clerk or the jury commission or their duly designated deputies to the marshal who shall make such service.

If such service is made by mail, the summons may be served by the marshal or by the clerk, the jury commission or their duly designated deputies, who shall make affidavit of service and shall attach thereto any receipt from the addressee for a registered or certified summons.

(c) Except as provided in section 1865 of this title or in any jury selection plan provision adopted pursuant to paragraph (5) or (6) of section 1863(b) of this title, no person or class of persons shall be disqualified, excluded, excused, or exempt from service as jurors: *Provided*, That any person summoned for jury service may be (1) excused by the court, or by the clerk under supervision of the court if the court's jury selection plan so authorizes, upon a showing of undue hardship or extreme inconvenience, for such period as the court deems necessary, at the conclusion of which such person either shall be summoned again for jury service under subsections (b) and (c) of this section or, if the court's jury selection plan so provides, the name of such person shall be reinserted into the qualified jury wheel for selection pursuant to subsection (a) of this section, or (2) excluded by the court on the ground that such person may be unable to render impartial jury service or that his service as a juror would be likely to disrupt the proceedings, or (3) excluded upon peremptory challenge as provided by law, or (4) excluded pursuant to the procedure specified by law upon a challenge by any party for good cause shown, or (5) excluded upon determination by the court that his service as a juror would be likely to threaten the secrecy of the proceedings, or otherwise adversely affect the integrity of jury deliberations. No person shall be excluded under clause (5) of this subsection unless the judge, in open court, determines that such is warranted and that exclusion of the person will not be inconsistent with sections 1861 and 1862 of this title. The number of persons excluded under clause (5) of this subsection shall not exceed one per centum of the number of persons who return executed jury qualification forms during the period, specified in the plan, between two consecutive fillings of the master jury wheel. The names of persons excluded under clause (5) of this subsection, together with detailed explanations for the exclusions, shall be forwarded immediately to the judicial council of the circuit, which shall have the power to make any appropriate order, prospective or retroactive, to redress any misapplication of clause (5) of this subsection, but otherwise exclusions effectuated under such clause shall not be subject to challenge under the provisions of this title. Any person excluded from a particular jury under clause (2), (3), or (4) of this subsection shall be eligible to sit on another jury if the basis for his initial exclusion would not be relevant to his ability to serve on such other jury.

(d) Whenever a person is disqualified, excused, exempt, or excluded from jury service, the jury commission or clerk shall note in the space provided on his juror qualification form or on the juror's card drawn from the qualified jury wheel the specific reason therefor.

(e) In any two-year period, no person shall be required to (1) serve or attend court for prospective service as a petit juror for a total of more than thirty days, except when necessary to complete service in a particular case, or (2) serve on more than one grand jury, or (3) serve as both a grand and petit juror.

(f) When there is an unanticipated shortage of available petit jurors drawn from the qualified jury wheel, the court may require the marshal to summon a sufficient number of petit jurors selected at random from the voter registration lists, lists of actual voters, or other lists specified in the plan, in a manner ordered by the court consistent with sections 1861 and 1862 of this title.

(g) Any person summoned for jury service who fails to appear as directed may be ordered by the district court to appear forthwith and show cause for failure to comply with the summons. Any person who fails to show good cause for noncompliance with a summons may be fined not more than $1,000, imprisoned not more than three days, ordered to perform community service, or any combination thereof.

§ 1867. Challenging compliance with selection procedures

(a) In criminal cases, before the voir dire examination begins, or within seven days after the defendant discovered or could have discovered, by the exercise of diligence, the grounds therefor, whichever is earlier, the defendant may move to dismiss the indictment or stay the proceedings against him on the ground of substantial failure to comply with the provisions of this title in selecting the grand or petit jury.

(b) In criminal cases, before the voir dire examination begins, or within seven days after the Attorney General of the United States discovered or could have discovered, by the exercise of diligence, the grounds therefor, whichever is earlier, the Attorney General may move to dismiss the indictment or stay the proceedings on the ground of substantial failure to comply with the provisions of this title in selecting the grand or petit jury.

(c) In civil cases, before the voir dire examination begins, or within seven days after the party discovered or could have discovered, by the exercise of diligence, the grounds therefor, whichever is earlier, any party may move to stay the proceedings on the ground of substantial failure to comply with the provisions of this title in selecting the petit jury.

(d) Upon motion filed under subsection (a), (b), or (c) of this section, containing a sworn statement of facts which, if true, would constitute a substantial failure to comply with the provisions of this title, the moving party shall be entitled to present in support of such motion the testimony of the jury commission or clerk, if available, any relevant records and papers not public or otherwise available used by the jury commissioner or clerk, and any other relevant evidence. If the court determines that there has been a substantial failure to comply with the provisions of this title in selecting the grand jury, the court shall stay the proceedings pending the selection of a grand jury in conformity with this title or dismiss the indictment, whichever is appropriate. If the court determines that there has been a substantial failure to comply with the provisions of this title in selecting the petit jury, the court shall stay the proceedings pending the selection of a petit jury in conformity with this title.

(e) The procedures prescribed by this section shall be the exclusive means by which a person accused of a Federal crime, the Attorney General of the United States or a party in a civil case may challenge any jury on the ground that such jury was not selected in conformity with the provisions of this title. Nothing in this section shall preclude any person or the United States from pursuing any other remedy, civil or criminal, which may be available for the vindication or enforcement of any law prohibiting discrimination on account of race, color, religion, sex, national origin or economic status in the selection of persons for service on grand or petit juries.

(f) The contents of records or papers used by the jury commission or clerk in connection with the jury selection process shall not be disclosed, except pursuant to the district court plan or as may be necessary in the preparation or presentation of a motion under subsection (a), (b), or (c) of this section, until after the master jury wheel has been emptied and refilled pursuant to section 1863(b)(4) of this title and all persons selected to serve as jurors before the master wheel was emptied have completed such service. The parties in a case shall be allowed to inspect, reproduce, and copy such records or papers at all reasonable times during the preparation and pendency of such a motion. Any person who discloses the contents of any record or paper in violation of this subsection may be fined not more than $1,000 or imprisoned not more than one year, or both.

HABEAS CORPUS

(28 U.S.C. §§ 2241–2244, 2253–2255, 2261–2266).

§ 2241. Power to grant writ

(a) Writs of habeas corpus may be granted by the Supreme Court, any justice thereof, the district courts and any circuit judge within their respective jurisdictions. The order of a circuit judge shall be entered in the records of the district court of the district wherein the restraint complained of is had.

(b) The Supreme Court, any justice thereof, and any circuit judge may decline to entertain an application for a writ of habeas corpus and may transfer the application for hearing and determination to the district court having jurisdiction to entertain it.

(c) The writ of habeas corpus shall not extend to a prisoner unless—

(1) He is in custody under or by color of the authority of the United States or is committed for trial before some court thereof; or

(2) He is in custody for an act done or omitted in pursuance of an Act of Congress, or an order, process, judgment or decree of a court or judge of the United States; or

(3) He is in custody in violation of the Constitution or laws or treaties of the United States; or

(4) He, being a citizen of a foreign state and domiciled therein is in custody for an act done or omitted under any alleged right, title, authority, privilege, protection, or exemption claimed under the commission, order or sanction of any foreign state, or under color thereof, the validity and effect of which depend upon the law of nations; or

(5) It is necessary to bring him into court to testify or for trial.

(d) Where an application for a writ of habeas corpus is made by a person in custody under the judgment and sentence of a State court of a State which contains two or more Federal judicial districts, the application may be filed in the district court for the district wherein such person is in custody or in the district court for the district within which the State court was held which convicted and sentenced him and each of such district courts shall have concurrent jurisdiction to entertain the application. The district court for the district wherein such an application is filed in the exercise of its discretion and in furtherance of justice may transfer the application to the other district court for hearing and determination.

(e)(1) No court, justice, or judge shall have jurisdiction to hear or consider an application for a writ of habeas corpus filed by or on behalf of an alien detained by the United States who has been determined by the United States to have been properly detained as an enemy combatant or is awaiting such determination.

(2) Except as provided in paragraphs (2) and (3) of section 1005(e) of the Detainee Treatment Act of 2005 (10 U.S.C. 801 note), no court, justice, or judge shall have jurisdiction to hear or consider any other action against the United States or its agents relating to any aspect of the detention, transfer, treatment, trial, or conditions of confinement of an alien who is or was detained by the United States and has been determined by the United States to have been properly detained as an enemy combatant or is awaiting such determination.

§ 2242. Application

Application for a writ of habeas corpus shall be in writing signed and verified by the person for whose relief it is intended or by someone acting in his behalf.

It shall allege the facts concerning the applicant's commitment or detention, the name of the person who has custody over him and by virtue of what claim or authority, if known.

It may be amended or supplemented as provided in the rules of procedure applicable to civil actions.

If addressed to the Supreme Court, a justice thereof or a circuit judge it shall state the reasons for not making application to the district court of the district in which the applicant is held.

§ 2243. Issuance of writ; return; hearing; decision

A court, justice or judge entertaining an application for a writ of habeas corpus shall forthwith award the writ or issue an order directing the respondent to show cause why the writ should not be granted, unless it appears from the application that the applicant or person detained is not entitled thereto.

The writ, or order to show cause shall be directed to the person having custody of the person detained. It shall be returned within three days unless for good cause additional time, not exceeding twenty days, is allowed.

The person to whom the writ or order is directed shall make a return certifying the true cause of the detention.

When the writ or order is returned a day shall be set for hearing, not more than five days after the return unless for good cause additional time is allowed.

Unless the application for the writ and the return present only issues of law the person to whom the writ is directed shall be required to produce at the hearing the body of the person detained.

The applicant or the person detained may, under oath, deny any of the facts set forth in the return or allege any other material facts.

The return and all suggestions made against it may be amended, by leave of court, before or after being filed.

The court shall summarily hear and determine the facts, and dispose of the matter as law and justice require.

§ 2244. Finality of determination

(a) No circuit or district judge shall be required to entertain an application for a writ of habeas corpus to inquire into the detention of a person pursuant to a judgment of a court of the United States if it appears that the legality of such detention has been determined by a judge or court of the United States on a prior application for a writ of habeas corpus, except as provided in section 2255.

(b)(1) A claim presented in a second or successive habeas corpus application under section 2254 that was presented in a prior application shall be dismissed.

(2) A claim presented in a second or successive habeas corpus application under section 2254 that was not presented in a prior application shall be dismissed unless—

> (A) the applicant shows that the claim relies on a new rule of constitutional law, made retroactive to cases on collateral review by the Supreme Court, that was previously unavailable; or

> (B)(i) the factual predicate for the claim could not have been discovered previously through the exercise of due diligence; and

> (ii) the facts underlying the claim, if proven and viewed in light of the evidence as a whole, would be sufficient to establish by clear and convincing evidence that, but for constitutional error, no reasonable factfinder would have found the applicant guilty of the underlying offense.

(3)(A) Before a second or successive application permitted by this section is filed in the district court, the applicant shall move in the appropriate court of appeals for an order authorizing the district court to consider the application.

(B) A motion in the court of appeals for an order authorizing the district court to consider a second or successive application shall be determined by a three-judge panel of the court of appeals.

(C) The court of appeals may authorize the filing of a second or successive application only if it determines that the application makes a prima facie showing that the application satisfies the requirements of this subsection.

(D) The court of appeals shall grant or deny the authorization to file a second or successive application not later than 30 days after the filing of the motion.

(E) The grant or denial of an authorization by a court of appeals to file a second or successive application shall not be appealable and shall not be the subject of a petition for rehearing or for a writ of certiorari.

(4) A district court shall dismiss any claim presented in a second or successive application that the court of appeals has authorized to be filed unless the applicant shows that the claim satisfies the requirements of this section.

(c) In a habeas corpus proceeding brought in behalf of a person in custody pursuant to the judgment of a State court, a prior judgment of the Supreme Court of the United States on an appeal or review by a writ of certiorari at the instance of the prisoner of the decision of such State court, shall be conclusive as to all issues of fact or law with respect to an asserted denial of a Federal right which constitutes ground for discharge in a habeas corpus proceeding, actually adjudicated by the Supreme Court therein, unless the applicant for the writ of habeas corpus shall plead and the court shall find the existence of a material and controlling fact which did not appear in the record of the proceeding in the Supreme Court and the court shall further find that the applicant for the writ of habeas corpus could not have caused such fact to appear in such record by the exercise of reasonable diligence.

(d)(1) A 1-year period of limitation shall apply to an application for a writ of habeas corpus by a person in custody pursuant to the judgment of a State court. The limitation period shall run from the latest of—

(A) the date on which the judgment became final by the conclusion of direct review or the expiration of the time for seeking such review;

(B) the date on which the impediment to filing an application created by State action in violation of the

Constitution or laws of the United States is removed, if the applicant was prevented from filing by such State action;

(C) the date on which the constitutional right asserted was initially recognized by the Supreme Court, if the right has been newly recognized by the Supreme Court and made retroactively applicable to cases on collateral review; or

(D) the date on which the factual predicate of the claim or claims presented could have been discovered through the exercise of due diligence.

(2) The time during which a properly filed application for State post-conviction or other collateral review with respect to the pertinent judgment or claim is pending shall not be counted toward any period of limitation under this subsection.

§ 2253. Appeal

(a) In a habeas corpus proceeding or a proceeding under section 2255 before a district judge, the final order shall be subject to review, on appeal, by the court of appeals for the circuit in which the proceeding is held.

(b) There shall be no right of appeal from a final order in a proceeding to test the validity of a warrant to remove to another district or place for commitment or trial a person charged with a criminal offense against the United States, or to test the validity of such person's detention pending removal proceedings.

(c)(1) Unless a circuit justice or judge issues a certificate of appealability, an appeal may not be taken to the court of appeals from—

(A) the final order in a habeas corpus proceeding in which the detention complained of arises out of process issued by a State court; or

(B) the final order in a proceeding under section 2255.

(2) A certificate of appealability may issue under paragraph (1) only if the applicant has made a substantial showing of the denial of a constitutional right.

(3) The certificate of appealability under paragraph (1) shall indicate which specific issue or issues satisfy the showing required by paragraph (2).

§ 2254. State custody; remedies in Federal courts

(a) The Supreme Court, a Justice thereof, a circuit judge, or a district court shall entertain an application for a writ of habeas corpus in behalf of a person in custody pursuant to the judgment of a State court only on the ground that he is in custody in violation of the Constitution or laws or treaties of the United States.

(b)(1) An application for a writ of habeas corpus on behalf of a person in custody pursuant to the judgment of a State court shall not be granted unless it appears that—

    (A) the applicant has exhausted the remedies available in the courts of the State; or

    (B)(i) there is an absence of available State corrective process; or

    (ii) circumstances exist that render such process ineffective to protect the rights of the applicant.

(2) An application for a writ of habeas corpus may be denied on the merits, notwithstanding the failure of the applicant to exhaust the remedies available in the courts of the State.

(3) A State shall not be deemed to have waived the exhaustion requirement or be estopped from reliance upon the requirement unless the State, through counsel, expressly waives the requirement.

(c) An applicant shall not be deemed to have exhausted the remedies available in the courts of the State, within the meaning of this section, if he has the right under the law of the State to raise, by any available procedure, the question presented.

(d) An application for a writ of habeas corpus on behalf of a person in custody pursuant to the judgment of a State court shall not be granted with respect to any claim that was adjudicated on the merits in State court proceedings unless the adjudication of the claim—

    (1) resulted in a decision that was contrary to, or involved an unreasonable application of, clearly established Federal law, as determined by the Supreme Court of the United States; or

    (2) resulted in a decision that was based on an unreasonable determination of the facts in light of the evidence presented in the State court proceeding.

(e)(1) In a proceeding instituted by an application for a writ of habeas corpus by a person in custody pursuant to the judgment of a State court, a determination of a factual issue made by a State court shall be presumed to be correct. The applicant shall have the burden of rebutting the presumption of correctness by clear and convincing evidence.

(2) If the applicant has failed to develop the factual basis of a claim in State court proceedings, the court shall not hold an evidentiary hearing on the claim unless the applicant shows that—

    (A) the claim relies on—

(i) a new rule of constitutional law, made retroactive to cases on collateral review by the Supreme Court, that was previously unavailable; or

(ii) a factual predicate that could not have been previously discovered through the exercise of due diligence; and

(B) the facts underlying the claim would be sufficient to establish by clear and convincing evidence that but for constitutional error, no reasonable factfinder would have found the applicant guilty of the underlying offense.

(f) If the applicant challenges the sufficiency of the evidence adduced in such State court proceeding to support the State court's determination of a factual issue made therein, the applicant, if able, shall produce that part of the record pertinent to a determination of the sufficiency of the evidence to support such determination. If the applicant, because of indigency or other reason is unable to produce such part of the record, then the State shall produce such part of the record and the Federal court shall direct the State to do so by order directed to an appropriate State official. If the State cannot provide such pertinent part of the record, then the court shall determine under the existing facts and circumstances what weight shall be given to the State court's factual determination.

(g) A copy of the official records of the State court, duly certified by the clerk of such court to be a true and correct copy of a finding, judicial opinion, or other reliable written indicia showing such a factual determination by the State court shall be admissible in the Federal court proceeding.

(h) Except as provided in section 408 of the Controlled Substances Act, in all proceedings brought under this section, and any subsequent proceedings on review, the court may appoint counsel for an applicant who is or becomes financially unable to afford counsel, except as provided by a rule promulgated by the Supreme Court pursuant to statutory authority. Appointment of counsel under this section shall be governed by section 3006A of title 18.

(i) The ineffectiveness or incompetence of counsel during Federal or State collateral post-conviction proceedings shall not be a ground for relief in a proceeding arising under section 2254.

§ 2255. Federal custody; remedies on motion attacking sentence

(a) A prisoner in custody under sentence of a court established by Act of Congress claiming the right to be released upon the ground that the sentence was imposed in violation of the Constitution or laws of the United States, or that the court was without jurisdiction to impose such sentence, or that the sentence was in excess of the maximum authorized by law, or is otherwise subject to collateral attack, may move the court which imposed the sentence to vacate, set aside or correct the sentence.

(b) Unless the motion and the files and records of the case conclusively show that the prisoner is entitled to no relief, the court shall cause notice thereof to be served upon the United States attorney, grant a prompt hearing thereon, determine the issues and make findings of fact and conclusions of law with respect thereto. If the court finds that the judgment was rendered without jurisdiction, or that the sentence imposed was not authorized by law or otherwise open to collateral attack, or that there has been such a denial or infringement of the constitutional rights of the prisoner as to render the judgment vulnerable to collateral attack, the court shall vacate and set the judgment aside and shall discharge the prisoner or resentence him or grant a new trial or correct the sentence as may appear appropriate.

(c) A court may entertain and determine such motion without requiring the production of the prisoner at the hearing.

(d) An appeal may be taken to the court of appeals from the order entered on the motion as from a final judgment on application for a writ of habeas corpus.

(e) An application for a writ of habeas corpus in behalf of a prisoner who is authorized to apply for relief by motion pursuant to this section, shall not be entertained if it appears that the applicant has failed to apply for relief, by motion, to the court which sentenced him, or that such court has denied him relief, unless it also appears that the remedy by motion is inadequate or ineffective to test the legality of his detention.

(f) A 1-year period of limitation shall apply to a motion under this section. The limitation period shall run from the latest of—

(1) the date on which the judgment of conviction becomes final;

(2) the date on which the impediment to making a motion created by governmental action in violation of the Constitution or laws of the United States is removed, if the movant was prevented from making a motion by such governmental action;

(3) the date on which the right asserted was initially recognized by the Supreme Court, if that right has been newly recognized by the Supreme Court and made retroactively applicable to cases on collateral review; or

(4) the date on which the facts supporting the claim or claims presented could have been discovered through the exercise of due diligence.

(g) Except as provided in section 408 of the Controlled Substances Act, in all proceedings brought under this section, and any subsequent proceedings on review, the court may appoint counsel, except as provided by a rule promulgated by the Supreme Court pursuant to statutory authority. Appointment of counsel under this section shall be governed by section 3006A of title 18.

(h) A second or successive motion must be certified as provided in section 2244 by a panel of the appropriate court of appeals to contain—

(1) newly discovered evidence that, if proven and viewed in light of the evidence as a whole, would be sufficient to establish by clear and convincing evidence that no reasonable factfinder would have found the movant guilty of the offense; or

(2) a new rule of constitutional law, made retroactive to cases on collateral review by the Supreme Court, that was previously unavailable.

§ 2261. Prisoners in State custody subject to capital sentence; appointment of counsel; requirement of rule of court or statute; procedures for appointment

(a) This chapter shall apply to cases arising under section 2254 brought by prisoners in State custody who are subject to a capital sentence. It shall apply only if the provisions of subsections (b) and (c) are satisfied.

(b) Counsel.—This chapter is applicable if—

(1) the Attorney General of the United States certifies that a State has established a mechanism for providing counsel in postconviction proceedings as provided in section 2265; and

(2) counsel was appointed pursuant to that mechanism, petitioner validly waived counsel, petitioner retained counsel, or petitioner was found not to be indigent.

(c) Any mechanism for the appointment, compensation, and reimbursement of counsel as provided in subsection (b) must offer counsel to all State prisoners under capital sentence and must provide for the entry of an order by a court of record—

(1) appointing one or more counsels to represent the prisoner upon a finding that the prisoner is indigent and accepted the offer or is unable competently to decide whether to accept or reject the offer;

(2) finding, after a hearing if necessary, that the prisoner rejected the offer of counsel and made the decision with an understanding of its legal consequences; or

(3) denying the appointment of counsel upon a finding that the prisoner is not indigent.

(d) No counsel appointed pursuant to subsections (b) and (c) to represent a State prisoner under capital sentence shall have previously represented the prisoner at trial in the case for which the appointment is made unless the prisoner and counsel expressly request continued representation.

(e) The ineffectiveness or incompetence of counsel during State or Federal post-conviction proceedings in a capital case shall not be a ground for relief in a proceeding arising under section 2254. This limitation shall not preclude the appointment of different counsel, on the court's own motion or at the request of the prisoner, at any phase of State or Federal post-conviction proceedings on the basis of the ineffectiveness or incompetence of counsel in such proceedings.

§ 2262. Mandatory stay of execution; duration; limits on stays of execution; successive petitions

(a) Upon the entry in the appropriate State court of record of an order under section 2261(c), a warrant or order setting an execution date for a State prisoner shall be stayed upon application to any court that would have jurisdiction over any proceedings filed under section 2254. The application shall recite that the State has invoked the post-conviction review procedures of this chapter and that the scheduled execution is subject to stay.

(b) A stay of execution granted pursuant to subsection (a) shall expire if—

(1) a State prisoner fails to file a habeas corpus application under section 2254 within the time required in section 2263;

(2) before a court of competent jurisdiction, in the presence of counsel, unless the prisoner has competently and knowingly waived such counsel, and after having been advised of the consequences, a State prisoner under capital sentence waives the right to pursue habeas corpus review under section 2254; or

(3) a State prisoner files a habeas corpus petition under section 2254 within the time required by section 2263 and fails to make a substantial showing of the denial of a Federal right or is denied relief in the district court or at any subsequent stage of review.

(c) If one of the conditions in subsection (b) has occurred, no Federal court thereafter shall have the authority to enter a stay of execution in the case, unless the court of appeals approves the filing of a second or successive application under section 2244(b).

§ 2263. Filing of habeas corpus application; time requirements; tolling rules

(a) Any application under this chapter for habeas corpus relief under section 2254 must be filed in the appropriate district court not later than 180 days after final State court affirmance of the conviction and sentence on direct review or the expiration of the time for seeking such review.

(b) The time requirements established by subsection (a) shall be tolled—

(1) from the date that a petition for certiorari is filed in the Supreme Court until the date of final disposition of the petition if a State prisoner files the petition to secure review by the Supreme Court of the affirmance of a capital sentence on direct review by the court of last resort of the State or other final State court decision on direct review;

(2) from the date on which the first petition for post-conviction review or other collateral relief is filed until the final State court disposition of such petition; and

(3) during an additional period not to exceed 30 days, if—

(A) a motion for an extension of time is filed in the Federal district court that would have jurisdiction over the case upon the filing of a habeas corpus application under section 2254; and

(B) a showing of good cause is made for the failure to file the habeas corpus application within the time period established by this section.

§ 2264. Scope of Federal review; district court adjudications

(a) Whenever a State prisoner under capital sentence files a petition for habeas corpus relief to which this chapter applies, the district court shall only consider a claim or claims that have been raised and decided on the merits in the State courts, unless the failure to raise the claim properly is—

(1) the result of State action in violation of the Constitution or laws of the United States;

(2) the result of the Supreme Court's recognition of a new Federal right that is made retroactively applicable; or

(3) based on a factual predicate that could not have been discovered through the exercise of due diligence in time to present the claim for State or Federal post-conviction review.

(b) Following review subject to subsections (a), (d), and (e) of section 2254, the court shall rule on the claims properly before it.

§ 2265. Certification and judicial review

(a) Certification.—

(1) In general.—If requested by an appropriate State official, the Attorney General of the United States shall determine—

(A) whether the State has established a mechanism for the appointment, compensation, and payment of reasonable litigation expenses of competent counsel in State postconviction proceedings brought by indigent prisoners who have been sentenced to death;

(B) the date on which the mechanism described in subparagraph (A) was established; and

(C) whether the State provides standards of competency for the appointment of counsel in proceedings described in subparagraph (A).

(2) Effective date.—The date the mechanism described in paragraph (1)(A) was established shall be the effective date of the certification under this subsection.

(3) Only express requirements.—There are no requirements for certification or for application of this chapter other than those expressly stated in this chapter.

(b) Regulations.—The Attorney General shall promulgate regulations to implement the certification procedure under subsection (a).

(c) Review of certification.—

(1) In general.—The determination by the Attorney General regarding whether to certify a State under this section is subject to review exclusively as provided under chapter 158 of this title.

(2) Venue.—The Court of Appeals for the District of Columbia Circuit shall have exclusive jurisdiction over matters under paragraph (1), subject to review by the Supreme Court under section 2350 of this title.

(3) Standard of review.—The determination by the Attorney General regarding whether to certify a State under this section shall be subject to de novo review.

§ 2266. Limitation periods for determining applications and motions

(a) The adjudication of any application under section 2254 that is subject to this chapter, and the adjudication of any motion under section 2255 by a person under sentence of death, shall be given priority by the district court and by the court of appeals over all noncapital matters.

(b)(1)(A) A district court shall render a final determination and enter a final judgment on any application for a writ of habeas corpus brought under this chapter in a capital case not later than 450 days after the date on which the application is filed, or 60 days after the date on which the case is submitted for decision, whichever is earlier.

(B) A district court shall afford the parties at least 120 days in which to complete all actions, including the preparation of all pleadings and briefs, and if necessary, a hearing, prior to the submission of the case for decision.

(C)(i) A district court may delay for not more than one additional 30-day period beyond the period specified in subparagraph (A), the rendering of a determination of an application for a writ of habeas corpus if the court issues a written order making a finding, and stating the reasons for the finding, that the ends of justice that would be served by allowing the delay outweigh the best interests of the public and the applicant in a speedy disposition of the application.

(ii) The factors, among others, that a court shall consider in determining whether a delay in the disposition of an application is warranted are as follows:

(I) Whether the failure to allow the delay would be likely to result in a miscarriage of justice.

(II) Whether the case is so unusual or so complex, due to the number of defendants, the nature of the prosecution, or the existence of novel questions of fact or law, that it is unreasonable to expect adequate briefing within the time limitations established by subparagraph (A).

(III) Whether the failure to allow a delay in a case that, taken as a whole, is not so unusual or so complex as described in subclause (II), but would otherwise deny the applicant reasonable time to obtain counsel, would unreasonably deny the applicant or the government continuity of counsel, or would deny counsel for the applicant or the government the reasonable time necessary for effective preparation, taking into account the exercise of due diligence.

(iii) No delay in disposition shall be permissible because of general congestion of the court's calendar.

(iv) The court shall transmit a copy of any order issued under clause (i) to the Director of the Administrative Office of the United States Courts for inclusion in the report under paragraph (5).

(2) The time limitations under paragraph (1) shall apply to—

(A) an initial application for a writ of habeas corpus;

(B) any second or successive application for a writ of habeas corpus; and

(C) any redetermination of an application for a writ of habeas corpus following a remand by the court of appeals or the Supreme Court for further proceedings, in which case the limitation period shall run from the date the remand is ordered.

(3)(A) The time limitations under this section shall not be construed to entitle an applicant to a stay of execution, to which the applicant would otherwise not be entitled, for the purpose of litigating any application or appeal.

(B) No amendment to an application for a writ of habeas corpus under this chapter shall be permitted after the filing of the answer to the application, except on the grounds specified in section 2244(b).

(4)(A) The failure of a court to meet or comply with a time limitation under this section shall not be a ground for granting relief from a judgment of conviction or sentence.

(B) The State may enforce a time limitation under this section by petitioning for a writ of mandamus to the court of appeals. The court of appeals shall act on the petition for a writ of mandamus not later than 30 days after the filing of the petition.

(5)(A) The Administrative Office of the United States Courts shall submit to Congress an annual report on the compliance by the district courts with the time limitations under this section.*

(B) The report described in subparagraph (A) shall include copies of the orders submitted by the district courts under paragraph (1)(B)(iv).

(c)(1)(A) A court of appeals shall hear and render a final determination of any appeal of an order granting or denying, in whole or in part, an application brought under this chapter in a capital case not later than 120 days after the date on which the reply brief is filed, or if no reply brief is filed, not later than 120 days after the date on which the answering brief is filed.

(B)(i) A court of appeals shall decide whether to grant a petition for rehearing or other request for rehearing en banc not later than 30 days after the date on which the petition for rehearing is filed unless a responsive pleading is required, in which case the court shall decide whether to grant the petition not later than 30 days after the date on which the responsive pleading is filed.

(ii) If a petition for rehearing or rehearing en banc is granted, the court of appeals shall hear and render a final determination of the appeal

---

*   The enacting legislation states that new sections 2261–2266 "shall apply to cases pending on or after the date of enactment of this Act."

not later than 120 days after the date on which the order granting rehearing or rehearing en banc is entered.

(2) The time limitations under paragraph (1) shall apply to—

(A) an initial application for a writ of habeas corpus;

(B) any second or successive application for a writ of habeas corpus; and

(C) any redetermination of an application for a writ of habeas corpus or related appeal following a remand by the court of appeals en banc or the Supreme Court for further proceedings, in which case the limitation period shall run from the date the remand is ordered.

(3) The time limitations under this section shall not be construed to entitle an applicant to a stay of execution, to which the applicant would otherwise not be entitled, for the purpose of litigating any application or appeal.

(4)(A) The failure of a court to meet or comply with a time limitation under this section shall not be a ground for granting relief from a judgment of conviction or sentence.

(B) The State may enforce a time limitation under this section by applying for a writ of mandamus to the Supreme Court.

(5) The Administrative Office of the United States Courts shall submit to Congress an annual report on the compliance by the courts of appeals with the time limitations under this section.*

PRIVACY PROTECTION ACT OF 1980

(42 U.S.C. §§ 2000aa–2000aa–12); Guidelines (28 C.F.R. § 59.4).

§ 2000aa. Searches and seizures by government officers and employees in connection with investigation or prosecution of criminal offenses

(a) Work product materials

Notwithstanding any other law, it shall be unlawful for a government officer or employee, in connection with the investigation or prosecution of a criminal offense, to search for or seize any work product materials possessed by a person reasonably believed to have a purpose to disseminate to the public a newspaper, book, broadcast, or other similar form of public communication, in or affecting interstate or foreign commerce; but this provision shall not impair or affect the ability of any

---

*   The enacting legislation states that the new §§ 2216–2266 "shall apply to cases pending on or after the date of enactment of this Act."

government officer or employee, pursuant to otherwise applicable law, to search for or seize such materials, if—

(1) there is probable cause to believe that the person possessing such materials has committed or is committing the criminal offense to which the materials relate: *Provided, however*, That a government officer or employee may not search for or seize such materials under the provisions of this paragraph if the offense to which the materials relate consists of the receipt, possession, communication, or withholding of such materials or the information contained therein (but such a search or seizure may be conducted under the provisions of this paragraph if the offense consists of the receipt, possession, or communication of information relating to the national defense, classified information, or restricted data under the provisions of section 793, 794, 797, or 798 of Title 18, or section 2274, 2275 or 2277 of this title, or section 783 of Title 50, or if the offense involves the production, possession, receipt, mailing, sale, distribution, shipment, or transportation of child pornography, the sexual exploitation of children, or the sale or purchase of children under section 2251, 2251A, 2252, or 2252A of Title 18); or

(2) there is reason to believe that the immediate seizure of such materials is necessary to prevent the death of, or serious bodily injury to, a human being.

(b) Other documents

Notwithstanding any other law, it shall be unlawful for a government officer or employee, in connection with the investigation or prosecution of a criminal offense, to search for or seize documentary materials, other than work product materials, possessed by a person in connection with a purpose to disseminate to the public a newspaper, book, broadcast, or other similar form of public communication, in or affecting interstate or foreign commerce; but this provision shall not impair or affect the ability of any government officer or employee, pursuant to otherwise applicable law, to search for or seize such materials, if—

(1) there is probable cause to believe that the person possessing such materials has committed or is committing the criminal offense to which the materials relate: *Provided, however*, That a government officer or employee may not search for or seize such materials under the provisions of this paragraph if the offense to which the materials relate consists of the receipt, possession, communication, or withholding of such materials or the information contained therein (but such a search or seizure may be conducted under the provisions of this

paragraph if the offense consists of the receipt, possession, or communication of information relating to the national defense, classified information, or restricted data under the provisions of section 793, 794, 797, or 798 of Title 18, or section 2274, 2275, or 2277 of this title, or section 783 of Title 50, or if the offense involves the production, possession, receipt, mailing, sale, distribution, shipment, or transportation of child pornography, the sexual exploitation of children, or the sale or purchase of children under section 2251, 2251A, 2252, or 2252A of Title 18);

(2) there is reason to believe that the immediate seizure of such materials is necessary to prevent the death of, or serious bodily injury to, a human being;

(3) there is reason to believe that the giving of notice pursuant to a subpena duces tecum would result in the destruction, alteration, or concealment of such materials; or

(4) such materials have not been produced in response to a court order directing compliance with a subpena duces tecum, and—

(A) all appellate remedies have been exhausted; or

(B) there is reason to believe that the delay in an investigation or trial occasioned by further proceedings relating to the subpena would threaten the interests of justice.

(c) Objections to court ordered subpoenas; affidavits

In the event a search warrant is sought pursuant to paragraph (4)(B) of subsection (b) of this section, the person possessing the materials shall be afforded adequate opportunity to submit an affidavit setting forth the basis for any contention that the materials sought are not subject to seizure.

§ 2000aa–5. Border and customs searches

This chapter shall not impair or affect the ability of a government officer or employee, pursuant to otherwise applicable law, to conduct searches and seizures at the borders of, or at international points of, entry into the United States in order to enforce the customs laws of the United States.

§ 2000aa–6. Civil actions by aggrieved persons

(a) Right of action

A person aggrieved by a search for or seizure of materials in violation of this chapter shall have a civil cause of action for damages for such search or seizure—

(1) against the United States, against a State which has waived its sovereign immunity under the Constitution to a claim for damages resulting from a violation of this chapter, or against any other governmental unit, all of which shall be liable for violations of this chapter by their officers or employees while acting within the scope or under color of their office or employment; and

(2) against an officer or employee of a State who has violated this chapter while acting within the scope or under color of his office or employment, if such State has not waived its sovereign immunity as provided in paragraph (1).

(b) Good faith defense

It shall be a complete defense to a civil action brought under paragraph (2) of subsection (a) of this section that the officer or employee had a reasonable good faith belief in the lawfulness of his conduct.

(c) Official immunity

The United States, a State, or any other governmental unit liable for violations of this chapter under subsection (a)(1) of this section, may not assert as a defense to a claim arising under this chapter the immunity of the officer or employee whose violation is complained of or his reasonable good faith belief in the lawfulness of his conduct, except that such a defense may be asserted if the violation complained of is that of a judicial officer.

(d) Exclusive nature of remedy

The remedy provided by subsection (a)(1) of this section against the United States, a State, or any other governmental unit is exclusive of any other civil action or proceeding for conduct constituting a violation of this chapter, against the officer or employee whose violation gave rise to the claim, or against the estate of such officer or employee.

(e) Admissibility of evidence

Evidence otherwise admissible in a proceeding shall not be excluded on the basis of a violation of this chapter.

(f) Damages; costs and attorneys' fees

A person having a cause of action under this section shall be entitled to recover actual damages but not less than liquidated damages of $1,000, and such reasonable attorneys' fees and other litigation costs reasonably incurred as the court, in its discretion, may award: *Provided, however,* That the United States, a State, or any other governmental unit shall not be liable for interest prior to judgment.

(g) Attorney General; claims settlement; regulations

The Attorney General may settle a claim for damages brought against the United States under this section, and shall promulgate regulations to provide for the commencement of an administrative inquiry following a determination of a violation of this chapter by an officer or employee of the United States and for the imposition of administrative sanctions against such officer or employee, if warranted.

(h) Jurisdiction

The district courts shall have original jurisdiction of all civil actions arising under this section.

§ 2000aa–7. Definitions

(a) "Documentary materials", as used in this chapter, means materials upon which information is recorded, and includes, but is not limited to, written or printed materials, photographs, motion picture films, negatives, video tapes, audio tapes, and other mechanically,[6] magentically or electronically recorded cards, tapes, or discs, but does not include contraband or the fruits of a crime or things otherwise criminally possessed, or property designed or intended for use, or which is or has been used as, the means of committing a criminal offense.

(b) "Work product materials", as used in this chapter, means materials, other than contraband or the fruits of a crime or things otherwise criminally possessed, or property designed or intended for use, or which is or has been used, as the means of committing a criminal offense, and—

> (1) in anticipation of communicating such materials to the public, are prepared, produced, authored, or created, whether by the person in possession of the materials or by any other person;

> (2) are possessed for the purposes of communicating such materials to the public; and

> (3) include mental impressions, conclusions, opinions, or theories of the person who prepared, produced, authored, or created such material.

(c) "Any other governmental unit", as used in this chapter, includes the District of Columbia, the Commonwealth of Puerto Rico, any territory or possession of the United States, and any local government, unit of local government, or any unit of State government.

§ 2000aa–11.   Guidelines for Federal officers and employees

(a) Procedures to obtain documentary evidence; protection of certain privacy interests

---

[6]   So in original. Probably should be "magnetically".

The Attorney General shall, within six months of October 13, 1980, issue guidelines for the procedures to be employed by any Federal officer or employee, in connection with the investigation or prosecution of an offense, to obtain documentary materials in the private possession of a person when the person is not reasonably believed to be a suspect in such offense or related by blood or marriage to such a suspect, and when the materials sought are not contraband or the fruits or instrumentalities of an offense. The Attorney General shall incorporate in such guidelines—

(1) a recognition of the personal privacy interests of the person in possession of such documentary materials;

(2) a requirement that the least intrusive method or means of obtaining such materials be used which do not substantially jeopardize the availability or usefulness of the materials sought to be obtained;

(3) a recognition of special concern for privacy interests in cases in which a search or seizure for such documents would intrude upon a known confidential relationship such as that which may exist between clergyman and parishioner; lawyer and client; or doctor and patient; and

(4) a requirement that an application for a warrant to conduct a search governed by this subchapter be approved by an attorney for the government, except that in an emergency situation the application may be approved by another appropriate supervisory official if within 24 hours of such emergency the appropriate United States Attorney is notified.

(b) Use of search warrants; reports to Congress

The Attorney General shall collect and compile information on, and report annually to the Committees on the Judiciary of the Senate and the House of Representatives on the use of search warrants by Federal officers and employees for documentary materials described in subsection (a)(3) of this section.

§ 2000aa–12.   Binding nature of guidelines; disciplinary actions for violations; legal proceedings for non-compliance prohibited

Guidelines issued by the Attorney General under this subchapter shall have the full force and effect of Department of Justice regulations and any violation of these guidelines shall make the employee or officer involved subject to appropriate administrative disciplinary action. However, an issue relating to the compliance, or the failure to comply, with guidelines issued pursuant to this subchapter may not be litigated, and a court may not entertain such an issue as the basis for the suppression or exclusion of evidence.

[EDITOR'S NOTE: These guidelines appear in 28 C.F.R. Pt. 59. The procedural provisions are set out below.]

GUIDELINES

(28 C.F.R. § 59.4).

§ 59.4   Procedures.[1]

(a) Provisions governing the use of search warrants generally.

(1) A search warrant should not be used to obtain documentary materials believed to be in the private possession of a disinterested third party unless it appears that the use of a subpoena, summons, request, or other less intrusive alternative means of obtaining the materials would substantially jeopardize the availability or usefulness of the materials sought, and the application for the warrant has been authorized as provided in paragraph (a)(2) of this section.

(2) No federal officer or employee shall apply for a warrant to search for and seize documentary materials believed to be in the private possession of a disinterested third party unless the application for the warrant has been authorized by an attorney for the government. Provided, however, that in an emergency situation in which the immediacy of the need to seize the materials does not permit an opportunity to secure the authorization of an attorney for the government, the application may be authorized by a supervisory law enforcement officer in the applicant's department or agency, if the appropriate U.S. Attorney (or where the case is not being handled by a U.S. Attorney's Office, the appropriate supervisory official of the Department of Justice) is notified of the authorization and the basis for justifying such authorization under this part within 24 hours of the authorization.

(b) Provisions governing the use of search warrants which may intrude upon professional, confidential relationships.

(1) A search warrant should not be used to obtain documentary materials believed to be in the private possession of a disinterested third party physician,[7] lawyer, or clergyman, under circumstances in which the materials sought, or other materials likely to be reviewed during the execution of the warrant, contain confidential information on patients,

---

[1]   Notwithstanding the provisions of this section, any application for a warrant to search for evidence of a criminal tax offense under the jurisdiction of the Tax Division must be specifically approved in advance by the Tax Division pursuant to section 6–2.330 of the U.S. Attorneys' Manual.

[7]   Documentary materials created or compiled by a physician, but retained by the physician as a matter of practice at a hospital or clinic shall be deemed to be in the private possession of the physician, unless the clinic or hospital is a suspect in the offense.

clients, or parishioners which was furnished or developed for the purposes of professional counseling or treatment, unless—

(i) It appears that the use of a subpoena, summons, request or other less intrusive alternative means of obtaining the materials would substantially jeopardize the availability or usefulness of the materials sought;

(ii) Access to the documentary materials appears to be of substantial importance to the investigation or prosecution for which they are sought; and

(iii) The application for the warrant has been approved as provided in paragraph (b)(2) of this section.

(2) No federal officer or employee shall apply for a warrant to search for and seize documentary materials believed to be in the private possession of a disinterested third party physician, lawyer, or clergyman under the circumstances described in paragraph (b)(1) of this section, unless, upon the recommendation of the U.S. Attorney (or where a case is not being handled by a U.S. Attorney's Office, upon the recommendation of the appropriate supervisory official of the Department of Justice), an appropriate Deputy Assistant Attorney General has authorized the application for the warrant. Provided, however, that in an emergency situation in which the immediacy of the need to seize the materials does not permit an opportunity to secure the authorization of a Deputy Assistant Attorney General, the application may be authorized by the U.S. Attorney (or where the case is not being handled by a U.S. Attorney's Office, by the appropriate supervisory official of the Department of Justice) if an appropriate Deputy Assistant Attorney General is notified of the authorization and the basis for justifying such authorization under this part within 72 hours of the authorization.

(3) Whenever possible, a request for authorization by an appropriate Deputy Assistant Attorney General of a search warrant application pursuant to paragraph (b)(2) of this section shall be made in writing and shall include:

(i) The application for the warrant; and

(ii) A brief description of the facts and circumstances advanced as the basis for recommending authorization of the application under this part.

If a request for authorization of the application is made orally or if, in an emergency situation, the application is authorized by the U.S. Attorney or a supervisory official of the Department of Justice as provided in paragraph (b)(2) of this section, a written record of the request including the materials specified in paragraphs (b)(3)(i) and (ii) of this section shall be transmitted to an appropriate Deputy Assistant Attorney General within 7 days. The Deputy Assistant Attorneys General shall keep a record of the disposition of all requests for authorizations of search warrant applications made under paragraph (b) of this section.

(4) A search warrant authorized under paragraph (b)(2) of this section shall be executed in such a manner as to minimize, to the greatest extent practicable, scrutiny of confidential materials.

(5) Although it is impossible to define the full range of additional doctor-like therapeutic relationships which involve the furnishing or development of private information, the U.S. Attorney (or where a case is not being handled by a U.S. Attorney's Office, the appropriate supervisory official of the Department of Justice) should determine whether a search for documentary materials held by other disinterested third party professionals involved in such relationships (e.g. psychologists or psychiatric social workers or nurses) would implicate the special privacy concerns which are addressed in paragraph (b) of this section. If the U.S. Attorney (or other supervisory official of the Department of Justice) determines that such a search would require review of extremely confidential information furnished or developed for the purposes of professional counseling or treatment, the provisions of this subsection should be applied. Otherwise, at a minimum, the requirements of paragraph (a) of this section must be met.

(c) Considerations bearing on choice of methods. In determining whether, as an alternative to the use of a search warrant, the use of a subpoena or other less intrusive means of obtaining documentary materials would substantially jeopardize the availability or usefulness of the materials sought, the following factors, among others, should be considered:

(1) Whether it appears that the use of a subpoena or other alternative which gives advance notice of the government's interest in obtaining the materials would be likely to result in the destruction, alteration, concealment, or transfer of the materials sought; considerations, among others, bearing on this issue may include:

(i) Whether a suspect has access to the materials sought;

(ii) Whether there is a close relationship of friendship, loyalty, or sympathy between the possessor of the materials and a suspect;

(iii) Whether the possessor of the materials is under the domination or control of a suspect;

(iv) Whether the possessor of the materials has an interest in preventing the disclosure of the materials to the government;

(v) Whether the possessor's willingness to comply with a subpoena or request by the government would be likely to subject him to intimidation or threats of reprisal;

(vi) Whether the possessor of the materials has previously acted to obstruct a criminal investigation or judicial proceeding or refused to comply with or acted in defiance of court orders; or

(vii) Whether the possessor has expressed an intent to destroy, conceal, alter, or transfer the materials;

(2) The immediacy of the government's need to obtain the materials; considerations, among others, bearing on this issue may include:

(i) Whether the immediate seizure of the materials is necessary to prevent injury to persons or property;

(ii) Whether the prompt seizure of the materials is necessary to preserve their evidentiary value;

(iii) Whether delay in obtaining the materials would significantly jeopardize an ongoing investigation or prosecution; or

(iv) Whether a legally enforceable form of process, other than a search warrant, is reasonably available as a means of obtaining the materials.

The fact that the disinterested third party possessing the materials may have grounds to challenge a subpoena or other legal process is not in itself a legitimate basis for the use of a search warrant.

FOREIGN INTELLIGENCE SURVEILLANCE ACT

(50 U.S.C. § 1861)

§ 1861. Access to certain business records for foreign intelligence and international terrorism investigations

(a)(1) Subject to paragraph (3), the Director of the Federal Bureau of Investigation or a designee of the Director (whose rank shall be no lower than Assistant Special Agent in Charge) may make an application for an order requiring the production of any tangible things (including books, records, papers, documents, and other items) for an investigation to obtain foreign intelligence information not concerning a United States person or to protect against international terrorism or clandestine intelligence activities, provided that such investigation of a United States person is not conducted solely upon the basis of activities protected by the first amendment to the Constitution.

(2) An investigation conducted under this section shall

(A) be conducted under guidelines approved by the Attorney General under Executive Order 12333 (or a successor order); and

(B) not be conducted of a United States person solely upon the basis of activities protected by the first amendment to the Constitution of the United States.

(3) In the case of an application for an order requiring the production of library circulation records, library patron lists, book sales records, book customer lists, firearms sales records, tax return records, educational records, or medical records containing information that would identify a person, the Director of the Federal Bureau of Investigation may delegate the authority to make such application to either the Deputy Director of the Federal Bureau of Investigation or the Executive Assistant Director for National Security (or any successor position). The Deputy Director or the Executive Assistant Director may not further delegate such authority.

(b) Each application under this section

(1) shall be made to—

(A) a judge of the court established by section 1803(a) of this title; or

(B) a United States Magistrate Judge under chapter 43 of Title 28, who is publicly designated by the Chief Justice of the United States to have the power to hear applications and grant orders for the production of tangible things under this section on behalf of a judge of that court; and

(2) shall include—

(A) a statement of facts showing that there are reasonable grounds to believe that the tangible things sought are relevant to an authorized investigation (other than a threat assessment) conducted in accordance with subsection (a)(2) of this section to obtain foreign intelligence information not concerning a United States person or to protect against international terrorism or clandestine intelligence activities, such things being presumptively relevant to an authorized investigation if the applicant shows in the statement of the facts that they pertain to—

(i) a foreign power or an agent of a foreign power;

(ii) the activities of a suspected agent of a foreign power who is the subject of such authorized investigation; or

(iii) an individual in contact with, or known to, a suspected agent of a foreign power who is the subject of such authorized investigation; and

(B) an enumeration of the minimization procedures adopted by the Attorney General under subsection (g) of this section that are applicable to the retention and dissemination by the Federal Bureau of Investigation of any tangible things to be made available to the Federal Bureau of Investigation based on the order requested in such application.

(c) (1) Upon an application made pursuant to this section, if the judge finds that the application meets the requirements of subsections (a) and (b) of this section, the judge shall enter an ex parte order as requested, or as modified, approving the release of tangible things. Such order shall direct that minimization procedures adopted pursuant to subsection (g) of this section be followed.

(2) An order under this subsection—

(A) shall describe the tangible things that are ordered to be produced with sufficient particularity to permit them to be fairly identified;

(B) shall include the date on which the tangible things must be provided, which shall allow a reasonable period of time within which the tangible things can be assembled and made available;

(C) shall provide clear and conspicuous notice of the principles and procedures described in subsection (d) of this section;

(D) may only require the production of a tangible thing if such thing can be obtained with a subpoena duces tecum issued by a court of the United States in aid of a grand jury investigation or with any other order issued by a court of the United States directing the production of records or tangible things; and

(E) shall not disclose that such order is issued for purposes of an investigation described in subsection (a) of this section.

(d) (1) No person shall disclose to any other person that the Federal bureau of investigation has sought or obtained tangible things pursuant to an order under this section, other than to

(A) those persons to whom disclosure is necessary to comply with such order;

(B) an attorney to obtain legal advice or assistance with respect to the production of things in response to the order; or

(C) other persons as permitted by the Director of the Federal Bureau of Investigation or the designee of the Director.

(2) (A) A person to whom disclosure is made pursuant to paragraph (1) shall be subject to the nondisclosure requirements applicable to a person to whom an order is directed under this section in the same manner as such person.

(B) Any person who discloses to a person described in subparagraph (A), (B), or (C) of paragraph (1) that the Federal Bureau of Investigation has sought or obtained tangible things pursuant to an order under this section shall notify such person of the nondisclosure requirements of this subsection.

(C) At the request of the Director of the Federal Bureau of Investigation or the designee of the Director, any person making or intending to make a disclosure under subparagraph (A) or (C) of paragraph (1) shall identify to the Director or such designee the person to whom such disclosure will be made or to whom such disclosure was made prior to the request.

(e) A person who, in good faith, produces tangible things under an order pursuant to this section shall not be liable to any other person for such production. Such production shall not be deemed to constitute a waiver of any privilege in any other proceeding or context.

(f) (1) In this subsection—

(A) the term "production order" means an order to produce any tangible thing under this section; and

(B) the term "nondisclosure order" means an order imposed under subsection (d) of this section.

(2)(A)

(i) A person receiving a production order may challenge the legality of that order by filing a petition with the pool established by section 1803(e)(1) of this title. Not less than 1 year after the date of the issuance of the production order, the recipient of a production order may challenge the nondisclosure order imposed in connection with such production order by filing a petition to modify or set aside such nondisclosure order, consistent with the requirements of subparagraph (C), with the pool established by section 1803(e)(1) of this title.

(ii) The presiding judge shall immediately assign a petition under clause (i) to 1 of the judges serving in the pool established by section 1803(e)(1) of this title. Not later than 72 hours after the assignment of such petition, the assigned judge shall conduct an initial review of the petition. If the assigned judge determines that the petition is frivolous, the assigned judge shall immediately deny the petition and affirm the production order or nondisclosure order. If the assigned judge determines the petition is not frivolous, the assigned judge shall promptly consider the petition in accordance with the procedures established under section 1803(e)(2) of this title.

(iii) The assigned judge shall promptly provide a written statement for the record of the reasons for any determination under this subsection. Upon the request of the Government, any order setting aside a nondisclosure order shall be stayed pending review pursuant to paragraph (3).

(B) A judge considering a petition to modify or set aside a production order may grant such petition only if the judge finds that such order does not meet the requirements of this section or is otherwise unlawful. If the judge does not modify or set aside the production order, the judge shall immediately affirm such order, and order the recipient to comply therewith.

(C) (i) A judge considering a petition to modify or set aside a nondisclosure order may grant such petition only if the judge finds that there is no reason to believe that disclosure may endanger the national security of the United States, interfere with a criminal, counterterrorism, or counterintelligence investigation, interfere with diplomatic relations, or endanger the life or physical safety of any person.

(ii) If, upon filing of such a petition, the Attorney General, Deputy Attorney General, an Assistant Attorney General, or the Director of the Federal Bureau of Investigation certifies that disclosure may endanger the national security of the United States or interfere with diplomatic relations, such certification shall be treated as conclusive, unless the judge finds that the certification as made in bad faith.

(iii) If the judge denies a petition to modify or set aside a nondisclosure order, the recipient of such order shall be precluded for a period of 1 year from filing another such petition with respect to such nondisclosure order.

(D) Any production or nondisclosure order not explicitly modified or set aside consistent with this subsection shall remain in full effect.

(3) A petition for review of a decision under paragraph (2) to affirm, modify, or set aside an order by the Government or any person receiving such order shall be made to the court of review established under section 1803(b) of this title, which shall have jurisdiction to consider such petitions. The court of review shall provide for the record a written statement of the reasons for its decision and, on petition by the Government or any person receiving such order for writ of certiorari, the record shall be transmitted under seal to the Supreme Court of the United States, which shall have jurisdiction to review such decision.

(4) Judicial proceedings under this subsection shall be concluded as expeditiously as possible. The record of proceedings, including petitions filed, orders granted, and statements of reasons for decision, shall be maintained under security measures established by the Chief Justice of the United States, in consultation with the Attorney General and the Director of National Intelligence.

(5) All petitions under this subsection shall be filed under seal. In any proceedings under this subsection, the court shall, upon request of the Government, review ex parte and in camera any Government submission, or portions thereof, which may include classified information.

(g) Minimization procedures

(1) In general. Not later than 180 days after March 9, 2006, the Attorney General shall adopt specific minimization procedures governing the retention and dissemination by the Federal Bureau of Investigation of any tangible things, or information therein, received by the Federal Bureau of Investigation in response to an order under this subchapter.

(2) Defined. In this section, the term "minimization procedures" means—

(A) specific procedures that are reasonably designed in light of the purpose and technique of an order for the production of tangible things, to minimize the retention, and prohibit the dissemination, of nonpublicly available information concerning unconsenting United States persons consistent with the need of the United States to obtain, produce, and disseminate foreign intelligence information;

(B) procedures that require that nonpublicly available information, which is not foreign intelligence information, as defined in section 1801(e)(1) of this title, shall not be disseminated in a manner that identifies any United States person, without such person's consent, unless such person's identity is necessary to understand foreign intelligence information or assess its importance; and

(C) notwithstanding subparagraphs (A) and (B), procedures that allow for the retention and dissemination of information that is evidence of a crime which has been, is being, or is about to be committed and that is to be retained or disseminated for law enforcement purposes.

(h) Use of information. Information acquired from tangible things received by the Federal Bureau of Investigation in response to an order under this subchapter concerning any United States person may be used and disclosed by Federal officers and employees without the consent of the United States person only in accordance with the minimization procedures adopted pursuant to subsection (g) of this section. No otherwise privileged information acquired from tangible things received by the Federal Bureau of Investigation in accordance with the provisions of this subchapter shall lose its privileged character. No information acquired from tangible things received by the Federal Bureau of Investigation in response to an order under this subchapter may be used or disclosed by Federal officers or employees except for lawful purposes.

APPENDIX C

FEDERAL RULES OF CRIMINAL PROCEDURE FOR THE UNITED STATES DISTRICT COURTS

■ ■ ■

I. SCOPE, PURPOSE AND CONSTRUCTION

Rule 1. Scope; Definitions

(a) Scope.

(1) In General. These rules govern the procedure in all criminal proceedings in the United States district courts, the United States courts of appeals, and the Supreme Court of the United States.

(2) State or Local Judicial Officer. When a rule so states, it applies to a proceeding before a state or local judicial officer.

(3) Territorial Courts. These rules also govern the procedure in all criminal proceedings in the following courts:

(A) the district court of Guam;

(B) the district court for the Northern Mariana Islands, except as otherwise provided by law; and

(C) the district court of the Virgin Islands, except that the prosecution of offenses in that court must be by indictment or information as otherwise provided by law.

(4) Removed Proceedings. Although these rules govern all proceedings after removal from a state court, state law governs a dismissal by the prosecution.

(5) Excluded Proceedings. Proceedings not governed by these rules include:

(A) the extradition and rendition of a fugitive;

(B) a civil property forfeiture for violating a federal statute;

(C) the collection of a fine or penalty;

(D) a proceeding under a statute governing juvenile delinquency to the extent the procedure is inconsistent with the statute, unless Rule 20(d) provides otherwise;

(E) a dispute between seamen under 22 U.S.C. §§ 256–258; and

(F) a proceeding against a witness in a foreign country under 28 U.S.C. § 1784.

(b) Definitions. The following definitions apply to these rules:

(1) "Attorney for the government" means:

(A) the Attorney General or an authorized assistant;

(B) a United States attorney or an authorized assistant;

(C) when applicable to cases arising under Guam law, the Guam Attorney General or other person whom Guam law authorizes to act in the matter; and

(D) any other attorney authorized by law to conduct proceedings under these rules as a prosecutor.

(2) "Court" means a federal judge performing functions authorized by law.

(3) "Federal judge" means:

(A) a justice or judge of the United States as these terms are defined in 28 U.S.C. § 451;

(B) a magistrate judge; and

(C) a judge confirmed by the United States Senate and empowered by statute in any commonwealth, territory, or possession to perform a function to which a particular rule relates.

(4) "Judge" means a federal judge or a state or local judicial officer.

(5) "Magistrate judge" means a United States magistrate judge as defined in 28 U.S.C. §§ 631–639.

(6) "Oath" includes an affirmation.

(7) "Organization" is defined in 18 U.S.C. § 18.

(8) "Petty offense" is defined in 18 U.S.C. § 19.

(9) "State" includes the District of Columbia, and any commonwealth, territory, or possession of the United States.

(10) "State or local judicial officer" means:

(A) a state or local officer authorized to act under 18 U.S.C. § 3041; and

(B) a judicial officer empowered by statute in the District of Columbia or in any commonwealth, territory, or possession to perform a function to which a particular rule relates.

(11) "Telephone" means any technology for transmitting live electronic voice communication.

(12) "Victim" means a "crime victim" as defined in 18 U.S.C. § 3771(e).

(c) Authority of a Justice or Judge of the United States. When these rules authorize a magistrate judge to act, any other federal judge may also act.

Rule 2. Interpretation

These rules are to be interpreted to provide for the just determination of every criminal proceeding, to secure simplicity in procedure and fairness in administration, and to eliminate unjustifiable expense and delay.

Rule 3. The Complaint

The complaint is a written statement of the essential facts constituting the offense charged. Except as provided in Rule 4.1, it must be made under oath before a magistrate judge or, if none is reasonably available, before a state or local judicial officer.

Rule 4. Arrest Warrant or Summons on a Complaint

(a) Issuance. If the complaint or one or more affidavits filed with the complaint establish probable cause to believe that an offense has been committed and that the defendant committed it, the judge must issue an arrest warrant to an officer authorized to execute it. At the request of an attorney for the government, the judge must issue a summons, instead of a warrant, to a person authorized to serve it. A judge may issue more than one warrant or summons on the same complaint. If a defendant fails to appear in response to a summons, a judge may, and upon request of an attorney for the government must, issue a warrant.

(b) Form.

(1) Warrant. A warrant must:

(A) contain the defendant's name or, if it is unknown, a name or description by which the defendant can be identified with reasonable certainty;

(B) describe the offense charged in the complaint;

(C) command that the defendant be arrested and brought without unnecessary delay before a magistrate judge or, if none is reasonably available, before a state or local judicial officer; and

(D) be signed by a judge.

(2) Summons. A summons must be in the same form as a warrant except that it must require the defendant to appear before a magistrate judge at a stated time and place.

(c) Execution or Service, and Return.

(1) By Whom. Only a marshal or other authorized officer may execute a warrant. Any person authorized to serve a summons in a federal civil action may serve a summons.

(2) Location. A warrant may be executed, or a summons served, within the jurisdiction of the United States or anywhere else a federal statute authorizes an arrest.

(3) Manner.

(A) A warrant is executed by arresting the defendant. Upon arrest, an officer possessing the original or a duplicate original warrant must show it to the defendant. If the officer does not possess the warrant, the officer must inform the defendant of the warrant's existence and of the offense charged and, at the defendant's request, must show the original or a duplicate original warrant to the defendant as soon as possible.

(B) A summons is served on an individual defendant:

(i) by delivering a copy to the defendant personally; or

(ii) by leaving a copy at the defendant's residence or usual place of abode with a person of suitable age and discretion residing at that location and by mailing a copy to the defendant's last known address.

(C) A summons is served on an organization by delivering a copy to an officer, to a managing or general agent, or to another agent appointed or legally authorized to receive service of process. A copy must also be mailed to the organization's last known address within the district or to its principal place of business elsewhere in the United States.

(4) Return.

(A) After executing a warrant, the officer must return it to the judge before whom the defendant is brought in accordance with Rule 5. The officer may do so by reliable electronic means. At the request of an attorney for the government, an unexecuted warrant must be brought back to and canceled by a magistrate judge or, if none is reasonably available, by a state or local judicial officer.

(B) The person to whom a summons was delivered for service must return it on or before the return day.

(C) At the request of an attorney for the government, a judge may deliver an unexecuted warrant, an unserved summons, or a copy of the warrant or summons to the marshal or other authorized person for execution or service.

(d) Warrant by Telephone or Other Reliable Electronic Means. In accordance with Rule 4.1, a magistrate judge may issue a warrant or summons based on information communicated by telephone or other reliable electronic means.

Rule 4.1.   Complaint, Warrant, or Summons by Telephone or Other Reliable Electronic Means

(a) In General. A magistrate judge may consider information communicated by telephone or other reliable electronic means when deciding whether to approve a complaint or to issue a warrant or summons.

(b) Procedures. If a magistrate judge decides to proceed under this rule, the following procedures apply:

(1) Taking Testimony Under Oath. The judge must place under oath—and may examine—the applicant and any person on whose testimony the application is based.

(2) Creating a Record of the Testimony and Exhibits.

(A) Testimony Limited to Attestation. If the applicant does no more than attest to the contents of a written affidavit submitted by reliable electronic means, the judge must acknowledge the attestation in writing on the affidavit.

(B) Additional Testimony or Exhibits. If the judge considers additional testimony or exhibits, the judge must:

(i) have the testimony recorded verbatim by an electronic recording device, by a court reporter, or in writing;

(ii) have any recording or reporter's notes transcribed, have the transcription certified as accurate, and file it;

(iii) sign any other written record, certify its accuracy, and file it; and

(iv) make sure that the exhibits are filed.

(3) Preparing a Proposed Duplicate Original of a Complaint, Warrant, or Summons. The applicant must prepare a proposed duplicate original of a complaint, warrant, or summons, and must read or otherwise transmit its contents verbatim to the judge.

(4) Preparing an Original Complaint, Warrant, or Summons. If the applicant reads the contents of the proposed duplicate original, the judge must enter those contents into an original complaint, warrant, or summons. If the applicant transmits the contents by reliable electronic means, the transmission received by the judge may serve as the original.

(5) Modification. The judge may modify the complaint, warrant, or summons. The judge must then:

    (A) transmit the modified version to the applicant by reliable electronic means; or

    (B) file the modified original and direct the applicant to modify the proposed duplicate original accordingly.

(6) Issuance. To issue the warrant or summons, the judge must:

    (A) sign the original documents;

    (B) enter the date and time of issuance on the warrant or summons; and

    (C) transmit the warrant or summons by reliable electronic means to the applicant or direct the applicant to sign the judge's name and enter the date and time on the duplicate original.

(c) Suppression Limited. Absent a finding of bad faith, evidence obtained from a warrant issued under this rule is not subject to suppression on the ground that issuing the warrant in this manner was unreasonable under the circumstances.

Rule 5. Initial Appearance

(a) In General.

(1) Appearance Upon an Arrest.

    (A) A person making an arrest within the United States must take the defendant without unnecessary delay before a magistrate judge, or before a state or local judicial officer as Rule 5(c) provides, unless a statute provides otherwise.

    (B) A person making an arrest outside the United States must take the defendant without unnecessary delay before a magistrate judge, unless a statute provides otherwise.

(2) Exceptions.

(A) An officer making an arrest under a warrant issued upon a complaint charging solely a violation of 18 U.S.C. § 1073 need not comply with this rule if:

(i) the person arrested is transferred without unnecessary delay to the custody of appropriate state or local authorities in the district of arrest; and

(ii) an attorney for the government moves promptly, in the district where the warrant was issued, to dismiss the complaint.

(B) If a defendant is arrested for violating probation or supervised release, Rule 32.1 applies.

(C) If a defendant is arrested for failing to appear in another district, Rule 40 applies.

(3) Appearance Upon a Summons. When a defendant appears in response to a summons under Rule 4, a magistrate judge must proceed under Rule 5(d) or (e), as applicable.

(b) Arrest Without a Warrant. If a defendant is arrested without a warrant, a complaint meeting Rule 4(a)'s requirement of probable cause must be promptly filed in the district where the offense was allegedly committed.

(c) Place of Initial Appearance; Transfer to Another District.

(1) Arrest in the District Where the Offense Was Allegedly Committed. If the defendant is arrested in the district where the offense was allegedly committed:

(A) the initial appearance must be in that district; and

(B) if a magistrate judge is not reasonably available, the initial appearance may be before a state or local judicial officer.

(2) Arrest in a District Other Than Where the Offense Was Allegedly Committed. If the defendant was arrested in a district other than where the offense was allegedly committed, the initial appearance must be:

(A) in the district of arrest; or

(B) in an adjacent district if:

(i) the appearance can occur more promptly there; or

(ii) the offense was allegedly committed there and the initial appearance will occur on the day of arrest.

(3) Procedures in a District Other Than Where the Offense Was Allegedly Committed. If the initial appearance occurs in a district other than where the offense was allegedly committed, the following procedures apply:

(A) the magistrate judge must inform the defendant about the provisions of Rule 20;

(B) if the defendant was arrested without a warrant, the district court where the offense was allegedly committed must first issue a warrant before the magistrate judge transfers the defendant to that district;

(C) the magistrate judge must conduct a preliminary hearing if required by Rule 5.1;

(D) the magistrate judge must transfer the defendant to the district where the offense was allegedly committed if:

(i) the government produces the warrant, a certified copy of the warrant, reliable electronic form of either; and

(ii) the judge finds that the defendant is the same person named in the indictment, information, or warrant; and

(E) when a defendant is transferred and discharged, the clerk must promptly transmit the papers and any bail to the clerk in the district where the offense was allegedly committed.

(4) Procedure for Persons Extradited to the United States. If the defendant is surrendered to the United States in accordance with a request for the defendant's extradition, the initial appearance must be in the district (or one of the districts) where the offense is charged.

(d) Procedure in a Felony Case.

(1) Advice. If the defendant is charged with a felony, the judge must inform the defendant of the following:

(A) the complaint against the defendant, and any affidavit filed with it;

(B) the defendant's right to retain counsel or to request that counsel be appointed if the defendant cannot obtain counsel;

(C) the circumstances, if any, under which the defendant may secure pretrial release;

(D) any right to a preliminary hearing; and

(E) the defendant's right not to make a statement, and that any statement made may be used against the defendant.

(2) Consulting with Counsel. The judge must allow the defendant reasonable opportunity to consult with counsel.

(3) Detention or Release. The judge must detain or release the defendant as provided by statute or these rules.

(4) Plea. A defendant may be asked to plead only under Rule 10.

(e) Procedure in a Misdemeanor Case. If the defendant is charged with a misdemeanor only, the judge must inform the defendant in accordance with Rule 58(b)(2).

(f) Video Teleconferencing. Video teleconferencing may be used to conduct an appearance under this rule if the defendant consents.

Rule 5.1.   Preliminary Hearing

(a) In General. If a defendant is charged with an offense other than a petty offense, a magistrate judge must conduct a preliminary hearing unless:

(1) the defendant waives the hearing;

(2) the defendant is indicted;

(3) the government files an information under Rule 7(b) charging the defendant with a felony;

(4) the government files an information charging the defendant with a misdemeanor; or

(5) the defendant is charged with a misdemeanor and consents to trial before a magistrate judge.

(b) Selecting a District. A defendant arrested in a district other than where the offense was allegedly committed may elect to have the preliminary hearing conducted in the district where the prosecution is pending.

(c) Scheduling. The magistrate judge must hold the preliminary hearing within a reasonable time, but no later than 14 days after the initial appearance if the defendant is in custody and no later than 21 days if not in custody.

(d) Extending the Time. With the defendant's consent and upon a showing of good cause—taking into account the public interest in the prompt disposition of criminal cases—a magistrate judge may extend the time limits in Rule 5.1(c) one or more times. If the defendant does not consent, the magistrate judge may extend the time limits only on a showing that extraordinary circumstances exist and justice requires the delay.

(e) Hearing and Finding. At the preliminary hearing, the defendant may cross-examine adverse witnesses and may introduce evidence but may not object to evidence on the ground that it was unlawfully acquired. If the magistrate judge finds probable cause to believe an offense has been committed and the defendant committed it, the magistrate judge must promptly require the defendant to appear for further proceedings.

(f) Discharging the Defendant. If the magistrate judge finds no probable cause to believe an offense has been committed or the defendant committed it, the magistrate judge must dismiss the complaint and discharge the defendant. A discharge does not preclude the government from later prosecuting the defendant for the same offense.

(g) Recording the Proceedings. The preliminary hearing must be recorded by a court reporter or by a suitable recording device. A recording of the proceeding may be made available to any party upon request. A copy of the recording and a transcript may be provided to any party upon request and upon any payment required by applicable Judicial Conference regulations.

(h) Producing a Statement.

(1) In General. Rule 26.2(a)–(d) and (f) applies at any hearing under this rule, unless the magistrate judge for good cause rules otherwise in a particular case.

(2) Sanctions for Not Producing a Statement. If a party disobeys a Rule 26.2 order to deliver a statement to the moving party, the magistrate judge must not consider the testimony of a witness whose statement is withheld.

Rule 6. The Grand Jury

(a) Summoning a Grand Jury.

(1) In General. When the public interest so requires, the court must order that one or more grand juries be summoned. A grand jury must have 16 to 23 members, and the court must order that enough legally qualified persons be summoned to meet this requirement.

(2) Alternate Jurors. When a grand jury is selected, the court may also select alternate jurors. Alternate jurors must have the same qualifications and be selected in the same manner as any other juror. Alternate jurors replace jurors in the same sequence in which the alternates were selected. An alternate juror who replaces a juror is subject to the same challenges, takes the same oath, and has the same authority as the other jurors.

(b) Objection to the Grand Jury or to a Grand Juror.

(1) Challenges. Either the government or a defendant may challenge the grand jury on the ground that it was not lawfully drawn, summoned, or selected, and may challenge an individual juror on the ground that the juror is not legally qualified.

(2) Motion to Dismiss an Indictment. A party may move to dismiss the indictment based on an objection to the grand jury or on an individual juror's lack of legal qualification, unless the court has previously ruled on the same objection under Rule 6(b)(1). The motion to dismiss is governed by 28 U.S.C. § 1867(e). The court must not dismiss the indictment on the ground that a grand juror was not legally qualified if the record shows that at least 12 qualified jurors concurred in the indictment.

(c) Foreperson and Deputy Foreperson. The court will appoint one juror as the foreperson and another as the deputy foreperson. In the foreperson's absence, the deputy foreperson will act as the foreperson. The foreperson may administer oaths and affirmations and will sign all indictments. The foreperson—or another juror designated by the foreperson—will record the number of jurors concurring in every indictment and will file the record with the clerk, but the record may not be made public unless the court so orders.

(d) Who May Be Present.

(1) While the Grand Jury Is in Session. The following persons may be present while the grand jury is in session: attorneys for the government, the witness being questioned, interpreters when needed, and a court reporter or an operator of a recording device.

(2) During Deliberations and Voting. No person other than the jurors, and any interpreter needed to assist a hearing-impaired or speech-impaired juror, may be present while the grand jury is deliberating or voting.

(e) Recording and Disclosing the Proceedings.

(1) Recording the Proceedings. Except while the grand jury is deliberating or voting, all proceedings must be recorded by a court reporter or by a suitable recording device. But the validity of a prosecution is not affected by the unintentional failure to make a recording. Unless the court orders otherwise, an attorney for the government will retain control of the recording, the reporter's notes, and any transcript prepared from those notes.

(2) Secrecy.

(A) No obligation of secrecy may be imposed on any person except in accordance with Rule 6(e)(2)(B).

(B) Unless these rules provide otherwise, the following persons must not disclose a matter occurring before the grand jury:

(i) a grand juror;

(ii) an interpreter;

(iii) a court reporter;

(iv) an operator of a recording device;

(v) a person who transcribes recorded testimony;

(vi) an attorney for the government; or

(vii) a person to whom disclosure is made under Rule 6(e)(3)(A)(ii) or (iii).

(3) Exceptions.

(A) Disclosure of a grand-jury matter—other than the grand jury's deliberations or any grand juror's vote—may be made to:

(i) an attorney for the government for use in performing that attorney's duty;

(ii) any government personnel—including those of a state, state subdivision, Indian tribe, or foreign government—that an attorney for the government considers necessary to assist in performing that attorney's duty to enforce federal criminal law; or

(iii) a person authorized by 18 U.S.C. § 3322.

(B) A person to whom information is disclosed under Rule 6(e)(3)(A)(ii) may use that information only to assist an attorney for the government in performing that attorney's duty to enforce federal criminal law. An attorney for the government must promptly provide the court that impaneled the grand jury with the names of all persons to whom a disclosure has been made, and must certify that the attorney has advised those persons of their obligation of secrecy under this rule.

(C) An attorney for the government may disclose any grand-jury matter to another federal grand jury.

(D) An attorney for the government may disclose any grand-jury matter involving foreign intelligence, counterintelligence (as defined in 50 U.S.C. § 401a), or foreign intelligence information (as defined in Rule 6(e)(3)(D)(iii)) to any federal law enforcement, intelligence, protective, immigration, national defense, or national security official to assist the official receiving the information in the performance of that official's duties. An attorney for the government may also disclose any grand jury matter involving, within the United States or elsewhere, a threat of attack or other grave hostile acts of a foreign power or its agent, a threat of domestic or international sabotage or terrorism, or clandestine intelligence gathering activities by an intelligence service or network of a foreign power or by its agent, to any appropriate federal, state, state subdivision, Indian tribal, or foreign government official, for the purpose of preventing or responding to such threat or activities.

(i) Any official who receives information under Rule 6(e)(3)(D) may use the information only as necessary in the conduct of that person's official duties subject to any limitations on the unauthorized disclosure of such information. Any state, state subdivision, Indian tribal, or foreign government official who receives information under Rule 6(e)(3)(D) may use the information only in a manner consistent with any guidelines issued by the Attorney General and the Director of National Intelligence.

(ii) Within a reasonable time after disclosure is made under Rule 6(e)(3)(D), an attorney for the government must file, under seal, a notice with the court in the district where the grand jury convened stating that such information was disclosed and the departments, agencies, or entities to which the disclosure was made.

(iii) As used in Rule 6(e)(3)(D), the term "foreign intelligence information" means:

(a) information, whether or not it concerns a United States person, that relates to the ability of the United States to protect against—

• actual or potential attack or other grave hostile acts of a foreign power or its agent;

• sabotage or international terrorism by a foreign power or its agent; or

• clandestine intelligence activities by an intelligence service or network of a foreign power or by its agent; or

(b) information, whether or not it concerns a United States person, with respect to a foreign power or foreign territory that relates to—

• the national defense or the security of the United States; or

• the conduct of the foreign affairs of the United States.

(E) The court may authorize disclosure—at a time, in a manner, and subject to any other conditions that it directs—of a grand-jury matter:

(i) preliminarily to or in connection with a judicial proceeding;

(ii) at the request of a defendant who shows that a ground may exist to dismiss the indictment because of a matter that occurred before the grand jury;

(iii) at the request of the government, when sought by a foreign court or prosecutor for use in an official criminal investigation;

(iv) at the request of the government if it shows that the matter may disclose a violation of State, Indian tribal, or foreign criminal law, as long as the disclosure is to an appropriate state, state-subdivision, Indian tribal, or foreign government official for the purpose of enforcing that law; or

(v) at the request of the government if it shows that the matter may disclose a violation of military criminal law under the Uniform Code of Military Justice, as long as the disclosure is to an appropriate military official for the purpose of enforcing that law.

(F) A petition to disclose a grand-jury matter under Rule 6(e)(3)(E)(i) must be filed in the district where the grand jury convened. Unless the hearing is ex parte—as it may be when the government is the petitioner—the petitioner must serve the petition on, and the court must afford a reasonable opportunity to appear and be heard to:

> **(i)** an attorney for the government;

> **(ii)** the parties to the judicial proceeding; and

> **(iii)** any other person whom the court may designate.

(G) If the petition to disclose arises out of a judicial proceeding in another district, the petitioned court must transfer the petition to the other court unless the petitioned court can reasonably determine whether disclosure is proper. If the petitioned court decides to transfer, it must send to the transferee court the material sought to be disclosed, if feasible, and a written evaluation of the need for continued grand-jury secrecy. The transferee court must afford those persons identified in Rule 6(e)(3)(F) a reasonable opportunity to appear and be heard.

(4) Sealed Indictment. The magistrate judge to whom an indictment is returned may direct that the indictment be kept secret until the defendant is in custody or has been released pending trial. The clerk must then seal the indictment, and no person may disclose the indictment's existence except as necessary to issue or execute a warrant or summons.

(5) Closed Hearing. Subject to any right to an open hearing in a contempt proceeding, the court must close any hearing to the extent necessary to prevent disclosure of a matter occurring before a grand jury.

(6) Sealed Records. Records, orders, and subpoenas relating to grand-jury proceedings must be kept under seal to the extent and as long as necessary to prevent the unauthorized disclosure of a matter occurring before a grand jury.

(7) Contempt. A knowing violation of Rule 6, or of guidelines jointly issued by the Attorney General and the Director of National Intelligence pursuant to Rule 6, may be punished as a contempt of court.

(f) Indictment and Return. A grand jury may indict only if at least 12 jurors concur. The grand jury—or its foreperson or deputy foreperson—must return the indictment to a magistrate judge in open court. To avoid unnecessary cost or delay, the magistrate judge may take the return by video teleconference from the court where the grand jury sits. If a complaint or information is pending against the defendant and

12 jurors do not concur in the indictment, the foreperson must promptly and in writing report the lack of concurrence to the magistrate judge.

(g) Discharging the Grand Jury. A grand jury must serve until the court discharges it, but it may serve more than 18 months only if the court, having determined that an extension is in the public interest, extends the grand jury's service. An extension may be granted for no more than 6 months, except as otherwise provided by statute.

(h) Excusing a Juror. At any time, for good cause, the court may excuse a juror either temporarily or permanently, and if permanently, the court may impanel an alternate juror in place of the excused juror.

(i) "Indian Tribe" Defined. "Indian tribe" means an Indian tribe recognized by the Secretary of the Interior on a list published in the Federal Register under 25 U.S.C. § 479a–1.

Rule 7. The Indictment and the Information

(a) When Used.

(1) Felony. An offense (other than criminal contempt) must be prosecuted by an indictment if it is punishable:

(A) by death; or

(B) by imprisonment for more than one year.

(2) Misdemeanor. An offense punishable by imprisonment for one year or less may be prosecuted in accordance with Rule 58(b)(1).

(b) Waiving Indictment. An offense punishable by imprisonment for more than one year may be prosecuted by information if the defendant—in open court and after being advised of the nature of the charge and of the defendant's rights—waives prosecution by indictment.

(c) Nature and Contents.

(1) In General. The indictment or information must be a plain, concise, and definite written statement of the essential facts constituting the offense charged and must be signed by an attorney for the government. It need not contain a formal introduction or conclusion. A count may incorporate by reference an allegation made in another count. A count may allege that the means by which the defendant committed the offense are unknown or that the defendant committed it by one or more specified means. For each count, the indictment or information must give the official or customary citation of the statute, rule, regulation, or other provision of law that the defendant is alleged to have violated. For purposes of an indictment referred to in section 3282 of title 18, United States Code, for which the identity of the defendant is unknown, it shall be sufficient for the indictment to describe the defendant as an individual whose name is unknown, but who has a particular DNA profile, as that term is defined in that section 3282.

(2) Citation Error. Unless the defendant was misled and thereby prejudiced, neither an error in a citation nor a citation's omission is a ground to dismiss the indictment or information or to reverse a conviction.

(d) Surplusage. Upon the defendant's motion, the court may strike surplusage from the indictment or information.

(e) Amending an Information. Unless an additional or different offense is charged or a substantial right of the defendant is prejudiced, the court may permit an information to be amended at any time before the verdict or finding.

(f) Bill of Particulars. The court may direct the government to file a bill of particulars. The defendant may move for a bill of particulars before or within 14 days after arraignment or at a later time if the court permits. The government may amend a bill of particulars subject to such conditions as justice requires.

Rule 8. Joinder of Offenses or Defendants

(a) Joinder of Offenses. The indictment or information may charge a defendant in separate counts with 2 or more offenses if the offenses charged—whether felonies or misdemeanors or both—are of the same or similar character, or are based on the same act or transaction, or are connected with or constitute parts of a common scheme or plan.

(b) Joinder of Defendants. The indictment or information may charge 2 or more defendants if they are alleged to have participated in the same act or transaction, or in the same series of acts or transactions, constituting an offense or offenses. The defendants may be charged in one or more counts together or separately. All defendants need not be charged in each count.

Rule 9. Arrest Warrant or Summons on an Indictment or Information

(a) Issuance. The court must issue a warrant—or at the government's request, a summons—for each defendant named in an indictment or named in an information if one or more affidavits accompanying the information establish probable cause to believe that an offense has been committed and that the defendant committed it. The court may issue more than one warrant or summons for the same defendant. If a defendant fails to appear in response to a summons, the court may, and upon request of an attorney for the government must, issue a warrant. The court must issue the arrest warrant to an officer authorized to execute it or the summons to a person authorized to serve it.

(b) Form.

(1) Warrant. The warrant must conform to Rule 4(b)(1) except that it must be signed by the clerk and must describe the offense charged in the indictment or information.

(2) Summons. The summons must be in the same form as a warrant except that it must require the defendant to appear before the court at a stated time and place.

(c) Execution or Service; Return; Initial Appearance.

(1) Execution or Service.

(A) The warrant must be executed or the summons served as provided in Rule 4(c)(1), (2), and (3).

(B) The officer executing the warrant must proceed in accordance with Rule 5(a)(1).

(2) Return. A warrant or summons must be returned in accordance with Rule 4(c)(4).

(3) Initial Appearance. When an arrested or summoned defendant first appears before the court, the judge must proceed under Rule 5.

(d) Warrant by Telephone or Other Means. In accordance with Rule 4.1, a magistrate judge may issue an arrest warrant or summons based on information communicated by telephone or other reliable electronic means.

Rule 10.   Arraignment

(a) In General. An arraignment must be conducted in open court and must consist of:

(1) ensuring that the defendant has a copy of the indictment or information;

(2) reading the indictment or information to the defendant or stating to the defendant the substance of the charge; and then

(3) asking the defendant to plead to the indictment or information.

(b) Waiving Appearance. A defendant need not be present for the arraignment if:

(1) the defendant has been charged by indictment or misdemeanor information;

(2) the defendant, in a written waiver signed by both the defendant and defense counsel, has waived appearance and has affirmed that the defendant received a copy of the indictment or information and that the plea is not guilty; and

(3) the court accepts the waiver.

(c) Video Teleconferencing. Video teleconferencing may be used to arraign a defendant if the defendant consents.

Rule 11.   Pleas

(a) Entering a Plea.

(1) In General. A defendant may plead not guilty, guilty, or (with the court's consent) nolo contendere.

(2) Conditional Plea. With the consent of the court and the government, a defendant may enter a conditional plea of guilty or nolo contendere, reserving in writing the right to have an appellate court review an adverse determination of a specified pretrial motion. A defendant who prevails on appeal may then withdraw the plea.

(3) Nolo Contendere Plea. Before accepting a plea of nolo contendere, the court must consider the parties' views and the public interest in the effective administration of justice.

(4) Failure to Enter a Plea. If a defendant refuses to enter a plea or if a defendant organization fails to appear, the court must enter a plea of not guilty.

(b) Considering and Accepting a Guilty or Nolo Contendere Plea.

(1) Advising and Questioning the Defendant. Before the court accepts a plea of guilty or nolo contendere, the defendant may be placed under oath, and the court must address the defendant personally in open court. During this address, the court must inform the defendant of, and determine that the defendant understands, the following:

> **(A)** the government's right, in a prosecution for perjury or false statement, to use against the defendant any statement that the defendant gives under oath;

> **(B)** the right to plead not guilty, or having already so pleaded, to persist in that plea;

> **(C)** the right to a jury trial;

(D) the right to be represented by counsel—and if necessary have the court appoint counsel—at trial and at every other stage of the proceeding;

(E) the right at trial to confront and cross-examine adverse witnesses, to be protected from compelled self-incrimination, to testify and present evidence, and to compel the attendance of witnesses;

(F) the defendant's waiver of these trial rights if the court accepts a plea of guilty or nolo contendere;

(G) the nature of each charge to which the defendant is pleading;

(H) any maximum possible penalty, including imprisonment, fine, and term of supervised release;

(I) any mandatory minimum penalty;

(J) any applicable forfeiture;

(K) the court's authority to order restitution;

(L) the court's obligation to impose a special assessment;

(M) in determining a sentence, the court's obligation to calculate the applicable sentencing-guideline range and to consider that range, possible departures under the Sentencing Guidelines, and other sentencing factors under 18 U.S.C. § 3553(a);

(N) the terms of any plea-agreement provision waiving the right to appeal or to collaterally attack the sentence; and

(O) that, if convicted, a defendant who is not a United States citizen may be removed from the United States, denied citizenship, and denied admission to the United States in the future.

(2) Ensuring That a Plea Is Voluntary. Before accepting a plea of guilty or nolo contendere, the court must address the defendant personally in open court and determine that the plea is voluntary and did not result from force, threats, or promises (other than promises in a plea agreement).

(3) Determining the Factual Basis for a Plea. Before entering judgment on a guilty plea, the court must determine that there is a factual basis for the plea.

(c) Plea Agreement Procedure.

(1) In General. An attorney for the government and the defendant's attorney, or the defendant when proceeding pro se, may discuss and reach a plea agreement. The court must not participate in these discussions. If the defendant pleads guilty or nolo contendere to either a charged offense or a lesser or related offense, the plea agreement may specify that an attorney for the government will:

(A) not bring, or will move to dismiss, other charges;

(B) recommend, or agree not to oppose the defendant's request, that a particular sentence or sentencing range is appropriate or that a particular provision of the Sentencing Guidelines, or policy statement, or sentencing factor does or does not apply (such a recommendation or request does not bind the court); or

(C) agree that a specific sentence or sentencing range is the appropriate disposition of the case, or that a particular provision of the Sentencing Guidelines, or policy statement, or sentencing factor does or does not apply (such a recommendation or request binds the court once the court accepts the plea agreement).

(2) Disclosing a Plea Agreement. The parties must disclose the plea agreement in open court when the plea is offered, unless the court for good cause allows the parties to disclose the plea agreement in camera.

(3) Judicial Consideration of a Plea Agreement.

(A) To the extent the plea agreement is of the type specified in Rule 11(c)(1)(A) or (C), the court may accept the agreement, reject it, or defer a decision until the court has reviewed the presentence report.

(B) To the extent the plea agreement is of the type specified in Rule 11(c)(1)(B), the court must advise the defendant that the defendant has no right to withdraw the plea if the court does not follow the recommendation or request.

(4) Accepting a Plea Agreement. If the court accepts the plea agreement, it must inform the defendant that to the extent the plea agreement is of the type specified in Rule 11(c)(1)(A) or (C), the agreed disposition will be included in the judgment.

(5) Rejecting a Plea Agreement. If the court rejects a plea agreement containing provisions of the type specified in

Rule 11(c)(1)(A) or (C), the court must do the following on the record and in open court (or, for good cause, in camera):

    (A) inform the parties that the court rejects the plea agreement;

    (B) advise the defendant personally that the court is not required to follow the plea agreement and give the defendant an opportunity to withdraw the plea; and

    (C) advise the defendant personally that if the plea is not withdrawn, the court may dispose of the case less favorably toward the defendant than the plea agreement contemplated.

    (d) Withdrawing a Guilty or Nolo Contendere Plea. A defendant may withdraw a plea of guilty or nolo contendere:

    (1) before the court accepts the plea, for any reason or no reason; or

    (2) after the court accepts the plea, but before it imposes sentence if:

    (A) the court rejects a plea agreement under Rule 11(c)(5); or

    (B) the defendant can show a fair and just reason for requesting the withdrawal.

    (e) Finality of a Guilty or Nolo Contendere Plea. After the court imposes sentence, the defendant may not withdraw a plea of guilty or nolo contendere, and the plea may be set aside only on direct appeal or collateral attack.

    (f) Admissibility or Inadmissibility of a Plea, Plea Discussions, and Related Statements. The admissibility or inadmissibility of a plea, a plea discussion, and any related statement is governed by Federal Rule of Evidence 410.

    (g) Recording the Proceedings. The proceedings during which the defendant enters a plea must be recorded by a court reporter or by a suitable recording device. If there is a guilty plea or a nolo contendere plea, the record must include the inquiries and advice to the defendant required under Rule 11(b) and (c).

    (h) Harmless Error. A variance from the requirements of this rule is harmless error if it does not affect substantial rights.

Rule 12. Pleadings and Pretrial Motions

(a) Pleadings. The pleadings in a criminal proceeding are the indictment, the information, and the pleas of not guilty, guilty, and nolo contendere.

(b) Pretrial Motions.

(1) In General. Rule 47 applies to a pretrial motion.

(2) Motions That May Be Made Before Trial. A party may raise by pretrial motion any defense, objection, or request that the court can determine without a trial of the general issue.

(3) Motions That Must Be Made Before Trial. The following must be raised before trial:

(A) a motion alleging a defect in instituting the prosecution;

(B) a motion alleging a defect in the indictment or information—but at any time while the case is pending, the court may hear a claim that the indictment or information fails to invoke the court's jurisdiction or to state an offense;

(C) a motion to suppress evidence;

(D) a Rule 14 motion to sever charges or defendants; and

(E) a Rule 16 motion for discovery.

(4) Notice of the Government's Intent to Use Evidence.

(A) At the Government's Discretion. At the arraignment or as soon afterward as practicable, the government may notify the defendant of its intent to use specified evidence at trial in order to afford the defendant an opportunity to object before trial under Rule 12(b)(3)(C).

(B) At the Defendant's Request. At the arraignment or as soon afterward as practicable, the defendant may, in order to have an opportunity to move to suppress evidence under Rule 12(b)(3)(C), request notice of the government's intent to use (in its evidence-in-chief at trial) any evidence that the defendant may be entitled to discover under Rule 16.

(c) Motion Deadline. The court may, at the arraignment or as soon afterward as practicable, set a deadline for the parties to make pretrial motions and may also schedule a motion hearing.

(d) Ruling on a Motion. The court must decide every pretrial motion before trial unless it finds good cause to defer a ruling. The court must not defer ruling on a pretrial motion if the deferral will adversely affect a party's right to appeal. When factual issues are involved in deciding a motion, the court must state its essential findings on the record.

(e) Waiver of a Defense, Objection, or Request. A party waives any Rule 12(b)(3) defense, objection, or request not raised by the deadline the court sets under Rule 12(c) or by any extension the court provides. For good cause, the court may grant relief from the waiver.

(f) Recording the Proceedings. All proceedings at a motion hearing, including any findings of fact and conclusions of law made orally by the court, must be recorded by a court reporter or a suitable recording device.

(g) Defendant's Continued Custody or Release Status. If the court grants a motion to dismiss based on a defect in instituting the prosecution, in the indictment, or in the information, it may order the defendant to be released or detained under 18 U.S.C. § 3142 for a specified time until a new indictment or information is filed. This rule does not affect any federal statutory period of limitations.

(h) Producing Statements at a Suppression Hearing. Rule 26.2 applies at a suppression hearing under Rule 12(b)(3)(C). At a suppression hearing, a law enforcement officer is considered a government witness.

Rule 12.1.   Notice of an Alibi Defense

(a) Government's Request for Notice and Defendant's Response.

    (1) Government's Request. An attorney for the government may request in writing that the defendant notify an attorney for the government of any intended alibi defense. The request must state the time, date, and place of the alleged offense.

    (2) Defendant's Response. Within 14 days after the request, or at some other time the court sets, the defendant must serve written notice on an attorney for the government of any intended alibi defense. The defendant's notice must state:

        (A) each specific place where the defendant claims to have been at the time of the alleged offense; and

        (B) the name, address, and telephone number of each alibi witness on whom the defendant intends to rely.

(b) Disclosing Government Witnesses.

(1) Disclosure.

(A) In General. If the defendant serves a Rule 12.1(a)(2) notice, an attorney for the government must disclose in writing to the defendant or the defendant's attorney:

(i) the name of each witness—and the address and telephone number of each witness other than a victim—that the government intends to rely on to establish that the defendant was present at the scene of the alleged offense; and

(ii) each government rebuttal witness to the defendant's alibi defense.

(B) Victim's Address and Telephone Number. If the government intends to rely on a victim's testimony to establish that the defendant was present at the scene of the alleged offense and the defendant establishes a need for the victim's address and telephone number, the court may:

(i) order the government to provide the information in writing to the defendant or the defendant's attorney; or

(ii) fashion a reasonable procedure that allows preparation of the defense and also protects the victim's interests.

(2) Time to Disclose. Unless the court directs otherwise, an attorney for the government must give its Rule 12.1(b)(1) disclosure within 14 days after the defendant serves notice of an intended alibi defense under Rule 12.1(a)(2), but no later than 14 days before trial.

(c) Continuing Duty to Disclose.

(1) In General. Both an attorney for the government and the defendant must promptly disclose in writing to the other party the name of each additional witness—and the address and telephone number of each additional witness other than a victim—if:

(A) the disclosing party learns of the witness before or during trial; and

(B) the witness should have been disclosed under Rule 12.1(a) or (b) if the disclosing party had known of the witness earlier.

(2) Address and Telephone Number of an Additional Victim Witness. The address and telephone number of an additional victim witness must not be disclosed except as provided in Rule 12.1 (b)(1)(B).

(d) Exceptions. For good cause, the court may grant an exception to any requirement of Rule 12.1(a)–(c).

(e) Failure to Comply. If a party fails to comply with this rule, the court may exclude the testimony of any undisclosed witness regarding the defendant's alibi. This rule does not limit the defendant's right to testify.

(f) Inadmissibility of Withdrawn Intention. Evidence of an intention to rely on an alibi defense, later withdrawn, or of a statement made in connection with that intention, is not, in any civil or criminal proceeding, admissible against the person who gave notice of the intention.

Rule 12.2.   Notice of an Insanity Defense; Mental Examination

(a) Notice of an Insanity Defense. A defendant who intends to assert a defense of insanity at the time of the alleged offense must so notify an attorney for the government in writing within the time provided for filing a pretrial motion, or at any later time the court sets, and file a copy of the notice with the clerk. A defendant who fails to do so cannot rely on an insanity defense. The court may, for good cause, allow the defendant to file the notice late, grant additional trial-preparation time, or make other appropriate orders.

(b) Notice of Expert Evidence of a Mental Condition. If a defendant intends to introduce expert evidence relating to a mental disease or defect or any other mental condition of the defendant bearing on either (1) the issue of guilt or (2) the issue of punishment in a capital case, the defendant must—within the time provided for filing a pretrial motion or at any later time the court sets—notify an attorney for the government in writing of this intention and file a copy of the notice with the clerk. The court may, for good cause, allow the defendant to file the notice late, grant the parties additional trial-preparation time, or make other appropriate orders.

(c) Mental Examination.

(1) Authority to Order an Examination; Procedures.

(A) The court may order the defendant to submit to a competency examination under 18 U.S.C. § 4241.

(B) If the defendant provides notice under Rule 12.2(a), the court must, upon the government's motion, order the defendant to be examined under 18 U.S.C. § 4242. If the defendant provides notice under Rule 12.2(b) the court may, upon the government's motion, order the defendant to be examined under procedures ordered by the court.

(2) Disclosing Results and Reports of Capital Sentencing Examination. The results and reports of any examination conducted solely under Rule 12.2(c)(1) after notice under Rule 12.2(b)(2) must be sealed and must not be disclosed to any attorney for the government or the defendant unless the defendant is found guilty of one or more capital crimes and the defendant confirms an intent to offer during sentencing proceedings expert evidence on mental condition.

(3) Disclosing Results and Reports of the Defendant's Expert Examination. After disclosure under Rule 12.2(c)(2) of the results and reports of the government's examination, the defendant must disclose to the government the results and reports of any examination on mental condition conducted by the defendant's expert about which the defendant intends to introduce expert evidence.

(4) Inadmissibility of a Defendant's Statements. No statement made by a defendant in the course of any examination conducted under this rule (whether conducted with or without the defendant's consent), no testimony by the expert based on the statement, and no other fruits of the statement may be admitted into evidence against the defendant in any criminal proceeding except on an issue regarding mental condition on which the defendant:

    (A) has introduced evidence of incompetency or evidence requiring notice under Rule 12.2(a) or (b)(1), or

    (B) has introduced expert evidence in a capital sentencing proceeding requiring notice under Rule 12.2(b)(2).

(d) Failure to Comply.

(1) Failure to Give Notice or to Submit to Examination. The court may exclude any expert evidence from the defendant on the issue of the defendant's mental disease, mental defect, or any other mental condition bearing on the defendant's guilt or the issue of punishment in a capital case if the defendant fails to:

    (A) give notice under Rule 12.2(b); or

    (B) submit to an examination when ordered under Rule 12.2(c).

(2) Failure to Disclose. The court may exclude any expert evidence for which the defendant has failed to comply with the disclosure requirement of Rule 12.2(c)(3).

(e) Inadmissibility of Withdrawn Intention. Evidence of an intention as to which notice was given under Rule 12.2(a) or (b), later withdrawn, is not, in any civil or criminal proceeding, admissible against the person who gave notice of the intention.

Rule 12.3.   Notice of a Public-Authority Defense

(a) Notice of the Defense and Disclosure of Witnesses.

(1) Notice in General. If a defendant intends to assert a defense of actual or believed exercise of public authority on behalf of a law enforcement agency or federal intelligence agency at the time of the alleged offense, the defendant must so notify an attorney for the government in writing and must file a copy of the notice with the clerk within the time provided for filing a pretrial motion, or at any later time the court sets. The notice filed with the clerk must be under seal if the notice identifies a federal intelligence agency as the source of public authority.

(2) Contents of Notice. The notice must contain the following information:

    (A) the law enforcement agency or federal intelligence agency involved;

    (B) the agency member on whose behalf the defendant claims to have acted; and

    (C) the time during which the defendant claims to have acted with public authority.

(3) Response to the Notice. An attorney for the government must serve a written response on the defendant or the defendant's attorney within 14 days after receiving the defendant's notice, but no later than 21 days before trial. The response must admit or deny that the defendant exercised the public authority identified in the defendant's notice.

(4) Disclosing Witnesses.

    (A) Government's Request. An attorney for the government may request in writing that the defendant disclose the name, address, and telephone number of each witness the defendant intends to rely on to establish a public-authority defense. An attorney for the government may serve the request when the government serves its response to the defendant's notice under Rule 12.3(a)(3), or later, but must serve the request no later than 21 days before trial.

(B) Defendant's Response. Within 14 days after receiving the government's request, the defendant must serve on an attorney for the government a written statement of the name, address, and telephone number of each witness.

(C) Government's Reply. Within 14 days after receiving the defendant's statement, an attorney for the government must serve on the defendant or the defendant's attorney a written statement of the name of each witness— and the address and telephone number of each witness other than a victim—that the government intends to rely on to oppose the defendant's public-authority defense.

(D) Victim's Address and Telephone Number. If the government intends to rely on a victim's testimony to oppose the defendant's public-authority defense and the defendant establishes a need for the victim's address and telephone number, the court may:

    (i) order the government to provide the information in writing to the defendant or the defendant's attorney; or

    (ii) fashion a reasonable procedure that allows for preparing the defense and also protects the victim's interests.

(5) Additional Time. The court may, for good cause, allow a party additional time to comply with this rule.

(b) Continuing Duty to Disclose.

(1) In General. Both an attorney for the government and the defendant must promptly disclose in writing to the other party the name of any additional witness—and the address, and telephone number of any additional witness other than a victim—if:

    (A) the disclosing party learns of the witness before or during trial; and

    (B) the witness should have been disclosed under Rule 12.3(a)(4) if the disclosing party had known of the witness earlier.

(2) Address and Telephone Number of an Additional Victim-Witness. The address and telephone number of an additional victim-witness must not be disclosed except as provided in Rule 12.3(a)(4)(D).

(c) Failure to Comply. If a party fails to comply with this rule, the court may exclude the testimony of any undisclosed witness regarding the public-authority defense. This rule does not limit the defendant's right to testify.

(d) Protective Procedures Unaffected. This rule does not limit the court's authority to issue appropriate protective orders or to order that any filings be under seal.

(e) Inadmissibility of Withdrawn Intention. Evidence of an intention as to which notice was given under Rule 12.3(a), later withdrawn, is not, in any civil or criminal proceeding, admissible against the person who gave notice of the intention.

Rule 12.4.   Disclosure Statement

(a) Who Must File.

(1) Nongovernmental Corporate Party. Any nongovernmental corporate party to a proceeding in a district court must file a statement that identifies any parent corporation and any publicly held corporation that owns 10% or more of its stock or states that there is no such corporation.

(2) Organizational Victim. If an organization is a victim of the alleged criminal activity, the government must file a statement identifying the victim. If the organizational victim is a corporation, the statement must also disclose the information required by Rule 12.4(a)(1) to the extent it can be obtained through due diligence.

(b) Time for Filing; Supplemental Filing. A party must:

(1) file the Rule 12.4(a) statement upon the defendant's initial appearance; and

(2) promptly file a supplemental statement upon any change in the information that the statement requires.

Rule 13.   Joint Trial of Separate Cases

The court may order that separate cases be tried together as though brought in a single indictment or information if all offenses and all defendants could have been joined in a single indictment or information.

Rule 14.   Relief from Prejudicial Joinder

(a) Relief. If the joinder of offenses or defendants in an indictment, an information, or a consolidation for trial appears to prejudice a defendant or the government, the court may order separate trials of counts, sever the defendants' trials, or provide any other relief that justice requires.

(b) Defendant's Statements. Before ruling on a defendant's motion to sever, the court may order an attorney for the government to deliver to the court for in camera inspection any defendant's statement that the government intends to use as evidence.

Rule 15.   Depositions

(a) When Taken.

(1) In General. A party may move that a prospective witness be deposed in order to preserve testimony for trial. The court may grant the motion because of exceptional circumstances and in the interest of justice. If the court orders the deposition to be taken, it may also require the deponent to produce at the deposition any designated material that is not privileged, including any book, paper, document, record, recording, or data.

(2) Detained Material Witness. A witness who is detained under 18 U.S.C. § 3144 may request to be deposed by filing a written motion and giving notice to the parties. The court may then order that the deposition be taken and may discharge the witness after the witness has signed under oath the deposition transcript.

(b) Notice.

(1) In General. A party seeking to take a deposition must give every other party reasonable written notice of the deposition's date and location. The notice must state the name and address of each deponent. If requested by a party receiving the notice, the court may, for good cause, change the deposition's date or location.

(2) To the Custodial Officer. A party seeking to take the deposition must also notify the officer who has custody of the defendant of the scheduled date and location.

(c) Defendant's Presence.

(1) Defendant in Custody. Except as authorized by Rule 15(c)(3), the officer who has custody of the defendant must produce the defendant at the deposition and keep the defendant in the witness's presence during the examination, unless the defendant:

(A) waives in writing the right to be present; or

(B) persists in disruptive conduct justifying exclusion after being warned by the court that disruptive conduct will result in the defendant's exclusion.

(2) Defendant Not in Custody. Except as authorized by Rule 15(c)(3), a defendant who is not in custody has the right upon request to be present at the deposition, subject to any conditions imposed by the court. If the government tenders the defendant's expenses as provided in Rule 15(d) but the defendant still fails to appear, the defendant—absent good cause—waives both the right to appear and any objection to the taking and use of the deposition based on that right.

(3) Taking Depositions Outside the United States Without the Defendant's Presence. The deposition of a witness who is outside the United States may be taken without the defendant's presence if the court makes case-specific findings of all the following:

(A) the witness's testimony could provide substantial proof of a material fact in a felony prosecution;

(B) there is a substantial likelihood that the witness's attendance at trial cannot be obtained;

(C) the witness's presence for a deposition in the United States cannot be obtained;

(D) the defendant cannot be present because:

(i) the country where the witness is located will not permit the defendant to attend the deposition;

(ii) for an in-custody defendant, secure transportation and continuing custody cannot be assured at the witness's location; or

(iii) for an out-of-custody defendant, no reasonable conditions will assure an appearance at the deposition or at trial or sentencing; and

(E) the defendant can meaningfully participate in the deposition through reasonable means.

(d) Expenses. If the deposition was requested by the government, the court may—or if the defendant is unable to bear the deposition expenses, the court must—order the government to pay:

(1) any reasonable travel and subsistence expenses of the defendant and the defendant's attorney to attend the deposition; and

(2) the costs of the deposition transcript.

(e) Manner of Taking. Unless these rules or a court order provides otherwise, a deposition must be taken and filed in the same manner as a deposition in a civil action, except that:

(1) A defendant may not be deposed without that defendant's consent.

(2) The scope and manner of the deposition examination and cross-examination must be the same as would be allowed during trial.

(3) The government must provide to the defendant or the defendant's attorney, for use at the deposition, any statement of the deponent in the government's possession to which the defendant would be entitled at trial.

(f) Admissibility and Use as Evidence. An order authorizing a deposition to be taken under this rule does not determine its admissibility. A party may use all or part of a deposition as provided by the Federal Rules of Evidence.

(g) Objections. A party objecting to deposition testimony or evidence must state the grounds for the objection during the deposition.

(h) Depositions by Agreement Permitted. The parties may by agreement take and use a deposition with the court's consent.

Rule 16. Discovery and Inspection

(a) Government's Disclosure.

(1) Information Subject to Disclosure.

(A) Defendant's Oral Statement. Upon a defendant's request, the government must disclose to the defendant the substance of any relevant oral statement made by the defendant, before or after arrest, in response to interrogation by a person the defendant knew was a government agent if the government intends to use the statement at trial.

(B) Defendant's Written or Recorded Statement. Upon a defendant's request, the government must disclose to the defendant, and make available for inspection, copying, or photographing, all of the following:

(i) any relevant written or recorded statement by the defendant if:

• the statement is within the government's possession, custody, or control; and

• the attorney for the government knows—or through due diligence could know—that the statement exists;

(ii) the portion of any written record containing the substance of any relevant oral statement made before or after arrest if the defendant made the statement in response to interrogation by a person the defendant knew was a government agent; and

(iii) the defendant's recorded testimony before a grand jury relating to the charged offense.

(C) Organizational Defendant. Upon a defendant's request, if the defendant is an organization, the government must disclose to the defendant any statement described in Rule 16(a)(1)(A) and (B) if the government contends that the person making the statement:

(i) was legally able to bind the defendant regarding the subject of the statement because of that person's position as the defendant's director, officer, employee, or agent; or

(ii) was personally involved in the alleged conduct constituting the offense and was legally able to bind the defendant regarding that conduct because of that person's position as the defendant's director, officer, employee, or agent.

(D) Defendant's Prior Record. Upon a defendant's request, the government must furnish the defendant with a copy of the defendant's prior criminal record that is within the government's possession, custody, or control if the attorney for the government knows—or through due diligence could know—that the record exists.

(E) Documents and Objects. Upon a defendant's request, the government must permit the defendant to inspect and to copy or photograph books, papers, documents, data, photographs, tangible objects, buildings or places, or copies or portions of any of these items, if the item is within the government's possession, custody, or control and:

(i) the item is material to preparing the defense;

(ii) the government intends to use the item in its case-in-chief at trial; or

(iii) the item was obtained from or belongs to the defendant.

(F) Reports of Examinations and Tests. Upon a defendant's request, the government must permit a defendant to inspect and to copy or photograph the results or reports of any physical or mental examination and of any scientific test or experiment if:

(i) the item is within the government's possession, custody, or control;

(ii) the attorney for the government knows—or through due diligence could know—that the item exists; and

(iii) the item is material to preparing the defense or the government intends to use the item in its case-in-chief at trial.

(G) Expert witnesses. At the defendant's request, the government must give to the defendant a written summary of any testimony that the government intends to use under Rules 702, 703, or 705 of the Federal Rules of Evidence during its case-in-chief at trial. If the government requests discovery under subdivision (b)(1)(C)(ii) and the defendant complies, the government must, at the defendant's request, give to the defendant a written summary of testimony that the government intends to use under Rules 702, 703, or 705 of the Federal Rules of Evidence as evidence at trial on the issue of the defendant's mental condition. The summary provided under this subparagraph must describe the witness's opinions, the bases and reasons for those opinions, and the witness's qualifications.

(2) Information Not Subject to Disclosure. Except as permitted by Rule 16(a)(1)(A)–(D), (F), and (G), this rule does not authorize the discovery or inspection of reports, memoranda, or other internal government documents made by an attorney for the government or other government agent in connection with investigating or prosecuting the case. Nor does this rule authorize the discovery or inspection of statements made by prospective government witnesses except as provided in 18 U.S.C. 3 § 3500.*

(3) Grand Jury Transcripts. This rule does not apply to the discovery or inspection of a grand jury's recorded proceedings, except as provided in Rules 6, 12(h), 16(a)(1), and 26.2.

(b) Defendant's Disclosure.

(1) Information Subject to Disclosure.

(A) Documents and Objects. If a defendant requests disclosure under Rule 16(a)(1)(E) and the government complies, then the defendant must permit the government,

---

    *   This provision is set out in Appendix B.

upon request, to inspect and to copy or photograph books, papers, documents, data, photographs, tangible objects, buildings or places, or copies or portions of any of these items if:

    (i) the item is within the defendant's possession, custody, or control; and

    (ii) the defendant intends to use the item in the defendant's case-in-chief at trial.

(B) Reports of Examinations and Tests. If a defendant requests disclosure under Rule 16(a)(1)(F) and the government complies, the defendant must permit the government, upon request, to inspect and to copy or photograph the results or reports of any physical or mental examination and of any scientific test or experiment if:

    (i) the item is within the defendant's possession, custody, or control; and

    (ii) the defendant intends to use the item in the defendant's case-in-chief at trial, or intends to call the witness who prepared the report and the report relates to the witness's testimony.

(C) Expert witnesses. The defendant must, at the government's request, give to the government a written summary of any testimony that the defendant intends to use under Rules 702, 703, or 705 of the Federal Rules of Evidence as evidence at trial, if—

    (i) the defendant requests disclosure under subdivision (a)(1)(G) and the government complies; or

    (ii) the defendant has given notice under Rule 12.2(b) of an intent to present expert testimony on the defendant's mental condition.

This summary must describe the witness's opinions, the bases and reasons for those opinions, and the witness's qualifications.

(2) Information Not Subject to Disclosure. Except for scientific or medical reports, Rule 16(b)(1) does not authorize discovery or inspection of:

    (A) reports, memoranda, or other documents made by the defendant, or the defendant's attorney or agent, during the case's investigation or defense; or

    (B) a statement made to the defendant, or the defendant's attorney or agent, by:

(i) the defendant;

(ii) a government or defense witness; or

(iii) a prospective government or defense witness.

(c) Continuing Duty to Disclose. A party who discovers additional evidence or material before or during trial must promptly disclose its existence to the other party or the court if:

(1) the evidence or material is subject to discovery or inspection under this rule; and

(2) the other party previously requested, or the court ordered, its production.

(d) Regulating Discovery.

(1) Protective and Modifying Orders. At any time the court may, for good cause, deny, restrict, or defer discovery or inspection, or grant other appropriate relief. The court may permit a party to show good cause by a written statement that the court will inspect ex parte. If relief is granted, the court must preserve the entire text of the party's statement under seal.

(2) Failure to Comply. If a party fails to comply with this rule, the court may:

(A) order that party to permit the discovery or inspection; specify its time, place, and manner; and prescribe other just terms and conditions;

(B) grant a continuance;

(C) prohibit that party from introducing the undisclosed evidence; or

(D) enter any other order that is just under the circumstances.

Rule 17.   Subpoena

(a) Content. A subpoena must state the court's name and the title of the proceeding, include the seal of the court, and command the witness to attend and testify at the time and place the subpoena specifies. The clerk must issue a blank subpoena—signed and sealed—to the party requesting it, and that party must fill in the blanks before the subpoena is served.

(b) Defendant Unable to Pay. Upon a defendant's ex parte application, the court must order that a subpoena be issued for a named witness if the defendant shows an inability to pay the witness's fees and the necessity of the witness's presence for an adequate defense. If the court orders a subpoena to be issued, the process costs and witness fees will be paid in the same manner as those paid for witnesses the government subpoenas.

(c) Producing Documents and Objects.

(1) In General. A subpoena may order the witness to produce any books, papers, documents, data, or other objects the subpoena designates. The court may direct the witness to produce the designated items in court before trial or before they are to be offered in evidence. When the items arrive, the court may permit the parties and their attorneys to inspect all or part of them.

(2) Quashing or Modifying the Subpoena. On motion made promptly, the court may quash or modify the subpoena if compliance would be unreasonable or oppressive.

(3) Subpoena for Personal or Confidential Information About a Victim. After a complaint, indictment, or information is filed, a subpoena requiring the production of personal or confidential information about a victim may be served on a third party only by court order. Before entering the order and unless there are exceptional circumstances, the court must require giving notice to the victim so that the victim can move to quash or modify the subpoena or otherwise object.

(d) Service. A marshal, a deputy marshal, or any nonparty who is at least 18 years old may serve a subpoena. The server must deliver a copy of the subpoena to the witness and must tender to the witness one day's witness-attendance fee and the legal mileage allowance. The server need not tender the attendance fee or mileage allowance when the United States, a federal officer, or a federal agency has requested the subpoena.

(e) Place of Service.

(1) In the United States. A subpoena requiring a witness to attend a hearing or trial may be served at any place within the United States.

(2) In a Foreign Country. If the witness is in a foreign country, 28 U.S.C. § 1783 governs the subpoena's service.

(f) Issuing a Deposition Subpoena.

(1) Issuance. A court order to take a deposition authorizes the clerk in the district where the deposition is to be taken to issue a subpoena for any witness named or described in the order.

(2) Place. After considering the convenience of the witness and the parties, the court may order—and the subpoena may require—the witness to appear anywhere the court designates.

(g) Contempt. The court (other than a magistrate judge) may hold in contempt a witness who, without adequate excuse, disobeys a subpoena issued by a federal court in that district. A magistrate judge may hold in contempt a witness who, without adequate excuse, disobeys a subpoena issued by that magistrate judge as provided in 28 U.S.C. § 636(e).

(h) Information Not Subject to a Subpoena. No party may subpoena a statement of a witness or of a prospective witness under this rule. Rule 26.2 governs the production of the statement.

Rule 17.1.   Pretrial Conference

On its own, or on a party's motion, the court may hold one or more pretrial conferences to promote a fair and expeditious trial. When a conference ends, the court must prepare and file a memorandum of any matters agreed to during the conference. The government may not use any statement made during the conference by the defendant or the defendant's attorney unless it is in writing and is signed by the defendant and the defendant's attorney.

Rule 18.   Place of Prosecution and Trial

Unless a statute or these rules permit otherwise, the government must prosecute an offense in a district where the offense was committed. The court must set the place of trial within the district with due regard for the convenience of the defendant, any victim, and the witnesses, and the prompt administration of justice.

Rule 19.   [Reserved]

Rule 20.   Transfer for Plea and Sentence

(a) Consent to Transfer. A prosecution may be transferred from the district where the indictment or information is pending, or from which a warrant on a complaint has been issued, to the district where the defendant is arrested, held, or present if:

> **(1)** the defendant states in writing a wish to plead guilty or nolo contendere and to waive trial in the district where the indictment, information, or complaint is pending, consents in writing to the court's disposing of the case in the transferee district, and files the statement in the transferee district; and

> **(2)** the United States attorneys in both districts approve the transfer in writing.

(b) Clerk's Duties. After receiving the defendant's statement and the required approvals, the clerk where the indictment, information, or complaint is pending must send the file, or a certified copy, to the clerk in the transferee district.

(c) Effect of a Not Guilty Plea. If the defendant pleads not guilty after the case has been transferred under Rule 20(a), the clerk must return the papers to the court where the prosecution began, and that court must restore the proceeding to its docket. The defendant's statement that the defendant wished to plead guilty or nolo contendere is not, in any civil or criminal proceeding, admissible against the defendant.

(d) Juveniles.

(1) Consent to Transfer. A juvenile, as defined in 18 U.S.C. § 5031, may be proceeded against as a juvenile delinquent in the district where the juvenile is arrested, held, or present if:

(A) the alleged offense that occurred in the other district is not punishable by death or life imprisonment;

(B) an attorney has advised the juvenile;

(C) the court has informed the juvenile of the juvenile's rights—including the right to be returned to the district where the offense allegedly occurred—and the consequences of waiving those rights;

(D) the juvenile, after receiving the court's information about rights, consents in writing to be proceeded against in the transferee district, and files the consent in the transferee district;

(E) the United States attorneys for both districts approve the transfer in writing; and

(F) the transferee court approves the transfer.

(2) Clerk's Duties. After receiving the juvenile's written consent and the required approvals, the clerk where the indictment, information, or complaint is pending or where the alleged offense occurred must send the file, or a certified copy, to the clerk in the transferee district.

Rule 21.   Transfer for Trial

(a) For Prejudice. Upon the defendant's motion, the court must transfer the proceeding against that defendant to another district if the court is satisfied that so great a prejudice against the defendant exists in the transferring district that the defendant cannot obtain a fair and impartial trial there.

(b) For Convenience. Upon the defendant's motion, the court may transfer the proceeding, or one or more counts, against that defendant to another district for the convenience of the parties, any victim, and the witnesses, and in the interest of justice.

(c) Proceedings on Transfer. When the court orders a transfer, the clerk must send to the transferee district the file, or a certified copy, and any bail taken. The prosecution will then continue in the transferee district.

(d) Time to File a Motion to Transfer. A motion to transfer may be made at or before arraignment or at any other time the court or these rules prescribe.

Rule 22.   [Transferred]

Rule 23.   Jury or Nonjury Trial

(a) Jury Trial. If the defendant is entitled to a jury trial, the trial must be by jury unless:

(1) the defendant waives a jury trial in writing;

(2) the government consents; and

(3) the court approves.

(b) Jury Size.

(1) In General. A jury consists of 12 persons unless this rule provides otherwise.

(2) Stipulation for a Smaller Jury. At any time before the verdict, the parties may, with the court's approval, stipulate in writing that:

(A) the jury may consist of fewer than 12 persons; or

(B) a jury of fewer than 12 persons may return a verdict if the court finds it necessary to excuse a juror for good cause after the trial begins.

(3) Court Order for a Jury of 11. After the jury has retired to deliberate, the court may permit a jury of 11 persons to return a verdict, even without a stipulation by the parties, if the court finds good cause to excuse a juror.

(c) Nonjury Trial. In a case tried without a jury, the court must find the defendant guilty or not guilty. If a party requests before the finding of guilty or not guilty, the court must state its specific findings of fact in open court or in a written decision or opinion.

Rule 24.   Trial Jurors

(a) Examination.

(1) In General. The court may examine prospective jurors or may permit the attorneys for the parties to do so.

(2) Court Examination. If the court examines the jurors, it must permit the attorneys for the parties to:

(A) ask further questions that the court considers proper; or

(B) submit further questions that the court may ask if it considers them proper.

(b) Peremptory Challenges. Each side is entitled to the number of peremptory challenges to prospective jurors specified below. The court may allow additional peremptory challenges to multiple defendants, and may allow the defendants to exercise those challenges separately or jointly.

(1) Capital Case. Each side has 20 peremptory challenges when the government seeks the death penalty.

(2) Other Felony Case. The government has 6 peremptory challenges and the defendant or defendants jointly have 10 peremptory challenges when the defendant is charged with a crime punishable by imprisonment of more than one year.

(3) Misdemeanor Case. Each side has 3 peremptory challenges when the defendant is charged with a crime punishable by fine, imprisonment of one year or less, or both.

(c) Alternate Jurors.

(1) In General. The court may impanel up to 6 alternate jurors to replace any jurors who are unable to perform or who are disqualified from performing their duties.

(2) Procedure.

(A) Alternate jurors must have the same qualifications and be selected and sworn in the same manner as any other juror.

(B) Alternate jurors replace jurors in the same sequence in which the alternates were selected. An alternate juror who replaces a juror has the same authority as the other jurors.

(3) Retaining Alternate Jurors. The court may retain alternate jurors after the jury retires to deliberate. The court must ensure that a retained alternate does not discuss the case with anyone until that alternate replaces a juror or is discharged. If an alternate replaces a juror after deliberations have begun, the court must instruct the jury to begin its deliberations anew.

(4) Peremptory Challenges. Each side is entitled to the number of additional peremptory challenges to prospective alternate jurors specified below. These additional challenges may be used only to remove alternate jurors.

> **(A) One or Two Alternates.** One additional peremptory challenge is permitted when one or two alternates are impaneled.

> **(B) Three or Four Alternates.** Two additional peremptory challenges are permitted when three or four alternates are impaneled.

> **(C) Five or Six Alternates.** Three additional peremptory challenges are permitted when five or six alternates are impaneled.

Rule 25. Judge's Disability

(a) During Trial. Any judge regularly sitting in or assigned to the court may complete a jury trial if:

> **(1)** the judge before whom the trial began cannot proceed because of death, sickness, or other disability; and

> **(2)** the judge completing the trial certifies familiarity with the trial record.

(b) After a Verdict or Finding of Guilty.

> **(1) In General.** After a verdict or finding of guilty, any judge regularly sitting in or assigned to a court may complete the court's duties if the judge who presided at trial cannot perform those duties because of absence, death, sickness, or other disability.

> **(2) Granting a New Trial.** The successor judge may grant a new trial if satisfied that:

>> **(A)** a judge other than the one who presided at the trial cannot perform the post-trial duties; or

> **(B)** a new trial is necessary for some other reason.

Rule 26. Taking Testimony

In every trial the testimony of witnesses must be taken in open court, unless otherwise provided by a statute or by rules adopted under 28 U.S.C. §§ 2072–2077.

Rule 26.1. Foreign Law Determination

A party intending to raise an issue of foreign law must provide the court and all parties with reasonable written notice. Issues of foreign law are questions of law, but in deciding such issues a court may consider any relevant material or source—including testimony—without regard to the Federal Rules of Evidence.

Rule 26.2.   Producing a Witness's Statement

(a) Motion to Produce. After a witness other than the defendant has testified on direct examination, the court, on motion of a party who did not call the witness, must order an attorney for the government or the defendant and the defendant's attorney to produce, for the examination and use of the moving party, any statement of the witness that is in their possession and that relates to the subject matter of the witness's testimony.

(b) Producing the Entire Statement. If the entire statement relates to the subject matter of the witness's testimony, the court must order that the statement be delivered to the moving party.

(c) Producing a Redacted Statement. If the party who called the witness claims that the statement contains information that is privileged or does not relate to the subject matter of the witness's testimony, the court must inspect the statement in camera. After excising any privileged or unrelated portions, the court must order delivery of the redacted statement to the moving party. If the defendant objects to an excision, the court must preserve the entire statement with the excised portion indicated, under seal, as part of the record.

(d) Recess to Examine a Statement. The court may recess the proceedings to allow time for a party to examine the statement and prepare for its use.

(e) Sanction for Failure to Produce or Deliver a Statement. If the party who called the witness disobeys an order to produce or deliver a statement, the court must strike the witness's testimony from the record. If an attorney for the government disobeys the order, the court must declare a mistrial if justice so requires.

(f) "Statement" Defined. As used in this rule, a witness's "statement" means:

  (1) a written statement that the witness makes and signs, or otherwise adopts or approves;

  (2) a substantially verbatim, contemporaneously recorded recital of the witness's oral statement that is contained in any recording or any transcription of a recording; or

  (3) the witness's statement to a grand jury, however taken or recorded, or a transcription of such a statement.

(g) Scope. This rule applies at trial, at a suppression hearing under Rule 12, and to the extent specified in the following rules:

  (1) Rule 5.1(h) (preliminary hearing);

  (2) Rule 32(i)(2) (sentencing);

(3) Rule 32.1(e) (hearing to revoke or modify probation or supervised release);

(4) Rule 46(j) (detention hearing); and

(5) Rule 8 of the Rules Governing Proceedings under 28 U.S.C. § 2255.

Rule 26.3.   Mistrial

Before ordering a mistrial, the court must give each defendant and the government an opportunity to comment on the propriety of the order, to state whether that party consents or objects, and to suggest alternatives.

Rule 27.   Proving an Official Record

A party may prove an official record, an entry in such a record, or the lack of a record or entry in the same manner as in a civil action.

Rule 28.   Interpreters

The court may select, appoint, and set the reasonable compensation for an interpreter. The compensation must be paid from funds provided by law or by the government, as the court may direct.

Rule 29.   Motion for a Judgment of Acquittal

(a) Before Submission to the Jury. After the government closes its evidence or after the close of all the evidence, the court on the defendant's motion must enter a judgment of acquittal of any offense for which the evidence is insufficient to sustain a conviction. The court may on its own consider whether the evidence is insufficient to sustain a conviction. If the court denies a motion for a judgment of acquittal at the close of the government's evidence, the defendant may offer evidence without having reserved the right to do so.

(b) Reserving Decision. The court may reserve decision on the motion, proceed with the trial (where the motion is made before the close of all the evidence), submit the case to the jury, and decide the motion either before the jury returns a verdict or after it returns a verdict of guilty or is discharged without having returned a verdict. If the court reserves decision, it must decide the motion on the basis of the evidence at the time the ruling was reserved.

(c) After Jury Verdict or Discharge.

(1) Time for a Motion. A defendant may move for a judgment of acquittal, or renew such a motion, within 14 days after a guilty verdict or after the court discharges the jury, whichever is later.

(2) Ruling on the Motion. If the jury has returned a guilty verdict, the court may set aside the verdict and enter an acquittal. If the jury has failed to return a verdict, the court may enter a judgment of acquittal.

(3) No Prior Motion Required. A defendant is not required to move for a judgment of acquittal before the court submits the case to the jury as a prerequisite for making such a motion after jury discharge.

(d) Conditional Ruling on a Motion for a New Trial.

(1) Motion for a New Trial. If the court enters a judgment of acquittal after a guilty verdict, the court must also conditionally determine whether any motion for a new trial should be granted if the judgment of acquittal is later vacated or reversed. The court must specify the reasons for that determination.

(2) Finality. The court's order conditionally granting a motion for a new trial does not affect the finality of the judgment of acquittal.

(3) Appeal.

(A) Grant of a Motion for a New Trial. If the court conditionally grants a motion for a new trial and an appellate court later reverses the judgment of acquittal, the trial court must proceed with the new trial unless the appellate court orders otherwise.

(B) Denial of a Motion for a New Trial. If the court conditionally denies a motion for a new trial, an appellee may assert that the denial was erroneous. If the appellate court later reverses the judgment of acquittal, the trial court must proceed as the appellate court directs.

Rule 29.1.   Closing Argument

Closing arguments proceed in the following order:

(a) the government argues;

(b) the defense argues; and

(c) the government rebuts.

Rule 30.   Jury Instructions

(a) In General. Any party may request in writing that the court instruct the jury on the law as specified in the request. The request must be made at the close of the evidence or at any earlier time that the court reasonably sets. When the request is made, the requesting party must furnish a copy to every other party.

(b) Ruling on a Request. The court must inform the parties before closing arguments how it intends to rule on the requested instructions.

(c) Time for Giving Instructions. The court may instruct the jury before or after the arguments are completed, or at both times.

(d) Objections to Instructions. A party who objects to any portion of the instructions or to a failure to give a requested instruction must inform the court of the specific objection and the grounds for the objection before the jury retires to deliberate. An opportunity must be given to object out of the jury's hearing and, on request, out of the jury's presence. Failure to object in accordance with this rule precludes appellate review, except as permitted under Rule 52(b).

Rule 31.   Jury Verdict

(a) Return. The jury must return its verdict to a judge in open court. The verdict must be unanimous.

(b) Partial Verdicts, Mistrial, and Retrial.

(1) Multiple Defendants. If there are multiple defendants, the jury may return a verdict at any time during its deliberations as to any defendant about whom it has agreed.

(2) Multiple Counts. If the jury cannot agree on all counts as to any defendant, the jury may return a verdict on those counts on which it has agreed.

(3) Mistrial and Retrial. If the jury cannot agree on a verdict on one or more counts, the court may declare a mistrial on those counts. The government may retry any defendant on any count on which the jury could not agree.

(c) Lesser Offense or Attempt. A defendant may be found guilty of any of the following:

(1) an offense necessarily included in the offense charged;

(2) an attempt to commit the offense charged; or

(3) an attempt to commit an offense necessarily included in the offense charged, if the attempt is an offense in its own right.

(d) Jury Poll. After a verdict is returned but before the jury is discharged, the court must on a party's request, or may on its own, poll the jurors individually. If the poll reveals a lack of unanimity, the court may direct the jury to deliberate further or may declare a mistrial and discharge the jury.

Rule 32.   Sentencing and Judgment

(a) [Reserved.]

(b) Time of Sentencing.

(1) In General. The court must impose sentence without unnecessary delay.

(2) Changing Time Limits. The court may, for good cause, change any time limits prescribed in this rule.

(c) Presentence Investigation.

(1) Required Investigation.

(A) In General. The probation officer must conduct a presentence investigation and submit a report to the court before it imposes sentence unless:

(i) 18 U.S.C. § 3593(c) or another statute requires otherwise; or

(ii) the court finds that the information in the record enables it to meaningfully exercise its sentencing authority under 18 U.S.C. § 3553, and the court explains its finding on the record.

(B) Restitution. If the law permits restitution, the probation officer must conduct an investigation and submit a report that contains sufficient information for the court to order restitution.

(2) Interviewing the Defendant. The probation officer who interviews a defendant as part of a presentence investigation must, on request, give the defendant's attorney notice and a reasonable opportunity to attend the interview.

(d) Presentence Report.

(1) Applying the Sentencing Guidelines. The presentence report must:

(A) identify all applicable guidelines and policy statements of the Sentencing Commission;

(B) calculate the defendant's offense level and criminal history category;

(C) state the resulting sentencing range and kinds of sentences available;

(D) identify any factor relevant to:

(i) the appropriate kind of sentence, or

(ii) the appropriate sentence within the applicable sentencing range; and

(E) identify any basis for departing from the applicable sentencing range.

(2) Additional Information. The presentence report must also contain the following:

    (A) the defendant's history and characteristics, including:

        (i) any prior criminal record;

        (ii) the defendant's financial condition; and

        (iii) any circumstances affecting the defendant's behavior that maybe helpful in imposing sentence or in correctional treatment;

    (B) information that assesses any financial, social, psychological, and medical impact on any victim;

    (C) when appropriate, the nature and extent of nonprison programs and resources available to the defendant;

    (D) when the law provides for restitution, information sufficient for a restitution order;

    (E) if the court orders a study under 18 U.S.C. § 3552(b), any resulting report and recommendation;

    (F) a statement of whether the government seeks forfeiture under Rule 32.2 and any other law; and

    (G) any other information that the court requires, including information relevant to the factors under 18 U.S.C. § 3553(a).

(3) Exclusions. The presentence report must exclude the following:

    (A) any diagnoses that, if disclosed, might seriously disrupt a rehabilitation program;

    (B) any sources of information obtained upon a promise of confidentiality; and

    (C) any other information that, if disclosed, might result in physical or other harm to the defendant or others.

(e) Disclosing the Report and Recommendation.

(1) Time to Disclose. Unless the defendant has consented in writing, the probation officer must not submit a presentence report to the court or disclose its contents to anyone until the defendant has pleaded guilty or nolo contendere, or has been found guilty.

(2) Minimum Required Notice. The probation officer must give the presentence report to the defendant, the defendant's attorney, and an attorney for the government at least 35 days before sentencing unless the defendant waives this minimum period.

(3) Sentence Recommendation. By local rule or by order in a case, the court may direct the probation officer not to disclose to anyone other than the court the officer's recommendation on the sentence.

(f) Objecting to the Report.

(1) Time to Object. Within 14 days after receiving the presentence report, the parties must state in writing any objections, including objections to material information, sentencing guideline ranges, and policy statements contained in or omitted from the report.

(2) Serving Objections. An objecting party must provide a copy of its objections to the opposing party and to the probation officer.

(3) Action on Objections. After receiving objections, the probation officer may meet with the parties to discuss the objections. The probation officer may then investigate further and revise the presentence report as appropriate.

(g) Submitting the Report. At least 7 days before sentencing, the probation officer must submit to the court and to the parties the presentence report and an addendum containing any unresolved objections, the grounds for those objections, and the probation officer's comments on them.

(h) Notice of Possible Departure from Sentencing Guidelines. Before the court may depart from the applicable sentencing range on a ground not identified for departure either in the presentence report or in a party's prehearing submission, the court must give the parties reasonable notice that it is contemplating such a departure. The notice must specify any ground on which the court is contemplating a departure.

(i) Sentencing.

(1) In General. At sentencing, the court:

(A) must verify that the defendant and the defendant's attorney have read and discussed the presentence report and any addendum to the report;

(B) must give to the defendant and an attorney for the government a written summary of—or summarize in camera—any information excluded from the presentence report under Rule 32(d)(3) on which the court will rely in sentencing, and give them a reasonable opportunity to comment on that information;

(C) must allow the parties' attorneys to comment on the probation officer's determinations and other matters relating to an appropriate sentence; and

(D) may, for good cause, allow a party to make a new objection at any time before sentence is imposed.

(2) Introducing Evidence; Producing a Statement. The court may permit the parties to introduce evidence on the objections. If a witness testifies at sentencing, Rule 26.2(a)–(d) and (f) applies. If a party fails to comply with a Rule 26.2 order to produce a witness's statement, the court must not consider that witness's testimony.

(3) Court Determinations. At sentencing, the court:

(A) may accept any undisputed portion of the presentence report as a finding of fact;

(B) must—for any disputed portion of the presentence report or other controverted matter—rule on the dispute or determine that a ruling is unnecessary either because the matter will not affect sentencing, or because the court will not consider the matter in sentencing; and

(C) must append a copy of the court's determinations under this rule to any copy of the presentence report made available to the Bureau of Prisons.

(4) Opportunity to Speak.

(A) By a Party. Before imposing sentence, the court must:

(i) provide the defendant's attorney an opportunity to speak on the defendant's behalf;

(ii) address the defendant personally in order to permit the defendant to speak or present any information to mitigate the sentence; and

(iii) provide an attorney for the government an opportunity to speak equivalent to that of the defendant's attorney.

(B) By a Victim. Before imposing sentence, the court must address any victim of the crime who is present at sentencing and must permit the victim to be reasonably heard.

(C) In Camera Proceedings. Upon a party's motion and for good cause, the court may hear in camera any statement made under Rule 32(i)(4).

(j) Defendant's Right to Appeal.

(1) Advice of a Right to Appeal.

(A) Appealing a Conviction. If the defendant pleaded not guilty and was convicted, after sentencing the court must advise the defendant of the right to appeal the conviction.

(B) Appealing a Sentence. After sentencing— regardless of the defendant's plea—the court must advise the defendant of any right to appeal the sentence.

(C) Appeal Costs. The court must advise a defendant who is unable to pay appeal costs of the right to ask for permission to appeal in forma pauperis.

(2) Clerk's Filing of Notice. If the defendant so requests, the clerk must immediately prepare and file a notice of appeal on the defendant's behalf.

(k) Judgment.

(1) In General. In the judgment of conviction, the court must set forth the plea, the jury verdict or the court's findings, the adjudication, and the sentence. If the defendant is found not guilty or is otherwise entitled to be discharged, the court must so order. The judge must sign the judgment, and the clerk must enter it.

(2) Criminal Forfeiture. Forfeiture procedures are governed by Rule 32.2.

Rule 32.1. Revoking or Modifying Probation or Supervised Release

(a) Initial Appearance.

(1) Person In Custody. A person held in custody for violating probation or supervised release must be taken without unnecessary delay before a magistrate judge.

(A) If the person is held in custody in the district where an alleged violation occurred, the initial appearance must be in that district.

(B) If the person is held in custody in a district other than where an alleged violation occurred, the initial appearance must be in that district, or in an adjacent district if the appearance can occur more promptly there.

(2) Upon a Summons. When a person appears in response to a summons for violating probation or supervised release, a magistrate judge must proceed under this rule.

(3) Advice. The judge must inform the person of the following:

    (A) the alleged violation of probation or supervised release;

    (B) the person's right to retain counsel or to request that counsel be appointed if the person cannot obtain counsel; and

    (C) the person's right, if held in custody, to a preliminary hearing under Rule 32.1(b)(1).

(4) Appearance in the District With Jurisdiction. If the person is arrested or appears in the district that has jurisdiction to conduct a revocation hearing—either originally or by transfer of jurisdiction—the court must proceed under Rule 32.1(b)–(e).

(5) Appearance in a District Lacking Jurisdiction. If the person is arrested or appears in a district that does not have jurisdiction to conduct a revocation hearing, the magistrate judge must:

    (A) if the alleged violation occurred in the district of arrest, conduct a preliminary hearing under Rule 32.1(b) and either:

        (i) transfer the person to the district that has jurisdiction, if the judge finds probable cause to believe that a violation occurred; or

        (ii) dismiss the proceedings and so notify the court that has jurisdiction, if the judge finds no probable cause to believe that a violation occurred; or

    (B) if the alleged violation did not occur in the district of arrest, transfer the person to the district that has jurisdiction if:

        (i) the government produces certified copies of the judgment, warrant, and warrant application or produces copies of those certified documents by reliable electronic means; and

(ii) the judge finds that the person is the same person named in the warrant.

(6) Release or Detention. The magistrate judge may release or detain the person under 18 U.S.C. § 3143(a)(1) pending further proceedings. The burden of establishing by clear and convincing evidence that the person will not flee or pose a danger to any other person or to the community rests with the person.

(b) Revocation.

(1) Preliminary Hearing.

(A) In General. If a person is in custody for violating a condition of probation or supervised release, a magistrate judge must promptly conduct a hearing to determine whether there is probable cause to believe that a violation occurred. The person may waive the hearing.

(B) Requirements. The hearing must be recorded by a court reporter or by a suitable recording device. The judge must give the person:

(i) notice of the hearing and its purpose, the alleged violation, and the person's right to retain counsel or to request that counsel be appointed if the person cannot obtain counsel;

(ii) an opportunity to appear at the hearing and present evidence; and

(iii) upon request, an opportunity to question any adverse witness, unless the judge determines that the interest of justice does not require the witness to appear.

(C) Referral. If the judge finds probable cause, the judge must conduct a revocation hearing. If the judge does not find probable cause, the judge must dismiss the proceeding.

(2) Revocation Hearing. Unless waived by the person, the court must hold the revocation hearing within a reasonable time in the district having jurisdiction. The person is entitled to:

(A) written notice of the alleged violation;

(B) disclosure of the evidence against the person;

(C) an opportunity to appear, present evidence, and question any adverse witness unless the court determines that the interest of justice does not require the witness to appear;

(D) notice of the person's right to retain counsel or to request that counsel be appointed if the person cannot obtain counsel; and

(E) an opportunity to make a statement and present any information in mitigation.

(c) Modification.

(1) In General. Before modifying the conditions of probation or supervised release, the court must hold a hearing, at which the person has the right to counsel and an opportunity to make a statement and present any information in mitigation.

(2) Exceptions. A hearing is not required if:

(A) the person waives the hearing; or

(B) the relief sought is favorable to the person and does not extend the term of probation or of supervised release; and

(C) an attorney for the government has received notice of the relief sought, has had a reasonable opportunity to object, and has not done so.

(d) Disposition of the Case. The court's disposition of the case is governed by 18 U.S.C. § 3563 and § 3565 (probation) and § 3583 (supervised release).

(e) Producing a Statement. Rule 26.2(a)–(d) and (f) applies at a hearing under this rule. If a party fails to comply with a Rule 26.2 order to produce a witness's statement, the court must not consider that witness's testimony.

Rule 32.2.   Criminal Forfeiture

(a) Notice to the Defendant. A court must not enter a judgment of forfeiture in a criminal proceeding unless the indictment or information contains notice to the defendant that the government will seek the forfeiture of property as part of any sentence in accordance with the applicable statute. The notice should not be designated as a count of the indictment or information. The indictment or information need not identify the property subject to forfeiture or specify the amount of any forfeiture money judgment that the government seeks.

(b) Entering a Preliminary Order of Forfeiture.

(1) Forfeiture Phase of the Trial.

(A) Forfeiture Determinations. As soon as practical after a verdict or finding of guilty, or after a plea of guilty or nolo contendere is accepted, on any count in an indictment or information regarding which criminal forfeiture is sought, the court must determine what property is subject to forfeiture under the applicable statute. If the government seeks forfeiture of specific property, the court must determine whether the government has established the requisite nexus between the property and the offense. If the government seeks a personal money judgment, the court must determine the amount of money that the defendant will be ordered to pay.

(B) Evidence and Hearing. The court's determination may be based on evidence already in the record, including any written plea agreement, and on any additional evidence or information submitted by the parties and accepted by the court as relevant and reliable. If the forfeiture is contested, on either party's request the court must conduct a hearing after the verdict or finding of guilty.

(2) Preliminary Order.

(A) Contents of a Specific Order. If the court finds that property is subject to forfeiture, it must promptly enter a preliminary order of forfeiture setting forth the amount of any money judgment, directing the forfeiture of specific property, and directing the forfeiture of any substitute property if the government has met the statutory criteria. The court must enter the order without regard to any third party's interest in the property. Determining whether a third party has such an interest must be deferred until any third party files a claim in an ancillary proceeding under Rule 32.2(c).

(B) Timing. Unless doing so is impractical, the court must enter the preliminary order sufficiently in advance of sentencing to allow the parties to suggest revisions or modifications before the order becomes final as to the defendant under Rule 32.2(b)(4).

(C) General Order. If, before sentencing, the court cannot identify all the specific property subject to forfeiture or calculate the total amount of the money judgment, the court may enter a forfeiture order that:

(i) lists any identified property;

(ii) describes other property in general terms; and

(iii) states that the order will be amended under Rule 32.2(e)(1) when additional specific property is identified or the amount of the money judgment has been calculated.

(3) Seizing Property. The entry of a preliminary order of forfeiture authorizes the Attorney General (or a designee) to seize the specific property subject to forfeiture; to conduct any discovery the court considers proper in identifying, locating, or disposing of the property; and to commence proceedings that comply with any statutes governing third-party rights. The court may include in the order of forfeiture conditions reasonably necessary to preserve the property's value pending any appeal.

(4) Sentence and Judgment.

(A) When Final. At sentencing—or at any time before sentencing if the defendant consents—the preliminary forfeiture order becomes final as to the defendant. If the order directs the defendant to forfeit specific property, it remains preliminary as to third parties until the ancillary proceeding is concluded under Rule 32.2(c).

(B) Notice and Inclusion in the Judgment. The court must include the forfeiture when orally announcing the sentence or must otherwise ensure that the defendant knows of the forfeiture at sentencing. The court must also include the forfeiture order, directly or by reference, in the judgment, but the court's failure to do so may be corrected at any time under Rule 36.

(C) Time to Appeal. The time for the defendant or the government to file an appeal from the forfeiture order, or from the court's failure to enter an order, begins to run when judgment is entered. If the court later amends or declines to amend a forfeiture order to include additional property under Rule 32.2(e), the defendant or the government may file an appeal regarding that property under Federal Rule of Appellate Procedure 4(b). The time for that appeal runs from the date when the order granting or denying the amendment becomes final.

(5) Jury Determination.

(A) Retaining the Jury. In any case tried before a jury, if the indictment or information states that the government is seeking forfeiture, the court must determine before the jury begins deliberating whether either party requests that the jury be retained to determine the forfeitability of specific property if it returns a guilty verdict.

(B) Special Verdict Form. If a party timely requests to have the jury determine forfeiture, the government must submit a proposed Special Verdict Form listing each property subject to forfeiture and asking the jury to determine whether the government has established the requisite nexus between the property and the offense committed by the defendant.

(6) Notice of the Forfeiture Order.

(A) Publishing and Sending Notice. If the court orders the forfeiture of specific property, the government must publish notice of the order and send notice to any person who reasonably appears to be a potential claimant with standing to contest the forfeiture in the ancillary proceeding.

(B) Content of the Notice. The notice must describe the forfeited property, state the times under the applicable statute when a petition contesting the forfeiture must be filed, and state the name and contact information for the government attorney to be served with the petition.

(C) Means of Publication; Exceptions to Publication Requirement. Publication must take place as described in Supplemental Rule G(4)(a)(iii) of the Federal Rules of Civil Procedure, and may be by any means described in Supplemental Rule G(4)(a)(iv). Publication is unnecessary if any exception in Supplemental Rule G(4)(a)(i) applies.

(D) Means of Sending the Notice. The notice may be sent in accordance with Supplemental Rules G(4)(b)(iii)–(v) of the Federal Rules of Civil Procedure.

(7) Interlocutory Sale. At any time before entry of a final forfeiture order, the court, in accordance with Supplemental Rule G(7) of the Federal Rules of Civil Procedure, may order the interlocutory sale of property alleged to be forfeitable.

(c) Ancillary Proceeding; Entering a Final Order of Forfeiture.

(1) In General. If, as prescribed by statute, a third party files a petition asserting an interest in the property to be forfeited, the court must conduct an ancillary proceeding, but no ancillary proceeding is required to the extent that the forfeiture consists of a money judgment.

(A) In the ancillary proceeding, the court may, on motion, dismiss the petition for lack of standing, for failure to state a claim, or for any other lawful reason. For purposes of the motion, the facts set forth in the petition are assumed to be true.

(B) After disposing of any motion filed under Rule 32.2(c)(1)(A) and before conducting a hearing on the petition, the court may permit the parties to conduct discovery in accordance with the Federal Rules of Civil Procedure if the court determines that discovery is necessary or desirable to resolve factual issues. When discovery ends, a party may move for summary judgment under Federal Rule of Civil Procedure 56.

(2) Entering a Final Order. When the ancillary proceeding ends, the court must enter a final order of forfeiture by amending the preliminary order as necessary to account for any third-party rights. If no third party files a timely petition, the preliminary order becomes the final order of forfeiture if the court finds that the defendant (or any combination of defendants convicted in the case) had an interest in the property that is forfeitable under the applicable statute. The defendant may not object to the entry of the final order on the ground that the property belongs, in whole or in part, to a codefendant or third party; nor may a third party object to the final order on the ground that the third party had an interest in the property.

(3) Multiple Petitions. If multiple third-party petitions are filed in the same case, an order dismissing or granting one petition is not appealable until rulings are made on all the petitions, unless the court determines that there is no just reason for delay.

(4) Ancillary Proceeding Not Part of Sentencing. An ancillary proceeding is not part of sentencing.

(d) Stay Pending Appeal. If a defendant appeals from a conviction or an order of forfeiture, the court may stay the order of forfeiture on terms appropriate to ensure that the property remains available pending appellate review. A stay does not delay the ancillary proceeding or the determination of a third party's rights or interests. If the court rules in favor of any third party while an appeal is pending, the court may amend the order of forfeiture but must not transfer any property interest to a third party until the decision on appeal becomes final, unless the defendant consents in writing or on the record.

(e) Subsequently Located Property; Substitute Property.

(1) In General. On the government's motion, the court may at any time enter an order of forfeiture or amend an existing order of forfeiture to include property that:

(A) is subject to forfeiture under an existing order of forfeiture but was located and identified after that order was entered; or

(B) is substitute property that qualifies for forfeiture under an applicable statute.

(2) Procedure. If the government shows that the property is subject to forfeiture under Rule 32.2(e)(1), the court must:

(A) enter an order forfeiting that property, or amend an existing preliminary or final order to include it; and

(B) if a third party files a petition claiming an interest in the property, conduct an ancillary proceeding under Rule 32.2(c).

(3) Jury Trial Limited. There is no right to a jury trial under Rule 32.2(e).

Rule 33.   New Trial

(a) Defendant's Motion. Upon the defendant's motion, the court may vacate any judgment and grant a new trial if the interest of justice so requires. If the case was tried without a jury, the court may take additional testimony and enter a new judgment.

(b) Time to File.

(1) Newly Discovered Evidence. Any motion for a new trial grounded on newly discovered evidence must be filed within 3 years after the verdict or finding of guilty. If an appeal is pending, the court may not grant a motion for a new trial until the appellate court remands the case.

(2) Other Grounds. Any motion for a new trial grounded on any reason other than newly discovered evidence must be filed within 14 days after the verdict or finding of guilty.

Rule 34.   Arresting Judgment

(a) In General. Upon the defendant's motion or on its own, the court must arrest judgment if:

(1) the indictment or information does not charge an offense; or

(2) the court does not have jurisdiction of the charged offense.

(b) Time to File. The defendant must move to arrest judgment within 14 days after the court accepts a verdict or finding of guilty, or after a plea of guilty or nolo contendere.

Rule 35.   Correcting or Reducing a Sentence

(a) Correcting Clear Error. Within 14 days after sentencing, the court may correct a sentence that resulted from arithmetical, technical, or other clear error.

(b) Reducing a Sentence for Substantial Assistance.

(1) In General. Upon the government's motion made within one year of sentencing, the court may reduce a sentence if the defendant, after sentencing, provided substantial assistance in investigating or prosecuting another person.

(2) Later Motion. Upon the government's motion made more than one year after sentencing, the court may reduce a sentence if the defendant's substantial assistance involved:

(A) information not known to the defendant until one year or more after sentencing;

(B) information provided by the defendant to the government within one year of sentencing, but which did not become useful to the government until more than one year after sentencing; or

(C) information the usefulness of which could not reasonably have been anticipated by the defendant until more than one year after sentencing and which was promptly provided to the government after its usefulness was reasonably apparent to the defendant.

(3) Evaluating Substantial Assistance. In evaluating whether the defendant has provided substantial assistance, the court may consider the defendant's presentence assistance.

(4) Below Statutory Minimum. When acting under Rule 35(b), the court may reduce the sentence to a level below the minimum sentence established by statute.

(c) "Sentencing" Defined. As used in this rule, "sentencing" means the oral announcement of the sentence.

Rule 36.   Clerical Error

After giving any notice it considers appropriate, the court may at any time correct a clerical error in a judgment, order, or other part of the record, or correct an error in the record arising from oversight or omission.

Rule 37.   Ruling on a Motion for Relief That Is Barred by a Pending Appeal

(a) Relief Pending Appeal. If a timely motion is made for relief that the court lacks authority to grant because of an appeal that has been docketed and is pending, the court may:

(1) defer considering the motion;

(2) deny the motion; or

(3) state either that it would grant the motion if the court of appeals remands for that purpose or that the motion raises a substantial issue.

(b) Notice to the Court of Appeals. The movant must promptly notify the circuit clerk under Federal Rule of Appellate Procedure 12.1 if the district court states that it would grant the motion or that the motion raises a substantial issue.

(c) Remand. The district court may decide the motion if the court of appeals remands for that purpose.

Rule 38.   Staying a Sentence or a Disability

(a) Death Sentence. The court must stay a death sentence if the defendant appeals the conviction or sentence.

(b) Imprisonment.

(1) Stay Granted. If the defendant is released pending appeal, the court must stay a sentence of imprisonment.

(2) Stay Denied; Place of Confinement. If the defendant is not released pending appeal, the court may recommend to the Attorney General that the defendant be confined near the place of the trial or appeal for a period reasonably necessary to permit the defendant to assist in preparing the appeal.

(c) Fine. If the defendant appeals, the district court, or the court of appeals under Federal Rule of Appellate Procedure 8, may stay a sentence to pay a fine or a fine and costs. The court may stay the sentence on any terms considered appropriate and may require the defendant to:

(1) deposit all or part of the fine and costs into the district court's registry pending appeal;

(2) post a bond to pay the fine and costs; or

(3) submit to an examination concerning the defendant's assets and, if appropriate, order the defendant to refrain from dissipating assets.

(d) Probation. If the defendant appeals, the court may stay a sentence of probation. The court must set the terms of any stay.

(e) Restitution and Notice to Victims.

(1) In General. If the defendant appeals, the district court, or the court of appeals under Federal Rule of Appellate Procedure 8, may stay—on any terms considered appropriate— any sentence providing for restitution under 18 U.S.C. § 3556 or notice under 18 U.S.C. § 3555.

(2) Ensuring Compliance. The court may issue any order reasonably necessary to ensure compliance with a restitution order or a notice order after disposition of an appeal, including:

(A) a restraining order;

(B) an injunction;

(C) an order requiring the defendant to deposit all or part of any monetary restitution into the district court's registry; or

(D) an order requiring the defendant to post a bond.

(f) Forfeiture. A stay of a forfeiture order is governed by Rule 32.2(d).

(g) Disability. If the defendant's conviction or sentence creates a civil or employment disability under federal law, the district court, or the court of appeals under Federal Rule of Appellate Procedure 8, may stay the disability pending appeal on any terms considered appropriate. The court may issue any order reasonably necessary to protect the interest represented by the disability pending appeal, including a restraining order or an injunction.

Rule 39.   [Reserved]

Rule 40.   Arrest for Failing to Appear in Another District

(a) In General. A person must be taken without unnecessary delay before a magistrate judge in the district of arrest if the person has been arrested under a warrant issued in another district for:

(i) failing to appear as required by the terms of that person's release under 18 U.S.C. §§ 3141–3156 or by a subpoena; or

(ii) violating conditions of release set in another district.

(b) Proceedings. The judge must proceed under Rule 5(c)(3) as applicable.

(c) Release or Detention Order. The judge may modify any previous release or detention order issued in another district, but must state in writing the reasons for doing so.

(d) Video Teleconferencing. Video teleconferencing may be used to conduct an appearance under this rule if the defendant consents.

Rule 41.   Search and Seizure

(a) Scope and Definitions.

(1) Scope. This rule does not modify any statute regulating search or seizure, or the issuance and execution of a search warrant in special circumstances.

(2) Definitions. The following definitions apply under this rule:

(A) "Property" includes documents, books, papers, any other tangible objects, and information.

(B) "Daytime" means the hours between 6:00 a.m. and 10:00 p.m. according to local time.

(C) "Federal law enforcement officer" means a government agent (other than an attorney for the government) who is engaged in enforcing the criminal laws and is within any category of officers authorized by the Attorney General to request a search warrant.

(D) "Domestic terrorism" and "international terrorism" have the meanings set out in 18 U.S.C. § 2331.

(E) "Tracking device" has the meaning set out in 18 U.S.C. § 3117(b).

(b) Authority to Issue a Warrant. At the request of a federal law enforcement officer or an attorney for the government:

(1) a magistrate judge with authority in the district—or if none is reasonably available, a judge of a state court of record in the district—has authority to issue a warrant to search for and seize a person or property located within the district;

(2) a magistrate judge with authority in the district has authority to issue a warrant for a person or property outside the district if the person or property is located within the district when the warrant is issued but might move or be moved outside the district before the warrant is executed; and

(3) a magistrate judge—in an investigation of domestic terrorism or international terrorism—with authority in any district in which activities related to the terrorism may have occurred has authority to issue a warrant for a person or property within or outside that district;

(4) a magistrate judge with authority in the district has authority to issue a warrant to install within the district a tracking device; the warrant may authorize use of the device to track the movement of a person or property located within the district, outside the district, or both; and

(5) a magistrate judge having authority in any district where activities related to the crime may have occurred, or in the District of Columbia, may issue a warrant for property that is located outside the jurisdiction of any state or district, but within any of the following:

(A) a United States territory, possession, or commonwealth;

(B) the premises—no matter who owns them—of a United States diplomatic or consular mission in a foreign state, including any appurtenant building, part of a building, or land used for the mission's purposes; or

(C) a residence and any appurtenant land owned or leased by the United States and used by United States personnel assigned to a United States diplomatic or consular mission in a foreign state.

(c) Persons or Property Subject to Search or Seizure. A warrant may be issued for any of the following:

(1) evidence of a crime;

(2) contraband, fruits of crime, or other items illegally possessed;

(3) property designed for use, intended for use, or used in committing a crime; or

(4) a person to be arrested or a person who is unlawfully restrained.

(d) Obtaining a Warrant.

(1) In General. After receiving an affidavit or other information, a magistrate judge—or if authorized by Rule 41(b), a judge of a state court of record—must issue the warrant if there is probable cause to search for and seize a person or property or to install and use a tracking device.

(2) Requesting a Warrant in the Presence of a Judge.

(A) Warrant on an Affidavit. When a federal law enforcement officer or an attorney for the government presents an affidavit in support of a warrant, the judge may require the affiant to appear personally and may examine under oath the affiant and any witness the affiant produces.

(B) Warrant on Sworn Testimony. The judge may wholly or partially dispense with a written affidavit and base a warrant on sworn testimony if doing so is reasonable under the circumstances.

(C) Recording Testimony. Testimony taken in support of a warrant must be recorded by a court reporter or by a suitable recording device, and the judge must file the transcript or recording with the clerk, along with any affidavit.

(3) Requesting a Warrant by Telephonic or Other Reliable Electronic Means. In accordance with Rule 4.1, a magistrate judge may issue a warrant based on information communicated by telephone or other reliable electronic means.

(e) Issuing the Warrant.

(1) In General. The magistrate judge or a judge of a state court of record must issue the warrant to an officer authorized to execute it.

(2) Contents of the Warrant.

(A) Warrant to Search for and Seize a Person or Property. Except for a tracking-device warrant, the warrant must identify the person or property to be searched, identify any person or property to be seized, and designate the magistrate judge to whom it must be returned. The warrant must command the officer to:

　　(i) execute the warrant within a specified time no longer than 14 days;

　　(ii) execute the warrant during the daytime, unless the judge for good cause expressly authorizes execution at another time; and

　　(iii) return the warrant to the magistrate judge designated in the warrant.

(B) Warrant Seeking Electronically Stored Information. A warrant under Rule 41(e)(2)(A) may authorize the seizure of electronic storage media or the seizure or copying of electronically stored information. Unless otherwise specified, the warrant authorizes a later review of the media or information consistent with the warrant. The time for executing the warrant in Rule 41(e)(2)(A) and (f)(1)(A) refers to the seizure or on-site copying of the media or information, and not to any later off-site copying or review.

(C) Warrant for a Tracking Device. A tracking-device warrant must identify the person or property to be tracked, designate the magistrate judge to whom it must be returned, and specify a reasonable length of time that the device may be used. The time must not exceed 45 days from the date the warrant was issued. The court may, for good cause, grant one or more extensions for a reasonable period not to exceed 45 days each. The warrant must command the officer to:

    (i) complete any installation authorized by the warrant within a specified time no longer than 10 days;

    (ii) perform any installation authorized by the warrant during the daytime, unless the judge for good cause expressly authorizes installation at another time; and

    (iii) return the warrant to the judge designated in the warrant.

(f) Executing and Returning the Warrant.

(1) Warrant to Search for and Seize a Person or Property.

    (A) Noting the Time. The officer executing the warrant must enter on it the exact date and time it was executed.

    (B) Inventory. An officer present during the execution of the warrant must prepare and verify an inventory of any property seized. The officer must do so in the presence of another officer and the person from whom, or from whose premises, the property was taken. If either one is not present, the officer must prepare and verify the inventory in the presence of at least one other credible person. In a case involving the seizure of electronic storage media or the seizure or copying of electronically stored information, the inventory may be limited to describing the physical storage media that were seized or copied. The officer may retain a copy of the electronically stored information that was seized or copied.

    (C) Receipt. The officer executing the warrant must give a copy of the warrant and a receipt for the property taken to the person from whom, or from whose premises, the property was taken or leave a copy of the warrant and receipt at the place where the officer took the property.

(D) Return. The officer executing the warrant must promptly return it—together with a copy of the inventory— to the magistrate judge designated on the warrant. The officer may do so by reliable electronic means. The judge must, on request, give a copy of the inventory to the person from whom, or from whose premises, the property was taken and to the applicant for the warrant.

(2) Warrant for a Tracking Device.

(A) Noting the Time. The officer executing a tracking-device warrant must enter on it the exact date and time the device was installed and the period during which it was used.

(B) Return. Within 10 days after the use of the tracking device has ended, the officer executing the warrant must return it to the judge designated in the warrant. The officer may do so by reliable electronic means.

(C) Service. Within 10 days after the use of the tracking device has ended, the officer executing a tracking-device warrant must serve a copy of the warrant on the person who was tracked or whose property was tracked. Service may be accomplished by delivering a copy to the person who, or whose property, was tracked; or by leaving a copy at the person's residence or usual place of abode with an individual of suitable age and discretion who resides at that location and by mailing a copy to the person's last known address. Upon request of the government, the judge may delay notice as provided in Rule 41(f)(3).

(3) Delayed Notice. Upon the government's request, a magistrate judge—or if authorized by Rule 41(b), a judge of a state court of record—may delay any notice required by this rule if the delay is authorized by statute.

(g) Motion to Return Property. A person aggrieved by an unlawful search and seizure of property or by the deprivation of property may move for the property's return. The motion must be filed in the district where the property was seized. The court must receive evidence on any factual issue necessary to decide the motion. If it grants the motion, the court must return the property to the movant, but may impose reasonable conditions to protect access to the property and its use in later proceedings.

(h) Motion to Suppress. A defendant may move to suppress evidence in the court where the trial will occur, as Rule 12 provides.

(i) Forwarding Papers to the Clerk. The magistrate judge to whom the warrant is returned must attach to the warrant a copy of the return, of the inventory, and of all other related papers and must deliver them to the clerk in the district where the property was seized.

Rule 42.   Criminal Contempt

(a) Disposition After Notice. Any person who commits criminal contempt may be punished for that contempt after prosecution on notice.

(1) Notice. The court must give the person notice in open court, in an order to show cause, or in an arrest order. The notice must:

(A) state the time and place of the trial;

(B) allow the defendant a reasonable time to prepare a defense; and

(C) state the essential facts constituting the charged criminal contempt and describe it as such.

(2) Appointing a Prosecutor. The court must request that the contempt be prosecuted by an attorney for the government, unless the interest of justice requires the appointment of another attorney. If the government declines the request, the court must appoint another attorney to prosecute the contempt.

(3) Trial and Disposition. A person being prosecuted for criminal contempt is entitled to a jury trial in any case in which federal law so provides and must be released or detained as Rule 46 provides. If the criminal contempt involves disrespect toward or criticism of a judge, that judge is disqualified from presiding at the contempt trial or hearing unless the defendant consents. Upon a finding or verdict of guilty, the court must impose the punishment.

(b) Summary Disposition. Notwithstanding any other provision of these rules, the court (other than a magistrate judge) may summarily punish a person who commits criminal contempt in its presence if the judge saw or heard the contemptuous conduct and so certifies; a magistrate judge may summarily punish a person as provided in 28 U.S.C. § 636(e). The contempt order must recite the facts, be signed by the judge, and be filed with the clerk.

Rule 43.   Defendant's Presence

(a) When Required. Unless this rule, Rule 5, or Rule 10 provides otherwise, the defendant must be present at:

(1) the initial appearance, the initial arraignment, and the plea;

(2) every trial stage, including jury impanelment and the return of the verdict; and

(3) sentencing.

(b) When Not Required. A defendant need not be present under any of the following circumstances:

(1) Organizational Defendant. The defendant is an organization represented by counsel who is present.

(2) Misdemeanor Offense. The offense is punishable by fine or by imprisonment for not more than one year, or both, and with the defendant's written consent, the court permits arraignment, plea, trial, and sentencing to occur by video teleconferencing or in the defendant's absence.

(3) Conference or Hearing on a Legal Question. The proceeding involves only a conference or hearing on a question of law.

(4) Sentence Correction. The proceeding involves the correction or reduction of sentence under Rule 35 or 18 U.S.C. § 3582(c).

(c) Waiving Continued Presence.

(1) In General. A defendant who was initially present at trial, or who had pleaded guilty or nolo contendere, waives the right to be present under the following circumstances:

(A) when the defendant is voluntarily absent after the trial has begun, regardless of whether the court informed the defendant of an obligation to remain during trial;

(B) in a noncapital case, when the defendant is voluntarily absent during sentencing; or

(C) when the court warns the defendant that it will remove the defendant from the courtroom for disruptive behavior, but the defendant persists in conduct that justifies removal from the courtroom.

(2) Waiver's Effect. If the defendant waives the right to be present, the trial may proceed to completion, including the verdict's return and sentencing, during the defendant's absence.

Rule 44.   Right to and Appointment of Counsel

(a) Right to Appointed Counsel. A defendant who is unable to obtain counsel is entitled to have counsel appointed to represent the defendant at every stage of the proceeding from initial appearance through appeal, unless the defendant waives this right.

(b) Appointment Procedure. Federal law and local court rules govern the procedure for implementing the right to counsel.

(c) Inquiry Into Joint Representation.

    (1) Joint Representation. Joint representation occurs when:

        (A) two or more defendants have been charged jointly under Rule 8(b) or have been joined for trial under Rule 13; and

        (B) the defendants are represented by the same counsel, or counsel who are associated in law practice.

    (2) Court's Responsibilities in Cases of Joint Representation. The court must promptly inquire about the propriety of joint representation and must personally advise each defendant of the right to the effective assistance of counsel, including separate representation. Unless there is good cause to believe that no conflict of interest is likely to arise, the court must take appropriate measures to protect each defendant's right to counsel.

Rule 45.   Computing and Extending Time

(a) Computing Time. The following rules apply in computing any time period specified in these rules, in any local rule or court order, or in any statute that does not specify a method of computing time.

    (1) Period Stated in Days or a Longer Unit. When the period is stated in days or a longer unit of time:

        (A) exclude the day of the event that triggers the period;

        (B) count every day, including intermediate Saturdays, Sundays, and legal holidays; and

        (C) include the last day of the period, but if the last day is a Saturday, Sunday, or legal holiday, the period continues to run until the end of the next day that is not a Saturday, Sunday, or legal holiday.

    (2) Period Stated in Hours. When the period is stated in hours:

        (A) begin counting immediately on the occurrence of the event that triggers the period;

(B) count every hour, including hours during intermediate Saturdays, Sundays, and legal holidays; and

(C) if the period would end on a Saturday, Sunday, or legal holiday, the period continues to run until the same time on the next day that is not a Saturday, Sunday, or legal holiday.

(3) Inaccessibility of the Clerk's Office. Unless the court orders otherwise, if the clerk's office is inaccessible:

(A) on the last day for filing under Rule 45(a)(1), then the time for filing is extended to the first accessible day that is not a Saturday, Sunday, or legal holiday; or

(B) during the last hour for filing under Rule 45(a)(2), then the time for filing is extended to the same time on the first accessible day that is not a Saturday, Sunday, or legal holiday.

(4) "Last Day" Defined. Unless a different time is set by a statute, local rule, or court order, the last day ends:

(A) for electronic filing, at midnight in the court's time zone; and

(B) for filing by other means, when the clerk's office is scheduled to close.

(5) "Next Day" Defined. The "next day" is determined by continuing to count forward when the period is measured after an event and backward when measured before an event.

(6) "Legal Holiday" Defined. "Legal holiday" means:

(A) the day set aside by statute for observing New Year's Day, Martin Luther King Jr.'s Birthday, Washington's Birthday, Memorial Day, Independence Day, Labor Day, Columbus Day, Veterans' Day, Thanksgiving Day, or Christmas Day;

(B) any day declared a holiday by the President or Congress; and

(C) for periods that are measured after an event, any other day declared a holiday by the state where the district court is located.

(b) Extending Time.

(1) In General. When an act must or may be done within a specified period, the court on its own may extend the time, or for good cause may do so on a party's motion made:

(A) before the originally prescribed or previously extended time expires; or

(B) after the time expires if the party failed to act because of excusable neglect.

(2) Exception. The court may not extend the time to take any action under Rule 35, except as stated in that rule.

(c) Additional Time After Certain Kinds of Service. Whenever a party must or may act within a specified period after service and service is made in the manner provided under Federal Rule of Civil Procedure 5(b)(2)(C), (D), (E), or (F), 3 days are added after the period would otherwise expire under subdivision (a).

Rule 46.   Release from Custody; Supervising Detention

(a) Before Trial. The provisions of 18 U.S.C. §§ 3142 and 3144 govern pretrial release.

(b) During Trial. A person released before trial continues on release during trial under the same terms and conditions. But the court may order different terms and conditions or terminate the release if necessary to ensure that the person will be present during trial or that the person's conduct will not obstruct the orderly and expeditious progress of the trial.

(c) Pending Sentencing or Appeal. The provisions of 18 U.S.C. § 3143 govern release pending sentencing or appeal. The burden of establishing that the defendant will not flee or pose a danger to any other person or to the community rests with the defendant.

(d) Pending Hearing on a Violation of Probation or Supervised Release. Rule 32.1(a)(6) governs release pending a hearing on a violation of probation or supervised release.

(e) Surety. The court must not approve a bond unless any surety appears to be qualified. Every surety, except a legally approved corporate surety, must demonstrate by affidavit that its assets are adequate. The court may require the affidavit to describe the following:

(1) the property that the surety proposes to use as security;

(2) any encumbrance on that property;

(3) the number and amount of any other undischarged bonds and bail undertakings the surety has issued; and

(4) any other liability of the surety.

(f) Bail Forfeiture.

(1) Declaration. The court must declare the bail forfeited if a condition of the bond is breached.

(2) Setting Aside. The court may set aside in whole or in part a bail forfeiture upon any condition the court may impose if:

(A) the surety later surrenders into custody the person released on the surety's appearance bond; or

(B) it appears that justice does not require bail forfeiture.

(3) Enforcement.

(A) Default Judgment and Execution. If it does not set aside a bail forfeiture, the court must, upon the government's motion, enter a default judgment.

(B) Jurisdiction and Service. By entering into a bond, each surety submits to the district court's jurisdiction and irrevocably appoints the district clerk as its agent to receive service of any filings affecting its liability.

(C) Motion to Enforce. The court may, upon the government's motion, enforce the surety's liability without an independent action. The government must serve any motion, and notice as the court prescribes, on the district clerk. If so served, the clerk must promptly mail a copy to the surety at its last known address.

(4) Remission. After entering a judgment under Rule 46(f)(3), the court may remit in whole or in part the judgment under the same conditions specified in Rule 46(f)(2).

(g) Exoneration. The court must exonerate the surety and release any bail when a bond condition has been satisfied or when the court has set aside or remitted the forfeiture. The court must exonerate a surety who deposits cash in the amount of the bond or timely surrenders the defendant into custody.

(h) Supervising Detention Pending Trial.

(1) In General. To eliminate unnecessary detention, the court must supervise the detention within the district of any defendants awaiting trial and of any persons held as material witnesses.

(2) Reports. An attorney for the government must report biweekly to the court, listing each material witness held in custody for more than 10 days pending indictment, arraignment, or trial. For each material witness listed in the report, an attorney for the government must state why the witness should not be released with or without a deposition being taken under Rule 15(a).

(i) Forfeiture of Property. The court may dispose of a charged offense by ordering the forfeiture of 18 U.S.C. § 3142(c)(1)(B)(xi) property under 18 U.S.C. § 3146(d), if a fine in the amount of the property's value would be an appropriate sentence for the charged offense.

(j) Producing a Statement.

(1) In General. Rule 26.2(a)–(d) and (f) applies at a detention hearing under 18 U.S.C. § 3142, unless the court for good cause rules otherwise.

(2) Sanctions for Not Producing a Statement. If a party disobeys a Rule 26.2 order to produce a witness's statement, the court must not consider that witness's testimony at the detention hearing.

Rule 47.   Motions and Supporting Affidavits

(a) In General. A party applying to the court for an order must do so by motion.

(b) Form and Content of a Motion. A motion—except when made during a trial or hearing—must be in writing, unless the court permits the party to make the motion by other means. A motion must state the grounds on which it is based and the relief or order sought. A motion may be supported by affidavit.

(c) Timing of a Motion. A party must serve a written motion—other than one that the court may hear ex parte—and any hearing notice at least 7 days before the hearing date, unless a rule or court order sets a different period. For good cause, the court may set a different period upon ex parte application.

(d) Affidavit Supporting a Motion. The moving party must serve any supporting affidavit with the motion. A responding party must serve any opposing affidavit at least one day before the hearing, unless the court permits later service.

Rule 48.   Dismissal

(a) By the Government. The government may, with leave of court, dismiss an indictment, information, or complaint. The government may not dismiss the prosecution during trial without the defendant's consent.

(b) By the Court. The court may dismiss an indictment, information, or complaint if unnecessary delay occurs in:

(1) presenting a charge to a grand jury;

(2) filing an information against a defendant; or

(3) bringing a defendant to trial.

Rule 49.   Serving and Filing Papers

(a) When Required. A party must serve on every other party any written motion (other than one to be heard ex parte), written notice, designation of the record on appeal, or similar paper.

(b) How Made. Service must be made in the manner provided for a civil action. When these rules or a court order requires or permits service on a party represented by an attorney, service must be made on the attorney instead of the party, unless the court orders otherwise.

(c) Notice of a Court Order. When the court issues an order on any post-arraignment motion, the clerk must provide notice in a manner provided for in a civil action. Except as Federal Rule of Appellate Procedure 4(b) provides otherwise, the clerk's failure to give notice does not affect the time to appeal, or relieve—or authorize the court to relieve—a party's failure to appeal within the allowed time.

(d) Filing. A party must file with the court a copy of any paper the party is required to serve. A paper must be filed in a manner provided for in a civil action.

(e) Electronic Service and Filing. A court may, by local rule, allow papers to be filed, signed, or verified by electronic means that are consistent with any technical standards established by the Judicial Conference of the United States. A local rule may require electronic filing only if reasonable exceptions are allowed. A paper filed electronically in compliance with a local rule is written or in writing under these rules.

Rule 49.1.   Privacy Protection for Filings Made with the Court

(a) Redacted Filings. Unless the court orders otherwise, in an electronic or paper filing with the court that contains an individual's social-security number, taxpayer-identification number, or birth date, the name of an individual known to be a minor, a financial-account number, or the home address of an individual, a party or nonparty making the filing may include only:

    (1) the last four digits of the social-security number and taxpayer-identification number;

    (2) the year of the individual's birth;

    (3) the minor's initials;

    (4) the last four digits of the financial-account number; and

    (5) the city and state of the home address.

(b) Exemptions from the Redaction Requirement. The redaction requirement does not apply to the following:

(1) a financial-account number or real property address that identifies the property allegedly subject to forfeiture in a forfeiture proceeding;

(2) the record of an administrative or agency proceeding;

(3) the official record of a state-court proceeding;

(4) the record of a court or tribunal, if that record was not subject to the redaction requirement when originally filed;

(5) a filing covered by Rule 49.1(d);

(6) a pro se filing in an action brought under 28 U.S.C. §§ 2241, 2254, or 2255;

(7) a court filing that is related to a criminal matter or investigation and that is prepared before the filing of a criminal charge or is not filed as part of any docketed criminal case;

(8) an arrest or search warrant; and

(9) a charging document and an affidavit filed in support of any charging document.

(c) Immigration Cases. A filing in an action brought under 28 U.S.C. § 2241 that relates to the petitioner's immigration rights is governed by Federal Rule of Civil Procedure 5.2.

(d) Filings Made Under Seal. The court may order that a filing be made under seal without redaction. The court may later unseal the filing or order the person who made the filing to file a redacted version for the public record.

(e) Protective Orders. For good cause, the court may by order in a case:

(1) require redaction of additional information; or

(2) limit or prohibit a nonparty's remote electronic access to a document filed with the court.

(f) Option for Additional Unredacted Filing Under Seal. A person making a redacted filing may also file an unredacted copy under seal. The court must retain the unredacted copy as part of the record.

(g) Option for Filing a Reference List. A filing that contains redacted information may be filed together with a reference list that identifies each item of redacted information and specifies an appropriate identifier that uniquely corresponds to each item listed. The list must be filed under seal and may be amended as of right. Any reference in the case to a listed identifier will be construed to refer to the corresponding item of information.

(h) Waiver of Protection of Identifiers. A person waives the protection of Rule 49.1(a) as to the person's own information by filing it without redaction and not under seal.

Rule 50.   Prompt Disposition

Scheduling preference must be given to criminal proceedings as far as practicable.

Rule 51.   Preserving Claimed Error

(a) Exceptions Unnecessary. Exceptions to rulings or orders of the court are unnecessary.

(b) Preserving a Claim of Error. A party may preserve a claim of error by informing the court—when the court ruling or order is made or sought—of the action the party wishes the court to take, or the party's objection to the court's action and the grounds for that objection. If a party does not have an opportunity to object to a ruling or order, the absence of an objection does not later prejudice that party. A ruling or order that admits or excludes evidence is governed by Federal Rule of Evidence 103.

Rule 52.   Harmless and Plain Error

(a) Harmless Error. Any error, defect, irregularity, or variance that does not affect substantial rights must be disregarded.

(b) Plain Error. A plain error that affects substantial rights may be considered even though it was not brought to the court's attention.

Rule 53.   Courtroom Photographing and Broadcasting Prohibited

Except as otherwise provided by a statute or these rules, the court must not permit the taking of photographs in the courtroom during judicial proceedings or the broadcasting of judicial proceedings from the courtroom.

Rule 54.   [Transferred [1]]

Rule 55.   Records

The clerk of the district court must keep records of criminal proceedings in the form prescribed by the Director of the Administrative Office of the United States courts. The clerk must enter in the records every court order or judgment and the date of entry.

---

[1]   All of Rule 54 was moved to Rule 1.

Rule 56.   When Court Is Open

(a) In General. A district court is considered always open for any filing, and for issuing and returning process, making a motion, or entering an order.

(b) Office Hours. The clerk's office—with the clerk or a deputy in attendance—must be open during business hours on all days except Saturdays, Sundays, and legal holidays.

(c) Special Hours. A court may provide by local rule or order that its clerk's office will be open for specified hours on Saturdays or legal holidays other than those set aside by statute for observing New Year's Day, Martin Luther King, Jr.'s Birthday, Washington's Birthday, Memorial Day, Independence Day, Labor Day, Columbus Day, Veterans' Day, Thanksgiving Day, and Christmas Day.

Rule 57.   District Court Rules

(a) In General.

(1) Adopting Local Rules. Each district court acting by a majority of its district judges may, after giving appropriate public notice and an opportunity to comment, make and amend rules governing its practice. A local rule must be consistent with—but not duplicative of—federal statutes and rules adopted under 28 U.S.C. § 2072 and must conform to any uniform numbering system prescribed by the Judicial Conference of the United States.

(2) Limiting Enforcement. A local rule imposing a requirement of form must not be enforced in a manner that causes a party to lose rights because of an unintentional failure to comply with the requirement.

(b) Procedure When There Is No Controlling Law. A judge may regulate practice in any manner consistent with federal law, these rules, and the local rules of the district. No sanction or other disadvantage may be imposed for noncompliance with any requirement not in federal law, federal rules, or the local district rules unless the alleged violator was furnished with actual notice of the requirement before the noncompliance.

(c) Effective Date and Notice. A local rule adopted under this rule takes effect on the date specified by the district court and remains in effect unless amended by the district court or abrogated by the judicial council of the circuit in which the district is located. Copies of local rules and their amendments, when promulgated, must be furnished to the judicial council and the Administrative Office of the United States Courts and must be made available to the public.

Rule 58.   Petty Offenses and Other Misdemeanors

(a) Scope.

(1) In General. These rules apply in petty offense and other misdemeanor cases and on appeal to a district judge in a case tried by a magistrate judge, unless this rule provides otherwise.

(2) Petty Offense Case Without Imprisonment. In a case involving a petty offense for which no sentence of imprisonment will be imposed, the court may follow any provision of these rules that is not inconsistent with this rule and that the court considers appropriate.

(3) Definition. As used in this rule, the term "petty offense for which no sentence of imprisonment will be imposed" means a petty offense for which the court determines that, in the event of conviction, no sentence of imprisonment will be imposed.

(b) Pretrial Procedure.

(1) Charging Document. The trial of a misdemeanor may proceed on an indictment, information, or complaint. The trial of a petty offense may also proceed on a citation or violation notice.

(2) Initial Appearance. At the defendant's initial appearance on a petty offense or other misdemeanor charge, the magistrate judge must inform the defendant of the following:

(A) the charge, and the minimum and maximum penalties, including imprisonment, fines, any special assessment under 18 U.S.C. § 3013, and restitution under 18 U.S.C. § 3556;

(B) the right to retain counsel;

(C) the right to request the appointment of counsel if the defendant is unable to retain counsel—unless the charge is a petty offense for which the appointment of counsel is not required;

(D) the defendant's right not to make a statement, and that any statement made may be used against the defendant;

(E) the right to trial, judgment, and sentencing before a district judge—unless:

(i) the charge is a petty offense; or

(ii) the defendant consents to trial, judgment, and sentencing before a magistrate judge;

(F) the right to a jury trial before either a magistrate judge or a district judge—unless the charge is a petty offense; and

(G) any right to a preliminary hearing under Rule 5.1, and the general circumstances, if any, under which the defendant may secure pretrial release.

(3) Arraignment.

(A) Plea Before a Magistrate Judge. A magistrate judge may take the defendant's plea in a petty offense case. In every other misdemeanor case, a magistrate judge may take the plea only if the defendant consents either in writing or on the record to be tried before a magistrate judge and specifically waives trial before a district judge. The defendant may plead not guilty, guilty, or (with the consent of the magistrate judge) nolo contendere.

(B) Failure to Consent. Except in a petty offense case, the magistrate judge must order a defendant who does not consent to trial before a magistrate judge to appear before a district judge for further proceedings.

(c) Additional Procedures in Certain Petty Offense Cases. The following procedures also apply in a case involving a petty offense for which no sentence of imprisonment will be imposed:

(1) Guilty or Nolo Contendere Plea. The court must not accept a guilty or nolo contendere plea unless satisfied that the defendant understands the nature of the charge and the maximum possible penalty.

(2) Waiving Venue.

(A) Conditions of Waiving Venue. If a defendant is arrested, held, or present in a district different from the one where the indictment, information, complaint, citation, or violation notice is pending, the defendant may state in writing a desire to plead guilty or nolo contendere; to waive venue and trial in the district where the proceeding is pending; and to consent to the court's disposing of the case in the district where the defendant was arrested, is held, or is present.

(B) Effect of Waiving Venue. Unless the defendant later pleads not guilty, the prosecution will proceed in the district where the defendant was arrested, is held, or is present. The district clerk must notify the clerk in the original district of the defendant's waiver of venue. The defendant's statement of a desire to plead guilty or nolo contendere is not admissible against the defendant.

(3) Sentencing. The court must give the defendant an opportunity to be heard in mitigation and then proceed immediately to sentencing. The court may, however, postpone sentencing to allow the probation service to investigate or to permit either party to submit additional information.

(4) Notice of a Right to Appeal. After imposing sentence in a case tried on a not-guilty plea, the court must advise the defendant of a right to appeal the conviction and of any right to appeal the sentence. If the defendant was convicted on a plea of guilty or nolo contendere, the court must advise the defendant of any right to appeal the sentence.

(d) Paying a Fixed Sum in Lieu of Appearance.

(1) In General. If the court has a local rule governing forfeiture of collateral, the court may accept a fixed-sum payment in lieu of the defendant's appearance and end the case, but the fixed sum may not exceed the maximum fine allowed by law.

(2) Notice to Appear. If the defendant fails to pay a fixed sum, request a hearing, or appear in response to a citation or violation notice, the district clerk or a magistrate judge may issue a notice for the defendant to appear before the court on a date certain. The notice may give the defendant an additional opportunity to pay a fixed sum in lieu of appearance. The district clerk must serve the notice on the defendant by mailing a copy to the defendant's last known address.

(3) Summons or Warrant. Upon an indictment, or upon a showing by one of the other charging documents specified in Rule 58(b)(1) of probable cause to believe that an offense has been committed and that the defendant has committed it, the court may issue an arrest warrant or, if no warrant is requested by an attorney for the government, a summons. The showing of probable cause must be made under oath or under penalty of perjury, but the affiant need not appear before the court. If the defendant fails to appear before the court in response to a summons, the court may summarily issue a warrant for the defendant's arrest.

(e) Recording the Proceedings. The court must record any proceedings under this rule by using a court reporter or a suitable recording device.

(f) New Trial. Rule 33 applies to a motion for a new trial.

(g) Appeal.

(1) From a District Judge's Order or Judgment. The Federal Rules of Appellate Procedure govern an appeal from a district judge's order or a judgment of conviction or sentence.

(2) From a Magistrate Judge's Order or Judgment.

(A) Interlocutory Appeal. Either party may appeal an order of a magistrate judge to a district judge within 14 days of its entry if a district judge's order could similarly be appealed. The party appealing must file a notice with the clerk specifying the order being appealed and must serve a copy on the adverse party.

(B) Appeal from a Conviction or Sentence. A defendant may appeal a magistrate judge's judgment of conviction or sentence to a district judge within 14 days of its entry. To appeal, the defendant must file a notice with the clerk specifying the judgment being appealed and must serve a copy on an attorney for the government.

(C) Record. The record consists of the original papers and exhibits in the case; any transcript, tape, or other recording of the proceedings; and a certified copy of the docket entries. For purposes of the appeal, a copy of the record of the proceedings must be made available to a defendant who establishes by affidavit an inability to pay or give security for the record. The Director of the Administrative Office of the United States Courts must pay for those copies.

(D) Scope of Appeal. The defendant is not entitled to a trial de novo by a district judge. The scope of the appeal is the same as in an appeal to the court of appeals from a judgment entered by a district judge.

(3) Stay of Execution and Release Pending Appeal. Rule 38 applies to a stay of a judgment of conviction or sentence. The court may release the defendant pending appeal under the law relating to release pending appeal from a district court to a court of appeals.

Rule 59.   Matters Before a Magistrate Judge

(a) Nondispositive Matters. A district judge may refer to a magistrate judge for determination any matter that does not dispose of a charge or defense. The magistrate judge must promptly conduct the required proceedings and, when appropriate, enter on the record an oral or written order stating the determination. A party may serve and file objections to the order within 14 days after being served with a copy of a written order or after the oral order is stated on the record, or at some other time the court sets. The district judge must consider timely objections and modify or set aside any part of the order that is contrary to law or clearly erroneous. Failure to object in accordance with this rule waives a party's right to review.

(b) Dispositive Matters.

(1) Referral to Magistrate Judge. A district judge may refer to a magistrate judge for recommendation a defendant's motion to dismiss or quash an indictment or information, a motion to suppress evidence, or any matter that may dispose of a charge or defense. The magistrate judge must promptly conduct the required proceedings. A record must be made of any evidentiary proceeding and of any other proceeding if the magistrate judge considers it necessary. The magistrate judge must enter on the record a recommendation for disposing of the matter, including any proposed findings of fact. The clerk must immediately serve copies on all parties.

(2) Objections to Findings and Recommendations. Within 14 days after being served with a copy of the recommended disposition, or at some other time the court sets, a party may serve and file specific written objections to the proposed findings and recommendations. Unless the district judge directs otherwise, the objecting party must promptly arrange for transcribing the record, or whatever portions of it the parties agree to or the magistrate judge considers sufficient. Failure to object in accordance with this rule waives a party's right to review.

(3) De Novo Review of Recommendations. The district judge must consider de novo any objection to the magistrate judge's recommendation. The district judge may accept, reject, or modify the recommendation, receive further evidence, or resubmit the matter to the magistrate judge with instructions.

Rule 60.   Victim's Rights

(a) In General.

(1) Notice of a Proceeding. The government must use its best efforts to give the victim reasonable, accurate, and timely notice of any public court proceeding involving the crime.

(2) Attending the Proceeding. The court must not exclude a victim from a public court proceeding involving the crime, unless the court determines by clear and convincing evidence that the victim's testimony would be materially altered if the victim heard other testimony at that proceeding. In determining whether to exclude a victim, the court must make every effort to permit the fullest attendance possible by the victim and must consider reasonable alternatives to exclusion. The reasons for any exclusion must be clearly stated on the record.

(3) Right to Be Heard on Release, a Plea, or Sentencing. The court must permit a victim to be reasonably heard at any public proceeding in the district court concerning release, plea, or sentencing involving the crime.

(b) Enforcement and Limitations.

(1) Time for Deciding a Motion. The court must promptly decide any motion asserting a victim's rights described in these rules.

(2) Who May Assert the Rights. A victim's rights described in these rules may be asserted by the victim, the victim's lawful representative, the attorney for the government, or any other person as authorized by 18 U.S.C. § 3771(d) and (e).

(3) Multiple Victims. If the court finds that the number of victims makes it impracticable to accord all of them their rights described in these rules, the court must fashion a reasonable procedure that gives effect to these rights without unduly complicating or prolonging the proceedings.

(4) Where Rights May Be Asserted. A victim's rights described in these rules must be asserted in the district where a defendant is being prosecuted for the crime.

(5) Limitations on Relief. A victim may move to reopen a plea or sentence only if:

    (A) the victim asked to be heard before or during the proceeding at issue, and the request was denied;

    (B) the victim petitions the court of appeals for a writ of mandamus within 10 days after the denial, and the writ is granted; and

    (C) in the case of a plea, the accused has not pleaded to the highest offense charged.

(6) No New Trial. A failure to afford a victim any right described in these rules is not grounds for a new trial.

Rule 61.   Title

These rules may be known and cited as the Federal Rules of Criminal Procedure.

APPENDIX D

PENDING AMENDMENTS TO FEDERAL RULES OF CRIMINAL PROCEDURE

■ ■ ■

[These amendments to Rules 5, 6, 12, 34 and 58 were approved by the Supreme Court on April 25, 201, and were forwarded to Congress. They will take effect on December 1, 2014, unless Congress enacts legislation to reject, modify or defer them.]

Rule 5. Initial Appearance

* * *

(d) Procedure in a Felony Case.

(1) Advice. If the defendant is charged with a felony, the judge must inform the defendant of the following:

* * *

(D) any right to a preliminary hearing;

(E) the defendant's right not to make a statement, and that any statement made may be used against the defendant; and

(F) that a defendant who is not a United States citizen may request that an attorney for the government or a federal law enforcement official notify a consular office from the defendant's country of nationality that the defendant has been arrested—but that even without the defendant's request, a treaty or other international agreement may require consular notification.

* * *

Rule 6. The Grand Jury

* * *

(e) Recording and Disclosing the Proceedings.

* * *

(3) Exceptions.

* * *

(D) An attorney for the government may disclose any grand-jury matter involving foreign intelligence, counterintelligence (as defined in 50 U.S.C. § 3003), or foreign intelligence information (as defined in Rule 16(e)(3)(D)(iii)) to any federal law enforcement, intelligence, protective, immigration, national defense, or national security official to assist the official receiving the information in the performance of that official's duties. An attorney for the government may also disclose any grand-jury matter involving, within the United States or elsewhere, a threat of attack or other grave hostile acts of a foreign power or its agent, a threat of domestic or international sabotage or terrorism, or clandestine intelligence gathering activities by an intelligence service or network of a foreign power or by its agent, to any appropriate federal, state, state subdivision, Indian tribal, or foreign government official, for the purpose of preventing or responding to such threat or activities.

* * *

Rule 12. Pleadings and Pretrial Motions

* * *

(b) Pretrial Motions.

(1) In General. A party may raise by pretrial motion any defense, objection, or request that the court can determine without a trial on the merits. Rule 47 applies to a pretrial motion.

(2) Motions That May Be Made at Any Time. A motion that the court lacks jurisdiction may be made at any time while the case is pending.

(3) Motions That May Be Made Before Trial. The following defenses, objections, and requests must be raised by pretrial motion if the basis for the motion is then reasonably available and the motion can be determined without a trial on the merits:

(A) a defect in instituting the prosecution, including:

(i) improper venue;

(ii) preindictment delay;

(iii) a violation of the constitutional right to a speedy trial;

(iv) selective or vindictive prosecution; and

(v) an error in the grand-jury proceeding or preliminary hearing;

(B) a defect in the indictment or information, including:

    (i) joining two or more offenses in the same count (duplicity);

    (ii) charging the same offense in more than one count (multiplicity);

    (iii) lack of specificity;

    (iv) improper joinder; and

    (v) failure to state an offense;

(C) suppression of evidence;

(D) severance of charges or defendants under Rule 14; and

(E) discovery under Rule 16.

(4) Notice of the Government's Intent to Use Evidence.

    (A) At the Government's Discretion. At the arraignment or as soon afterward as practicable, the government may notify the defendant of its intent to use specified evidence at trial in order to afford the defendant an opportunity to object before trial under Rule 12(b)(3)(C).

    (B) At the Defendant's Request. At the arraignment or as soon afterward as practicable, the defendant may, in order to have an opportunity to move to suppress evidence under rule 12(b)(3)(C), request notice of the government's intent to use (in its evidence-in-chief at trial) any evidence that the defendant may be entitled to discover under Rule 16.

(c) Deadline for a Pretrial Motion; Consequences of Not Making a Timely Motion.

    (1) Setting the Deadline. The court may, at the arraignment or as soon afterward as practicable, set a deadline for the parties to make pretrial motions and may also schedule a motion hearing. If the court does not set one, the deadline is the start of trial.

    (2) Extending or Resetting the Deadline. At any time before trial, the court may extend or reset the deadline for pretrial motions.

    (3) Consequences of Not Making a Timely Motion Under Rule 12(b)(3). If a party does not meet the deadline for making a Rule 12(b)(3) motion, the motion is untimely. But a court may consider the defense, objection, or request if the party shows good cause.

    (d) Ruling on a Motion. The court must decide every pretrial motion before trial unless it finds good cause to defer a ruling. The court must not defer ruling on a pretrial motion if the deferral will adversely affect a party's right to appeal. When factual issues are involved in deciding a motion, the court must state its essential findings on the record.

(e) [Reserved]

* * *

Rule 34. Arresting Judgment

(a) In General. Upon the defendant's motion or on its own, the court must arrest judgment if the court does not have jurisdiction of the charged offense.

* * *

Rule 58. Petty Offenses and Other Misdemeanors

* * *

(b) Pretrial Procedure.

* * *

(2) Initial Appearance. At the defendant's initial appearance on a petty offense or other misdemeanor charge, the magistrate judge must inform the defendant of the following:

* * *

(F) the right to a jury trial before either a magistrate judge or a district judge—unless the charge is a petty offense;

(G) any right to a preliminary hearing under Rule 5.1, and the general circumstances, if any, under which the defendant may secure pretrial release; and

(H) that a defendant who is not a United States citizen may request that an attorney for the government or a federal law enforcement official notify a consular officer from the defendant's country of nationality that the defendant has been arrested—but that even without the defendant's request, a treaty or other international agreement may require consular notification.

* * *